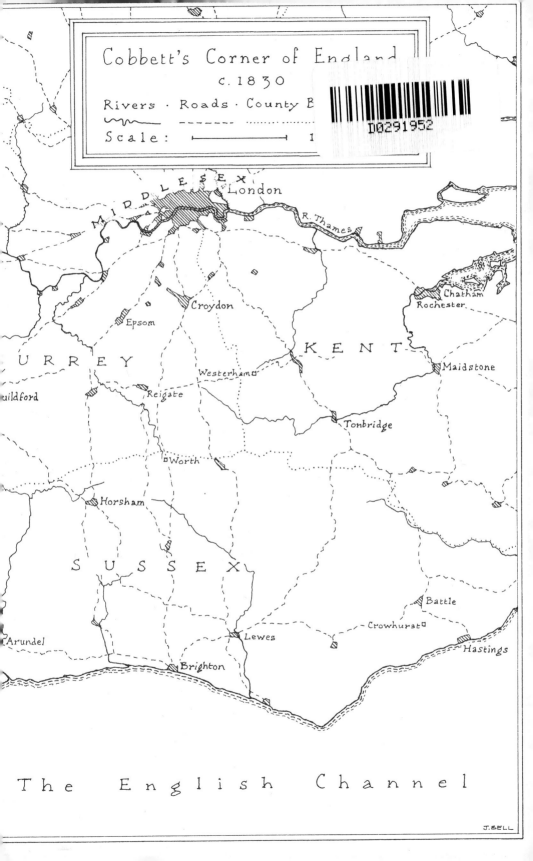

Cobbett's Corner of England
c. 1830

Rivers · Roads · County B[oundaries]

Scale:

D0291952

MIDDLESEX
London
R. Thames
Chatham
Rochester
Croydon
Epsom
K E N T
Maidstone
Westerham
URREY
Reigate
uildford
Tonbridge
Worth
Horsham
S U S S E X
Battle
Crowhurst
Arundel
Lewes
Hastings
Brighton

The English Channel

J. BELL

William Cobbett
The Poor Man's Friend

Volume 2

Cobbett in about 1830

WILLIAM COBBETT
The Poor Man's Friend

GEORGE SPATER

Volume 2

CAMBRIDGE UNIVERSITY PRESS

Cambridge

London   New York   New Rochelle

Melbourne   Sydney

Published by the Press Syndicate of the University of Cambridge
The Pitt Building, Trumpington Street, Cambridge CB2 1RP
32 East 57th Street, New York, NY 10022, USA
296 Beaconsfield Parade, Middle Park, Melbourne 3206, Australia

First published 1982

Printed in the United States of America

Library of Congress catalogue card number: 81-3859

British Library cataloguing in publication data
Spater, George
William Cobbett.
Vol. 2
1. Cobbett, William – Biography
I. Title
828'.6'08   PR4461.C324
ISBN 0 521 22216 8 vol. 1
ISBN 0 521 24077 8 vol. 2

Contents

v

Illustrations

LIST OF ILLUSTRATIONS

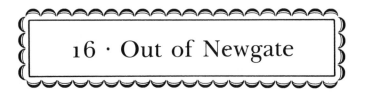

16 · Out of Newgate

It is my duty to copy and to animadvert upon what is *published by others*; and, I am not without hopes, that it is a duty, the performance of which has done, is doing, and will yet do the country no little good.

A NEWSPAPER editor housed in a London prison could hardly be expected to act as a reporter of the events of the outside world – he must, of necessity, limit himself to comment on the news as it was reported by others. This had been largely true since Cobbett had moved to Botley, but even there he had made occasional trips to London, attended county meetings, and made use of the eyes and ears of his colleague John Wright. Committal to Newgate and the casting off of Wright left Cobbett with no choice. He read the principal papers of the day: the *Morning Post,* the *Courier, The Times,* and the *Morning Chronicle,* and he received the official *London Gazette,* and, thus equipped, singlehanded became, as Hazlitt expressed it, "a kind of *fourth estate* in the politics of the country."[1]

During this two-year interval the major news topic – as it had been since 1793 and would continue to be until 1815 – was the war with France. The progress of the war on sea and land was itself in the forefront of public interest. In addition, there were always important issues created by the existence of the war: the raising and discipline of troops, the taxation and borrowing of money required by the war effort, the oppression or appeasement of Ireland for reasons of defense, the interdiction of the normal flow of goods to and from the warring parties. The war was also constantly used as a justification for taking certain measures and as an excuse for not taking others. Reform, for example, fell in the latter category. That no sensible man would repair his house in a hurricane was still the ruling philosophy. Moderate reform proposals by a few liberal whigs were halfheartedly put to the House of Commons and defeated by large majorities in May 1810 and again in May 1812.[2] The more radical reformers had lost some of their public attractiveness as the result of various personal involvements. Wardle, the hero of the Duke of York affair, had been discredited as a result of a pair of lawsuits with Mrs. Clarke from which it appeared not only that Wardle was something of a liar, but that he had covertly promised to furnish a house for Mrs. Clarke in return for her testimony against the duke.[3] Lord Folkestone, Cobbett's particular friend, became slightly tarnished when his indiscretions with the same lady were revealed by her.[4] Francis Place and Sir Francis Burdett had quarrelled and broken off relations following Burdett's release from the Tower in 1810, and Sir Francis's image suffered a devaluation when his adulterous liaison with the beautiful Lady Oxford became public knowledge.[5] Lord Cochrane, although distinguishing himself at sea, had been edged out of the navy after he had courageously brought charges of incompetence against his incompetent but well-connected superior, Admiral Gambier.[6] To complete the picture, the principal protagonist of the radical reformers, after an extended lambasting for his inconsistencies, his retreat from the 1792 court-martial, and his "oppression" of domestic servants, was in jail for libel.

For these reasons among others, the reform activity in parliament during the period 1810 to 1817 was limited to an occasional speech and the two moderate whig bills already referred to, which had been quietly and quickly cast into outer darkness. Yet there were plenty of other issues that provided opportunities for critical comment of a type that kept the reform question alive. One of the principal subjects of this character was the economic crisis that struck England in the middle of 1810. Production and employment had been dislocated by the war itself and by the various government embargoes on trade: the Berlin and Milan decrees of Napoleon barring British goods from continental Europe, the British orders in council prohibiting neutrals from trading with French-occupied territory, and the retaliatory American acts outlawing commerce with Britain and France. The poor, and particularly the farm laborers and others whose employment had been disrupted by the war or by war-related measures, were hard hit by rising inflation and heavy taxes on articles of consumption. In July 1810 the failure of a bank in London was followed by another in Exeter and a third in Salisbury. The merchants in Salisbury refused to accept banknotes in payment for provisions:

the poor people were, in many cases, without victuals or drink for some time, and many persons, in a respectable way of life, were for many days together, obliged to sit down to dine upon little more than bread ... many of these very best of people, saw their little all vanish in a moment, and themselves reduced to the same state with the improvident, the careless, the lazy, the spendthrift, the drunkard, and the glutton.[7]

The want of confidence spread rapidly. Within a week there were a number of failures on the London stock exchange. Then loans were hurriedly arranged to prop up overextended London merchants. In August another London bank failed, this time one of the old-established houses, bringing down a number of country banks in its train. The *Monthly Commercial Report* announced that the "stoppages and compositions are equal in number to one-half the traders in the Kingdom . . . In Manchester and other places, houses stop not only every day but every hour."[8] Severe unemployment developed in the manufacturing areas affected by the fall in trade. In Nottinghamshire, knitting frames were broken by the workers in protest against reduced wages, declining employment, and a variety of abuses in the hosiery industry. The war, the commercial embargoes, the heavy taxes, the new machinery, and the paper money were all blamed for the distress of the people.

The troubles in Salisbury were not the first suggestion that paper money might create problems in England. In an essay published in 1796 Thomas Paine had claimed that the English system of finance "is on the verge – nay – even in the gulph of bankruptcy."[9] He was referring to the fact that for a hundred years the government had borrowed to meet the ever-increasing cost of wars, and during the same period had caused the issue of more and more paper money to pay the annual interest on such borrowings. The paper money was convertible on demand into gold and silver, but according to Paine's estimates, the precious metals then held by the Bank of England amounted to less than £2 million, whereas the banknotes outstanding totalled £60 million – even if they were "but a third part of sixty millions, the bank cannot pay half a crown on the pound." Paine predicted a continued worsening of the country's financial condition as more notes were issued, for – in accordance with what later became known as the "quantity theory of money" – an increase in the quantity of money results in a decline in its purchasing power. And, he added, if it should happen that the paper should no longer be convertible into metal currency, two separate prices would be established, so that goods purchased with paper would cost more, in nominal terms, than goods purchased with gold. The continental currency of America and the assignats of France provided Paine with recent examples of this phenomenon.

Paine's predictions proved too quickly correct. In 1797, the year after his essay was published, parliament under Pitt's leadership passed a bill forbidding the Bank of England to convert its banknotes into metal currency, thereby preventing a run on the bank. Cobbett put the situation tersely: "It was said of some Roman that he found the city *stone,* and that he left it *marble.* It was said of Pitt that he found England *gold* and that he left it *paper.*" By 1811 the gold guinea, nominally worth twenty-one shillings, was selling for twenty-seven shillings in banknotes, a devaluation of 22 percent.[10] There was also a steady rise in the price of commodities as the quantity of money increased.

In June 1810 a select committee of the House of Commons, chaired by Francis Horner ("that stupid oaf, who always looked as if he had just had a bout of sucking his thumbs"), issued a report finding that there had been an overissue of paper money in the form of banknotes.[11] These had been issued without restraint by both county banks and the Bank of England, causing a rise in commodity prices, including that of gold bullion, and the decline in the value of the pound on European exchanges. The committee recommended that "with as much speed as [is] compatible with a wise and necessary caution" the currency should be brought back to "the original principle of cash payments at the option of the holder of the Bank paper."[12]

The enormously complicated questions raised by the report, still far from resolved at the end of the twentieth century, were the principal subjects to which Cobbett directed his attention as he began to serve his term of imprisonment. At first, he described developments in the financial crisis from week to week.[13] Then, beginning with the *Political Register* of September 1, 1810, Cobbett projected a treatise: "Paper against Gold: Being an Examination of the Report of the Bullion Committee: In a Series of Letters to the Tradesmen and Farmers in and near Salisbury."[14] There were twenty-nine of these letters written from Newgate in the period September 1810 to August 1811. With the first of them Cobbett announced that "in consequence of the increase of time that I have now upon my hands" the *Political Register* would thereafter be published twice weekly, on Wednesday and Saturday. This was continued for ten months, by which time it must have become as apparent to him (as it is to the modern reader) that his type of publication – a commentary on the news – could not support two issues a week without introducing boring repetition. But the letters relating to the monetary issue, which did not depend on developments from day to day, were in a different category. While they were as rambling and repetitious as twenty-nine separate conversations on a single subject tend to be, this was one of their virtues, since by repetition the reader was enabled to grasp the essentials of a subject that is commonly regarded as too difficult for anyone but a monetary expert. As a result the articles had a remarkable life. The twenty-nine letters from Newgate plus three others written several years later, thirty-two in all, were published in book form in 1815 in the midst of a serious depression due in part to the attempt that was then made to cut back on the quantity of outstanding paper. By 1817 150,000 copies had been sold, and editions continued to be printed for another dozen years.[15] *Paper against Gold* was probably the most widely read book ever written purely on monetary questions.[16]

In this work Cobbett expressed his debt to Paine:

In 1803, when there was much apprehension of invasion, and when great complaints were made of the *scarcity of change*, I began to read some books upon the subject; and, after reading several without coming to any thing like a clear notion of the real state of our currency, I took up the little essay of Paine. Here I saw to the bottom at once. Here was no bubble, no mud to obstruct my view: the stream was clear and strong: I saw the whole matter in its true light, and neither pamphleteers nor speech-makers were, after that, able to raise even a momentary puzzle in my mind. Paine not only told me what would come to pass, but shewed me, gave me convincing reasons, *why it must come to pass*; and he convinced me also, that it was my duty to endeavour to open the eyes of my countrymen to the truths which I myself had learnt from him: because his reasoning taught me, that, the longer those truths remained hidden from their view, the more fatal must be the consequences.[17]

Cobbett's thesis was that paper money was a consequence of the national debt and that while a return to a metallic currency was desirable, he could see no way to accomplish this, short of repudiating the debt on which such enormous annual interest payments were due.[18] How could the gold which was being hoarded in England or had been exported to foreign countries be bought back with paper money, since with every transaction more paper money had to be issued, causing further devaluation? If the quantity of paper money were lessened, the resulting deflation would produce "ruin amongst all persons in trade" and make the country unable to pay taxes at the nominal amount.[19] To complicate matters further, Britain's debt had risen to more than £800 million by 1811 and was growing every year. The interest on the debt was £33 million annually, or nearly half the government's total annual tax revenues, and it was generally accepted that taxes, which were already burdensome, could not be increased.[20] Although Cobbett covered much the same ground as Paine, touching on the quantity theory of money ("when apples are plenty, apples are cheap"), he spent far more time making it possible for the subject to be understood by the average man. He explained the role of money as medium of exchange; the meaning of such mysterious words as "funds," "sinking fund," "national debt"; the relationship of the private Bank of England to the government; the history behind the stoppage of cash payments. And he emphasized two points that were typically Cobbettian: that the present state of affairs, including the huge national debt encumbering the country, could in no way be blamed on the reformers (who were ordinarily used as scapegoats by the ministerial press), but was due wholly to those who had been running the government for the past many years; and that the destruction of the debt and of paper money would not in the slightest affect the safety of the nation or the happiness of the people:

No: the corn and the grass and the trees will grow without paper-money; the Banks may all break in a day, and the sun will rise the next day, and the lambs will gambol and the birds will sing and the carters and country girls will grin at each other and all will go on just as if nothing had happened.[21]

When Cobbett asserted that "all will go on just as if nothing had happened," he was speaking of the life of the lambs, birds, and country girls. Paine had declared that "every case of failure in finances, since the system of paper began, has produced a revolution in government, either total or partial." Cobbett accepted as certainties two of Paine's principles: first, that the paper system or funding system was sure to collapse in the near future, and second, when it did, there would be a revolution in government. To this Cobbett added a third principle, peculiarly his own, but an extension of Paine's ideas, that there would be no change in government, and no reform, *until* the funding system collapsed. This for many years was an essential feature of Cobbett's views on parliamentary reform – whereas most of the reformers believed that other pressures, chiefly public demand, would precipitate changes in the methods of selecting members of the House of Commons.

The view expressed by the Horner committee that Britain should return to a hard-currency system, that gold was preferable to paper as a medium of exchange, was thrust aside by Perceval and the ruling party. As has so often been the case, the decision on the currency issue was made on political rather than economic grounds. The ministry was convinced that it must continue the war against France. To do so required money, and the only way to get it was by more loans and more banknotes.[22] Cobbett, in contrast, had considerable doubts about the desirability of continuing the war. Despite reports of British "victories," Wellington had made little evident progress in the peninsular campaign. In 1809, after advancing into Spain and fighting at Talavera, he had promptly withdrawn to the Portuguese frontier. In 1810 he again campaigned in Spain, but after one major battle – that at Bussaco in September 1810 – he again retreated, this time to Torres Vedras, within twenty-five miles of Lisbon. In 1811, when Wellington reentered Spain, a major battle was fought at Albuera, where the British and their Portuguese allies, although performing with unparalleled bravery, lost nearly 6,000 troops out of the 35,000 engaged. More than two-thirds of the British infantry were killed or wounded. Wellington refused to send off Beresford's account of the losses: "That wont do; it will drive the people in England mad. Write me down a victory."[23] When the rewritten report reached the capital, the House of Commons unanimously voted its thanks for the "glorious victory" to those who had commanded the British forces.

Cobbett was too wily a reader to be taken in by such display. He followed the practice of looking at the figures in preference to the summaries, of reading the French bulletins as well as the British, and of carrying on a steady campaign against the uncritical accounts put out by the ministerial papers. Now Cobbett claimed, and rather convincingly demonstrated, that even the obviously incomplete British dispatches on the battle of Albuera showed that the allegations of victory were unwarranted.[24] But apart from the results of particular battles, Cobbett had three misgivings about the war as a whole: the cost in men, the cost in money, and the terrible suffering at home due to economic dislocation. Of equal concern was the objective of the war. At the outset it was to defend the British people against the "French principles" of atheism and republicanism, both of which had disappeared as reasons with the advent of Bonaparte. What was the objective now? Was Britain fighting to put the despotic regimes of Spain and Portugal back on the thrones? Finally, Cobbett doubted whether it was possible to win the war. Napoleon, he thought, was trifling with the British.[25] He was allowing them to wear themselves down in the peninsula. Anytime he wanted to do so he could take over the command in Spain instead of leaving it to subordinates, and whether he did this or not, he could pour 200,000 more trained troops into Spain to join the large French force already there. Wellington with his 45,000 or 50,000 British troops would be overwhelmed by numbers alone. Yes, and all this *might* have happened (Sir Charles Robertson called it one of the most fascinating "might have beens" in history) had not Napoleon at this point turned his eyes toward Russia.[26]

Cobbett was not the only one in England who had doubts about the British position in Spain. A large part of the whig party shared his doubts and opposed a continuation of the war. But the whigs were very much a minority party, with the likelihood that they would remain such for some time. Then, in October 1810, whig fortunes had taken a sudden turn. George III had another of his recurring lapses into insanity. Although at first there was a noticeable reluctance to name the malady ("we have been refined out of our veracity," Cobbett remarked), the seriousness of the illness soon became manifest.[27] Perceval and his colleagues, as long as they could, held to the hope that the king would recover, since if he did not, a regency would put the Prince of Wales on the throne, and the prince was a whig. Whigs had been his advisers and companions in debauchery since he came of age more than twenty-five years before. When his friend Fox died in 1806, the prince had written to the whig leader, Charles Grey: "But as to ourselves, my friend, the old & steady adherents & friends of Fox, we have but one line to pursue, one course to steer, to stick together, to remain united."[28]

In view of this history, one could hardly be surprised at the whigs' high expectation during the winter of 1810–11. But Cobbett, harking back to the days of Fox as leader of the liberal wing of the whig party, hoped for something more than the restoration of a Grenville ministry. The people of England, he declared, cared no more for the whigs than they did about "who is sweeper of the Mall."[29] Cobbett preferred there to be no change in ministry unless it be accompanied by a change in the system. Two things were needed – the same two things – conciliation of the Irish by relaxing the laws discriminating against them and a reform of parliament. Cobbett was quite certain that the prince was friendly to both propositions, and suddenly became strongly pro-prince, defending him against charges of unpopularity and of extravagance, although no defense could obscure the fact that the prince was both unpopular and extravagant.[30] Further, Cobbett argued that no parliamentary limitation should be imposed on the regent's powers; he should be given the authority he would have had if George III had died instead of going mad.[31]

The king's illness, the terms of the regency, and what would happen when the regency was finally declared were the principal topics of London conversation from October to December 1810. On the last day of the year the Ministry – being able to put off the evil day no longer – introduced resolutions declaring a regency and providing that for a period of a year, if the regency lasted that long, the regent would be prohibited from the grant of any rank or dignity of the peerage except for "singular naval or military achievement," and from the grant of any office for any term other than His Majesty's pleasure except for offices which by law were required to be for life or during good behavior.[32] These conditions, although originally resisted by the prince, were accepted by him on January 11, 1811. For nearly a month thereafter the town was wild with rumors about who would lead the new ministry. The conclusion, announced on February 4, was a stunning anticlimax: The prince intended to make no change – Spencer Perceval would continue as prime minister! The prince's decision was allegedly based on his "dread that any act of the Regent might, in the smallest degree, have the effect of interfering with the progress of his Sovereign's recovery."[33] Cobbett commented: "There were, in all human probability, more lying and hypocrisy in England during that month, than ever have been witnessed in any other country in the course of a year." The prince's decision made it plain that there would be no conciliation of the Irish, that there would be no reform of parliament, and that the war would go on.[34]

The war against France did not, however, require that the British also go to war with the Americans, although, by the time the regency had been declared, relations between the two countries had again become increasingly strained over the impressment of American sailors by British men-of-war and the enforcement of the British orders in council. The British minister to the United States had promised that his government would withdraw the orders as they applied to the United States if the French government would do the same with their Berlin and Milan decrees. The French announced in August 1810 that the decrees were revoked with effect from three months away, on November 1, 1810. When this news was relayed to the British foreign office, the Americans were told that no action would be taken to revoke the orders in council until the repeal of the French decrees had actually taken effect, and then not until commerce was restored to the condition in which it stood prior to the decrees.[35] As a result the Americans resumed trade with France but angrily forbade intercourse with Britain.

The general belief in England was that there would be no war. The Americans would back down: They could not afford a war; their merchants with business in England were against it; the American president, James Madison, who was responsible for the complaints, was unpopular in the United States. If, however, there was a war, it was believed that the Americans could be easily defeated without seriously detracting from concurrent efforts against Napoleon. And, as usual, the bumptious Americans needed to be taught a lesson.

These arguments were curiously like those that Cobbett had urged several years before at the time of the *Chesapeake* affair. On June 22, 1807, the British frigate *Leopard* had demanded the right to examine the crew of the U.S.S. *Chesapeake* for the purpose of impressing British deserters alleged to be on board. When this was refused, the *Leopard* poured three broadsides into the American ship, rendering her helpless. Four sailors were forcibly removed from the *Chesapeake*. Overnight, talk of war spread across America. The president, Thomas Jefferson, issued a proclamation ordering British warships out of U.S. territorial waters, and, at his request, congress passed an embargo act, virtually closing off all commerce with foreign nations.

The *Chesapeake* incident had brought to a head antagonisms that had been accumulating for years. Cobbett defended the search and impressment on his theory of the "dominion of the seas": Britain, having mastery of the seas, had the right to do on the ocean whatever any nation could do on land that it exclusively occupied.[36] He was in full agreement with the British orders in council restricting American trade with France and French-occupied Europe. He argued that there was no reason to fear the Americans. British goods were "indispensably necessary" to the Americans, who had neither wool nor the machinery to convert wool into the clothes they wore; the Americans were dependent on Britain for tools; they had no navy and no internal revenues to pay for a navy if they wanted to build one; the president, Thomas Jefferson, did not have the support of the American merchants and shipowners. The Americans would have to back down.[37] And Cobbett was right. There was no war; the self-imposed embargo of the Americans lasted only fourteen months – it was repealed in March 1809.

Outwardly, the same issues were involved when another surge of American war fever developed in 1811 as a result of the continued search for sailors on American ships and the continued restrictions on commerce imposed by the British orders in council. But this time Cobbett took exactly the opposite position to that which he had so heatedly defended three and four years before. He now contended, just as warmly, that the British position was unjust and unreasonable; that the government had welshed on its promise to revoke the orders in council if the French rescinded their decrees; that the American president, James Madison, represented a majority of the people in the United States; and that the Americans would go to war unless their demands were met by the British – not only in respect of the orders in council, but the impressment of sailors as well.[38] Nor did Cobbett share the popular illusion – which he had earnestly championed a short time before – that the British would be able to subdue the Americans with ease. In 1807 Cobbett had written: "We are for war, rather than yield to these demands"; in 1811 he favored yielding to the demands rather than have war.[39] But this time he was a lone voice. "Whatever the liberal opposition thought in private," wrote Henry Adams many years afterwards, "no one but Cobbett ventured in public to oppose the war."[40]

Although Cobbett never directly discussed the inconsistencies between his two positions, there are some clues which suggest what he might have said if he had been challenged to explain. He still held, for a time, at least, to his "dominion of the seas" principle, but explained that it was *expediency*, rather than *right*, that settled matters between nations.[41] Two new elements had entered the picture: The French had announced the revocation of their decrees in 1810, and Cobbett believed that the British were honor-bound to follow; and, as a wholly unrelated point, it was now "expedient" for the Americans to go to war on the issues involved. In the past few years the Americans had imported large numbers of sheep and were rapidly developing their own manufacturing capabilities. Being cut off from Britain would only accelerate the trend toward industrial independence.[42]

These elements do not, however, fully reconcile the views of 1807–8 with those of 1811–12. In the earlier period Cobbett had expressed the belief that America was "the most unprincipled country in the world," with no public morality; that the American government was "one of the very worst" and would not last long; that the Americans had been the aggressors for the previous fifteen years, during which time they had outrageously abused the king and the people of England; and that the Americans had "inveigled" thousands of British sailors to desert their ships.[43] In a mood close to hysteria, Cobbett wrote:

I hate the United States and all their mean and hypocritical system of rule . . . and I have further frequently declared, that, if I, or any one most dear to me, were destined to lose my or his life in a *just* war, I knew of no case, in which that life would be lost with so little regret, on my part, as in demolishing the towns of America and in burying their unprincipled inhabitants under the rubbish.[44]

By 1811 all this was forgotten. Indeed, in this short period Cobbett had become an advocate of cooperation, even some sort of union, between Britain and America:

A system that would combine the powers of England with those of America, and that would thus set liberty to wage war with despotism, dropping the Custom House and all its pitiful regulations as out of date, would give new life to an enslaved world, and would ensure the independence of England for a time beyond calculation.[45]

Presumably, in the years between 1808 and 1811, Cobbett's changing views of the government of his own country – changes resulting from the exposure of new corruption, the increasing belief that the English war in Europe was to restore the old despotic regimes rather than to bring freedom to the people, and the personal attacks on him leading to his imprisonment – gave him a fresh basis for transatlantic comparison.[46] The unjust $5,000 judgment of 1799 was not quite so heavy in the scales when weighed against the unjust jail sentence and £1,000 fine of 1810.[47] Thus in issue after issue of the *Political Register* this new admirer of America and Americans hammered away for a revocation of the orders in council.[48] When this finally occurred at the end of a campaign that lasted for nearly two years, Cobbett thought – and, typically, expressed the thought – that he was entitled to some of the credit for the change.

The revocation took place on June 23, 1812. But what might have prevented hostilities if done in November 1810 came too late when done nineteen months afterwards. The American government, with the approval of both houses of congress, had declared war five days before, on June 18, 1812.

This issue was still an open one on May 11, 1812 when the prime minister, Spencer Perceval, rushed into the House of Commons to attend a debate on the objectionable orders in council. As he entered the lobby, a quietly dressed man moved toward him, pulled a pistol out of his pocket, and fired point-blank at Perceval's chest. Perceval fell, mortally wounded. Despite his majorities in parliament, wrote Cobbett, "those mighty majorities, by the means of which he had so often yielded protection to others when assailed with all the artillery of political warfare, he was not able to protect himself against a little bit of lead scarcely surpassing in bulk a knot in a cat o'nine tails!"[49] It is the only time in England's history that a prime minister has been assassinated.[50]

Spencer Perceval had never been a popular prime minister. It is likely that most of the people living in the kingdom at the time could not have named the man who headed their government, and he is little remembered today. But the prime minister was a symbol, and his death provided the people with an opportunity of showing what they thought of their country's leadership and the Pitt system. Among

The assassination of the prime minister by John Bellingham

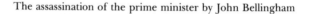

Mr Perceval Assassinated in the lobby of the House of Commons by John Bellingham May 11 1812

the multitude assembled outside Westminster "the most savage expressions of joy and exultation were heard; accompanied with regret that others, and particularly the Attorney-General, had not shared the same fate."[51] That evening the poet Coleridge went into a large public house in London:

It was really shocking – Nothing but exultation – Burdett's Health drank with a Clatter of Pots – & a Sentiment given to at least 50 men & women – May Burdett soon be the man to have Sway over us! – These were the very words. "This is but the beginning" – "more of these damned Scoundrels must go the same way – & then poor people may live" – "Every man might maintain his family decent & comfortable if the money were not picked out of pockets by them damned Placemen" – "God is above the Devil, *I* say – & down to Hell with Him & all his brood, the Minister Men & Parliament Fellows" – "They won't hear Burdett – No! he is a Christian Man & speaks for the Poor" – &c &c – I do not think, I have altered a word.[52]

Cobbett reported that "it is very notorious" that "the news of the death of Mr Perceval excited demonstrations of joy, the most unequivocal, amongst the people in several of the most populous parts of England; that at Nottingham the church bells were rung, at Leicester there was a supper and songs, at Sheffield there were sheep roasted whole."[53] Those in authority thought that the assassination of Perceval might be the signal for a general uprising. Troops were ordered out in London, at Windsor, and at other points where disorder might occur. Members of parliament who were lord lieutenants of their counties hurried home to take charge of local precautions.

Perceval's assassin, John Bellingham, was rushed to trial, presumably to demonstrate the strong hand with which any disturbance would be met. He was not allowed time to talk to counsel before being put to his defense at the Old Bailey, four days after the incident. To the impartial observer he seemed quite mad, but this was quickly brushed aside by the court. The story told by Bellingham in justification for his act fitted in well with the common man's image of the government: He had a grievance and no one would give him a hearing. Bellingham, who had been engaged in trade in Russia, had been held in various Russian prisons for approximately five years under false charges, while the British embassy in St. Petersburg had refused to assist him.[54] After finally gaining his freedom, he had spent two additional years back in England seeking recompense from the foreign office, the home office, the privy council, the prime minister, the prince regent, even the Bow Street magistrates. His "uniform and undeviating object" was "an endeavour to obtain justice, according to law." After exhausting all other avenues, he was told that his sole means of redress was a petition to parliament, but because money was involved, the petition required the sanction of the ministers, which Perceval refused to give. Bellingham asserted that he had no personal animosity against Perceval, but that justice is a matter of right, not of favor, and that by refusing him justice, Perceval, at his personal risk, had set himself above both the sovereign and the laws.

After a trial taking most of the day, it required only ten minutes for the jury to conclude that Bellingham was guilty. His execution was carried out three days later under Cobbett's windows at Newgate. A few minutes before the assigned time, Bellingham walked the few steps from the jail door to the scaffold.

... he looked attentively at the people, who were assembled to the amount of many thousands, who filled the opposite windows and parapets of the houses, and who, notwithstanding an almost continual heavy rain, crowded the sort of triangle which the streets here form, as thick as they could well stand upon the ground ... It was now, at the moment that he was going out of the world; at the moment when he was expecting every breath to be his last, that his ears were saluted with, *"God bless you! God bless you! God Almighty bless you! God Almighty bless you!"* issuing from the lips of thousands.[55]

Cobbett used the Perceval episode as the basis for two moralizing lectures in the form of letters to the prince regent appearing in the *Political Register* in May and June 1812:

It was not at the *shedding of Mr Perceval's blood* that they rejoiced; it was not that, but it was at the death of a man whom they regarded as being, in part at least, the cause of what, in various ways, the country has so long been suffering. They did not, in their view of the matter, bestow their blessings on a *murderer,* but on an Englishman, whom they regarded (perhaps erroneously) as having been grievously ill used by the government, and who had taken vengeance into his own hands. It is quite useless to inquire how far these popular feelings square with the rules laid down by moralists. Such have been, and such are, the feelings, and a wise politician will clearly perceive, that they are merely indications of what the people feel towards the ministers and their system generally; he will perceive, that they are clear indications of a spirit of hostility to the public measures, which, for a long time past, have been adopted.[56]

What was the remedy? In the first of the letters, Cobbett urged the prince regent to eschew force in favor of gentleness and persuasion. He should shun "as you would shun the bite of a mad dog" anyone who advised reliance on troops. Instead of threats of punishment directed at the unemployed weavers of Nottinghamshire who were breaking the frames they believed responsible for their unemployment, the prince should issue a proclamation expressing his feelings at their sufferings, and "speaking to them in a cheering language as to the future; after which might come denunciations against violators of the law."[57] In the second of the letters (after objecting to what he thought was the overgenerous provision for Perceval's family to come out of the pockets of the people whom he had oppressed) Cobbett returned to his usual thesis: the need for a reform in the House of Commons. "To the want of this reform *every* evil we experience may be traced."[58] The speechmakers of the two parties talked of the "alarming situation of the country" and called on the prince regent for a strong ministry, but they were the very people who had produced the situation. "What is wanted," Cobbett wrote, "is, not a *strong* ministry; but an *honest* ministry, who would soon give us a reformed House of Commons, who, by a great reduction in the expenditure and the taxes, would give us the best chance of content, tranquillity and happiness."[59]

Death had removed one of Cobbett's prosecutors; promotion took another. Three weeks after Perceval's assassination, Cobbett announced the "unexpected retreat of Sir Vicary Gibbs," who had been appointed, he roguishly emphasized, "to a PUISNE judgeship in the Court of Common Pleas." Although Cobbett had no taste for puns, he unquestionably relished the thought of the tiny (five feet four inches) narrow-minded lawyer becoming a "puisne" judge.[60]

Thus one might assume that Cobbett's closing days at Newgate – the two-year term ended on July 9, 1812 – were made reasonably pleasant by outside events. But apart from this type of intermittent distraction, and despite the brave face he attempted to show to the world, life in prison had been hard on Cobbett. It was common enough for journalists of the period to spend time in jail for libels on the government, but most of them were city men. In contrast, Cobbett, who seems "to have been born to love rural life," was very much a man of the country. He never liked London – after the first three months of living there in 1800 he found it a "scene of noise & nonsense" – and Newgate represented everything that he disliked most about the city.[61] His view of felons in the stone exercise yard awkwardly playing fives while wearing irons secured from the knee to the ankle, or the noises arising from the place of execution on the other side of his rooms, or the "black snow" perpetually falling in winter from the clouds of smoke that terminated "the length of every street with a fixed gray mist,"[62] were hardly satisfactory substitutes for the woods and meadows, the farms and neat little cottages, the clean country air that he loved so dearly. It is also possible that this disruption of Cobbett's outward image was paralleled by a disruption of Cobbett's image of himself. He was, as we have seen, a proud man. He made it clear, over and over again, that he hated to be thought "low and insignificant."[63] Yet is not this what people must have thought of him when he was sent to prison for a few words of justifiable indignation, while high and important men of the day could, with impunity, violate laws against bribery, corruption, and misuse of public funds? This kind of reasoning may have had its impact on Cobbett. His daughter Anne noticed that he had changed during his imprisonment. Before he entered Newgate "the black ox had not trod on his foot."[64] Thereafter, for the remaining twenty-odd years of his life, its heavy impress was never eradicated from his mind. Reference to the trial and imprisonment, always tinged with bitterness, was dragged into his writings time after time on the slightest provocation – often when there seemed to be no provocation.[65] Imprisonment had also sharpened the focus of Cobbett's objectives. Whereas he had previously never talked politics in society, after Newgate he talked little else: "He was so *angry* at being so ill used." He was more severe and less good humored with the children than before. They were puzzled by his apparent inability to throw off this bitterness, and thought that his alteration in manner may have been due to the type of people he met in prison.[66]

Yet Cobbett's associations at Newgate were not limited to the other inmates and the jailers. Old friends called on him frequently. They included Lord Cochrane, Lord Folkestone, Sir Francis Burdett, Major Cartwright, Henry Hunt, Thomas Creevey, and William Bosville in his coach and four. Francis Maseres, cursitor baron of the exchequer and senior judge of the sheriff's court in the city of London, visited Cobbett wearing his wig and gown to show his abhorrence of the sentence inflicted on his friend. John Philpot Curran, master of the rolls in 1806 and member of the privy council, one of the great wits of the time, came to make Cobbett laugh. And there were James Swann and Peter Finnerty and Peter Walker and George Crosby and Asbury Dickins and Timothy Brown and dozens of others of whom we have no record.[67] Casual visitors came to see him as a curiosity, while others came with a more flattering purpose:

during the two years, I was visited by persons, whom I have never seen before, from one hundred and ninety-seven cities and towns of England, Scotland and Ireland; the greatest part of whom came to me as the deputies of some society, club, or circle of people in their respective places of residence. I had the infinite satisfaction to learn from the gentlemen who thus visited me, that my writings had induced those who had read them to think.[68]

Henry Crabb Robinson's report of a visit to Newgate by a grand jury inspecting prison conditions reflects the special status occupied by Cobbett as a national celebrity. "Hammond mentioned that recently, when he was on the Grand Jury, and they visited Newgate prison, he proposed inquiring of Cobbett whether he had anything to complain of. Cobbett answered, 'Nothing but the being here.' Hammond said, the reverent bows his fellow-jurymen made to Cobbett were quite ludicrous."[69]

Throughout this period Cobbett's weekly articles in the *Political Register* invariably ended with his address: "State Prison, Newgate." The last of the articles, dated July 8, 1812, added: "where I have just paid a thousand pounds fine to the King: and much good may it do his Majesty!"[70] The following day he left Newgate. He was greeted by a grand dinner at the Crown and Anchor attended by 600 admirers, with Sir Francis Burdett in the chair.[71] Cobbett's enemies were determined that his triumphant reentry into the world should not be unadulterated joy. *The Times* of that date carried a scurrilous letter "From a Fellow Sufferer Under Unjust Persecution," which claimed that Cobbett was a man whom the people had raised "from the lowest poverty to the greatest affluence"; that in light of his affluence he had been guilty of "one of the meanest and dirtiest suggestions that ever disgraced" even an oppressor of public freedom, by proposing, through a notice in the *Political Register,* that his friends buy bound copies of the back numbers of the paper rather than subscribe to a fund for his benefit; that after Cobbett was found guilty he "would have sacrificed his wife and children" in order to save himself, and had, in fact, proposed to give up the cause of freedom by sacrificing the *Political Register* in order to escape punishment.[72] Those entering the Crown and Anchor to attend the dinner in Cobbett's honor were given handbills containing additional charges. The allegations were summarized by Cobbett in the following passage:

1st, That I had, ten years ago, expressed my decided disapprobation of the conduct and even of the principles of Sir Francis Burdett; 2nd, That, in the time between my conviction and my being brought up to judgment, I formed the design of dropping my Register, to announce which design I had prepared and actually caused to be printed an advertisement; 3rd, That this design was coupled with a negociation with the government for making the dropping of the Register a condition upon which forgiveness was to be obtained; 4th, That this offer on my part having being refused by the government, I next offered to turn about and write for them; 5th, That on account of this having been rejected, I abandoned the design, and continued the Register. – I shall answer these one by one. – As to the first, I had as much *right* to express my disapprobation of the conduct and principles of Sir Francis Burdett ten years ago as I have now to express my approbation of them. Whether this change has been produced by *conviction,* or proceeded from some *selfish motive,* the reader must be the judge, though I must say, that I think it would be very difficult to make out the probability of the latter. At any rate, it was *impossible* that the change should arise out of a desire to get at *any share in the public money*; and that is the great point to keep in view. – As to the second, it is perfectly *true*; and surely I had a perfect right to cease writing *whenever I pleased.* That man must have but little consideration who does not see many good reasons for my adopting such a course; but, my answer to the charge is this; that I had, and have, a *right* to cease writing whenever I pleased or shall please; and that, if I were to give up this right, I should, while I am endeavouring to ensure freedom to my country, be myself a *slave*. – As to the third, fourth, and fifth propositions, all I can say of them is, that they are FALSE; that they are *wholly* destitute of truth; that they have been invented as much as any fairy tale ever was invented; and, indeed, their falsehood is *proved* by the advertisement itself, which says, that I intended to discontinue the Register; *because . . . what*? Why, because I feared, that it would be impossible for me to continue it WITHOUT SOFTENING MY TONE. This was stated as the reason; it was so to be stated in *print*; who, then, will believe either of the three last propositions to contain a single word of truth? – Having made this denial, I make it *once for all*.[73]

Cobbett's answer, one is forced to say, was less than honest regarding the third proposition. One might quibble about whether there was any "negociation" with the government, on the ground that Cobbett's proposal was withdrawn before it could be acted on. There might be other quibbles as well, but it is difficult to understand why Cobbett made the denial at all. It would have been so easy, and not seriously damaging, to have admitted that such an arrangement with the government had been contemplated for a period of a week or so. Cobbett may have had some technical grounds for his flat denial; but unless those are better than anything that can be conjectured at this point, it is not possible to excuse his evasive answer.[74] Since the charges against Cobbett were premised on the assumption that he was affluent – that he had made a great fortune out of the cause that he proposed to desert – whereas he had not made even a small fortune, one wonders whether it was his pride that prevented him from explaining his true condition.[75] Or possibly his quick temper had led him into making a false reply that he felt obliged to defend, rather than manfully confessing the falsity of his initial response.

The day after the Crown and Anchor dinner, Cobbett, in "a carriage full of gentlemen," left London for Botley, accompanied by his eldest daughter, Anne, now a young lady of seventeen. They spent the night at Bagshot. The next day, rising early, they crossed into Hampshire for a public breakfast at Alton, the home of Cobbett's friend James Baverstock. There Anne

received a great set-down, for instead of being allowed to enjoy this beautiful repast, all over fruit and flowers and food and speeches, Mr Baverstock came to rescue her from the company of so many gentlemen, to seat her down in his own house to breakfast alone with Mrs Baverstock. Anne never all her life forgot her mortification.[76]

After Alton on they went another fifteen miles to Winchester, where they arrived at around one. "About five minutes after we got there

Mama came in a post-chaise with all the children."[77] More speeches and more bells and now a public dinner. Cobbett declared: "there were gentlemen, whom I had never seen, who had come thirty miles to meet me."[78] After Winchester, the procession travelled the ten miles or so to Botley along the new turnpike road running through Botley from Winchester to Gosport, a project begun by Cobbett before Newgate and completed in his absence. But at Botley, of all places, there were no bells! Cobbett's falling out with the local vicar, Mr. Baker (soon to enter Cobbett's pantheon of notable scoundrels), had created an irremediable breach:

Parson Baker refused the keys of the Church so that the people could not ring the bells which they wished very much to do. However, they sufficiently testified their respect to Papa, and their pleasure at his return, without the assistance of the Church. For a party of young men, I should think about a hundred, or a hundred and fifty, accompanied by a band of music which they had hired themselves for the purpose, met him about a mile out of Botley, on the new Winchester road, where they insisted on taking the horses out of the carriage, which they did, and, with colours flying and the band of music marching before them, they brought him into Botley.[79]

"When we got into the village," wrote Cobbett, "there was a sight for Sir Vicary Gibbs, and Lord Ellenborough, and his brother judges to see!"[80]

At the entrance of the village they gave three cheers and, after taking him round the village, they stopped opposite Mr Smith's, where he addressed them in a very appropriate speech, thanking them for the joy they testified at his return, and, after explaining why he was prosecuted, and what he had done to deserve such a punishment, he assured them that in the same cause he would suffer the same again, and ten times more. This met with unbounded cheers, but by this [time] all the men, women and children in the parish were assembled. They then, with the music playing, brought him down to the house, and upon his getting out of the carriage gave him three hearty cheers.

Mama had ordered four hogsheads of ale, one at each of the public houses, in the morning, but she had no idea of what was to be done. Papa arrived here about eight o'clock, and after we had drank tea about nine, the band came and stationed themselves on the lawn, where they continued playing for some time, after which we called them into the Hall, and I gave the young men and young women of the village a dance. Mr Walker and your humble Servant opening the Ball. They danced till Sunday morning, and then dispersed.[81]

17 · Peace

Were I to choose the words of my epitaph, they should be these: "He was a friend of Liberty, his power he derived from the spirit of freedom, and his exertions were directed to the benevolent purpose of bettering the condition of England".

WHEN COBBETT entered Newgate in July 1810 Britain was engaged in a single war – that with France. When he left Newgate in July 1812 Britain was engaged in two wars – its long struggle with France had been augmented by the little American war, barely a month old. To the government and the main body of the British public, the overriding objective of the nation was to defeat the enemy, and to continue fighting until that was accomplished. Not so to Cobbett. His objective was limited to the defense of England. He wanted to make peace as soon as that was secured. The government favored fighting to recover Hanover, the hereditary property of the British royal family. Cobbett was opposed to the expenditure of British lives or money for that purpose. The government favored fighting for what was grandiloquently described as the "deliverance of Europe." Cobbett favored intervention in the affairs of the continent only to the extent that it was in aid of the freely expressed will of the people; he was opposed to fighting for the restoration of the old order of hereditary despots. The government favored the extirpation of Napoleon. Cobbett favored leaving Napoleon as the ruler of France if that was the desire of the French people.

The government to which Cobbett was thus opposed was headed by Lord Liverpool, who had succeeded Spencer Perceval as prime minister. He had been in the somnolent House of Lords since the death of his father in 1808; there, combining his "respectable mediocrity of talents" with an "extreme measure of discretion in the use of them," he had the good sense to speak plainly and not too often. To this as much as anything may be attributed his uninterrupted tenure as prime minister from 1812 to 1827.[1] His inveterate habit of picking his nose in public seems to have annoyed Cobbett more than it detracted from Liverpool's success as prime minister.[2] Lord Castle-reagh, foreign secretary in Liverpool's cabinet, was ministerial leader in the House of Commons. In Cobbett's view, Castlereagh was "the aptest of all Pitt's disciples" and thus an enemy of freedom – an enmity further demonstrated by his involvement in the corruption that secured Ireland's acceptance of the union with England in 1800; his desertion of the cause of catholic emancipation; his unqualified support of Spencer Perceval; and, later, his part in reestablishing the old order throughout Europe at the end of the war and in sponsoring the repressive domestic legislation adopted by parliament shortly afterwards.[3] The references to Castlereagh in the *Political Register* during this period would almost certainly have been more memorable had it not been for the requirement of the court in the libel case that Cobbett provide surety in the sum of £5,000 for his good behavior during the seven years following his release from prison. Cobbett amused himself by converting this constraint into a game by which asterisks or other marks of deletion were used in place of the words of abuse that formerly had flowed so easily. The "times are likely to be ticklish," wrote Cobbett in an article addressed to Castlereagh, and "the mere sound of your well-known name is enough to fill any man living with . . . *prudence,* my Lord."[4]

The new ministry of Liverpool and Castlereagh, which began on June 8, 1812, coincided with a new course in the European war, which began two weeks later when Napoleon invaded Russia. By mid December of that year, Napoleon had returned to Paris without an army. Most of the half million troops with which he had commenced the campaign had been lost in Russia; the small remainder struggled home in the trail of their emperor. Thus encouraged, a new coalition of Russia, Prussia, and Austria, supported by British subsidies, threat-ened France from the east in the summer of 1813, while Wellington and his army, having fought their way through Spain, stood at the southern frontier of France by the end of the year. Paris fell in March 1814. Within a matter of weeks Napoleon was lodged on Elba and the Bourbons had been restored to the throne in the person of the cor-pulent, gout-ridden Louis XVIII – Louis "le gros," as he was famil-iarly known among the French lower classes. The coalition, the mili-tary campaigns, the abdication of Napoleon, and the return of the Bourbons were detailed, week by week, in the *Political Register* with the single exception of the exploits of Wellington, whose ultimate suc-cess in Spain and victories in southern France were largely ignored by Cobbett. While the British public exulted in these victories and the fall of Napoleon, Cobbett expressed quite different thoughts. Unlike the editor of *The Times,* who called Napoleon a "butcher," a "monster," an "odious, disgusting, contemptible hypocrite," and every other repulsive name that came to mind, the editor of the *Political Register* saw much in him that was attractive.[5]

Cobbett's assessment of Napoleon's virtues and vices tells us a great deal about Cobbett's own character. He had read the Code Napoléon, both civil and criminal, and admired it because it "effectually secured to every Frenchman an *equal* distribution of Justice" by sweeping away the tyranny that had prevailed under the Bourbons: "The letters de cachet; the game laws; the gabelles, the seigneurial jurisdiction; the arbitrary taxation; the accursed parliaments; the sale of Justice; the dominion and oppressions of the church; the cruel corvées; the endless vexations of the feudal system; the murderings of the provincial judges. All are done away, not a trace of them remains."[6] Under Napoleon freedom of worship was restored; "all *party distinctions* were disregarded; all were admissible to public offices, and places of trust, without any regard to their religious or even political opinions – whether they were catholics or protestants, royalists or republicans."[7] Immediately after the French entered Spain, the imprisonments and cruelties of the Inquisition were abolished. The sciences and arts in France during Napoleon's reign had "surpassed, in the midst of war, all the other nations of Europe put together."[8]

He even found leisure to organize public *schools* and *colleges,* to visit them occasionally, and to provide them with masters properly qualified to superintend the education of youth. France owes also her present organization of *charitable institutions* to the exertions of Napoleon. In the hospitals, the care of attending the sick was committed to persons chosen with the greatest circumspection; the old and infirm, and particularly the insane, were under the special protection of the Government. An asylum was built for the reception of foundlings; and here, as well as in the schools for orphans, the children were brought up in the habits of industry, and taught the first principles of education; after which they were apprenticed to such occupations as suited their inclinations. Even in the workhouses, of which there were comparatively few in France, every one who was able to work was furnished with employment, by which a fund was raised that rendered the exaction of poor rates merely nominal.[9]

Napoleon was obviously a great general ("the most skilful and brave captain that ever lived"), but Cobbett's admiration was broader-based: Napoleon had shared the "toils and dangers of his armies"; he had no officers who had not first served in the ranks – "the soldiers in the French army do not see strangers brought and put in command over them" – and promotions were made on the basis of merit alone.[10] Cobbett saw true greatness, "surpassing anything which is recorded of Alexander, of Scipio, of Hannibal, or of Caesar," when Napoleon, to remove the alarm of his soldiers in Egypt, went to the pesthouse and touched the bodies of soldiers suffering from the plague.[11] Cobbett found greatness, too, in the "honest, though dismal, account which Buonaparte gave of his retreat from Moscow."[12]

This oblique criticism of the heavily edited military bulletins which were then standard practice in England is paralleled by criticism in other directions. "Napoleon has many qualities . . . calculated to make him an object of respect with the people," wrote Cobbett, following this with examples which contrasted markedly with the habits of the notoriously unpopular prince regent and his friends:

He is sober. His associates, or those who appear to be most confided in by him, are men famed for their talents, in their several stations, for their wisdom, for their application to business. His hours of recreation are not spent at the gaming table, but in the manly exercises of the field.

He seldom dismounted from his horse but to retire to his study, and the greater part of that time which other Statesmen usually devote to pleasure and to repose, was employed by him in his closet on matters that concerned the welfare of the State.[13]

Finally Cobbett declared that Napoleon had ended his career (for so it was first thought when he was bundled off to Elba) with another act of greatness by abdicating while he still had strong forces loyal to him, rather than plunging the nation into a civil war for his personal rights.[14]

But Cobbett, admirer that he was, was not oblivious to Napoleon's faults. He condemned Napoleon's failure to give the Poles their freedom.[15] He condemned his ambition and his inordinate desire to aggrandize his own family.[16] He condemned his marriage to Princess Maria Louisa, daughter of the Austrian emperor, not only as an evidence of Napoleon's excessive vanity leading to his downfall, but as an act of treason against the cause of democracy: "he ought to have married the poorest girl in all France."[17] Cobbett was no starry-eyed hero-worshipper. He made it plain that he admired freedom more than he admired Napoleon. He declared that he preferred a free republican government to that of Napoleon; that he would even be willing to accept the restoration of the Bourbons if he could be sure they would not oppress their subjects "but would, in future, treat them well, and give them so much freedom and happiness, that they would desire no change."[18] Napoleon's unforgivable sin was his offenses against the republican cause:

They put him at the head of a *republic*; they placed an army of *republicans* in his hands; they sent him forth to pull down thrones. He betrayed his trust; he upheld thrones: he raised himself to a throne; he allied himself by marriage with a family, whom they regarded as their greatest enemy. He sold the liberties of his country, and, as far as he could, of Europe, for a wife and a dynasty.[19]

334

Napoleon had been accused of various criminal acts in territory occupied by his armies. Cobbett disagreed: "The only crime, in my opinion, of which Napoleon has been guilty, is that against liberty."[20] Yet, as a true lover of freedom, Cobbett believed that it was up to the French themselves to decide whether they would have this betrayer of liberty or Louis XVIII as their ruler; it was not an issue that should be decided for them by their victors.[21]

This principle was violated by the allies as they reestablished the old order in Europe, endowing future generations with a legacy of misery and discontent that produced wars and revolutions lasting into the twentieth century. Ferdinand VII, as soon as installed on the throne of Spain with the help of the British government, reinstated the Inquisition, dissolved the Cortes, abolished the constitution, and imprisoned or executed the leading liberals who had fought to save the country from its foreign enemies. Louis XVIII's return to France, greeted unenthusiastically by the people he expected to rule, was accomplished only through the assistance of the allied armies. Cobbett confidently predicted that dynasties so established after people had heard the doctrines expounded by the French revolution could not survive.[22] In 1811, when a revolution against Spanish rule had broken out in South America, Cobbett perceptively defined the future of the ancient governments:

There is a great moral cause at work: there is a change *in the mind of man*, of which the leaders in revolutions have been merely the *expositors*. The writings of Paine and Condorcet have been the effect and not the cause of this change, which has been gradually taking place, which gradually advances in its progress, and which cannot be arrested in that progress any more than human power can arrest the progress of nature in any of her operations . . . Whether it be better or worse for mankind that *rank* and *birth* should fall into contempt is a question which is beyond my humble capacity to answer; but, it is a fact, that they have fallen and are daily falling into contempt. What has been and is going on, is an insurrection of talents and courage and industry against birth and rank. Men have not, at bottom, been contending about *forms of government*. Writers and orators have; but the mass of nations do not enter into the theories; they look to the practical effects. They have been seeking such *a change* as will render their lives more happy and less humiliating, with very little regard as to *names* and *forms*.[23]

The restoration of the old order in Europe was viewed by Cobbett as proof that the British ruling class hated liberty when it meant giving the people any voice in the government, and would stamp it out wherever it appeared. He found further support for this view in two contemporaneous events: The ministerial newspapers in London, within weeks after the installation of Louis XVIII, began complaining that his government was too permissive. The *Courier* flatly stated that "the people of France, at present, are not in a condition to bear the representative system" and that if a representative legislature was attempted, it would fail.[24] Pointing in the same direction, Cobbett thought, was the course of the British war with the Americans, a war caused by the British orders in council forbidding neutral trade with French-occupied Europe and the British impressment of sailors on American ships. The conflict with France had ended in April 1814, and with it the grounds for the American war: Neutrals were allowed to trade with all parts of Europe, and the British navy ceased to impress sailors. But even though the grounds had disappeared, the war continued.

One possible explanation was that the Americans had done too well in the twenty-odd months that had elapsed since the beginning of the war in 1812 and the time Napoleon had surrendered in 1814. From the outset it had been accepted doctrine in Britain that the Americans needed a good drubbing. To a nation proud of its unbeaten ships of oak, it seemed natural and just to refer to the tiny American fleet as "half a dozen fir frigates with bits of striped bunting at their mast heads." But to everyone's surprise on the eastern side of the Atlantic (except Cobbett, who had predicted that the Americans would prove to be indigestible), the drubbing had not yet been managed.[25] The land war had been limited to short skirmishes along the Canadian border. There had been seven saltwater encounters between American and British ships, and the Americans had come off the victor in five of these trials. In the battle for control of Lake Erie, the British fleet had been entirely destroyed. According to Lloyds, American privateers had captured 825 British merchant ships by the summer of 1814. Thus, immediately after the French war had ended there was a demand for attention to the unfinished affair in America. *The Times* declared that "The American Government is in point of fact as much a tyranny . . . as was that of Buonaparte: and as we firmly urged the principle of No Peace with Buonaparte; so to be consistent with ourselves, we must in like manner maintain the doctrine of no peace with James Madison."[26] This view was confirmed by Sir Joseph Yorke, one of the lords of the admiralty, who told the House of Commons that "although one great enemy of this country, Buonaparte, had been deposed, there was another gentleman whose deposition was also necessary to our interest; he meant Mr. President Madison; and with a view to that deposition, a considerable naval force must be kept up."[27]

Thus, some 15,000 to 20,000 British veterans of the peninsular campaign and a squadron of men-of-war from the fleet that had blockaded all of Europe for the past twenty years were dispatched to America. They had not been engaged by August 1, 1814, when

England celebrated the centenary of the Hanoverian succession. One of the spectacles of the jubilee was a battle on the Hyde Park Serpentine between models of British ships of oak and American "fir frigates," both fitted with miniature cannon:

> Here the English fleet performed wonders against the Americans, whose frigates they sometimes sunk, sometimes burnt, sometimes destroyed, and sometimes captured. There were some *hottish* fights; but our tars always, in the end, overcame the Yankee dogs; and, at the close of the day, the Yankee flag was seen flying reversed, under the English, in token of the defeat and disgrace of the former.[28]

Three weeks later the real British expeditionary force was involved in its first action. A contingent which had sailed up Chesapeake Bay, making what the *Morning Chronicle* called "one of the most gallant dashes of the war," burned the Library of Congress and other public buildings in the Americans' newly built capital at Washington, and gallantly dashed back to their ships.[29] Two weeks afterwards, when attacking Baltimore, the force was repulsed and its commanding general killed. A northern contingent of 11,000 veterans under Sir George Prevost pressed down from Canada to Plattsburg, New York, supported by a fleet of small ships on Lake Champlain to protect the right flank. The British fleet was defeated and Prevost was forced to retreat with a large loss of supplies and some desertions. A third contingent led by Sir Edward Pakenham, one of Wellington's generals and his brother-in-law, was cut to pieces in an attack on New Orleans by a force under the command of the lawyer Andrew Jackson, whose frontiersmen from Kentucky and Tennessee, with their long rifles, shot down 2,000 redcoats (more than a quarter of the whole force) as though they were so many wild turkeys. Pakenham and two other British generals were killed. The battle of New Orleans took place on January 8, 1815. There was no way of advising the forces that a peace treaty between Britain and America had been signed at Ghent fifteen days before.[30]

Two behind-the-scenes episodes played a part, perhaps a controlling part, in bringing the war to an end. Wellington, when asked to assume the command of the war against the Americans in November 1814, declared that there could be no success without "naval superiority on the Lakes," which by then was firmly held by the Americans.[31] About the same time, the serious quarrels that had arisen between the allies meeting in Vienna to settle the shape of postwar Europe (Russia and Prussia taking sides against Britain, Austria, and France) made it desirable that the British rid themselves of all extraneous diversions.[32]

The British–American war of 1812–14 was not, to Cobbett, simply a war between two nations. To him it was primarily a war between two conceptions which were slowly heading for a confrontation in Britain itself.[33] The system of government specifically founded on the principle of equality, in which the people ruled themselves, stood opposed to the system which took for granted the existence of inequality, in which the people were ruled by an elite. The attitude of the British ruling class toward the rival system was expressed by *The Times*, which described the enemy across the seas as "the mischievous example of the existence of a Government founded on democratic rebellion."[34] President Madison's leadership was "a lamentable evil to the civilized world," and mild little Madison himself, America's greatest political philosopher, was "a military despot of the most sanguinary character."[35] *The Times* asserted that every man who had a regard for "rational liberty" devotedly wished to see the "subversion of that system of fraud and malignity, which constitutes the whole policy of the Jeffersonian school . . . The American Government must be displaced, or it will, sooner or later, plant its poisoned dagger into the heart of the parent State."[36]

These hysterical fulminations, typical of what the "respectable" London newspapers spewed out daily, provide some measure of the deeply rooted antagonism toward government founded on the principle of equality. Although the words themselves were directed against America, they consciously or subconsciously represented a defense against proposals to popularize the government of Britain.[37] Cobbett's reply to these attacks, in form directed to the American scene, was surely written with an eye to the situation at home. Week after week Cobbett regaled his readers with the more outrageous statements from *The Times* and the *Courier,* followed by his editorial comment. When the ministerial papers claimed that the war was unpopular in the United States, as demonstrated by articles appearing there in the federalist press, Cobbett turned the argument on his opponents; the articles only proved the remarkable freedom of the press in America, which permitted the publication of such attacks on the government:

Out of the three or four hundred newspapers, published in America, there are probably ten or twelve who proceed in this tone . . . But, the hireling prints here do one thing for us: they, by their extracts, prove to us *how great is freedom in America.* The *Times* tells us, that one paper in America expresses its opinion, that the President himself had a narrow escape from Washington; and, that another *expresses its regret that he was not taken by the enemy.* Now, reader, imagine, for a moment, the case of an enemy landed in England, and some writer expressing *his regret, that the said enemy had not captured the king!* – You tremble for the unfortunate creature. I see you tremble. Your teeth chat-

338

ter in your head. I hear them chatter; and well they may. How many *loyal* men do I hear exclaim: "send the traitor to the gallows! rip out his bowels and throw them in his face! Cut off his head! Quarter his vile carcase, and put the quarters at the king's disposal!" – Yet, we hear the American writers wishing that their chief magistrate had been taken by the enemy; and we do not find that any thing is either done or said to them. Their publications are suffered to take their free course. If they be true, and speak sense and reason, they will gain adherents, as they ought. If false, or foolish, they will only gain for the writers hatred or contempt, which, I dare say, has been the case in the instance before us. – But, reader, let us not, with this fact full in our eyes, be induced to believe that the Americans have nothing to fight for; or, that any man who loves freedom, can wish to see a change in the Government; or, at least, in the *sort* of Government which exists in that country.[38]

In other articles, Cobbett pointed to the modest salaries paid to American government officials; the absence of sinecures, hereditary titles, and the trappings of office; and the reliance for the country's defense on the ablebodied citizenry rather than on a huge standing army. When it was reported in *The Times* that Sir John Hippisley had said, at a Somerset county meeting, that he "hated" the Americans, Cobbett wrote:

But, Sir John, why do you HATE the Americans? You cannot, surely, hate them because they pay their President only about six thousand pounds a year, not half so much as our Apothecary General receives . . . You, surely, cannot hate them because they keep no sinecure placemen, and no pensioners, except to such as have actually rendered them services, and to them grant pensions only by vote of their real representatives. You, surely, cannot hate them because in their country, the press is *really* free, and *truth* cannot be a *libel*. You, surely, cannot hate them because they have shewn that a *cheap* government is, in fact, the strongest of all governments, standing in no need of the troops or of treason laws to defend it in times even of actual invasion. You may, indeed, *pity* them because they are destitute of the honour of being governed by some illustrious family; because they are destitute of Dukes, Royal and others, of Most Noble Marquises, of Earls, of Viscounts and Barons; because they are destitute of Knights of the Garter, Thistle and Bath, Grand-Crosses, Commanders and Companions . . . because they are destitute of a Church established by law and of tythes: you, may, indeed, *pity* the Republicans on these accounts; but, Sir John, it would be cruel to *hate* them.[39]

When Cobbett asserted that the American constitution "which the war had put upon its trial . . . has come out of it like pure gold out of the fire," he was thinking of the principles in that constitution which were of English origin, or so he believed.[40]

What are those principles? – That governments were made for the people, and not the people for governments. – That sovereigns reign legally only by virtue of the people's choice. – That birth without merit ought not to command merit without birth. – That all men ought to be equal in the eye of the law. – That no man ought to be taxed or punished by any law to which he has not given his assent by himself or by his representative. – That taxation and representation ought to go hand in hand. – That every man ought to be judged by his peers, or equals. – That the press ought to be free.[41]

Cobbett exulted in the peace with America, not because it was a defeat for English forces, but because he thought it foretold a victory for the future of English freedom.[42]

Within three months of the signing of the British–American peace of Ghent, Napoleon had returned from Elba. He was back in Paris on March 20, 1815.[43] Then, in quick succession, came the battle of Waterloo, the reoccupation of the French capital by the allies, and Napoleon's banishment to St. Helena. It was only then that the Pax Britannica could be said to have commenced. "The play is over," wrote the editor of the *Courier* in a fine dramatic mood, "and now let us go to supper." This evoked a sobering reply from Cobbett: "No," said he, "we cannot go to supper yet. We must first pay for the pleasure of the play."[44] For Britain's long wars had cost the country more than £1,000 million, of which only the smaller part had been collected out of current taxes. Most of the money had been borrowed, and this would have to be repaid out of future taxes. The national debt at the end of 1815 stood at more than £700 million, bearing interest of more than £30 million a year. The annual interest alone, without regard to the other expenses of government, was almost twice the total tax burden in 1792, the last prewar year. And what, Cobbett asked, had been accomplished for these millions of pounds and the thousands of lives that had been lost? The Bourbon dynasty – always hated in England, and one of the most tyrannous and corrupt in Europe – had been restored!

The truth is, that we have, in the course of this long war, lost sight of its origin. We now rejoice at a result, which, at the outset, we should have deplored . . . The injuries we can, with all our subsidized armies, inflict upon the French people, will be of short duration: those which we have inflicted on ourselves will last for ages, or will more speedily terminate after some great convulsion.[45]

Britain had already experienced, as the end of the war neared, something perilously close to a "great convulsion." In 1811 and 1812 extreme distress developed among workers in the textile industry, where an abrupt fall in work due to the war embargoes coincided with poor harvests.[46] At the same time, the competition from newly introduced steam machinery reduced the pay of hand-loom workers to half of what they had formerly received.[47] While many had to content themselves with these drastic cuts in pay, others had no work at all. There was "not more than half work in the cotton trade," and at Bolton, famous for its woolen manufacturers, 3,000 of its 17,000 popu-

lation were in need of relief.[48] Workers at Nottingham began breaking frames and machinery early in 1811. The movement, known as
"Luddism" (those involved in it as "Luddites") shortly spread into
Lancashire, Cheshire, and Yorkshire, where, throwing off previous
restraint, the Luddites, often masked and under cover of darkness,
gathered arms, committed robberies, and threatened more obdurate
employers with physical violence. One was murdered. Cobbett
described it as "a state of confusion approaching a civil war."[49] Hunger, he believed, was at the root of the problem:

It has been proved, in the clearest possible manner, that, in the troubled
counties, the people have suffered and are suffering, in a most cruel manner;
that the food of many of them is of the worst sort and not half sufficient in
quantity; that hundreds and thousands of poor mothers and their children
are wholly destitute of *bread,* and that even *potatoes are too dear for them to get
at*; that the food of these unfortunate creatures is *oatmeal and water,* and that
they have not a sufficiency of that. It is proved that many have *died,* actually
expired from want of food.[50]

The ministerial papers called the rioters miscreants, robbers, assas-
sins. "They speak of them as a contemptible rabble at the same time
. . . But, never does a word of pity for their sufferings find its way into
their writings."[51] The inexorable laws of supply and demand were the
refuge of many a scoundrel. "One must be cruel to be kind," said the
editor of the *Courier.*[52] While Cobbett condemned violence, he sympathized with those who were induced by circumstances to make use
of it. His way to stop the violence was to cure the cause. The government way was to punish. *The Times* disposed of the lawbreakers in a
riddlelike formula: "they put themselves out of the protection of the
law, and justice must be done upon them."[53] Of the editor of the
Courier, whose solution was "more vigorous measures," Cobbett
wrote: "This pampered hireling does not know what *hunger* is."[54] The
same comment might with equal propriety have been applied to
Spencer Perceval and his successor, Lord Liverpool, whose response
to the suffering of the people was force, and always more force.

Outside Nottingham a military camp was established for 3,000
infantry and 500 cavalry. Another such camp was set up at Kersal
Moor near Manchester.[55] Eight regiments of militia were distributed
around the troubled area.[56] Detachments of soldiers and guards provided by local property owners were stationed in the villages. A thousand troops were billeted in the thirty public houses of Huddersfield,
making the total military force for the suppression of the Luddites
more than 12,000 men.[57] Spies were also sent in to assist in ferreting
out the Luddite leaders. Early in 1812 parliament prescribed the
death penalty for frame breaking and for the administering or taking

of "unlawful oaths" of secrecy. The culprits seized in Nottingham during the 1811 episodes had been sentenced to transportation, but at Lancaster and Chester in 1812 and at York in January 1813 there were mass hangings – a total of more than twenty. Of this total, three were for the single murder that had been committed, while the others were for the lesser offenses of frame breaking, oath taking, and robbery.[58] One of the victims was a boy "not fourteen years old; and when he was about to be hanged, actually called out for his 'mammy' to come and save him!"[59] A woman at Manchester was hanged for stealing potatoes from a cart. The result was reassuring to the advocates of force. On March 11, 1813 Lord Sidmouth, the home secretary, wrote: "the people are sound and firm. A most material and happy change has taken place in their temper and disposition in the last few months."[60] That there had been a material change no one could doubt. There is some question, though, whether the change had been a particularly happy one for all who were concerned.

A superb harvest in the autumn of 1813, bringing down bread prices, provided some small relief to the textile workers, but the volume of production continued low even after raw cotton again became available from America.[61] Thus many remained unemployed while those who were working were paid about half of what they had earned ten years before. An unsuccessful strike against Nottingham hosiery manufacturers from April to July 1814 and a renewed burst of frame breaking produced nothing but more misery.[62] By that time, fissures had begun to appear elsewhere in the British economy. The high price of grain that had prevailed since 1805 had pushed up farm rents and induced the farmers to expand their acreage by cultivating marginal lands. Two million acres were added to the productive capacity in the ten years preceding 1816.[63] The good harvests beginning in 1813 and continuing into 1815, together with large imports in 1814, brought down the price of wheat to roughly half of what it had been three years before.[64] The farmers contended that the new prices were inadequate to cover their costs.

As farm prices came down, so did farm wages. Those in the Botley area had been 15s. to 18s. a week; now they were 10s. to 12s.[65] In Cambridgeshire, wage rates for single men fell to 8d. a day – 4s. a week.[66] Many employers could not afford even these wages. Laborers by the thousands were released at the same time as thousands were being discharged from the armed forces.

George Rose, Cobbett's neighbor at Lyndhurst in Hampshire, placeman and sinecurist for the past forty years, complained in the House of Commons about the 30,000 beggars in London. Sending them out of London into the country, Cobbett asserted, was no solution: "We are over-stocked already. Observe, trifling as is this village, scarcely a day passes without bringing one, and generally more, beggars to my door . . . They swarm over the country like vermin upon their own bodies; and are produced by causes nearly similar."[67] To the twentieth-century observer it is obvious that a "general depression was under way by the close of 1815."[68]

In 1816, the agricultural distress expanded into the industrial economy. Cobbett had seen in mid 1815 that the peace, "instead of crowding our ports with ships and goods, and filling our streets with the bustle of trade, produced a calm, a stillness, as to trade, truly gloomy."[69] But at the opening of parliament on February 1, 1816 the prince regent in his speech to the House of Commons was allowed to say that "the manufactures, commerce and revenue of the United Kingdom are in a flourishing condition."[70] That, however, was not the view of the majority of the House. Within three weeks of the speech, the parliament, contrary to the recommendations of the ministers, had refused to extend the 10 percent income tax on the ground that the people would no longer tolerate it. The economy fully justified their concern. Goods manufactured for export glutted foreign markets, and were finally sold at heavy losses.[71] Employment in the London dockyards fell from 1,500 to 500.[72] The price of iron dropped from £20 a ton to £8.[73] Colliers from the north of England, hitching themselves to wagons loaded with coal, dragged them towards London with placards proclaiming "rather work than beg."[74] Clock and watch workers pawned their tools in order to provide money for living expenses.[75] The *London Gazette* reported an average of six bankruptcies a day for the year 1816, an all-time record.[76] Those dispossessed of their businesses were also dispossessed of their homes and their personal possessions. Two paintings by Claude purchased three years before for £2,100 were sold for £150.[77]

By December 1816 the prince regent found it appropriate to acknowledge publicly the existence of the "distress and difficulties of the country," but his private actions belied his words, for despite the miseries of the people, he continued, at the age of fifty-four, the self-indulgent pattern that had been characteristic of his entire adult life.[78] His household was maintained at £40,000 for a quarter year; his wine bill alone was more than £2,000.[79] As a means of relieving distress, he fatuously directed his court attendants to wear clothes of domestic manufacture, those of the highest rank to be "of dark purple with crimson velvet collars, richly ornamented all over with gold."[80] At the prince's request, parliament generously voted £60,000 of the public money for the trousseau of his daughter on her marriage to the Prince of Saxe-Coburg, with annual payments of an equal amount for life.[81] This was not taken by all taxpayers in the same generous spirit as it was granted. At a Kent county meeting held in Maidstone on June 17, the assembled throng, by a vote of ten to one, rejected a proposed address to his royal highness on these "auspicious nuptials," with mutterings of "send up a petition for employment for the poor" and "we can't afford to keep foreigners."[82] This was the atmosphere in which Cobbett and his colleagues mounted their renewed attack for parliamentary reform after four or five years of relative inactivity.[83]

The three most prominent reformers in 1815 and the years following were Cobbett, Cartwright, and Hunt. Burdett was still nominally their leader, but he was almost imperceptibly losing enthusiasm as the reform program became increasingly a popular movement. Lord Cochrane, although discredited with much of the respectable public as the result of involvement in a stock exchange scandal, became, for a brief period, the voice in parliament of the radical reformers.[84] Lord Folkestone remained friendly with Cobbett but was not prepared to advocate universal suffrage; he had allied himself with such liberal whigs as Brougham and Creevey, and took little part in action outside the halls of parliament.[85]

While Cobbett, Cartwright, and Hunt cooperated closely, each had a separate, distinctive role. Cobbett made his principal contribution in the forceful articles appearing in the *Political Register*. Cartwright, seventy-five years old in 1815, toured the country promoting reform in the quiet, gentlemanly manner that was natural to him, and busied himself with the affairs of the Hampden Club, a society of conservative reformers (Cobbett and Hunt did not belong) which he had founded in 1812.[86] As a result of Cartwright's touring, independent Hampden Clubs were established in a number of cities outside London, although Cobbett (who had always heartily despised clubs and societies of every kind) was not sympathetic to this side of Cartwright's activity.[87] Henry Hunt, drawing on the material produced by Cobbett, proved capable of enthralling and exciting large crowds at public gatherings. Hunt lived with a Mrs. Vince on a farm near Andover twenty-five miles from Botley. As early as 1809 the two radicals began exchanging ideas on farming as well as on parliamentary reform.[88] In 1812 Cobbett supported Hunt's unsuccessful candidacy for parliament at Bristol. Hunt's national career dates from February 1816, when he spoke at a great meeting held at Palace Yard in Westminster. Cobbett's report of the meeting suggests that Hunt gained his mastery over the audience by the "numerous, the interesting, the apt facts, and home truths" (they seem to have been derived from the *Political Register*), adding generously, "and by the bold and manly way of stat-

344

ing them."[89] This bold and manly way of speaking, coupled with a clear and powerful voice and a fine touch of the dramatic, soon known throughout England, earned the tall and virile possessor of these attributes the name "Orator" Hunt.

The program that united these most prominent reformers was that of "restoring to the people . . . the most essential of all their rights, and without which all else is delusion, the right of freely, equally and annually electing their own representatives."[90] The word "annually" was clear enough – its purpose was to insure that parliament always reflected the most current views of their electors – but "freely" and "equally" were subject to interpretation and some controversy. The former could be construed to include the requirement for the secret ballot, and this interpretation was accepted by Cobbett although not always strenuously urged by him or his colleagues. The word "equally" to some meant granting suffrage to all adult males who were subject to direct taxation, as implied in "no taxation without representation." To others it meant all householders. To Cartwright it had always, since 1789, meant universal suffrage, and this view, accepted by Cobbett late in 1816, was also held by Hunt.[91] Thus the two essentials of the program were annually elected parliaments and universal suffrage.[92] The need for those reforms was inextricably linked to "the unexampled distress which now unhappily afflicts alike our agriculture, manufactures, and commerce." It was claimed that the government was controlled by a "borough faction" or, alternatively, "seatfillers" or "borough-mongers" – "lords, some baronets, and some esquires, as they call themselves, who fill, or nominate others to fill, the seats in the House of Commons" – who had, in their own interest, "plunged and continued the nation in sanguinary, unjust and protracted conflicts"; had heaped on the people a huge debt and intolerable taxes; and had promoted wrongful and wasteful expenditure, including a standing army in time of peace.[93] In addition to the general correction of wrongs and elimination of inefficiencies that could be expected from a freely and equally elected parliament, Cobbett had some favorite proposals which he and Hunt strenuously urged. These included the reduction of salaries of judges and other public officials which had been raised in times past because of higher living costs; the recouping by the government of excess past payments to sinecurists and contractors; the rooting out of lawyers from public office and their return to private practice; the reduction of payments to each of the junior members of the royal family to a maximum of £6,000 a year; and finally, and most important, an equitable adjustment of the national debt so as to bring down the annual interest expense.[94] The primary thrust of the argument in 1816, stated in its barest form, was that people were miserable because of the heavy tax burden caused by the "borough faction" and that the cure was a reform of parliament. Obviously this was a vast oversimplification of both the problem and the solutions proposed by the reformers, but it probably accurately reflected the view of the majority of those who signed the petitions for reform.

Early in 1816 Cobbett became convinced that the critical nature of the country's financial problems would force reform. Government expenditure in 1815 had been £113 million. About £78 million had been raised in taxes; the balance had been borrowed. Parliament's refusal to extend the income tax meant a £14 million loss in revenue; and another £2.7 million was lost by reducing the malt tax. The indirect taxes on articles of consumption would decline sharply because of the depression. The Bank of England was rapidly reducing the money in circulation, thereby accelerating the deflation and making tax collection more difficult. Cobbett concluded that the tax revenue would be so inadequate that the government would be forced to default on its obligations.[95] "The thing, the whole concern, is now got into such a state; there is such a *mess* of it altogether, that I defy any body to prevent a radical change."[96] This was published on March 9. Two weeks later he wrote: "It is impossible for things to go on in this course. There must be some *great change by law.*"[97] In April and May there were "bread or blood" riots in Norfolk, Suffolk, Devon, Huntingdonshire, and Cambridgeshire accompanied by a revival of rick and barn burnings and the destruction of machines.[98] This was met by what by now had become the standard repressive routine. Soldiers and spies were sent into the area. Seventy-three rioters were arrested. Five of these were hanged at Ely.

The distress was compounded by a cruel act of nature. Due to unprecedented volcanic eruptions in the Pacific obscuring the sky throughout the northern hemisphere for months on end, the mean temperature in England during July 1816 was the lowest registered in that month in any year since recordkeeping began in 1698. "Never was there such a backward season," wrote farmer Cobbett to farmer Hunt in June 1816.[99] Between June 17 and September 13, more than sixteen inches of rain fell in the London area. This extraordinary weather resulted in "the most severe scarcity of food since the 17th century."[100] Wheat had sold for 52s. a quarter in January 1816. In December it sold for 103s. On November 6, Cobbett flatly predicted that the desire of the people for reform "will be gratified . . . within one year from this very day."[101] This conclusion was reinforced in his mind by the recollection that Thomas Paine, in 1796, had declared that the English funding system had "now advanced into the last twenty years of its existence."[102] Because of the entrenched position of those in power, Cobbett believed reform would come only as a result of the collapse that would occur when the interest on the debt could no longer be paid.[103]

All Cobbett's efforts were now concentrated on one objective. He trimmed the *Political Register* by dropping official bulletins and letters from correspondents.[104] Nearly every issue was devoted to a single article bearing on the subject of reform. On November 2 the article was addressed to "The Journeymen and Labourers of England, Wales, Scotland, Ireland."[105] Although the paper had been read previously by workers meeting in public houses who had clubbed together to buy a copy, this was the first issue specifically directed to a working men's audience.[106] The cost of the paper, 1s. 0½d. (the tax alone was 4d.), was prohibitive to any single reader in that class, being more than a day's pay at the 8d. rate received in Cambridge. Cobbett decided to supplement the regular edition with a cheap edition printed on both sides of a single open sheet – a broadsheet approximately 18 by 22 inches – which, under existing law, was not subject to tax.[107] The sheet was to sell for 2d. It was an immediate success beyond all expectations: 6,000 of the address to journeymen and laborers were sold on the first day (the circulation of *The Times* was about 5,000), 20,000 in the first week, 44,000 in the first month.[108]

Those reading the address were told that the misery of the people was attributable to the high taxes – every family of five paid at least £10 a year (more than half a laborer's wages at 7s. a week) in indirect taxes – which "the government requires us to pay for the support of its army, its placemen, its pensioners, etc. and for the payment of the interest of its debt." This could be remedied only by a change in parliament, not by venting rage on the baker, or brewer, or butcher, or even the employer; they, too, were in distress because of the heavy tax burden. The journeymen and laborers needed not be quiet about the state of affairs, but should proceed to demand their rights in "peaceable and lawful manner"; that is, by petitioning for reform.[109]

There was nothing new in Cobbett's arguments. What was new was his deliberate attempt to induce the "swinish multitude" to participate in the government. Many times in the past they had seen proclamations stating what the government expected of them. Here, though, was a suggestion that they might have a voice in deciding what was expected of the government. Moreover, they were told that it was important for them to play an active part in shaping the political system, since the strength and resources of England, the most powerful nation in the world, "ever have sprung and must spring, from the *labour* of its people." Thus the cheap *Political Register* represented three significant steps in the making of the English working class: it gave them a feeling of their worth, it was a manifesto of their political rights, and it was a means of educating them in the exercise of such rights.[110] Leigh Hunt thought that Cobbett's innovation – a newspaper selling at a price within the reach of everybody – deserved "eternal commemoration" as a revolution in press history comparable to "the invention of printing itself."[111] The "Bourbon paper" (Cobbett's newest name for *The Times*) honored the innovation in a different manner. It ran a "five column" attack on Cobbett based on many of the old charges: his negotiations with the government to avoid punishment at the time of the 1810 libel case and the inconsistency between his 1802–3 and 1816 positions on such matters as Napoleon, parliamentary reform, and Sir Francis Burdett.[112] Cobbett's reply was brief: "it is what I *write*, and not what I *have been*, or what *I am*, which is the subject of interest with the people."[113]

When Cobbett decided to issue the broadsheet addressed to journeymen and laborers, there was no indication that he intended it as anything other than a single shot in that direction. But because of its reception, he decided to continue printing the two versions, the regular edition and the cheap edition, side by side. He took a house in London at 8 Catherine Street so he could be close to the main scene of activity, and used that address as a separate office for the sale of the cheap edition. To promote its widest possible distribution, he offered a substantial discount to purchasers of a hundred or more copies.[114] Hawkers of the cheap edition appeared everywhere, to the dismay of local authorities and to the even greater dismay of the editors of rival publications. The *Courier* called it "two penny trash," a name which Cobbett adopted in derision of his enemies.[115] The *Quarterly Review* declared that "Its ignorant readers receive it with entire faith: it serves them for law and for gospel – for their Creed and their Ten Commandments."[116] *The Times* gratuitously printed a "Caution to hawkers of Cobbett's register" warning them that they could not sell the paper in the streets without a pedlar's license.[117] At Wolverhampton a man selling the *Register* was taken into custody, although released the next day, and similar incidents took place at Coventry and in London itself. At Romsey, in Hampshire, the keepers of public houses were warned that they might endanger their licenses if the *Political Register* was allowed on their premises. "I am informed of one master manufacturer in Lancashire," wrote Cobbett, "who has threatened to turn off every man to starve, 'who shall *even read* Cobbett.' " Two men selling the new publication in Shropshire were flogged by order of a clerical magistrate, "since which," wrote an observer to Lord Sidmouth, "I have heard of no others being circulated in this neighbourhood." Still, the sale went on elsewhere. "I have heard of one man," wrote Cobbett, "who has sold 1,800 of these Registers, by which he has cleared three pounds fifteen shillings."[118] By January 1817, three months after the start of the new venture, Cobbett claimed that his circulation was greater than that of all the other London papers combined.[119] At the end of six months, more than a million copies had been sold.[120] The American secretary of state, reporting to Washington from London in January 1817, stated that Cobbett was "the most popular writer in Britain."[121]

Despite the suspicions about Cobbett's intentions, the immediate impact of the articles receiving such wide circulation was to quiet the people by inducing them to pursue lawful channels. As Cobbett himself was quick to point out, the petitions had given people hope, and they tended to be more tranquil than in those places where all reform activity was stamped out.[122] In his article of November 30 addressed "to the Luddites" he patiently explained that the worker would ultimately benefit from the introduction of new equipment; that the laborer "must be injured by the destruction of machinery."[123] One of the classic nineteenth-century accounts of the Luddites states flatly that "Beyond all question" the decline of Luddism "was hastened materially by the writings of the famous William Cobbett."[124]

Cobbett's appeal to the laboring class through the cheap edition was met by parallel activity on the part of Hunt. Hunt had been wildly applauded at Westminster meetings held in February and September 1816; there was nothing out of the ordinary, though, in those meetings, since they followed a standard pattern of at least semirespectability, being attended by members of parliament and local business people as well as the usual hangers-on. In November Hunt was invited to appear before a quite different audience. It was to be a public meeting, not of any parliamentary constituency, but of the distressed inhabitants of London for the alleged purpose of petitioning for such measures "as will relieve the sufferers from the misery which now overwhelms them."[125] The meeting, to be held on November 15, at Spa Fields in north London, was called by a small group who called themselves the Society of Spencean Philanthropists.[126] "Mr Hunt went over to Botley to me, to ask what I thought he had better do." It was agreed that Hunt should go, but should not allow the "cause of reform to be mixed up with what was called the Spencean Project" for the public ownership of land.[127] Hunt duly attended, made one of his stirring speeches to an audience of six to eight thousand, and (in place of the memorial that had been prepared in advance by the Spenceans) obtained the approval of a petition to the prince regent supporting universal suffrage and other reform objectives. The meeting was peaceful enough, but in the evening of the same day a mob attacked some bakers' and butchers' shops and the office of the *Morning Chronicle*.[128] A second meeting was held on December 2.[129] On the morning of that day, a handbill was handed about the crowd that had begun to assemble, with these words: "A pot of beer for a penny and bread for two pence: HUNT REGENT and COBBETT KING: Go it, my Boys!"[130] As Hunt approached Spa Fields he observed an excited crowd headed in the opposite direction. Hunt was told by one of them – "a damn'd scoundrel who had been guilty of conveying French prisoners out of the country" – that he should turn around and go with them, that the Tower was in their hands.[131] Disregarding the invitation, Hunt continued to the assigned meeting place, where he promptly called on those remaining to adopt a resolution condemning violence.[132] This obviously came too late. The early leavers broke into gunshops and stole arms, a few shots were fired (a spectator was injured), and one unidentified man, waving what was said to be a cutlass, proposed that the Tower surrender. When this did not happen the crowd dispersed. In a calmer atmosphere this relatively mild outburst might have been quickly forgotten. But two years of sporadic riots and violence, at a time when the excesses of the French revolution were hardly ancient history, had brought a large part of the population close to hysteria. The Spa Fields episode produced the wildest rumors: In Manchester it was believed that the Tower had surrendered and the Bank of England had been destroyed.[133] In Dublin, "the Royal family were flying for protection to Ireland . . . the populace had possession of London . . . the soldiers were in league with them."[134] The leaders of the Spencean Philanthropists were arrested and their papers seized. The *Courier* immediately claimed that one of the Spenceans had confessed to a conspiratorial "plan of insurrection" in which 300,000 persons were enrolled.[135] In the end all the Spenceans were released, but not until after a trial that took place in June 1817.[136]

The riot was grist to the conspiratorial mythmakers who visualized a vast national network of agitators with Cobbett and Hunt at the center. "They sigh for a PLOT," wrote Cobbett. "Oh, how they sigh! They are working and slaving and fretting and stewing; they are sweating all over; they are absolutely pining and dying for a plot!"[137] *The Times* and *Courier* thought they had found it. They reported "on authority" that Cobbett and Hunt were "in close consultation" with Lord Cochrane on the Sunday before the Spa Fields riots. It was a bad guess; on the day referred to, Cobbett was in Surrey, Hunt was in Essex, and Lord Cochrane was in London.[138]

Meanwhile, the petition gathering went on, stimulated by Cartwright's Hampden Clubs and similar reform societies, by Hunt's oratory, and by Cobbett's writings. An estimated 600,000 to 1,000,000 signatures were obtained, amounting, perhaps, to as much as 25 percent of the adult male population.[139] The objective was to present the petitions immediately after the opening of parliament on January 28, 1817. The week before that date seventy deputies from the various petitioning organizations (including Cobbett, Hunt, and Cartwright) met at the Crown and Anchor tavern in London in response to a printed circular signed by Sir Francis Burdett, and passed resolutions in support of specific reform proposals.[140] Since Burdett failed to appear at the meeting and could not be found at his London home, there was some confusion as to what should be done. Finally Hunt assembled the petition bearers at Charing Cross; from there they moved in a procession to the house of Lord Cochrane on the terrace in Palace Yard directly opposite the entrance to Westminster Hall. The crowd, now an estimated 20,000 persons, carried Cochrane to the door of Westminster with the Bristol petition in his arms, "a roll of parchment about the size of a tolerable barrel."[141] It was not until January 29, the day after the opening of parliament, that Lord Cochrane had the opportunity of offering the first petition. The others "filled the whole space of several yards, from the Bar to the Table."[142] The drama, however, was obscured by a more dramatic episode that had taken place the day before. The prince regent had hardly left parliament after delivering his opening address when Viscount Sidmouth announced to the House of Lords that he had "one of the most important communications that had ever been made to parliament": The prince regent had been attacked on his return from Westminster. The glass on the left side of his carriage had been pierced by two small bullets fired from an air gun or air pistol, a large stone had been thrown against the glass of the carriage which broke it, and three or four other stones were thrown which struck the carriage.[143]

Thus the petitions came as an anticlimax. The huge Bristol document containing nearly 16,000 signatures was received by the House and permitted to lie on the table, "where it still lies, in the legal construction of the thing, ungranted its prayer, undiscussed its contents, and unanswered its allegations."[144] Most of the other petitions became the playthings of the experts on arcane parliamentary procedure: Many were rejected on the ground that they were printed rather than handwritten; others because they were not sufficiently respectful of the House of Commons or because the signatures were on one piece of paper and the body of the petition on another.[145] The thoughts of the ministry had quickly turned to more practical matters,

Cobbett on the *Importer* in Liverpool harbor, November 1817

for the attack on the prince was all that was needed to set in motion the machinery of oppression. Secret committees were established in both houses of parliament. To these committees were delivered reports made during the past few months by the small army of spies and spies-turned-provocateurs employed by Lord Sidmouth for the purpose of tracking down Luddites and attending meetings of the suspected reform clubs. The secret committee of the House of Lords, reporting on February 18, found that the Spa Fields meetings were part of a traitorous conspiracy formed for "the purpose of overthrowing, by means of a general insurrection, the established Government . . . and of effecting a general plunder and division of property." These designs were furthered by the "unremitting activity which has been employed throughout the kingdom in circulating to an unprecedented extent, at the lowest prices or gratuitously, publications of the most seditious and inflammatory nature."[146] The House of Commons committee, adopting the same general theme, concluded that the ultimate object of the societies supporting parliamentary reform was to overthrow by force the existing form of government.[147]

Matters now moved rapidly. Lord Sidmouth urged the need for additional legislation: The law officers of the crown had decided that the allegedly "seditious and inflammatory" publications "were drawn up with so much dexterity – the authors had so profited from former lessons of experience" – that it would be difficult to succeed by prosecution in the courts.[148] This strange argument proved convincing. An act declaring that "a traitorous Conspiracy has been formed for the Purpose of overthrowing by means of a general Insurrection, the established Government, Laws and Constitution of this Kingdom" and providing that any person imprisoned by warrant signed by Sidmouth or Castlereagh might be detained without bail and without trial – that is, nullifying the Habeas Corpus Act – was rushed through parliament.[149] Quickly following it were several other strong measures, including a bill familiarly known as the "gagging act," placing all public meetings under the thumb of local authorities. The suspension of the writ of habeas corpus became effective on March 4. "I did hope," wrote the impatient poet laureate Southey to Lord Liverpool on March 19, "that the first measure after the suspension of the Habeas Corpus Act would have been to place the chief incendiary writers in safe custody."[150] A more conciliatory move was tried first. Cobbett received a proposal, from a person he believed to be acting for Lord Sidmouth, that he drop the *Political Register* and retire to his farm at Botley "with a compensation for the loss of the income from my writings."[151] Cobbett gave no immediate answer. Instead, at four

18 · America again

I will die an Englishman in exile, or an Englishman in England free.

WILLIAM COBBETT and his two sons arrived in New York on May 5, 1817. The six weeks' voyage had been perilous and disagreeable. The ship was twice struck by lightning, which shivered the masts and killed a man. The Cobbett boys were seasick and had to be nursed by their father. One of the eleven passengers sharing the Cobbett cabin (eight men, a woman, and two small children) died at the end of three weeks of "a lingering disease, the effects of which . . . formed a subject not only of horrible disgust, but of some apprehension on account of probable infection." Apart from the "perfectly civil and polite" Mr. Astor, son of "a respectable merchant of New York," their cabin companions were unpleasant. This was particularly true of a youngish Mr. Bostick (or Bostwick) from Connecticut, a commercial traveller who had a voice that was "half nasal and half squeak" and a nose "like that of Mrs Towhouse in Joseph Andrews," and who owed "pretty nearly half his weight to the taylor and shoe-maker." Bostick amused Cobbett by saying that a Dr. Mitchell of New York was writing an interesting work, as he described it, on "the theology of fishes" (a confusion, presumably, of theology with ichthyology), and irritated him in innumerable ways, including making the shocking assertion that the Episcopal church in America was the same as the church of England, whereas, as Cobbett made clear, the former had "abandoned the auricular confession and absolution of sins which our Church enjoins, and . . . has thrown out the whole of the Athanasian Creed!"[1]

The Cobbetts manifested their attitude toward their cabin mates by speaking French among themselves, so "we could talk and laugh about all sorts of things quite at our ease."[2] They found better use for their French – and one of the redeeming features of the trip – in conversations with two passengers elsewhere on the ship: Messieurs Archambault and Rousseau, "two gentlemen . . . lately of Buonaparte's suite . . . out of the four that our government would not allow to remain with him at St. Helena." They were on their way to join Joseph Bonaparte, former king of Spain, now living near Philadelphia.[3]

Cobbett pronounced Captain Ogden sober, active, and vigilant, always attentive to his duty, and endued with great presence of mind in very difficult circumstances, but he nonetheless conceived an early dislike of him. In Liverpool harbor the captain had refused to pay a part of the bill rendered by the boatman he had employed to bring the passengers out to the *Importer,* and had finally cut the matter short by telling the boatman that he might take the sum offered or not; but that if he was not out of the ship in five minutes he would be flung overboard. Once under way, the passengers were allowed only one tumblerful of water a day to wash in, and sea biscuit rather than bread was part of the daily diet. When Cobbett complained of the lack of bread, the captain took his revenge (as Cobbett saw it) by addressing the two Cobbett boys, aged eighteen and sixteen, as "plain William and John, while he accosted every other person, at the same table, by the usual term of *Mr.*" One night at supper, before the whole company, Cobbett said: "John, I perceive, that the Captain has taken to the addressing of you with the omission of the usual appellation of civility, which he uses toward other passengers. Now, the very first time he does so again, you have my free leave to resent it upon the spot." When John dutifully responded that he "certainly would," a "warm altercation ensued; great blustering on the part of our Commander; but, he, at last, begged pardon for his omission, said it was not intentional, and promised he would not omit the word in future." The problem, quite obviously, was that Cobbett did not think that he and his entourage were getting all the respect they deserved. When the *Importer* docked in New York Cobbett was delighted at the annoyance caused to the captain and the unpleasant cabin companions when they were asked, by the crowd of welcomers that boarded the ship, "Which is Mr. Cobbett? Where is Mr. Cobbett? Pray, Sir, tell me which is Mr. Cobbett?" Yet, after all this, Cobbett thought it outrageous that English and American papers carried an article, probably from Bostick's pen, which read: "A republican passenger from England to America with Cobbett, writes, that he was never in company with a greater blackguard; and that he is besides a lordly disagreeable person, and wanted every one to cringe to him."[4]

On the day after their arrival in New York, Cobbett began a search on Long Island for a place to live. He found, and leased for a year, a house and farm of 300 to 400 acres at what was then known as Hyde Park (now New Hyde Park), about eighteen miles from New York City. The house had been built by one of the early colonial governors of New York and later had been occupied by Judge George Ludlow, a keen loyalist during the revolution, who had removed himself and his family to New Brunswick. There, perhaps, he and Cobbett had met. The house was a fine one, but "has been deserted and haunted for years" and was out of repair. The Cobbetts moved into the house early in June. Meanwhile, they lived a few miles away at an inn run by a Mr. and Mrs. Wiggins, and worked during the day on the large garden attached to the Ludlow house "gone wholly into ruins" – this they cleaned and sowed from one end to the other. Livestock and equipment were purchased: "two pretty greys and a light waggon, green outside, and painted like a harlequin's jacket inside," two yoke of oxen, a cow, sheep, pigs, turkeys, and chickens. Two ploughmen – an Englishman and a Scotsman – were hired and set to work on the farm.[5]

The obvious reason for Cobbett's flight from England, but possibly not the only one, was the suspension of the Habeas Corpus Act. During an earlier wartime suspension (1798–1800), approximately seventy-five persons were confined without trial, and as Cobbett departed from Liverpool he left behind a manuscript for immediate publication explaining that the only way he could continue his campaign for reform was by leaving the country: "I do not retire from a combat with the Attorney-General, but from a combat with a dungeon, deprived of pen, ink, and paper."[6] The *Political Register,* he declared, would be resumed in about three months with material sent from America, where Cobbett could write without a halter about his neck. There was no exultation in the message. He was not exiling himself, as thousands of his countrymen were, to start a new life in America; he was sadly making a strategic withdrawal:

Never will I own as my friend him who is not a friend of the people of England. I will never become a *subject* or a *citizen* in any other state, and will always be a *foreigner* in every country but England . . . and my beloved countrymen, be you well assured, that the last beatings of that heart will be, love for the people, for the happiness and the renown of England; and hatred of their corrupt, hypocritical, dastardly and merciless foes.[7]

The farewell address, published on April 5, 1817 as "Mr. Cobbett's Taking Leave of His Countrymen," produced a varied response. His closest associates – Hunt and Cartwright – thought that Cobbett had acted wisely. T. J. Wooler, editor of the *Black Dwarf,* a new weekly paper which had started the month before Cobbett's departure, declared that his retreat was cowardly and a betrayal of the cause.[8] But this was the voice of hot-blooded youth; Wooler was about thirty years old, without any family, and unscarred by the law, whereas Cobbett, fifty-four years old with wife and seven children, knew what imprisonment meant and was still subject to a £5,000 bond conditional on his good behavior. A no more flattering but different view than that of Wooler was expressed by the progovernment publications. Cobbett had fled from his creditors, proclaimed the *Quarterly Review*. "That he should do this is perfectly natural; the thing to be admired is – that such a man should have creditors to flee from!"[9]

The charge was probably not true as stated, but it was so close to the truth that it must have been doubly goading to Cobbett. He was in perilous financial straits. If he had stayed in England and if his writings had in any way been interrupted – even by action short of imprisonment – he would have been in deep difficulty. Cobbett was in debt when he entered Newgate; his living accommodations there cost him over £2,000; he had suffered a loss in an unknown amount on the disposal of his interest in the *Parliamentary Debates* and the *Parliamentary History* to Hansard and the *State Trials* to Howell; he had paid the £1,000 fine.[10] During the Wright arbitration it developed that Wright had borrowed £300 from Sir Francis Burdett, a debt which Cobbett agreed to assume although Wright had used it for his own purposes, and before Cobbett left Newgate he borrowed another £2,000 from the baronet, so he emerged from prison far more heavily indebted than when he entered.[11] On returning to Botley in 1812, he moved his family out of the big house and rented a smaller one, with forty-five acres of land, from Sir James Kempt, at £300 a year.[12] In 1814, when farm prices began to fall, Cobbett felt the pinch like everyone else, and in 1816, the year without a summer, he found it necessary to borrow another £700 from Sir Francis Burdett, bringing the total to £3,000.[13] Cobbett's financial situation, always precarious, steadily deteriorated from 1810, when he entered Newgate, until November 1816, when he began the cheap edition of the *Political Register*.[14] This seems to have produced profits of at least £100 a week and at that rate would have enabled Cobbett within a few years to pay off all his debts, even the two mortgages on the Botley property totalling £16,000.[15] But within five months of the publication of the first "cheap *Register*" Cobbett was forced to flee the country, leaving everything behind in turmoil: his family, his farm and home in Botley, his publishing business and only source of income, and his on-the-scene participation in the campaign against corruption.

From the point of view of his family, Botley had lost some of the idlyllic characteristics that Cobbett had observed when they moved there in 1805. They had begun on the friendliest terms with the vicar, the Reverend Richard Baker.[16] In 1807 Cobbett publicly applauded him for his "wisdom," and in the following year at one of the Winchester meetings Baker seconded Cobbett's motion for an inquiry into the Cintra convention.[17] But about this time relations began to wear thin. Baker had sold some straw to Cobbett by weight, and the center proved to have been watered. When daughter Anne Cobbett wrote to John Wright in October 1808 she mentioned Baker's "little monkey of a wife," adding: "I am really afraid we shall not be treated any more with his large round of beef and delicious wine" nor "charmed any more by his delightful voice squeaking, *Hannah bring in the tray*."[18] On Cobbett's return from Newgate, bells rang along the line of his progress towards home, but the bells of All Saints, Botley, had remained silent. The church was not the only chilly shoulder. Because of its proximity to Portsmouth and Southampton, Botley became increasingly populated by army and navy officers, dockyard and barracks officials, government contractors, nabobs, and others dependent on government favors – all part of the system Cobbett derided in his weekly articles.[19] As a result, by the time Cobbett left his family for America, Botley had become hostile territory.[20] The Cobbett–Baker feud was continued, despite the distance that now lay between them, Cobbett utilizing the *Political Register* ("I could fill a volume with anecdotes of the meanness and dishonesty of this man") and Baker *The Times*. The remnants of the Cobbett family, in the meantime, had taken refuge in London.[21] All of Cobbett's farming stock at Botley and all of his household goods – furniture, books, and other movables – were seized and sold to satisfy mortgage interest, taxes, and other debts including the unpaid rent on the Kempt property, which was repossessed by the owner.[22]

The arrangements made for the continuation of the *Political Register* were not wholly satisfactory either. Responsibility had been turned over to William Jackson, man of affairs and sometime secretary to Cobbett's friend Lord Cochrane. This had been so hurriedly accomplished that no agreement had been made about how Jackson was to be compensated.[23] "I can surely have no hesitation in relying implicitly on your honour as to all matters connected with money," wrote Cobbett from America.[24] Jackson had authority to "alter and correct" according to his own taste the articles sent to him by Cobbett, and was free to stop publishing any time that he thought it might jeopardize his safety.[25] Despite the liberality of those terms, no publication dealing with current events was ever conducted under greater difficulty.[26] The continuation of the enterprise depended on the good will of creditors. There was no cash in the till; Cobbett had to borrow the money needed to get himself and his sons to New York.[27] Once there, Cobbett's information on events in England was derived almost entirely from London newspapers. They were often six weeks to two months on their way, and a period nearly as long was required between the time Cobbett wrote out his observations and the time they could appear in print in London. The result was a four months' lapse between the event in England and the printed comment. What little information we have on the circulation of the *Political Register* during this period suggests that it had fallen drastically from the peak circulation earlier attained.[28]

At one time Cobbett had believed that he could develop an American audience for his articles. His pro-American writings during the 1812–14 war had brought him a large American readership. Because of this he had sent his nephew Henry Cobbett and a G. S. Oldfield to New York in 1816 for the purpose of publishing an American edition of the *Political Register* with supplementary material that could not safely be released in England. The project, which began in May 1816, lasted only a few months. Cobbett, learning that "the numbers began to find their way back to Lord Castlereagh's office," stopped sending manuscript to America.[29] When he arrived on the scene in May 1817, he reestablished an American edition, but it was limited to what was published in England.[30] The office which Henry Cobbett had taken at 19 Wall Street was soon abandoned.[31]

The events that had occurred late in 1816 and early in 1817 did far more than send Cobbett scurrying across the Atlantic. They were responsible for the rise of a whole new group of younger adherents to the cause of reform, and for a serious split in the ranks of the older reformers. Three individuals stand out among the newcomers: William Hone, friend and collaborator of the artist George Cruikshank, who began publishing the *Reformists' Register* on February 1, 1817, and shortly was to become famous for his parodies directed at church and state; Thomas Jonathan Wooler, whose first issue of the *Black Dwarf*, published on February 27, 1817, was cynically dedicated to Cobbett "in evidence that the Liberty of the Press is not entirely destroyed in England"; and Richard Carlile, whose public career began in March 1817 with his vigorous promotion of Wooler's *Black Dwarf* and was made memorable by his fearless publication of the proscribed works of Thomas Paine. All three were at various times admirers of Cobbett; all three followed Cobbett's practice of writing and publishing under their own names; all three, like Cobbett, were prosecuted by the government: The intransigent and truculent Carlile, who died when he was fifty-three years old, bore imprisonment during nearly one-third of his adult life for his belief in the freedom of the press.

The stirring incidents that seem to have stimulated the reform activity of these younger individuals brought to a head some basic differences among the older participants. Prior to the Spa Fields episodes, the violence that occurred – the burning of ricks and the breaking of frames – was clearly due to economic distress.[32] But the involvement of Hunt in the Spa Fields rioting on December 2, 1816, closely following Cobbett's appeal to "the Journeymen and Labourers," and the attack on the prince regent while the reform petitions were being delivered to parliament, gave credence to the claim that the reformers were covertly engaged in fomenting lawless disorder. Cobbett's articles included a plea for peaceful petitioning rather than the use of violence, but his close associate Hunt – a forceful and exciting speaker – implied violence in his mode of delivery, regardless of his words; and these were not always restrained. Although Hunt was "gentlemanly in his manner and attire ... with a most agreeable expression" in amicable discussion, when he became excited while speaking, wrote Samuel Bamford, his eyes "seemed to distend and protrude; and if he worked himself furious, as he sometimes would, they became blood-streaked and almost started from their sockets."

Then it was that the expression of his lip was to be observed – the kind smile was exchanged for the curl of scorn, or the curse of indignation. His voice was bellowing; his face swollen and flushed; his griped hand beat as if to pulverize; and his whole manner gave token of a painful energy, struggling for utterance.[33]

Burdett almost certainly became frightened at the course the reform movement was taking: "in the precise degree that he perceived the people to wax warm, he appeared to wax cold."[34] Burdett refused to attend the meeting of the petitioning delegates before the opening of parliament in January 1817, going directly from his fox-hunting in Leicestershire to the House of Commons so as to avoid any contact with those who had attended the meeting. During the long debate on the gagging bills, in which the reformers were charged with rebellion, he uttered not a single word in their defense: "he sat silent while he saw the chains forging for us."[35] When Lord Cochrane made a motion which contained the statement that the House "have not been able to discover one single instance in which meetings to petition for parliamentary reform have been accompanied with any attempt to disturb the public tranquillity," Burdett had astutely left the House, so the motion failed for want of a second.[36] All this and more was charged to Burdett in the fourth and fifth of a series of six articles which Cobbett wrote from Long Island under the provocative title "A History of the Last Hundred Days of English Freedom."[37]

The fact that the charges were true did not make them more acceptable to Burdett; truths uttered by a debtor to a creditor come particularly hard. In November 1817, after Cobbett had been in America for six months, he wrote to Sir Francis about the debt, enclosing a letter on the same subject that he had sent to a Mr. Tipper, who had supplied paper used for the *Political Register*. In the letter to Tipper, Cobbett explained that his inability to pay was due to despotic acts of the government, and therefore he held it to be "perfectly just" that he should never give up future earnings to pay off his debts in England. However, he continued with the declaration that he waived this principle "and shall neglect no means within my power fully to pay and satisfy every demand" so far as was consistent with his duty to provide for his wife and children. Cobbett stated to Burdett that "as to the debt due you, no pains shall be spared by me to obtain the means of paying it as soon as possible."

Burdett, obviously enraged by Cobbett's repeated public attacks on him as a defected reformer, did not read Cobbett's communications very carefully. Or perhaps he read them too carefully and assumed that Cobbett charged him (Burdett) with responsibility for the despotic acts of the government because of his inaction. Burdett's bitter and sarcastic reply written in January 1818 proceeded on the premise that Cobbett had renounced his obligation to pay his debts; it ended with the comment that "nothing can or ought to stifle the expression of disgust every honest mind must feel at the want of integrity in the principles you proclaim." Burdett's reply, first displayed at "Brooks's in the Strand," shortly found its way into the press, and was widely published in both England and America.[38]

Cobbett's exchange with Burdett over the debt was a sideshow to the political issues between them. In June 1817 there had been another outbreak of violence in England. A group of two or three hundred workmen from the neighborhood of Pentrich, Derbyshire set off to march to Nottingham, armed with a few guns and some pikes and pitchforks. They were led by Jeremiah Brandreth, a stocking knitter, who believed that at Nottingham they would find thousands of aroused men from other towns in the distressed area. On the way they stopped at houses to collect men, arms, and money. At one of these, Brandreth shot through a window and accidentally killed a farm laborer. As they neared Nottingham (their number had fallen to fifty or so) they were met by a small government force. Brandreth and others were arrested: Forty-five in all were arraigned for high treason, punishable by the barbaric ritual of hanging, disemboweling, beheading, quartering, and placing head and quarters "at the king's disposal." After hearings before a special commission held in Derby, Brandreth and two others were executed. Most of those arraigned were sentenced to transportation for varying periods. The government, through its spy network, had been warned well in advance of the "rising"; indeed, within a week after the event the *Leeds Mercury* revealed that the rising had actually been fomented by the notorious informer Oliver (W. J. Richards), who had masqueraded as an agent of revolutionary clubs in London. Yet the court-appointed counsel for Brandreth, a lawyer from Manchester named Cross, did nothing to develop this point; instead he insisted that Brandreth had been deluded by the writings of Cobbett. The address to "the Journeymen and Labourers" was, Cross claimed, "one of the most malignant and diabolical publications ever issued from the English press."[39]

Hunt's efforts to provide independent counsel for the prisoners had been unsuccessful. He had applied to Thomas Cleary, an associate of Burdett in the London Hampden Club and sometime secretary of the Burdett-controlled "Rump," Cobbett's name for the vestigial remnants of the Westminster committee which had been formed to back the candidacy of James Paull in 1806. Cleary had turned down Hunt's appeal for funds:

We Reformers are far from wishing to countenance or identify ourselves with any men guilty of murder, robbery, or riot. Had it not been for acts of this kind, the people would by this time have been united as one man, in demanding their rights in a way the borough-mongers would have found irresistible. Instead of this, what a situation are we brought to, by the foolish, not to say wicked, conduct of violent and imprudent men! . . . By them, and them only, has our friend Cobbett, our stay and pillar, been expatriated. By them, and them only, have our lives and liberties been taken from the protection of the law . . . I could almost hang them myself for playing the game of tyrants, so convinced am I of the irreparable mischief they have done.[40]

Burdett, whose ancestral home was five miles south of Derby, made no effort to assist Brandreth and his misguided followers, or to relieve their families. He took himself off to Ireland, where, according to Cobbett, he was "carouzing . . . with the placemen and boroughmongers" and taking part in "dancings and paradings amongst crowds of baronial slaves."[41]

Additional fervor in the rising Cobbett–Burdett feud was evoked by the rumor that Lord Cochrane, about to leave England in order to help the Chileans in their struggle against Spain, would resign his Westminster seat and would be replaced by Burdett's friend Roger O'Connor.[42] To Cobbett, there were only three conceivable replacements: Cartwright, Hunt, or himself, all time-tested reformers who endorsed annual parliaments and universal suffrage. He was convinced that "nothing short of a very vile intrigue can have given rise to the idea of an intention to propose Mr O'Connor for Westminster," and that the central parties in the intrigue were Burdett and Burdett's tool, the Rump.[43] Cobbett was outraged by the suggestion that Burdett could bring in one of his personal friends. Ten years before,

Westminster had become freed from the domination of the two aristocratic parties through Cobbett's efforts. He was determined that it should not now become the close borough of Sir Francis Burdett.[44] The issues of the *Political Register* appearing in London during the first few months of 1818 contained a recapitulation of Burdett's recent shortcomings, from which Cobbett concluded that Burdett had, for all practical purposes, abandoned the reform movement – that a separation must take place; no, "it *has* taken place. It has always happened thus in every great public cause; in every struggle against tyranny. Some men, very ardent for a while, become cool. They drop off. They sometimes become opponents; and, then they are sure to accuse their former associates of going *too far,* of becoming *too violent.*"[45] As it turned out, Cochrane did not immediately resign, and so the O'Connor issue never came to a head. Parliament was dissolved in June 1818 and a general election was held, at which Lord Cochrane did not propose to stand. Hence both Westminster seats were open. Burdett, of course, would be a candidate, and it was decided by Burdett and the Rump that his running mate, instead of O'Connor, should be the banker Douglas Kinnaird, another friend of Burdett's, who had no previous association with Westminster and little reputation as a reformer. Sir Samuel Romilly was put up by the whigs, presumably with the backing of such reformers as Francis Place.[46] Sir Murray Maxwell, a naval officer, was nominated by the tories. Hunt and Cartwright were independent candidates, which meant that the reform cause, instead of being concentrated, was split five ways among Burdett, Kinnaird, Romilly, Hunt, and Cartwright.

Burdett did not appear at the hustings. After the third day of the fifteen-day polling period, Cartwright and Kinnaird withdrew, so Thomas Cleary, who had been supporting Cartwright, shifted to Burdett. Hunt attacked Burdett and Cleary, claiming that they had abandoned the cause of reform and pointing to the Derbyshire trials, where, he claimed, they were glad to see the rioters hanged. When Cleary denied the allegation, Hunt produced Cleary's letter to him of October 10, 1817, written before the wretched men had been tried, in which Cleary had declared: "I could almost hang them myself." Cleary quickly retaliated. On the day before the polls closed, he read from the hustings the following letter allegedly written by Cobbett to an unnamed addressee:

All the gentlemen whom I met with are loud in Sir Francis Burdett's praise. His motion about the cashiering of officers has gained him thousands of valuable friends ... It is impossible for both factions united to calumniate our motives if we proceed as we ought, and do not mix with men of bad character. There is one *Hunt,* the Bristol man. Beware of him! he rides about the country with a whore, the wife of another man, having deserted his own. A sad fellow! Nothing to do with him. Adieu.[47]

These squabbles among the reformers did Burdett no good. He was reelected, but – "having been shorn of his beams of popularity by Cobbett" (so wrote the novelist Thomas Love Peacock to the poet Shelley) – Burdett ran second to Romilly and polled only 400 more than the tory candidate, Maxwell.[48] Hunt, whose chief objective seems to have been dragging down Burdett, received fewer than 100 votes.[49]

The letter condemning Hunt's immorality did not come to Cobbett's attention until two months later when he was reading a New York paper's account of the election and there found references to the letter along with a statement made by Burdett that he could not "as an honest man" wish Cobbett in parliament. Cobbett immediately wrote that Burdett's "pretended bad opinion can surprise nobody, who reflects that it was I, with my long arm, reaching across the Atlantic, who brought him within an inch of being rejected in Westminster, and who have put him down from an eminence, which he will never dare to look up to again."[50] As to the letter about Hunt, Cobbett declared it to be a forgery, and accused Cleary of having forged it or "of having obtained it from a man who had forged it, and which man he well knew to have been guilty of forging my writing and name, for fraudulent purposes, many times" – referring, obviously, to his erstwhile associate John Wright.[51] When Cobbett's response appeared in the *Political Register,* Cleary replied that he knew nothing about a forgery; the letter had been given to him by Francis Place.[52] And time proved that it was no forgery; it had been written by Cobbett to Wright and not, as Cobbett suspected, forged by him. Is it possible that Cobbett could have forgotten that he wrote such a letter? When Cleary used the letter he did not disclose its date, so that to Cobbett in New York it would seem that he was being charged with having recently written a letter for the purpose of defeating Hunt's candidacy. In fact, the letter had been written in 1808, and the way the issue had been raised gave Cobbett no clue that it related to an earlier period.[53] Finally, while this does not dispose of the question, the conclusion that Cobbett by 1818 had forgotten the offhand remark made in a letter written ten years before is reinforced by a recently located communication from Cobbett to Cleary asking that he show the controverted letter to Cobbett's son for the purpose of determining its authenticity.[54]

It is difficult to leave the subject without commenting on the light that it sheds on Francis Place, who was willing to become the bearer of this bit of scandal at a time when it could serve no purpose other than to embarrass Cobbett, Hunt, and Hunt's mistress, Mrs. Vince. There can be little doubt why Cobbett refused, thereafter, to have anything to do with Place. One wonders to what extent Place may not have been trying to justify his own shabby conduct when he later referred to Cobbett, behind his back, as an "impudent mountebank" and "unprincipled cowardly bully."[55]

The breach between Burdett and Cobbett was also irreconcilable. Burdett's remark that he did not, as "an honest man," wish to see Cobbett in parliament was more than Cobbett could bear.[56] Burdett, he claimed, was his creature; he had made him "by our words put into his mouth; by our writings transcribed by him" – and he would break him.

I have sacrificed greatly to the wooden god too; but, I, for my part, am resolved, not only to sacrifice to him no more, but to knock him to pieces, as the man did his wooden god in the fable. I will (all in due course) beat him and thump him about, and kick him up and down and to and fro, till the most stupid amongst his adorers shall be ashamed of their adoration. He has deserted us; but, in the end, he shall get nothing by his desertion.[57]

The production of Hunt's letter by Cleary, and the use of "go home to your wife" election placards addressed to Hunt, stimulated some oblique comments on Burdett's domestic life and his illicit relations with Lady Oxford. "We shall not retaliate," wrote Cobbett, "by holding forth any body as a 'whore'. We, or I, at least, shall not go this length."[58]

Cartwright, too, broke with Burdett. Burdett's excuse for not suggesting the veteran reformer as his running mate for the 1818 general election was that he "thought that the major did not wish for a seat in parliament." Eight months later, in the March 1819 by-election to fill the vacancy created by Romilly's suicide, Burdett's choice was still another friend, John Cam Hobhouse. This time his explanation for excluding the kindly old gentleman who had given his life to the cause of reform was that "it was impossible that the major should be elected."[59] As it turned out, Hobhouse was not able to win either. The whig candidate George Lamb was successful in a hard-fought election enlivened by the antics of his sister-in-law Lady Caroline Lamb and by resort to some of the traditional corrupt practices of the period.[60] Young John Cobbett, who attended the election with two silk handkerchiefs he had brought from America, waggishly claimed that "reformers took them one after the other out of his pocket."[61]

The quarrels among reformers were not the only effects of the dramatic episodes of 1816–17. The average Englishman, or at least the average Londoner, became far more critical of the government's efforts to shackle freedom of speech and freedom of the press. That the most prominent journalist of the day was forced to flee the country was one element – Cobbett thought a major element – in the development of this more critical attitude.[62] Another was the disclosure that the government had spies, and in some cases provocateurs, in its employ.

In June 1817, Dr. James Watson, leader of the Spenceans at Spa Fields, was acquitted by a London jury when it was disclosed that John Castle, an active participant in the rioting and a witness for the prosecution, was a government informer. London juries in the same month were responsible for the victory of T. J. Wooler, editor of the *Black Dwarf*, in two actions for seditious libel brought against him by the attorney general. And in December 1817, London juries acquitted William Hone, who had been charged with seditious and blasphemous libels for his popular parodies. Lord Ellenborough presided at the final two of Hone's three successive trials. When the jury, despite Ellenborough's charge that Hone was guilty of "a most impious and profane libel," found that Hone had committed no libel at all, the lord chief justice allegedly took to his bed, from which he never emerged to try another case. Cobbett exulted almost as much over these victories as if they had been his own: "this is a most glorious triumph indeed . . . [Wooler's] defence . . . was a most noble one and also a most able one"; "Mr Hone's trial and his meritorious conduct will be . . . ranked along with those of William Penn . . . and the rest of the brave men who have resisted tyranny's favourite weapon."[63] Cobbett rightly saw these cases as milestones in the fight for freedom of speech: "Men dare publish, now, under the well-known protection of juries, what they have not dared publish during any time within the last twenty years," and although these were not the last of the attempts to enforce an oppressive interpretation of the law of criminal libel, from now on the prosecutor preferred the safer provincial juries to those of London and, wherever actions were brought, faced lengthening odds.[64]

Even more encouraging, Cobbett thought, was the progress of the paper money system. Payments in specie had been prohibited since 1797. The first suspension act was for a period of forty-seven days; the next, for four months. And so it went, one small bite after another, for twenty-two consecutive years.[65] In 1819 the outstanding notes of the Bank of England and country banks exceeded £100 million. Yet the total specie held by the banks was only £8 million. The trend was toward more paper (there was no legal restriction on the amount that could be issued), which would stimulate runaway inflation. The other course would be to cut down on the quantity of paper money, but when this was attempted in 1816, the resulting deflation brought about bankruptcy and universal distress. Even if this were braved out, tax revenues would be so reduced that it would be impossible to pay the interest on the national debt. The resulting default would create a convulsion so severe as to bring down the governing system; parliamentary reform would follow as a matter of course. Cobbett saw no escape from this dilemma. His own solution (repudiation of the debt in whole or part) having been rejected as a breach of faith with creditors, he saw every further suspension of payment in specie as simply putting off the evil day and making default increasingly inevitable.[66] He was vastly amused, therefore, when parliament in 1819 approved a bill sponsored by the young Robert Peel, which provided for still another suspension for four years while stoutly resolving that beginning in 1823, after twenty-six years of nonconvertibility, the Bank would finally pay in coin.[67] Cobbett was sure this was impossible:

> To resolve, my friends, is an easy matter; but, as our pretty fellows will find, to *execute* a resolution is sometimes a very difficult matter; and, if they execute their resolution, though it has now assumed the shape of a law, I will give Castlereagh leave to put me upon a gridiron, while Sidmouth stirs the fire, and Canning stands by making a jest of my writhing and my groans.[68]

While the expected blowout of the paper money system had thus been deferred until 1823, Cobbett concluded that an earlier crisis might occur through what he called a "puff-out" of that system. An engraver of ordinary ability ("any boy of common capacity can learn in six months") could produce good imitations of the existing banknotes. If a large quantity of the bogus notes were put into circulation at one time – for example, by dropping parcels of them on the streets of London on some dark night – such a panic would occur that everyone would refuse to accept paper money. "In 48 hours not a note would pass. The mails would carry the news to the land's end. A dread, such as never was before heard of, would spread over the country like lightning."[69] The poet Shelley, a regular reader of the *Political Register,* exclaimed, "Cobbett still more and more delights me, with all my horror of the sanguinary consequences of his creed. His design to overthrow Bank notes by forgery is very comic."[70] There were some, however, to whom the humor may have been obscure. The mere suggestion of such wholesale counterfeiting was enough to send a shudder through every banker in England. The problem was already an acute one. From 1797 to 1818 the Bank of England had prosecuted over 900 persons for forgery. More than 300 of these had been executed.[71]

While the quarrelling reformers and the paper money system occupied a large part of Cobbett's American writing for the *Political Register*, two other subjects need to be mentioned. First, Cobbett strongly supported the struggle for independence in the South American colonies of Spain, directing his arguments to both British and American governments, where some indecision had been evidenced. Policy, rivalships, and personal interests, Cobbett declared, should have nothing to do "with a moral question of so determinate a character, that it is impossible to be misunderstood by any human being."[72] Second, one perceives an evolutionary development of Cobbett's attitude toward reform. Although he still spoke of the need to pursue peaceful methods, his writings contain an increasing number of references to the right to resist oppression, and even passages that could be interpreted as incitements to use force, as for example: "It is nothing to tell us, that we cannot relieve ourselves without running a *risk* of great trouble, turmoil, and, perhaps, bloodshed ... a third part of the nation destroyed would be preferable to the present state of things. The mass of the people do not now live; they crawl about, and die by inches."[73] This more frequent reference to the use of force was accompanied by more talk about revenge, about retribution, about the right of those injured under existing conditions to be compensated when parliamentary reform should occur.[74] There was also a shift in nomenclature. In 1806 Cobbett had hated "the system" and those administering it. Ten years later the system had become anthropomorphized: Cobbett now hated the "boroughmongers" – the two or three hundred families responsible for the system through their control of the majority of seats in the House of Commons – and the individuals who were the "tools" of the boroughmongers.[75] The tools of the boroughmongers in 1818 constituted a large class. They included the chief ministers: Canning, Liverpool, Castlereagh, Eldon, and Sidmouth. They also included those who cooperated with the ministers: whigs like Charles Wynne, "squeaking" Wynne, nephew of Lord Grenville; and the allegedly independent Saints led by William Wilberforce. Wynne and the sanctimonious Wilberforce talked about liberty, but both voted to suspend the Habeas Corpus Act. And finally, the "tools" included the system utilized by the boroughmongers to maintain their control over the people: tax collectors; repressive legislation; the standing army; bankers who managed the national debt and paper money; the corrupt press of Daniel Stuart and James Perry, editors of the *Courier* and the *Morning Chronicle*; and Lord Ellenborough's efficient law enforcement machinery which, during the trials at Derby, used packed juries of tenant farmers, a court-appointed lawyer too friendly with the prosecution (lawyer Cross of Manchester), and provocateur spies, such as Castle and

Oliver, working under the vigilant eye of that old bloodhound, Colonel Fletcher of Bolton.[76] These elements of control were thrown together by Cobbett in one forceful paragraph contrasting America and England:

And, then, to see a free country for once, and to see every labourer with plenty to eat and drink! Think of *that*! And never to see the hang-dog face of a tax-gatherer. Thank of *that*! No Alien Acts here. No long-sworded and whiskered Captains. No Judges escorted from town to town and sitting under the guard of dragoons. No packed juries of tenants. No Crosses. No Bolton Fletchers. No hangings and rippings up. No Castles and Olivers. No Stewarts and Perries. No Cannings, Liverpools, Castlereaghs, Eldons, Ellenboroughs or Sidmouths. No Bankers. No Squeaking Wynnes. No Wilberforces. Think of *that*. No Wilberforces![77]

Hypocrisy, to Cobbett, was the greatest of all sins, and Wilberforce, with his concern for the black slaves of the West Indies and apparent lack of interest in the "white slaves" of England, was the embodiment of hypocrisy.[78]

Cobbett's reformer friends in England – particularly Hunt and Cartwright – urged him to return in order to fight the boroughmongers on their own ground. The act suspending the writ of habeas corpus had terminated in January 1818, no evidence ever having been produced to support the existence of the organized conspiracy on which the suspension had been premised. Cobbett at first evaded the urgings, saying only that the reasons for remaining away were not "public" ones and he realized that he was in "no personal danger."[79] A little later he explained: The tyranny of the boroughmongers, by depriving him of his ability to write in England, had placed him in a state "as to pecuniary matters, which disables me, for the present, from coping with it *there*."[80] He was working diligently on two books which he hoped would relieve his financial situation before returning. One of these was an account of life in America; the other, an English grammar. The first, entitled *A Year's Residence in the United States of America*, began with a journal from the date Cobbett landed in New York in May 1817 and continued until the following April. It described the weather and Cobbett's farming activities interlarded with bits of advice, political commentary, amusing gossip about himself and his acquaintances, and lists of things he liked and did not like about America and Americans:

My driver, who is a tavern-keeper himself, would have been a very pleasant companion, if he had not drunk so much spirits on the road. This is the *great misfortune* of America! As we were going up a hill very slowly, I could perceive him looking very hard at my cheek for some time. At last, he said: "I am wondering, Sir, to see you look so *fresh* and so *young*, considering what you have gone through in the world"; though I cannot imagine *how* he learnt who I was. "I'll tell you," said I, how I have contrived the thing. I rise early, go to bed early, eat sparingly, never drink any thing stronger than small beer, shave once a day, and wash my hands and face clean three times a day, at the very least." He said, that was *too much* to think of doing.[81]

Following the journal there is a typically Cobbettian mélange: culture of the rutabaga, cabbage, and potato; the cost of living in America; the customs and character of the people; rural sports; the government and religion; and, inevitably, more about the writer himself –all entertaining to the reader because they were entertaining to Cobbett: "When I make up my hogs' lodging place for winter, I look well at it, and consider, whether, upon a pinch, I could, for once and away, make shift to lodge in it myself. If I *shiver at the thought,* the place is not good enough for my hogs."[82] The book ends with a part devoted to a description (written by Cobbett's friend Thomas Hulme) of a trip to Illinois to visit a colony organized by an English settler and promoter, Morris Birbeck.[83] To this there are tacked on two postscripts by Cobbett: one criticizing Birbeck for his "romantic chaff" about life in Illinois and the other claiming that Henry Fearon, an Englishman who had visited Cobbett on Long Island, had grossly misrepresented Cobbett's mode of living.[84] Fearon, who had come to America for the purpose of advising a number of English families thinking of moving there, produced a delightful account of his experiences, which he published in 1818 as *Sketches of America.* He was obviously intelligent and observant, and he described the Cobbett residence as it was when he visited it in August 1817, two months after Cobbett had moved in: "a path rarely trod, fences in ruins, the gate broken, a house mouldering to decay." The front parlor "contained nothing but a single chair and several trunks of sea-clothes." The description of the master of the establishment also rings true:

A print by Bartollotzi [Bartolozzi], executed in 1801, conveys a correct outline of his person. His eyes are small, and pleasingly good-natured. To the French gentleman he was attentive; with his sons familiar; to his servants easy; but to all, in his tone and manner resolute and determined. He feels no hesitation in praising himself, and evidently believes that he is eventually destined to be the Atlas of the British nation. His faculty of relating anecdotes is amusing . . .
My impressions of Mr Cobbett are, that those who know him would like him, if they can be content to submit unconditionally to his dictation. "Obey me, and I will treat you kindly; if you do not, I will trample on you," seemed visible in every word and feature. He appears to feel, in its fullest force, the sentiment,

> "I have no brother, am like no brother,
> I am myself alone."[85]

Cobbett did not like Fearon's descriptions, but his reply was largely limited to abusing Fearon and emphasizing the beauties of the Ludlow orchards, which Fearon had not mentioned.[86]

The other book produced by Cobbett in America was *Cobbett's English Grammar*, a series of letters to Cobbett's third son, James Paul Cobbett, aged fourteen. The book was intended, as its subtitle suggests, for schools and young persons in general, *but, More Especially for the Use of Soldiers, Sailors, Apprentices, and Plough-Boys*. So successful was it for these classes, and for others as well, that by 1834 100,000 copies had been sold. Since then, there have been several dozen editions including three in German, many pirated editions in odd parts of the world, and at least two editions in the twentieth century.[87] There is no way in which a grammar can be made exciting, but Cobbett came as close to doing it as is humanly possible. And again it is his own enthusiasm for the subject that carries the book along – his belief in the magical properties of grammar "in affording protection to innocence and securing punishment to guilt" – and his whimsical humor, most often exemplified by his reference to nouns of number – "such as Mob, Parliament, Rabble, House of Commons, Regiment, Court of King's Bench, Den of Thieves, and the like." And Cobbett kept the *Grammar* up to date. In the editions published after the 1820 quarrel between George IV and Queen Caroline, a previous example was updated to explain the verb forms expressing time of action: "The Queen *defies* the tyrants; the Queen *defied* the tyrants; the Queen *will defy* the tyrants."[88]

The little book was not simply a grammar; it contained some excellent advice on both substance and style, warning the reader against writing about any matter which he does not well understand and against the use of figures of speech, superlatives, and the type of affectation which from the beginning of the written word has characterized official communications. Later editions were enlivened by examples of poor writing taken from the correspondence of distinguished contemporaries including Lord Castlereagh and the Duke of Wellington. The article on education in the *Encyclopoedia Edinensis*, after disclosing its disagreement with Cobbett on "points both of politics and literature," found that his book on grammar was "the best treatise we possess, and that it is entitled to supersede all the popular, and many of the scientific, productions on the subject in our language."[89] We must note, however, that while Cobbett was often overcritical of the grammar of others, he was not always letter-perfect himself. Yet who cannot admire the ploughboy who learned his grammar out of a book well enough to teach others?

When Cobbett had arrived in New York in 1817 he had made it plain that he did not intend to involve himself in American affairs. It was an intention he respected, with two exceptions: his opposition to any move that would interfere with the effort of the South American colonies of Spain to free themselves from the mother country, and a personal matter between himself and the state of Pennsylvania dating back to his earlier residence in America. He was determined to recover the money the state had taken on the forfeiture of the surety bonds conditioned on Cobbett's good behavior, which his old enemy Judge McKean had required in the Yrujo case in 1797. Cobbett, it will be recalled, was exonerated by both federal and state grand juries, but the state attorney general proceeded against the sureties in an independent action, claiming that Cobbett, by libels against various other persons, had violated the bonds. Cobbett had a reasonably good case for reimbursement, both legally and equitably.[90] The right mood had been set, too, by the action of the federal government in reimbursing, with interest, all the fines that had been imposed under the Alien and Sedition Act of 1798. Cobbett's claim, including interest, amounted to more than $6,000, money that he much needed. However, the petition filed by Cobbett in 1818 was hardly the type that was best calculated to produce a favorable result.[91] Thomas McKean as chief justice and later governor of the state was responsible for most, if not all, of the injustice Cobbett claimed, but McKean had died only seven months before Cobbett made his application, and it would have been indeed strange if his associates in the legislature could have been induced to authorize the payment of public money to one who claimed, as Cobbett did, that their recently departed colleague had been as wicked as England's bloody Judge Jeffreys of the seventeenth century. When, as may have been expected, the state senate turned down the petition, Cobbett left the visitors' gallery where he had been listening to the debate and, "Braving the rules of the Senate, he pushed through the door-keepers' barrier, entered without notice on the floor of the chamber," and delivered to the speaker a request that he be heard in person before the bar of the house.[92] He followed this with a petition to the other branch of the legislature, but, without waiting for a decision, immediately left town by stagecoach.[93] Cobbett at first vowed that he would disclose to the world the infamy of the Pennsylvania legislature, but then decided to give it one more chance to do him justice. He chose Joseph Nancrede, a well-known bookseller, to assist him in a second attempt, to be made at the next annual session of the legislature. Nancrede, after "many inquiries" into the first effort, advised Cobbett that the "general apology for not doing what is evidently right in your case, is that *you were too stiff.*"[94]

Cobbett was not disposed to do much easing off. He looked on his claim as no ordinary one; to him it was an issue affecting "the character of free institutions of government."[95] He drafted a new petition, and although no copy seems to have survived, we can guess its tone

Nancy Cobbett in 1818. This silhouette was made in Philadelphia during Nancy Cobbett's brief stay in America

by Cobbett's letter forwarding the document to Nancrede: "To you, indeed, I leave the whole matter, excepting only, the mere words of the Petition itself, which must remain as they are." Continuing, he added:

For, though I must necessarily wish to have my money, because it is mine; I will not *bend* a single hair's breadth to get it. I am well aware of the temporary injury that the pertinacious injustice of the Republican Government of Pennsylvania will, through me, do to the cause of freedom; but, *I will do what is right, let what will come of it.* I know well, that every man of mind and of honour, in the state, is indignant at the conduct of the vulgar beasts, who oppose or reject, this claim of mine; but, then, there comes the damning question: "*What a state of things must that be,* where the men of mind and honour are under the sway of vulgar beasts?" However, let us hope, that a year's reflec-

Anne Cobbett in 1818. Silhouette made in Philadelphia

tion may have produced some sense of shame in those who opposed my demand of justice.[96]

It seems probable that the petition finally filed by Nancrede was moderated, but the harm that had been done in the first round could not be rectified.[97] Cobbett was so much more interested in having McKean officially declared a rascal than he was in getting his money back that he accomplished neither.[98]

Except for this trip to the Pennsylvania capital at Harrisburg (with a stop at Philadelphia to see old friends) and an occasional journey to New York, Cobbett stuck to his farm on Long Island. There he lived a simple life, rising before the sun, eating mainly the vegetables he grew, drinking nothing but water and milk. Sometimes, in hot weather, he rode out in a Long Island farm wagon pulled by a pair of oxen which he drove with a long stick – "He with only a shirt, a pair of nankin trowsers, yellow buckskin shoes & a broad-brimmed straw hat."[99] His wife and five younger children had followed him at the end of 1817, but, after only a brief stay, Mrs. Cobbett with most of the family returned to England in the summer of 1818.[100] The Ludlow house was hardly ideal and probably a source of contention between husband and wife: "As to our living *here* in a way suitable to my state in life, the thing is out of the question. I will make no alteration in any respect. Simply to preserve *life* and *health* is all that reason, or common sense, will permit me to go to the expense of."[101] Events beyond Cobbett's control made the accommodation even less suitable. In May 1819 the house burned down. Cobbett built himself a tent lined with old English newspapers and furnished with a table made of a mahogany slab supported by stakes driven into the ground and bedsteads made of wood so green that it threw out shoots and leaves, on which were placed mattresses and pillows stuffed with rye straw; there he stayed for several months with his third son, James, as his only company.[102] He announced, with some consciousness of the humor of the remark, that he was going to strike his tent, but not "till the fall"; that he would be in England before parliament assembled again.[103] James, now sixteen years old, would remain to carry on the seed, book, and pig business Cobbett had established in New York City at 63 Fulton Street.[104] Cobbett himself would sail for England in October. But at this point some trouble developed about getting a ship to take him. We do not know whether the trouble related to the yellow fever epidemic that struck New York in 1819, or whether Cobbett was personally objectionable, or whether it had something to do with Cobbett's luggage. Cobbett, who had planned to sail on the *Amity*, owned by Captain Isaac Wright, "a very cunning old Quaker," was refused passage on that ship, and shifted himself and his belongings to Captain Nathan Cobb's ship, the *Hercules*.[105]

The "luggage" about which the quaker captain might have raised some question was a coffin containing a body; more specifically, the coffin and body of Thomas Paine, who had been denied the right of burial by the quaker church when he had died ten years before in 1809. At the time of his death, Paine had been living with old friends, M and Mme Bonneville, at 59 Grove Street in Greenwich Village, New York. Because of the refusal of the quakers to accept his body, Paine had been buried on the farm that he owned in New Rochelle, about twenty miles from the city.[106]

Paine had been very much on Cobbett's mind since he had arrived in New York; almost every one of Cobbett's articles on paper money referred to Paine's views on the subject. It was natural, therefore, that

Cobbett should also interest himself in Paine as an individual. Cobbett made a point of learning what he could about Paine. He became acquainted with Mme Bonneville and with Colonel John Fellows, one of Paine's most intimate friends.[107] He involved himself in a public controversy concerning the claim that Paine had recanted his deism shortly before dying.[108] He proposed writing a life of Paine and publishing a complete edition of his works, and although this project was never completed, Cobbett did rewrite (but never published) a short life of Paine which had been begun by Mme Bonneville.[109] In an article written in February 1819 discussing Paine and the English paper money system, Cobbett declared: "I hope yet to see an Act of Parliament to cause his bones to be conveyed to England and deposited in the stead of those of Pitt, whose system he opposed, the ruin attending whose schemes he foretold, and for which foretelling he was per-

An English print entitled "Transatlantic luxury." Cobbett, seated in the farmyard outside his dilapidated Long Island house, writes: "My Dear Hunt . . ."

secuted."[110] Six months later in another article on the same subject, Cobbett stated: "Paine lies in a little hole under the grass and weeds of an obscure farm in America. There, however, *he shall not lie, unnoticed, much longer*. He belongs to England. His fame is the property of England; and, if no other people will show, that they value that fame, the people of England will."[111] These statements, however, hardly prepared the world for Cobbett's subsequent conduct. Setting out from New York one night late in September 1819, Cobbett and several helpers arrived in New Rochelle "at the peep of day, took up the coffin entire, brought it off to New York; and just as we found it, it goes to England."

Let this be considered the act of the *reformers of England, Scotland, and Ireland*. In their name we opened the grave, and in their name will the tomb be raised. We do not look upon ourselves as adopting *all* Paine's opinions upon *all* subjects. He was a *great man*, an *Englishman*, a *friend of freedom*, and the *first and greatest enemy of the Borough and Paper System*. This is enough for us.[112]

On October 30, 1819, the *Hercules*, bearing the extraordinary William Cobbett and his even more extraordinary baggage, set sail for England.

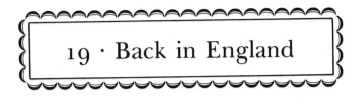

19 · Back in England

The Queen *defies* the tyrants; the Queen *defied* the tyrants; the Queen *will defy* the tyrants.

COBBETT'S DISINTERMENT of the body of Thomas Paine had created quite a stir in America.[1] It came as something of a surprise to him to find that Paine's bones provoked so little excitement in England. But when the *Hercules* anchored in Liverpool harbor on November 21, 1819, the event that still dominated serious conversation and filled the newspaper editorials was the so-called Peterloo massacre that had occurred on August 16.[2] On that day 60,000 men, women, and children of the working classes had gathered in a small area at the center of Manchester near St. Peter's Church, known as St. Peter's Fields, to demonstrate their sympathy for parliamentary reform. Henry Hunt was to be the principal speaker. The huge numbers – probably larger than any crowd previously assembled in England – and their ordered columns as they marched in military style to the meeting place with banners proclaiming "Parliaments Annual and Suffrage Universal" or, more provocatively, "Let Us Die like Men, and Not Be Sold as Slaves" alarmed the magistrates watching from a nearby house. Hunt had scarcely started to speak when a detachment of mounted yeomanry was ordered to arrest him. These volunteer cavalrymen, drawn from the middle classes, had neither the experience nor the inclination to effect their purpose gracefully. Then too, the particular moment they were called upon was not auspicious, since they had been drinking heavily. Jostling, and being jostled, as they moved through the densely packed crowd toward the speakers' platform, they became confused and frightened and began using their sabres. They were followed by a troop of hussars who had been directed to disperse the meeting. The crowd panicked. Among sword cuts, horse hooves, and the crush of the terrified victims, nine men and two women were killed and four or five hundred were wounded.[3]

In ten minutes . . . the field was an open and almost deserted space . . . The hustings remained, with a few broken and hewed flag-staves erect, and a torn and gashed banner or two dropping [drooping?], whilst over the whole field were strewed caps, bonnets, hats, shawls, and shoes, and other parts of male and female dress, trampled, torn, and bloody. The yeomanry had dismounted – some were easing their horses' girths, others adjusting their accoutrements, and some were wiping their sabres. Several mounds of human beings still remained where they had fallen, crushed down and smothered. Some of these were still groaning . . . All was silent save those low sounds, and the occasional snorting and pawing of steeds.[4]

The "victory" of the yeomanry over the peaceful gathering at St. Peter's Fields, in contrast to the glorious final battle against Napoleon four years before, evoked the cynical name "Peterloo."

The first comments on Peterloo came from the government. The prince regent, sailing off the Hampshire coast, whose knowledge of what had occurred was limited to a secondhand account of a report made by the Manchester magistrates, sent a message through the home secretary, Lord Sidmouth, congratulating the magistracy and military for their "prompt, decisive and efficient measures for the preservation of the public tranquillity." But within a few days it became obvious to a large part of the British public, including many persons who had no radical sympathies, that it was exceedingly doubtful whether there had been any threat to the "public tranquillity" except that created by those in authority. Sir Francis Burdett, throwing off the lethargy with which he had been charged by the more active reformers, promptly condemned the action of the government in a public letter to the electors of Westminster, and the attorney general proceeded against him by an ex officio information for libel. A huge mass meeting held in Palace Yard on September 2 was addressed by Cartwright as well as Burdett and Hobhouse; the animosities of the previous year were forgotten in presenting a united opposition to this newest act of tyranny.[5] Hobhouse followed up with a pamphlet on Peterloo that sent the author to Newgate. Cartwright, Wooler (editor of the *Black Dwarf*), and Sir Charles Wolseley, an old friend of Cartwright, were all implicated in incidents that were regarded as the preamble to Peterloo. The first two were indicted for participation in a public meeting held in Birmingham in July 1819 at which Sir Charles Wolseley had been elected "legislatorial attorney" to represent the city, otherwise unrepresented in parliament. Sir Charles himself was indicted for a speech made at Stockport the month before.[6]

After Hunt had been arrested at Peterloo he and his companions had been lodged in Manchester's New Bailey. They were then moved to Lancaster Castle, from which they were released on bail provided by Wolseley. Hunt left Lancaster for London, where, on September 13, he was given a hero's welcome by no fewer than 300,000 persons. "The whole distance from the Angel at Islington to the Crown and Anchor [in the Strand] was lined with multitudes," wrote the poet John Keats.[7]

Radical criticism could have been more or less expected. But condemnation of Peterloo did not stop there. *The Times*, whose reporter at the scene on August 16 had been mistakenly arrested as an agitator, pressed questions that seriously embarrassed the Manchester magistrates, the military forces, and Lord Liverpool's government. Protest meetings were held from Bristol and London in the south to the lowland towns of Scotland in the north, and seemed to increase rather than decrease with the passage of time. Earl Fitzwilliam was deposed as lord lieutenant of the West Riding for participation in such a meeting held in York on October 14.[8]

Shelley was in Italy when he learned of Peterloo. He wrote a long poem picturing "Lord Liverpool's ministers riding the horses which trampled down the English crowd", with the memorable lines

> I met Murder in the way –
> He had a mask like Castlereagh – [9]

A host of pamphlets, cartoons, and parodies were hawked on the streets of every major town. The most effective shot at the government was almost certainly that fired by William Hone, whose *The Political House That Jack Built* with caricatures by Cruikshank became a spectacular bestseller when published in September 1819.

> These are
> THE PEOPLE
>   all tatter'd and torn,
> Who curse the day
>   wherein they were born,
> On account of Taxation
>   too great to be borne,
> And pray for relief,
>   from night to morn;
> Who, in vain, Petition
>   in every form,
> Who, peaceably Meeting
>   to ask for Reform
> Were sabred by Yeomanry Cavalry,
>   who,
> Were thank'd by THE MAN,
>   all shaven and shorn,
> All cover'd with Orders –
>   and all forlorn;
> THE DANDY OF SIXTY,

———————— " Great offices will have
Great talents."

This is THE MAN—all shaven and shorn,
All cover'd with Orders—and all forlorn ;

The prince regent as seen by the radicals. This was one of the George Cruikshank
illustrations in the *Political House That Jack Built* by William Hone. The pamphlet
went into more than fifty editions

The prince regent as seen by his friends. This was one of the illustrations in the *Real Constitutional House That Jack Built*, which the friends of the prince regent, no doubt assisted by government funds, issued in response to Hone's pamphlet

who bows with a grace,
And has taste in wigs, collars,
    cuirasses, and lace:
Who, to tricksters, and fools,
    leaves the State and its treasure,
And when Britain's in tears,
    sails about at his pleasure;
Who spurn'd from his presence
    the Friends of his youth,
And now has not one
    who will tell him the truth.

Hone's parody, which eventually went into more than fifty editions, was in its sixteenth at the time Cobbett arrived in Liverpool – a rough measure of the rising tide of indignation produced by Peterloo. Thus Cobbett found the reform movement with many new faces devoted wholeheartedly to a new and unfamiliar subject. A special session of parliament to consider the state of the country, i.e. the Peterloo affair, had been convened on November 23, the day after Cobbett disembarked. It was, presumably, more Cobbett's sense of humor than his enlarged ego that caused him to write to his son James, just before leaving the ship, "You see, they have really called the Parliament to *meet me,* or, rather, to *receive me.*"[10]

Parliament's reception, if it may be called that, came in the form of repressive legislation that forced another drastic change in the *Political Register,* but this was not apparent at the time of Cobbett's arrival. The veteran reformer did receive a heartening personal welcome at Liverpool: "An immense number of people met him on the beach, and cheered him to the inn, which is a considerable distance from the docks." He addressed a large crowd in Clayton Square and was entertained at a public dinner on November 26. The unfriendly *Liverpool Mercury* declared that Cobbett "possesses an almost unbounded influence over the minds of the people of this country"; this was confirmed at Bolton, in Lancashire, the home of the bloodthirsty Colonel Fletcher, where the town crier was jailed – and held there ten weeks without trial – for announcing Cobbett's return to England.[11] All we know about Cobbett's curious luggage is that when he opened a certain wooden box at the customs house he declared: "There, gentlemen, are the mortal remains of the immortal Thomas Paine." According to the same account, "The skull was shown ... Cobbett was extremely attentive to the box, and looked rather serious during the exhibition." At a later point the report adds: "He came in for a considerable share of what the theatrical gentry term *goose,* in the neighbourhood of the custom-house."[12]

On November 28, Cobbett set off for Manchester, thirty miles

"The Political Champion turned Resurrection Man." Cobbett with Paine's bones is welcomed to England by Hunt and Wooler (the black dwarf) while Bonaparte on St. Helena exclaims: "Ah! Ça ira," and the quakers in America "rejoice, that the Evil Spirit hath departed from us!" Cobbett wrote to his son James in January 1820: "I will send you a caricature that they have published here representing me flying over the sea and old Isaac Wright dancing with the Devil upon the American shore, rejoicing at my departure." 35 *PR* 573

away, in the company of his eldest sons, William and John. When they reached Irlam, ten miles from their destination, they were stopped by a messenger on horseback sent by the Manchester authorities to caution Cobbett against any "public entry" into that city, since "in the present situation of the country" a large assemblage of people would be "necessarily attended with considerable danger to the public peace." Cobbett's reply angrily denounced this threatened interference with the right to move freely from one point to another, and refused to declare whether he intended to enter Manchester or not.[13] In the end he decided to proceed towards London; a wise move, it would seem, as *The Times* reported a few days later that the military preparations at Manchester, in anticipation of Cobbett's arrival, were comparable to those at Peterloo.[14] After spending the next night in

Cobbett leaves Liverpool with Paine's bones. No single event in Cobbett's full life was the subject of more humor than Paine's bones. Here Cobbett, Liverpool harbor on the horizon, heads for London with Paine's coffin on his back

Coventry, Cobbett addressed several thousand persons who had followed him out of the city, stopping his horse in an open space on the
side of the road, and standing on the footboard of the chaise to speak
to the crowd.[15] In London, Cobbett was entertained at a public dinner
for 400 reformers at the Crown and Anchor tavern on December 4.
Hunt, harboring no grudge for the "whore" letter, acted as chairman,
and Woolner, after recommending "a general oblivion of all private
feuds between the real friends of reform," apologized to Cobbett for

what "he might have said to that gentleman's disadvantage."[16] This was a good start toward a reunion among the principal reformers, but a subsequent effort to reconcile Cobbett with Burdett (who did not attend) proved fruitless.[17]

A toast at the dinner to the health of William Cobbett "having been drank with almost nine times nine," the prodigal son of reform "returned his sincere thanks for the honour; at the same time, he observed, he did not feel that he was altogether unworthy of it." In the speech that followed Cobbett reasserted the familiar theme he had obliquely derived from Paine: that there would be no reform until those in power were convinced that they could no longer carry on the funding system; that is, until they ran out of money. Much of the rest of Cobbett's talk was related directly or indirectly to Paine's bones, and the context suggests his disappointment at the reception thus far accorded to these relics.[18] One looking at the facts today sees clearly what had gone wrong: Cobbett thought that he was bringing back the bones of Thomas Paine, author of the economic essay *The Decline and Fall of the English System of Finance,* but discovered that to most Englishmen he had brought back the bones of Thomas Paine, author of the *Age of Reason,* the book that defended deism and taught that the Bible was largely mythology.[19] For publishing that book, Richard Carlile had been found guilty of blasphemy and sentenced to two years' imprisonment only the week before Cobbett's return.[20] Thus it seems quite reasonable that those attending the Crown and Anchor dinner should have been given an explanation for the presence of the bones in England. Cobbett did this at some length: Paine had been refused burial in consecrated ground in America. Under such circumstances, Cobbett would have brought back the bones of any Englishman, "but the hypocrites were in alarm, it appeared, lest the bones of this man . . . should injure the cause of religion." So far as Cobbett was concerned,

he begged distinctly to disavow having in view the propagation of any opinions connected with religion: he had never even read his theological works, for, in his opinion, religion ought to be left to the individual consciences of men; and his sole object, in bringing over the bones of Paine for re-interment in this country, was from a desire to atone, in some degree, for the injustice he had himself formerly done him in his writings . . . and, if he lived another year, he intended to erect a colossal statue, in bronze, in honour of his memory.

At a later point in the evening, Hunt found it necessary to explain that for humanitarian reasons he had offered to stand bail for Carlile at the time of his arrest, but that he had never read the theological works of Paine until Carlile's trial.[21] These protestations demonstrate the extent to which English society of the period was "religious, and even pietist."[22]

Cobbett did live "another year" – another sixteen years – but he erected no bronze statue of Paine. His proposal for a great public dinner on Paine's birthday had to be abandoned. So too did his proposal for the sale of gold rings containing strands of Paine's hair.[23] Paine's bones became an object of "laughter, contempt and derision" rather than reverence.[24] Byron was only one of the poets and would-be poets who found the subject irresistible:

> In digging up your bones, Tom Paine,
>   Will. Cobbett has done well;
> You visit him on earth again,
>   He'll visit you in hell.[25]

An American ship putting in to Cowes reported that Cobbett had made a mistake: Instead of bringing the bones of Paine, he had brought those of an unidentified Negro, a story that may account for the following stanza by an unknown author:

> The radicals seem quite elated,
>   And soon will be intoxicated
> For Cobbett means to turn their brain
>   With his American SHAM PAINE.[26]

A surprised Cobbett, viewing the mixed reception of humor and abuse aroused by Paine's bones, wrote: "No one dared to move a pen or tongue in my defence . . . Former friends, or pretended friends, shrugged up their shoulders."[27] He ascribed the lack of enthusiasm to envy, and this conclusion (for which there seems little justification) may explain Cobbett's growing coolness to his former colleagues. Daughter Anne wrote to James: "He has cut the Old Major, as he ought, and there is a fair prospect of his cutting somebody else too, our friend Chasse [Hunt]; Papa begins to be sick of him, and to find out that he is envious as well as the rest."[28]

Following the Crown and Anchor dinner, Cobbett stayed on in London for another ten days, and then left for Botley to join his wife and the younger children, whom he had not seen since they left America in mid 1818. He arrived in Botley with his eldest son on December 15. The people of the village met the homecomers "upon the hill in Winchester road" – presumably the turnpike for which Cobbett had secured parliamentary approval and in which he had invested some of his money.

The men took the horses out of the chaise and brought them home, filling the air with most tremendous shouts, which must have grated the Parson's ear, who was one amongst the throng. He had been for several days previous poking about in the village, telling the people they would do very wrong in doing such honour as they intended to P's [Papa's] return. He told them they would draw the devil into Botley for *beer,* and they civilly told him they would "dra him out for nothen". But one man "told me to us head" (so Punch says) that so far from expecting beer from Mr Cobbett they would rather give him some, if he should want it. When Papa got out of the chaise at our door, poor Jurd burst into tears, and I could have cried too, to hear the hearty cheers the men gave. Papa gave them a little speech in the village, though it was dark.[29]

This performance was another of the strange episodes in Cobbett's life. His wife and younger children, since their return from America, had been living in a small furnished house on King's Road, Chelsea. Cobbett refused to meet the family there and, "to the regret of all," wrote his daughter Susan, "said that he would only return upon condition of returning to Botley."

This was imperative but most difficult to perform, for how to furnish the larger house and get the furniture down was impossible, particularly as the house (which had stood empty since he left for America) was in the possession

"The Hampshire Hog with Paine's bones." Cobbett's home at Botley in Hampshire earned him the unfriendly name "the Hampshire Hog." In this cartoon the Hampshire Hog, with forked tail, carries Paine's skeleton. Hunt, wearing the white hat that was an invariable part of his showmanship, marches behind

of Mr Tunno, the mortgagee; but he was very kind about it, and *lent* the house to Mrs C; so William bought a little second-hand furniture for a few of the rooms, and Mrs C and the family went down to Botley to be there to receive Mr C when he came.[30]

When "Mr C" finally did come, a year and a half had passed since wife and husband had separated in New York, and three weeks had elapsed since Cobbett's arrival in Liverpool – another bit of evidence that there had been some disagreement in America accounting for Nancy's premature return to England. Daughter Anne in Botley wrote to her brother James in New York: "You will be delighted to hear that dear Papa & Mama are as happy as ever they were, and we all seem more united [wanted?] and happy together than ever."[31] The happy stay at Botley was a brief one. Cobbett and the two older boys returned to London on January 2. The rest of the family followed in May. This was the last time any of the Cobbetts occupied Botley House.

Two principal motivations (neither of which explains the Botley reunion) dominated Cobbett's conduct at this period: his urgent need for money and his desire to resume his role as leader of the reform movement. Cobbett's seed, book, and pig business in New York, now being conducted by James, had been sold to his friend and former partner, John Morgan of Philadelphia, possibly as a device to protect the assets against creditors, but more likely as a means of reimbursing Morgan for the advances he had made to Cobbett since his arrival in America.[32] Waiting to disembark from the *Hercules* at Liverpool, Cobbett began to make inquiries about a by-election to be held in Chichester – for as a member of parliament he would be immune from arrest for debt – but the Chichester move proved impracticable.[33] As soon as his arrival was announced in the press, petty creditors began to plague him. On the night of the Crown and Anchor dinner on December 4, he was served with a writ sworn out by a maltster at Droxford, near Botley, to whom Cobbett owed £35.[34] Cobbett's ability to make money out of the *Political Register* was abruptly curtailed by the new laws Lord Liverpool's government rushed through parliament. One of these – directly aimed at Cobbett and his imitators – put an end to cheap unstamped pamphlets commenting on affairs of the day. The newspaper tax of fourpence a copy was made specifically applicable to pamphlets "containing any public news, intelligence, or occurrences, or any remarks or observations thereon, or upon any matter in Church or State" printed on not more than "two sheets" or sold for less than sixpence.[35] Thus the price of the *Political Register* to the reader would be tripled, rising from twopence to sixpence – reducing its circulation, Cobbett estimated, by more than 80 percent.[36] Five other acts were adopted before parliament adjourned on December 29.[37] Meetings to teach marching or drilling were made unlawful; magistrates were empowered to enter private homes to search and seize arms in fourteen named counties; open-air gatherings of more than fifty persons were, with minor exceptions, limited to residents of the parish in which the meeting was held; the right of an accused to obtain an adjournment of trial to prepare his defense was limited; a blasphemous or seditious libel, punishable by banishment for a second offense, was defined as language "tending to bring into hatred or contempt" the king, regent, or either house of parliament or to "excite his Majesty's subjects to attempt the alteration of any matter in church or state . . . otherwise than by lawful means." These laws, known to history as the Six Acts, added a heavy weight to the already accumulated mass of hatred borne by the principal ministers: Liverpool, Sidmouth, and Castlereagh.[38]

To offset the loss of income caused by the expected decline in circulation of the *Political Register,* Cobbett resorted to a risky expedient: He would publish a daily newspaper as he had from 1800 to 1801.[39] Although this would place a further strain on his overextended credit, Cobbett saw only the opportunity of profiting from his national reputation for lively journalism. The newspaper, *Cobbett's Evening Post,* began on January 29, 1820. George III died the same day, which meant that there would be an immediate general election. Cobbett promptly decided to run for Coventry, which he had been eyeing with interest for the past several years, although it was "a corrupt borough whose 'politics' were shunned by most of its neighbours."[40] The result, as might have been predicted, was the failure of both undertakings. The paper was doomed from the day it began, since Cobbett put all his efforts into the election. He had an orderly mind, and its order required that he do one thing at a time. He refused to combine even two relatively simple things such as eating an apple and reading a book. He read, or he ate, but not both at once.[41] *Cobbett's Evening Post,* without Cobbett, lasted fifty-five issues, expiring on April 1.[42] Its sole interest today is what it said about the Coventry election. This was a disaster, despite heroic efforts by Cobbett. The fault lay in his initial assumption that he could win an election singlehanded against the forces of corruption.

The struggle began with the difficult task of raising money. Even a no-corruption candidate for a parliamentary seat faced heavy bills. At the 1807 election for Westminster, nearly £800 had been spent during the polling period for such routine items as advertisements, stationery, flags, music, and constables' charges.[43] At Coventry another large charge was involved: Freemen of that city living elsewhere were entitled to be conveyed to the polling place at the expense of the candidate for whom they were voting. This came to about £15 a head for voters living in London.[44] Cobbett at first estimated that the total cost of standing at Coventry would be £2,000.[45] "The enemies of the people," wrote T. J. Wooler, "have cunningly rendered elections *expensive*, that honest, well-meaning men might be deterred from the contest."[46]

The money problem had concerned Cobbett from the outset. The *Political Register* of December 24, 1819 contained an article by him stating that he could be far more effective if he were in the House of Commons. "I am thinking of a mode of acquiring the means to effect this object."[47] Two weeks later he announced "Cobbett's Fund for Reform," which was for the purpose of "furthering the cause of Reform in a way such as my discretion shall point out." He estimated that the sum required would be £5,000 "to be used solely by me, of course, and without the check or controul of any-body; and without any one ever having a right to ask me what I was going to do with it."[48] In succeeding issues he continued advertising the fund and acknowledging contributions as received, but without further edification as to purpose.[49] When Cobbett announced his candidacy for Coventry and the opening of a subscription to defray the expenses, he proposed that "Cobbett's Fund for Reform" be diverted to his election campaign. At that point the fund was six weeks old; "something approaching nearly two hundred pounds" had been received by him, and sums in unknown amounts had been collected but not yet remitted.[50] Whatever this was, it was far from enough. On February 25 Cobbett mailed a printed circular letter to seventy persons asking for £10 each.[51] According to Cobbett, a large amount was raised by subscription, "principally coming from one generous man," and yet Cobbett still had to lay out more than £500, presumably of his own money, after the election was over.[52]

Cobbett's intention to run for Coventry had hardly been announced when he found it necessary to reply to the "calumnies which have been heaped upon me by the atrocious daily press of the metropolis, by the still more atrocious *Quarterly Review*, and by almost the whole of the country newspapers."[53] Cobbett's reply consisted of an abbreviated life history including that charming account of the eleven-year-old boy in his blue smock frock and red garters tied under his knees who walked from Farnham to Richmond in order to find employment in the royal gardens at Kew. It contained a good deal of background to Cobbett's current financial affairs, ending with an admission that if he had been more careful of his own money, it would not have been necessary to appeal for funds. "Very true; but, then, I should not have been *the man I am*: observe that. To be careful of money; to sue and be sued; to squabble about shillings and pennies: these are wholly incompatible with the pursuit of great public objects."[54] The little-blue-smock-frock story, according to Cobbett, "produced a prodigious effect all over the country." When he made his preliminary survey of Coventry in the middle of February 1820, his friends there urged him to republish it, and so copies were circulated throughout that city. Cobbett was elated by his initial reception: "our friends there are so warm, so kind, so respectable too."[55]

The election was scheduled to begin on March 8. The week before, Cobbett returned to Coventry with his eldest daughter, Anne, and his brother-in-law, Captain Reid. They travelled by post chaise from London to Dunchurch, eleven miles from Coventry. There they were told that a gang of ruffians who had proposed to prevent Cobbett's entry into Coventry had been defeated when "our friends sallied forth upon them, took away their banners, staved in their drums, dispersed them in all directions, and set off on their march to meet me." Although this action had cleared the road, the landlords of Dunchurch, "who had doubtless been prepared," refused to let Cobbett have a chaise to continue his journey. Friends again came to the rescue. They provided an old post chaise which they pulled through the streets of the city for two hours while Cobbett, standing on the footboard with his hat off, greeted the cheering crowds in the chilly night air. He had left London with a cold. When he arrived at the house of Mr. Sergeant, with whom he was staying in Coventry, he discovered that he had lost his voice "nearly as complete as if I had been dumb from my birth."[56]

As this preamble suggests, the atmosphere was charged with violence. Peterloo was a reflection of current passions. The duc de Berry, heir to the French throne, had been assassinated in Paris on February 13. Ten days later, in London, a gang meeting in Cato Street, just off Edgware Road, was arrested a matter of hours before its planned assassination of the entire cabinet.[57] On the night of Cobbett's arrival in Coventry, February 29, the windows of Sergeant's house were smashed, and several stabbings occurred in the streets. Four days later when Cobbett's rivals, the whig incumbents Peter Moore and Edward Ellice, appeared in Coventry, Sergeant's windows were again smashed.[58]

The polling began on Wednesday, March 8. At the end of the day Cobbett stood at the head of the list. On the next day "the Savages came." They were brought in "by sixes, eights or tens" from the mines

393

Cobbett's triumphal entry into Coventry. I. R. Cruikshank in 1821 parodied Cobbett's account of the Coventry election in the same way Gillray, in 1809, had parodied Cobbett's account of his life as a soldier.

Cobbett's obligation to Burdett, his diatribes against tea drinking, and his inconsistencies were obvious targets for the cartoonist. Less obvious is "St. Pacomo's Bree-[ches]," a story Cobbett levelled at Burdett about a lecherous monk whose trousers became an object of local reverence.

at Bedworth, Longford, and Nuneaton, so that by the hour of closing "an immense multitude of these wretches, roaring like wolves, and foaming with rage and drink, were collected around the Booth."

I that day saw above twenty of my voters actually torn away from the polling place, and ripped up behind, and stripped of their coats, and sometimes, even of their waistcoats! Nevertheless, in spite of all this destruction ... my voters persevered to such a degree as to put me nearly on a level with my opponents at the close of the poll; and, if the *infirm persons,* whom I had got *into* the Booth, had been permitted to poll, I should have stood above Moore at the end of the second day.

As Cobbett left the booth he was personally attacked by the savages. Defending himself as best he could with the sharp end of a snuffbox held in his hand, he was saved by the prompt intervention of Frank Sergeant, the son of his host: "To him I certainly owe my life."[59]

On the beginning of the third day, Friday, three to four hundred of Cobbett's voters were arranged by the side of the booth ready to vote. By eleven o'clock Cobbett was again heading the poll when the savages arrived in full force: "not less than five hundred in number, in regular order, about eight or ten deep, with drums and banners at their head." In five minutes "three hundred of my voters were as completely driven away as if an army had made an attack upon them."

After this, not a man dare to shew his face in order to vote for me, during that whole day. If a man crept in unperceived, he was, as soon as discovered, pulled back, dragged away, jostled, beaten, or cut. The ferocity of the Savages, this day, was such as I thought human beings incapable of. I have seen parcels of drunken soldiers. I have seen gangs of furious and drunken sailors. I have seen roaring mobs in London. I have seen whole bands of American Indians, drunk with rum. But, never did my eyes behold any thing in human shape so ferocious, so odiously, so diabolically ferocious, as those bands of villains, hired, paid, fed, and drenched by the Rich Ruffians of Coventry.[60]

On Saturday there was another attack on Sergeant's house – this time in earnest. The windows were again broken, the shutters torn off, the street door smashed open. Entering the house, the howling mob tried to force its way along the twenty-foot passage leading to the bedroom where Cobbett, suffering severely from his cold, was sitting with his daughter. The men of the house met the savages with pokers and tongs, while Cobbett and Anne fixed the bedstead in a way to let the door open no wider than to admit one man at a time, while Cobbett stood with drawn sword to meet any one who might manage to enter. Fortunately, the constables appeared, the riot act was read, and the crowd dispersed.[61] According to the account that appeared in the *Sun*, "the professed design of the mob was to kill Cobbett, if they could have laid hold of him."[62]

Cobbett at the Coventry hustings. Another in the series of I. R. Cruikshank's cartoons. This one was derived from Cobbett's statement "My way was to stand and look upon the yelling beasts with a most good-humoured smile . . ."

Despite Cobbett's appeals to the mayor and the sheriffs for protection, he was no longer able to get his voters to the poll.[63] The savages, backed by new recruits pouring in from the surrounding country, were too much for him. Instead of quitting when this became obvious, he held on for another four days in the belief that his opponents' display of force was costing them £1,000 a day. He took satisfaction, too, in a strange Cobbettian way of dealing with the savages themselves:

My way was to stand and look upon the yelling beasts with a most good-humoured smile; turning my head now and then, and leaning it, as it were to take different views of the same person, or same group. I now and then substituted something of *curiosity* instead of the general total *unconcern*, that was seated upon my face. Now and then, I would put my mouth close to the ear of some friend that stood by me, and then point to some beast that was foaming with rage, giving him at the same time a laughing look; such as we bestow on a dog that is chained up and barking at us. Then, another time, when half a dozen fresh-drenched brutes were bursting forth close under my nose, I would stretch up my neck, and look, with apparently great curiosity and anxiousness towards a distant part of the crowd, as if to ascertain what was passing there; and this I would do with so much apparent earnestness and continue in the attitude so long, that the beasts really seemed, sometimes, as if they were going mad![64]

On March 16, after eight days of polling, Cobbett had collected 517 votes, some 900 behind Ellice and Moore. The day before the close Cobbett was so ill that he and his daughter had withdrawn to Meriden, five miles from Coventry. After three nights there, they were hounded out of the Bull's Head inn by the Earl of Aylesford and other gentlemen of the neighborhood, who threatened the landlord with the loss of his license for accommodating such discreditable guests.[65] The charges of "infidel" and "apostate" levelled against Cobbett by the daily papers as a result of the Paine episode almost certainly colored the entire Coventry experience. "At Coventry, my opponents took 'loyalty and religion' to themselves, and allotted to me 'sedition and blasphemy'."[66]

Cobbett "seated" at Coventry. Cobbett's seat is on an ass, which he rides backwards. *Paper against Gold* is discharged from the rear of the animal while Cobbett prepares to beat the "Rump," his pet name for the Westminster committee allegedly controlled by Burdett. The ass exclaims: "Ize be Jesse Burges[s]" (a reference to the 1809 runaway) and heads for Botley

After a brief visit to Botley, Cobbett was back in London at the end of March, still ill and now, more than ever, beset by creditors. He was twice arrested for debts: by a Mr. Buckland of Hampshire, for money borrowed for the Winchester turnpike, for which Cobbett had made himself responsible in the amount of £272, and by the printers Hay and Turner for a bill amounting to £400. Timothy Brown, a friendly creditor for £1,600, who had stood surety for Cobbett when he had left Newgate, urged Cobbett to seek the protection of the bankruptcy laws, and at his own expense undertook all the necessary procedures. To avoid further arrests before his surrender, Cobbett, still "very poorly, coughing all the time" and not warmly dressed ("somehow there never was money for these things"), left London for Westerham, where there was an inn conveniently located on the Surrey–Kent border. He was accompanied by his daughter Anne. They moved on, after a few days, to Reigate, and finally at the end of April, when all the papers had been prepared and the commission in bankruptcy arranged, Cobbett returned to London, where he surrendered and entered the Rules of the King's Bench prison.[67]

Cobbett's debts amounted to £28,000, of which £16,000 was secured by mortgages on the Botley property.[68] This was the only asset of substance, and although valued by Cobbett at £30,000, it seems likely – in view of the abrupt decline in land prices since the end of the war – that if sold, the property would not have brought enough to cover the amount for which it was mortgaged.[69] Thus the bankruptcy decree generously allowed Cobbett a period of years in which to redeem the property by paying off the mortgages, but since the deflation following the Napoleonic wars continued for nearly a century, Cobbett's right of redemption proved valueless. It is unlikely that the unsecured creditors, to whom Cobbett was indebted for an aggregate of £12,000, received anything from the bankrupt estate.[70]

From these debts Cobbett was finally released on October 12, 1820. The crusty Lord Eldon had finished his business for the day, but, to oblige the man who had so often attacked him, he graciously signed the certificate that ended the bankruptcy. For five months Cobbett, Anne, and John had been living within the Rules in lodgings at 15 Lambeth Road – "a small dirty place in a dusty road." They were very poor. Much of the time they lived on the cheapest food available: cauliflowers and other garden vegetables. Years later Anne wrote: "I, for my part think that Papa never would have got thro' that hard time so well, if it had not been for the Queen's affair."[71]

The "queen's affair" became everyone's affair from the middle to the end of 1820. Cobbett's interest dated back to 1806, when articles began to appear in the *Political Register* under the heading "Delicate Investigation," a typically English euphemism for what eventually became the most indelicate investigation in royal history. In 1795 the Prince of Wales, aged thirty-two, had married his first cousin Princess Caroline of Brunswick, aged twenty-six. The prince – fat, dissolute, selfish – had been secretly married ten years before to a Roman catholic widow, Mrs. Fitzherbert, in an alliance that was invalid under the Royal Marriage Act. He now undertook to marry his cousin, sight unseen, to induce parliament to pay off his debts. The princess was generous, high-spirited, and good-natured but also ill-educated, impulsive, untidy about her person, and – even her father admitted it – lacking in judgment, although she was not allowed much opportunity to exercise it in the choice of a husband.[72] Nine months after the marriage a daughter, Princess Charlotte, was born. Three months later Caroline received a letter from her husband declaring that "nature has not made us suitable to each other," and suggesting that they maintain "tranquil and comfortable society" by going their separate ways.[73] The prince returned to Mrs. Fitzherbert for a time, then took up with younger court ladies. The princess set up her own residence where she entertained her friends. This "tranquil and comfortable society" ended in 1806 when, at the urging of the prince, the king issued a warrant initiating an investigation – the "delicate investigation" – into the claim that Caroline had given birth to an illegitimate child. The first news Caroline had of this proceeding was the discovery that her servants and confidants, one by one, were being interrogated. The resulting report of the royal commission concluded that there was "no foundation whatever" for the charge, but added that there were "other particulars" that "gave occasion to very unfavourable interpretations."[74] To put it briefly, she had a number of male visitors with whom she was on familiar terms. Where she drew the line (if she drew one), and where the line for the cast-off wife of a dissolute prince should be drawn, became questions debated by the British public for the next fifteen years.

The charges against Caroline, the evidence educed by the royal commission, and the conclusions of the commission, even the creation of the commission itself, were officially secret, but not secret enough to avoid widely disseminated gossip that continued from 1806 to 1813. In that year Cobbett, with the assistance of his friend Andrew Cochrane Johnstone, then a member of parliament, forced the publication of the complete story.[75] The prince, who had never been popular with the people, became noticeably less popular. The falsely accused Caroline was a heroine overnight, but forgoing her popularity, left England for the continent after Napoleon's surrender in

Queen Caroline and Bartolomeo Bergami. The queen's buxom figure, her extravagant dress, and her apparent infatuation with Bergami were obvious targets for the king's friends

1814. There she stayed until 1820, seemingly unconcerned about the interpretation given to her open relations with a handsome Italian soldier, Bartolomeo Bergami. Bergami, beginning service as her courier, soon assumed the role of constant companion – "even at dinner," the *Dictionary of National Biography* discreetly reveals. In 1818 the prince sent a delegation of lawyers to Milan for the express purpose of collecting evidence on the indiscretions of his wife. When he was proclaimed George IV on January 31, 1820, two days after the death of his father, he made it plain that Caroline was not to be treated as his queen. This advice was sent to all British ambassadors abroad. The king also ordered that her name be excluded from the liturgy of the church of England, and demanded that his ministers procure a divorce using the materials collected by the Milan commission. The ministers nervously agreed that they would do so if the queen returned to England, although under the prevailing law a divorce was not obtainable for a wife's adultery if the husband had been first to break the marriage vows.

Early in June 1820 Caroline appeared at St. Omer, twenty-five miles from Calais. She had been persuaded by Alderman Matthew Wood of London to return to England. At St. Omer she was met by a representative of the ministers and her legal adviser, Henry Brougham, prepared to discuss a settlement. She could have £50,000 a year for life if she would renounce her title and remain abroad.[76] If she came to England, criminal proceedings would be instituted against her. She immediately left for Calais, where she embarked on an English packet bound for Dover. On June 6, Cobbett stood on Shooter's Hill with his daughter Anne and waved a bough of laurel as they saw the queen pass "in a miserable half broken down carriage covered with dust, followed by a post chaise and a calash."[77] But despite such appearances, it was a triumphal return for Queen Caroline. "The Queen of England is at present everything with everybody," declared *The Times*.[78] Throughout the summer and autumn of 1820, admirers by the thousands assembled around her residence, followed her, and saluted her wherever she went. No sovereign, before or since, has been greeted by such unsponsored throngs, such enthusiastic cheering, such voluntary illuminations as Queen Caroline.

This phenomenon was, in part, due to a hearty dislike of George IV. But there were other elements. Some believed in Caroline's innocence.[79] "She is a real *good woman*," wrote Anne Cobbett, "kind, charitable, feeling and condescending towards every creature, she possesses wonderful courage, presence of mind, fortitude and promptness in action . . . She is very industrious, for when sitting still she is always at work, and if anything ails any of her servants she waits upon them."[80] Others thought that, innocent or guilty, she had suffered more than any woman should suffer: She had been rejected by her dissolute husband, been denied the company of her daughter, been excluded from court, been falsely charged with bearing an illegitimate child, been spied on by a team of government-paid lawyers.[81]

Now she bravely faced a high-handed ministry that was prepared to bribe her to stay away from England and to threaten her with criminal prosecution if she did not. Cobbett and his fellow reformers saw Caroline as a representative of all those oppressed by acts of the government. Her enemies, they declared, were their enemies: "The case of Her Majesty then, is the case of us all."[82] The ministers quickly confirmed the propriety of this comparison. The Milan commission's materials, inviolable in a green bag, were referred to a secret committee without opportunity for rebuttal, just as had occurred at the time of the suspension of the Habeas Corpus Act in 1817. The ministry held no old-fashioned nonsense about a presumption of innocence until proof of guilt. On the contrary, Lord Castlereagh asserted on the floor of the House of Commons that "a charge of crime necessarily implied a presumption of guilt."[83] Thus, relying on the report of the secret committee that had examined the contents of the green bag, a Bill of Pains and Penalties introduced on July 7 in the House of Commons by Castlereagh and in the House of Lords by Liverpool flatly declared that the queen, having carried on "a licentious, disgraceful and adulterous intercourse" with Bergami, was "hereby deprived of the title of Queen," and her marriage with the king was "hereby from henceforth for ever wholly dissolved." The queen was denied a list of the witnesses to be called against her and even a statement of where or when the alleged offenses had been committed.[84] The whole proceeding was dominated by the same arrogance, self-righteousness, and partiality that were characteristic of all proceedings by the government against those it regarded as enemies. Fortunately for the queen, the Bill of Pains and Penalties was only a bill. To become effective it had to pass both houses of Parliament.

On the evening of Caroline's arrival in London, Cobbett had offered his services to Alderman Wood. In the next three weeks he addressed eight letters to the queen containing advice on her conduct.[85] Cobbett's advice may have been in the best interest of the queen, but it also fitted in well with the interests of the reformers, who needed a leader able to stand up to parliament and the crown.[86] Cobbett asserted that the queen should demand her full rights. She must not compromise. She must not agree to leave England. She must rely wholly on the public for her support. These views were generally endorsed by Alderman Wood, who was something of a reformer himself.

The other avenue of advice being received by the queen came from her legal advisor, Henry Brougham. His advice was colored by three elements: He was the queen's lawyer, and thus had information not known to Cobbett or other members of the public; he was a member of the whig opposition that was interested in returning to power; he had his own career to consider. His advice to the queen may have been for her advantage, but it was also fully compatible with his several other concerns.[87] As a result, his advice was almost the reverse of that urged by Cobbett. Brougham favored a compromise settlement which would have involved Caroline giving up most of her rights as well as leaving the country. He was opposed to any acts of the queen that associated her with the disreputable reformers.

Because of such opposing forces, the queen's policy seemed to change from day to day, depending on which force was dominant. The negotiations for a settlement that had commenced at St. Omer were reopened by Brougham in London and continued for several weeks while Cobbett denounced this course in his letters to the queen and in his pronouncements appearing in the *Political Register*. On June 24, to Cobbett's delight, the queen put an end to the negotiations by stating that she would not consent to "the sacrifice of any essential privilege."[88]

Cobbett won another round when, on August 7, ten days before the opening of the trial, the queen wrote a bitter, stinging letter to the king referring to the "unparalleled and unprovoked persecution" carried on against her "under the name and authority of your Majesty."[89] The letter listed the injuries she had suffered at his hands between the time of marriage and her departure for Europe in 1814 (a subject which Brougham expressly excluded from his presentation), and attacked the lack of disinterestedness of the House of Lords, before which she was to be tried (Brougham extolled the virtue and fair-mindedness of the same group).[90] *The Times* thought that the queen's letter was "calculated to rouse every generous and manly moral feeling."[91] But the *Courier* declared it to be a "libel" and a "shameless publication." The *New Times* claimed that it contained "seditious and treasonable doctrines."[92]

Although it was never admitted, the letter itself had been written by Cobbett. "We were in absolute terror when the queen's letter first appeared in the newspapers," wrote daughter Anne. "Young Mr Bryant came over to us with one in his hand, and read it out with great feeling. Papa and I affecting wonder and admiration the while. He the writer; I the copyer. Papa got up and went away and tore up his rough copy." The queen had signed the letter and sent it off immediately after receiving it from Cobbett, knowing that "her legal advisers might, if they arrived before it was gone, advise her to the contrary." She liked it so much that "when she had her portrait painted for the City of London, she desired Mr. Lonsdale, the artist, to represent her with this document in her hand."[93]

Queen Caroline: portrait by James Lonsdale. This portrait, which hangs today in the Guildhall, London, shows the queen holding in her right hand a letter "For His Majesty The King" – the stinging attack on her husband which Cobbett wrote for her and which the artist included in the picture at the specific request of the queen

Cobbett also managed to reverse a decision made by Caroline's two vice-chamberlains, who suddenly announced, late in October, that the queen would receive no more addresses from the people – presumably to avoid offending those in power. Up to that point, deputations from all over the nation had besieged the queen with statements of their support for her cause and their condemnation of the government. On the day of the announcement some thirty addresses were presented while 70,000 enthusiastic supporters had milled round her residence. Cobbett's heated attack on this disclaimer of public support brought about a reversal the following week.[94]

While shaping the queen's policy, Cobbett also maintained a continuous barrage directed at the prosecution. The case opened with a two-day speech by the attorney general delivered on August 19 and 21. Five days later Cobbett wrote in the *Political Register*: "I have the report of the speech made by the Attorney General . . . now lying before me. I have read it with attention and, in *it alone*, without waiting to hear any contradiction of its assertions, I see enough to convince me, *that the charges are* false."[95] And Cobbett produced a convincing demonstration of his conclusion. At the end of the prosecutor's case he landed another solid blow, pointing out that the attorney general's own witnesses had failed to prove many of the points he had asserted at the outset.[96]

Brougham, in the meantime, tried the queen's case before the House of Lords on his own theory of appealing to the fair-mindedness of the judges and endeavoring not to cause more offense than necessary. And he did his job well despite the constant public hectoring by Cobbett, who spent almost as much time expressing his disapproval of Brougham's performance as he did in attacking that of the prosecution.[97] Brougham, a skilled trial lawyer, demolished the foreign witnesses – mainly Italians – who had been brought up the river at night in an armed ship and kept secreted from view in accommodations adjacent to Westminster Hall. They were principally disgruntled ex-servants of the queen who had been promised substantial rewards for their testimony. One of the key witnesses closely pressed by Brougham's searching examination finally fell back on a repetitive answer: "Non mi ricordi," a phrase that quickly became a part of the popular humor of the day.[98]

The case against the queen went steadily downhill from the time the trial began until its close. On November 6 the House of Lords voted 123 to 95 on the second reading of the bill, giving the ministers a majority of 28. Three days later the majority on the third reading had shrunk to 9, a sure sign that the bill could never pass the House of Commons in view of the strongly expressed public opinion. Lord

Liverpool gave up the fight, withdrawing the bill by the parliamentary device of moving that "This bill do pass this day six months" – that is, after prorogation, which automatically extinguished all pending bills. His motion had come at four o'clock in the afternoon, and the news spread as rapidly as the communication system of 1820 would allow. Stagecoaches leaving the capital that evening for all parts of the country "carried white flags on their tops with bunches of laurel; while the horses, and the whips of the coachmen, were decorated with bows and streamers of white ribband. Away went the tidings, carrying pleasure to every honest heart in the kingdom."[99] All through the night and into the early hours of the morning, the church bells of England, in an ever widening circle, rang out the message. London itself was a riot of noise and lights from the Friday on which the bill was withdrawn to the following Tuesday. On two of those nights the Cobbetts roamed the streets in a hired coach, looking upon "such a scene of rejoicing as I believe never was before witnessed in this world": All the ships in the river were lighted to the mast heads; processions bearing torches marched to bands of music playing "God Save the Queen," many carrying busts of the queen wearing a crown and covered with laurels. The demonstrations came mainly from the "industrious classes." The streets they occupied, as distinguished from those occupied by the aristocracy, the bankers, and other "tax-eaters," were one blaze of illumination, while "guns, pistols, blunderbusses and cannons kept firing during the whole of the night, from sun set nearly till day light."

To the noise of these was added that of squibs, crackers, rockets, fire-balls and all sorts of fire-works, so that not only in the streets, but also up in the air there was continual light blazing over this immense space.

The means were, in short, proportioned to the end. It was THE PEOPLE'S TRIUMPH over those who had so long triumphed over them.[100]

It was a triumph that had important long-term consequences. What the reformers had been saying about the failure of the boroughmongers' government to represent the main body of the people was proved to be true in a clear-cut situation; that is, one in which the oppressive acts of the ministry could not be justified as necessary to preserve private property or to protect established religion, the standard excuses for past acts of tyranny.[101] "It required her case to be before us," wrote Cobbett, "to convince a certain portion of the people of the lengths to which this system could go."[102] *The Times*, to its credit, no longer sided with the ministry, right or wrong; it had taken a critical stance at the time of the Peterloo affair and did so again in the contest involving the queen. The episode also had a levelling influence. Those at the center of power, when stripped of their sanctity, were revealed as mediocre men, whose actions could not be accepted on faith as they had been in the past.[103] The question so often posed by Cobbett became less silly: Were there not men, even from the lower classes of society, who were equally, or perhaps even better, qualified to hold these positions of responsibility and trust?

These were some of the long-term benefits of the events of 1820. The short-term consequences fell short of Cobbett's predictions.[104] The ministry was not forced to resign after its defeat. The queen's success, which at first had seemed so complete, allowed her only one further blaze of glory: when she went to St. Paul's late in November to give thanks for the victory.[105] This was nearly the end. She forgot Cobbett's warnings that she must depend on public support, and when, without advance notice to her followers, she tried to enter Westminster Abbey to attend the coronation in July 1821, she found herself excluded.[106] Then she was suddenly taken ill. Within three weeks she was dead. As the martyred queen she was as popular as she had been when she was the persecuted queen. The government had prescribed a route for the funeral procession that would have taken the coffin through the back streets of London, but the people would have none of it. They built barricades; they fought the soldiers leading the procession; they fought the constables called to assist the soldiers. Two men were killed, many were wounded. After hours of obstruction and delay, the government forces surrendered. The body of the queen, without further disturbance, was carried through the principal streets of the city and past St. Paul's, where the bells were solemnly tolled, before it set off on its journey to Germany.[107]

Cobbett wrote: "She did us more good in six months than ever was before done to any people in scores of years."[108] He had thrown himself into her cause with the single-minded concentration that characterized whatever he undertook. Between the time when the queen arrived in England in June 1820 and the withdrawal of the Bill of Pains and Penalties, all Cobbett's efforts were directed to her affairs. There were the *Political Register* articles week after week, some 1,500 pages of them in the aggregate, almost wholly devoted to this one subject. There were the many personal letters of advice. In between, Cobbett had drafted addresses to the queen on behalf of various communities and had prepared the queen's replies to these and other addresses.[109] He had written and published handbills in support of the queen that were distributed in London by the tens of thousands.[110] He and his daughter Anne had produced two pamphlets: *A Peep at the Peers* and *The Links of the Lower House*, designed to show the bias of the members of the two houses of parliament and the ulterior motives they would have in supporting the king against the queen.[111] Of Cobbett's share in the final victory, Anne wrote: "Every body gives *him* the credit for it, solely and unreservedly," and although we must discount the testimony of a devoted daughter, we have the independent conclusion of Sheriff Williams, although possibly not of the poet Coleridge, who reported the conversation with Williams, that "without this alliance the Queen must have been overwhelmed."[112]

Cobbett had harvested his own reward in mid October, while the case was at its peak, when he called on the queen with addresses from the towns of Warwick and Bury St. Edmunds. An account of the "Governor's" visit was written by Anne to her brother James in New York:

Papa has been to Court and kissed the Queen's hand, and a very pretty little hand he says it is. We made the gentleman dress himself very smart, and powder his head, and I assure you he cut a very different appearance to what he used to do on Long Island with the straw hat slouched over his eyes . . . The Queen made him a little speech, in which she thanked him for the great services he had rendered her, and conveyed to him some handsome compliments about his talents and so forth. This was in public, of course, that is to say, her Chamberlains, Major Domos and Dames of Honour standing about. Her Chaplain, the gentleman who writes her answers for her (all those that the Govr. has not written) told us the next day, that when Papa left the room, she turned round and said in her lively manner, "well now, if that is Mr. C no wonder such fine writing comes from him, he is the finest man I have seen since I came to England, aye, aye, if there be only a few such men as that to stand by me, I shall not care for the Lords".

And the letter continues:

All of which the Govr. says is nothing more than bare justice, for he saw no man there anything to compare to himself; you know the gentleman has by no means a contemptible notion of his person.[113]

"I think," wrote Anne several months later, after Cobbett had made another call on the queen, "the Govr. is the man of all men to be her Prime Minister."[114]

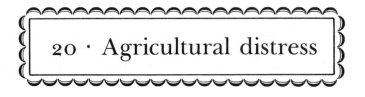

20 · Agricultural distress

The sheep must necessarily have wishes in opposition to those of the wolf.

I N 1 8 2 1 T H E nation's attention was forcibly diverted from the queen's affair to a more critical problem. The course of economic distress that had been plaguing the country for the past twenty years reached a third stage in its evolution. In Cobbett's opinion it was approaching the point at which a collapse of the hated Pitt system was inevitable.

During the first stage of distress, the poorest class in England, the farm laborers, had been the principal sufferers. Almost immediately after the outbreak of war in 1793, the price of food began to climb steeply. By 1800 bread – the chief item in the farm laborer's diet – cost over twice what it had cost in 1792.[1] In addition, heavy taxes had been levied on articles of daily consumption: salt, sugar, tea, candles, leather.[2] Yet the pay of the farm laborer lagged so far behind the increased cost of living that he could no longer afford the food needed to maintain his family at a decent level, and he was forced to dip into what little capital he may have had. By the time the long war ended

The clock was gone; the brass kettle was gone; the pewter plates were gone; the beer-barrel was gone; the brass candlesticks were gone; the warming pan was gone; the brass-topped dog-irons were gone; the half-dozen silver spoons and the two table spoons were gone; the feather bed was gone; the Sunday-coat was gone. All was gone! How miserable, how deplorable, how changed that labourer's dwelling, which I, only twenty years before, had seen so neat and so happy![3]

In the second stage, workers in industry and trade intermittently shared the plight of the farm laborers. Beginning in 1811, considerable hardship was caused by the curtailed production of export goods in consequence of the British, French, and American trade embargoes. The cessation of military orders at the end of the war and the introduction of new machinery brought another wrench to many of those employed in manufacture and trade.

During most of the first two stages of the developing crisis, the large landowners and their tenant farmers had prospered. In the twenty years prior to the start of the war, the average annual price of wheat had been 46s. a quarter. In the next twenty years it rose to an unprecedented 83s. a quarter.[4] The farmers grew rich. While their income had nearly doubled, wages paid to their laborers had been increased by only about one-third.[5] In those areas where the Speenhamland system operated, the laborer was forced to seek poor relief to avoid starvation at the same time as his employer was enabled to take on a new character:

A fox-hunting horse; polished boots; a spanking trot to market; a "get out the way, or by G—d I'll ride over you" to every poor devil upon the road; wine at his dinner; a carpet on his floor; a bell in his parlour; a servant (and sometimes in *livery*) to wait at his table; a painted lady for a wife; novel-reading daughters; sons aping the young 'squires and lords; a house crammed up with sofa's, piano's, and all sorts of fooleries.[6]

Most of these farmers were tenants of the large landowners; nine-tenths of all the agricultural land of England was farmed under lease.[7] As the leases expired during the war they were replaced by new ones at greatly increased rentals reflecting the wartime prices of farm produce. The good times continued until 1814, when the peace of that year coincided with a fine harvest, and the price of wheat began to fall. In 1815 it was 65s.[8] A panicked agricultural interest prevailed on a landowner parliament, despite the opposition of those who ate bread, to pass a corn law forbidding the importation of wheat when the price was below 80s. The next few years brought firmer prices, but this was probably due more to poor harvests than to the corn law.[9] Then came 1821, when wheat fell to 56s. Few farmers were able to operate profitably at this price. Some survived by living on their savings. Many were forced into bankruptcy.

The condition of the country in 1821 brought into sharp focus many of the things that Cobbett believed had gone wrong in England since Pitt had assumed office in 1783. The government had become enormously expensive: £58 million in 1821 as compared with £17 million in 1790. The largest item of cost was the interest on the debt, which alone accounted for an annual charge of £32 million by 1821. The debt had been created by the twenty-three-year war against France; a war that Cobbett claimed was "wholly unnecessary for any good purpose," that had been precipitated by Pitt to prevent the spread of the democratic principles proclaimed in France, and that ended only when the despotic Bourbons were returned to the French throne by Pitt's successors.[10] Thus, in Cobbett's view, the debt represented money that need not have been spent if the ruling class had been prepared to allow the common people of England a voice in the government.[11] And interest on the debt was not the only item in the budget expended to maintain the ascendancy of the ruling class. There was the "dead-weight" of around £5 million a year, representing another war cost, made up chiefly of retirement pay and benefits to military personnel (mainly officers) and their families. There were the pensions and sinecures to friends of the government, relatively small in amount, but "they are the grease and tar ... without them the waggon can't stir."[12] There was a large standing army, staffed by the aristocracy and strategically located to put down disaffection among the starving. There was the heavy cost of civil servants: The salary of judges, to take a favorite Cobbett example, had been doubled during the war to offset the effects of inflation, but had not been reduced when prices were halved after the war had ended. Hence in terms of purchasing power these government officials were now receiving four times their prewar remuneration. These items and others like them accounted for the heavy taxes the people of England were expected to bear in 1821. "I leave you to the Exchequer in this world and to Hell in the next" is the remark Cobbett puts into the mouth of Tax-Eater (a government payee), speaking to Clodpole (a farmer taxpayer).[13]

Following the repeal of the income tax in 1816, the burden fell mostly on consumer goods. The taxes amounted to about £4 per year per capita, or £8 per year for a man and wife (taking no account of children), at a time when the largest group of gainfully employed, the farm laborers, earned £20–30 a year. The fall in prices after 1814 brought some relief to the hard-pressed laborer, as wages lagged behind prices ("A mechanic can now have a joint of lamb for his Sunday's dinner"), but this did not last long.[14] Wages were shortly down to 1792 levels, and many agricultural workers were released. In 1822 Cobbett indicated that everywhere the laborers were "assembling in bands to demand or beg for food" and were "almost ready to burst forth into open violence."[15]

The employers of the farm laborers were caught between the sharply falling prices on the one hand and, on the other, the high taxes, the increasingly heavy poor rates, the exorbitant rents based on war prices, and the obligation to turn 10 percent of their produce over to the clergy as tithes. There was no agreement on either the cause of their plight or its cure. The ministerial view was that the distress was due to the transition from war to peace and the recent good harvests – nothing that the government had caused or could remedy. The Malthusians argued that agriculture was unfairly burdened by the heavy poor law assessments as a result of an excess population: Between 1801 and 1821 the population of England and Wales had risen from 8.9 million to 12 million, a 35 percent increase. Newly formed farmers' associations put the blame for the farmers' hardship on low prices resulting from foreign competition, and petitioned parliament for a high protective duty on agricultural imports.[16]

Cobbett vigorously attacked the proposal of the farm associations, not only because it would increase the cost of the laborer's food, but also because such a tariff would not, in Cobbett's opinion, constitute a cure for the farmers' ailments. According to his view, the problem was caused by the simultaneous action of two elements: the heavy taxes and the deflation brought about by Peel's bill of 1819, which provided for the gradual return to metallic currency (and the reestablishment of the gold standard) in place of the paper money that had been issued to finance the war.[17] This shift from paper to gold was to be accomplished during the period 1820 to 1823. The critical final date was May 1, 1823. On that day gold again became legal tender, and all outstanding banknotes were convertible into gold coin at full face value.[18] Prices of farm produce fell to reflect the diminution in the quantity of money circulating in the country as the Bank of England put itself in a position to replace the paper money with gold. Yet the farmers' rents and taxes remained at the same nominal figures as before. Thus, in physical terms, the farmer now had to give up two to three times as many bushels of wheat in order to pay his taxes (or to meet his rent) as he had had to give up a few years earlier. The landowner, the holder of government securities, and the mortgagee were, in contrast, getting correspondingly more in purchasing power than at the time the leases had been executed or the money invested.

Three major solutions for this situation were proposed. First, to continue with the hard currency program embodied in Peel's bill without change, thereby allowing the holders of fixed obligations, the rentier class, to benefit at the expense of the rest of the community.[19] Second, to abandon the hard currency program by abrogating Peel's bill and returning to an inflationary course. Third, to continue with the hard currency program, but accompany this with a legalized adjustment of all obligations (the national debt, leases, mortgages, and other contracts) so that the burdens on the one side and the benefits on the other would be approximately the same as they had been before the government began its deflationary policy – in other words, to reduce the obligations to match the new price level.[20]

The third solution – the most complicated one and the most difficult to administer but possibly the fairest to all interests – was Cobbett's proposal.[21] He believed, however, that whichever course was followed the end result would be the same: The national debt would have to be reduced, since the people were unable to pay the taxes needed to meet the interest payments. He had offered to submit himself for broiling on a gridiron if parliament were able to carry out Peel's bill by resuming cash payments without defaulting on the debt. So certain was he of this prediction that he had an iron gridiron made, seven feet long and six feet wide, which he proposed to suspend over the *Political Register* shop in Fleet Street when he was proved to be correct; the *Political Register* of February 1821 appeared with the gridiron on its masthead, and this was repeated at frequent intervals; and Cobbett often regaled his readers with a description of the celebration, the Feast of the Gridiron, that he would sponsor when his prediction was verified.[22]

At the root of Cobbett's analysis was his firm belief that the debt was too large ever to be paid off.[23] Hence it would have to be wiped out by a default (solution one) or by a revaluation of the currency through inflation (solution two) or by government fiat (solution three). In the background was Paine's observation "that every case of failure in finances, since the system of paper began, had produced a revolution in government, either total or partial."[24] Each of the three

The gridiron in 1821. This cut first appeared in the masthead of the *Political Register* in February 1821 and appeared irregularly thereafter until the financial crisis of 1825. Then it became a feature of every weekly issue until Cobbett's death ten years later

413

solutions led to a failure in finances which would make parliamentary reform possible.

Cobbett's interest in the agricultural distress was not because of a desire to rescue the farmers. Although he had friends among the farmers, he had little sympathy with them as a group. He thought they had unconscionably ground down the laborer during the profitable war years: "It was out of his bones that the means came . . . it was the means . . . that put pianos into the farm houses, and set the farmer up upon a cavalry horse."[25] The prosperity of the nation as a whole, as well as that of the farmers, came about "not by conjuration; not by witchcraft; but by deductions made from the meals of the millions; by making the millions go half-naked; by making the millions sit shivering in the cold; by making the millions creep under rugs [rags?] laid on beds of straw."[26] Then too, the farmers as a class had opposed all efforts at reform and had supported the oppressive measures of the government against the reformers. They were personified, in Cobbett's mind, by the yeomen cavalry at Peterloo.[27] Cobbett's appeal to the farmers at this point was not because he believed they were deserving, but because he regarded them as a means of gaining his objectives.[28] It had been possible for the government to put down the protests of the farm laborers and the industrial workers by strong-arm methods, but nothing like this would do for the tenant farmers who provided the principal source of income of the landed gentry and aristocracy. If this group could be sufficiently motivated, it would precipitate the changes in the system of government he believed necessary.

Cobbett opened his agricultural campaign in "A New Year's Gift to the Farmers," which appeared in the first issue of the *Political Register* for 1821.[29] In this he berated the farmers for seeking higher prices through protective tariffs instead of demanding a reduction in their expenses, particularly in their taxes and rents. Throughout the year he continued the same theme, devoting most of his leading articles to this subject.[30] Despite the abject state of the farmers – in five contiguous parishes in Kent 3,000 acres of farmland had already been abandoned[31] – Cobbett assured them that they had not seen the worst; prices would continue to fall, since the full effect of Peel's bill would not be felt until May 1823.

During the latter part of 1821 Cobbett began travelling around the country on horseback, observing what was happening on the farms and in the villages. He often took one of his children as a companion. They visited friends en route, staying in Hampshire with William Budd at Burghclere and Joseph Blount at Hurstbourne Tarrant, in Kent with William Waller at Elverton Farm near Faversham, in Herefordshire with William Palmer at Bollitree Castle, and in Norfolk with Samuel Clarke at Burgh-Apton – all prosperous farmers. While staying with Clarke, Cobbett was entertained at public dinners in Great Yarmouth and Norwich, and met many of the farmers at both places. Cobbett's reception was recorded by his daughter Anne:

He was received with unbounded applause, and as he walked through the market at Norwich where there were about two thousand rich farmers assembled, and there as he passed through the crowd they took off their hats and bowed to him and those who were near enough pressed forward to shake him by the hand. These were not *rabble* but rich farmers, all of whom keep hunters and some of them hounds. At the village of Cawston where Baker was born the ringers were in waiting to ring the bells as Papa passed through. We were staying at the house of Mr. Clarke, and every day while we were there we had a large dinner party of three or four and twenty people to meet Papa, or else he went out to dine at the house of somebody else; and really you can imagine nothing like the respect and admiration with which the people behaved towards him. They really appeared to make a little God of him . . . And in Norfolk we found what we owe and shall always owe to the poor Queen, for many places where Papa was received with unbounded admiration he would not have dared to shew his nose before the Queen's cause turned so many hundreds of hearts from the side of the government.[32]

When Cobbett resumed his travels early in 1822 he made a point of attending the meetings that were being held to consider the agricultural distress. The first of these was a gathering of landlords and farmers at Battle, in Sussex, on January 3, which had been called for the purpose of agreeing on a petition to parliament. E. J. Curteis, member of parliament for Sussex and the principal speaker, urged the need for protective tariffs. Cobbett said nothing at the meeting, but at the dinner that immediately followed: "Mr Britton having proposed my health, and Mr. Curteis, who was in the chair, having given it, I thought it would have looked like mock modesty . . . to refrain from expressing my opinions."[33] He made three points: A protective tariff would do the farmer no good; Peel's bill for resuming cash payments without adjusting other obligations was the true cause of the farmers' distress; and prices of farm produce would continue to fall.

A week later Cobbett appeared at a gathering in Lewes, Sussex, because, he explained, someone at the Battle meeting had "observed to me that I would do well *not to go to Lewes*." During the dinner at the Star inn, Cobbett's health was again proposed. "This was the signal for the onset." One of the crowd got up on a table and read a garbled extract from the *Political Register* that contained some uncomplimentary references to farmers, while another, "all [having] been duly prepared . . . moved that I might be put out of the room," whereupon "six or eight of the dark, dirty, half-whiskered, tax eaters from Brighton (which is only eight miles off) joined in this cry." Nothing could have been more congenial to Cobbett: "I rose, that they might see the man that they had to put out." This proved to be a convincing argument to the gentlemen from Brighton. Cobbett's health was drunk and he was allowed to speak without interruption. "Even those who, upon my health being given, had taken their hats and gone out of the room . . . came back, formed a crowd, and were just as silent and attentive as the rest of the company." He told them that the deflation caused by Peel's bill had made it impossible to pay rents and taxes; that the sole remedy was to reduce taxes by cutting payments of interest on the national debt; and that the prices of farm produce would continue to fall.[34]

Anne wrote: "Papa is going about the country, making fine speeches at great dinners and making such a stir as you never heard. To be sure if his head *can* be turned by the applauses and homage he meets with, it certainly will be. He and John are just gone off to Huntingdon, where . . . he has been invited to a dinner, and there are all sorts of preparations making to do him honour."[35] At the Huntingdon meeting a petition to the House of Commons was adopted based on Cobbett's precepts, "with only three hands held up in the negative."[36] In the next few months Cobbett carried his message to gatherings at King's Lynn, Epsom, Chichester, Brighton, Norwich, and Farnham.[37] He reported the talks in the *Political Register,* where he expounded, over and over, principles stressed in the talks. Parliament was flooded with petitions. The economic annalist William Smart reported: "By the month of May, some 500 petitions had been presented from the agricultural classes, and supported generally by the country gentlemen; the strange spectacle was presented of the classes dependent on land as owners and farmers, hitherto notorious for their conservatism, suddenly assuming the character of political agitators and joining hands with the Radicals." "The petitions on the whole," Smart added, "are so many echoes of Cobbett's *Register*."[38] Two of Cobbett's contentions had even acquired a substantial following in parliament. There were a large number in parliament who, after much elucidation, had finally accepted Cobbett's belief that the deflation resulting from Peel's bill of 1819 could be blamed, at least in part, for the fall in prices.[39] There were a large number who agreed with Cobbett's claim that the heavy taxes, coming on top of the decline in prices, were a cause of much of the distress. However, there were only a handful of brave legislators willing to consider for a moment Cobbett's key proposal to reduce taxes by cutting the interest on the national debt.[40] English hackles rose at the mere suggestion of such a "breach of faith," notwithstanding Cobbett's observation that the problem had largely been created by an earlier breach of faith: the law passed in 1797 forbidding the Bank of England from paying its notes in cash, an action which contributed to the wartime inflation.

Up to this point, that is, up to the end of May 1822, Cobbett's appearances had been limited to local gatherings of landlords and farmers, mostly farmers. In June he attended a meeting of a different sort – one "enjoying the consecration of custom" – a county meeting of freeholders called by the high sheriff of Kent, who summoned all eligible parties within the county to a gathering at Maidstone on the tenth of that month.[41] The Kent meeting had been requested, in accordance with tradition, by the aristocracy and gentry of Kent, including seven members of the House of Lords and the two county members in the House of Commons, W. P. Honeywood and Sir Edward Knatchbull.[42] The two last and the Earl of Darnley were the advocates of a polite petition to parliament calling for "reform and retrenchment" in general, but nothing in particular. Cobbett provided the excitement by proposing a clause which asked the Commons for "a just reduction of the interest of the national debt, as soon as you have completed a reform of your honourable house."[43] Despite the opposition of Lord Darnley, Honeywood, and Knatchbull, Cobbett's proposal was carried "by an immense majority, there being scarcely three hands held up against it."[44]

Four days later, when the Kent petition was presented to the House of Commons, Knatchbull staunchly asserted that nine-tenths of the freeholders would have rejected the proposition for breaking faith with the public creditors. This was sharply met by a question from C. C. Western: "why had not the nine-tenths come forward to oppose it?"[45] A brave claim by John Calcraft that if he had been at Maidstone "he would have made the proposer take his horse and get away home as fast as he could" evoked a challenge from Cobbett to meet Calcraft face to face at another county meeting to see who would be required to take horse.[46] These exchanges were momentarily amusing, but of little long-term significance. What was of lasting importance, but little recognized at the time, was the groanlike utterance of Lord Clifton, son of the Earl of Darnley whose estates in Kent yielded rents of more than £4,000 a year but who, on his own ground, had been bested by Cobbett at Maidstone.[47] Lord Clifton "could hardly conceive" how it was that Cobbett "had got possession of the meeting." This perplexity was resolved by Lord Grey's observation four years later that "The charm of the power of the landed interest is gone."[48] Lord Clifton's groan was a monument attesting to the passing of influence based solely on family, rank, and property. It was a groan that foretold the ultimate success of the reform movement.

But that success was still a long way ahead. The action taken at the 1822 session of parliament was a series of wobbly compromises. The ministers denied that taxation was a cause of the distress, but taxes were reduced by £3 million by lowering the impositions on salt, malt, and leather. The ministers doubted whether import restrictions would assist the farmers, but approved a bill which excluded foreign wheat until the home price exceeded 70s., at which point a scale of duties would become operative.[49] The ministers denied that the reductions in currency pursuant to Peel's bill had affected the economy to any substantial extent, but agreed to borrow £4 million from the Bank of England which would be spent in order "to extend and quicken the general circulation," and at the same time continued until 1833 the right of the Bank of England and country banks to issue notes under £5, a right that would otherwise have expired in May 1823.[50] The latter was accomplished by the Small Note Act of 1822. Thus, while the Peel bill of 1819 had decreed that after 1823 there should be an all-metal currency (silver coins for amounts less than a pound, and gold coins for a pound or over), the Small Note Act provided for a supplementary paper currency. And while the Peel bill had decreed that after May 1823 the currency should be contracted to the amount of gold and silver in circulation, the Small Note Act provided that the currency should be expanded to include notes in an unlimited amount.

By the time parliament had adjourned in August 1822, wheat had fallen to 40s. a quarter, one-third of its average price in 1812. Although it was below 1792 levels, Cobbett continued to predict further declines until after gold payments were resumed on May 1, 1823. Beginning in September 1822, the current prices of corn, meat, butter, and cheese became a weekly feature of the *Political Register*. As conditions turned increasingly critical, Cobbett again took to the road. He spoke to farmers at dinners in Winchester, Andover, Salisbury, Newbury, Reading, and Guildford, urging the need for a change in government.[51] By change he did not mean a substitution of whigs for tories; he referred to entirely new men:

A general may be the best soldier in the world: singularly able in laying his plans, in marching and countermarching; he ought, according to all the rules of war, to beat the enemy; but he is *unfortunate,* and therefore he is beaten. There requires nothing more; we change him without scruple. Why should not the same rule meet with application here? Why should we not try new men?[52]

The charge commonly levelled against Cobbett that he carried his audience with him by demagogic appeals is belied by the talks he made in 1822. Over and over again he reminded the farmers (whose survival was threatened by the falling prices for their products) that their first duty was to the men they employed. The laborer had "first claim" to the crop which the land produced, he told his audience at Salisbury. "Were I a farmer; were I pushed to the very end of ruin, my labourers would share with me to the last."[53] At Reading he told his listeners that the pay of the farm laborer had fallen below that of the common soldier, "who has clothing, lodging, firing and candle, into the bargain."[54]

These "rustic harangues" were warm-up sessions for the huge Norfolk county meeting held at Norwich on January 3, 1823, which was attended by 7,000 persons, the most numerous ever assembled at such a meeting in Norfolk.[55] It had been called by the large whig landowners, chief among them being the famous Thomas Coke of Holkham, the greatest commoner in England (later Earl of Leicester), who had been a member of parliament for the past forty-six years.[56] Both he and his fellow county member, Edmund Wodehouse, expected that the meeting would result in a polite petition to parliament requesting relief from the agricultural distress – hence, a goad to the tory ministry, which stoutly claimed that the problem was one that could not be cured by parliamentary action.[57] This hypocritical tactic of seeking popular support by vague proposals for relief or reform without the intention of pressing for any real change was one of Cobbett's frequent accusations against the whigs. Cobbett said to Lord Suffield: "You are really one of those reformers, who, like the Westminster Rump, do not want reform itself, but want the want of reform."[58] This may, indeed, have been the motivation for his attendance at the Norwich meeting, where he wrecked the plans of Coke and Wodehouse by persuading the ordinarily docile Norfolk freeholders to support the most drastic program he had ever put before any public assembly. Thus, at Cobbett's urging, the meeting endorsed the sale of church property and crown lands for the purpose of reducing the national debt. It supported "an equitable adjustment with regard to the public debt and also with regard to all debts and contracts between man and man." It asserted that the standing army should be reduced, sinecures should be abolished, and that the taxes on malt, hops, leather, soap, and candles should be repealed. It recommended that parliament suspend for a year all distraints for rent and all legal processes for tithes or arising out of mortgages or other contracts affecting real property.[59]

A startled Coke pleaded with his fellow countrymen to reverse their decision: "he really believed that neither the resolutions or the amendment had been sufficiently heard . . . to enable them to form a correct opinion of their contents." But a second vote resulted in a worse defeat for Coke than before.[60] The whig strategy of mildly reproving the tory government had been converted by Cobbett into a condemnation of whig moderation. Coke wrote to a friend: "That old vagabond, I am satisfied, is in the pay of the Government, and has been rewarded for that day's iniquity." Coke's whig associate, Lord Suffield, declared that "We were noodled by old Cobbett!" The *Norwich Mercury* screamed: "There is not a man of any sense or any honesty in Norfolk who would not gladly reverse this proceeding."[61] Thus stimulated, Coke and Lord Suffield attempted to minimize the impact of the county determination through what Cobbett called "hole-and-corner" meetings of several Norfolk hundreds, where, free from the danger of Cobbett's presence, the selected groups disclaimed what had been specifically approved at Norwich.[62] No one, however, was willing to act on Cobbett's roguish suggestion that a second county meeting be held to see whether there was any widespread desire to reverse the decisions made on January 3.

Reverberations from the Norfolk action rolled across England. The *Worcester Journal* "seemed incredulous that Coke had been deserted by the farmers of his own county." *The Times*, after asking what should be done with the Norfok petition, declared: "Why, spit upon it: first for its stupid malignity, and next on account of the character of its author." The economist David Ricardo wrote to James Mill: "Mr. Coke and Mr. Wodehouse must be very much mortified at the success of Cobbett at their Norfolk meeting. I confess I am astonished by it."[63] Well might Ricardo, who still felt the "charm of the power of the landed interest," be astonished. But the Norfolk farmers were desperate, and, in contrast to the prayerful generalities of the whigs, Cobbett offered a specific program of action that would provide immediate relief. Cobbett's method of presentation, too, was unique. He had none of the oratorical flourish that was characteristic of the period. He spoke plainly; he relied on facts; he radiated confidence. We can see this in the account given by Richard Monckton Milnes (later Lord Houghton) of a talk Cobbett made in the neighborhood of Cambridge:

He spoke in a barn to about one hundred farmers and Cambridge men. It lasted full three hours, and he never paused, sat down, or recalled a word, but went through the whole series of the causes of the distress: currency; poor laws; Church property; Crown lands; standing army, &c., and wound up with radical reform. He was at one time conversational, at another humorous, at another eloquent, yet all in the same idiomatic phraseology. The impression on the farmers was decidedly favourable, and I was much pleased with the whole.[64]

After Norwich, Cobbett went on to other county meetings at Hereford and Epsom.[65] At the former, where he submitted the language approved at Norfolk, he was attacked as "a one day old" Hereford freeholder, "a political itinerant tinker" who "travelled about from county to county, and from town to town as the apostle of discontent and spoliation."[66] He was not permitted to reply. And while the meeting might be said to have rejected Cobbett, it accepted all the main points of his program excepting only the appropriation of church property and crown lands. Thus the Hereford petition placed the blame for the distress on the government; condemned the "unfortunate wars" and the "debased paper currency"; and recommended the adjustment of both public and private contracts, the elimination of sinecures, and the reduction of government salaries to the scale of 1792.[67] After Cobbett had recovered from the blow to his pride, he regarded the Hereford petition as no different from that adopted by the Kent and Norfolk freeholders.[68] His next appearance, the Surrey county meeting at Epsom, was an unambiguous success, although on this occasion Cobbett wisely made no effort to press the Norfolk language on the Surrey freeholders.[69]

Despite these triumphs in the field, the strength of Cobbett's appeal for parliamentary action was being undermined by an abrupt turn-around in the price of farm produce. At the end of January 1823, wheat had risen from 32s. to 40s.; by the middle of March it was 45s. Two months later it was 57s., adequate to yield a profit at the drastically reduced rents and declining taxes.[70] To the farmer who once again had coins to jingle in his pockets, parliamentary reform and the other changes urged by Cobbett no longer seemed so urgent.

As the prices of farm produce continued to advance, the agricultural distress receded into the distance.[71] May 1, 1823 – the final date under Peel's bill for the return to gold currency after a quarter century of paper money – came and went without incident. The holder of a banknote was now legally entitled to receive, on request, gold coin for the full face value of the note. All such requests were accommodated without anything approaching a run on the Bank. The government of Lord Liverpool, still firmly in the saddle, had not been obliged to default on the debt. Cobbett's enemies were exultant.[72] Claiming that his predictions had been disproved, they called for the gridiron and hot coals. He stoutly asserted that his conditions had not been fulfilled. The broiling was to occur only if Peel's bill went into *full effect*, and this had been prevented by the Small Note Act. "Now here," wrote Cobbett, "was a repeal of a good third part, at least, of

Peel's bill," and he claimed that the very purpose of the Small Note Act was to raise the price of wheat by expanding the quantity of currency.[73] The rise in price enabled the farmers and their landlords to pay their taxes, and this, in turn, avoided a default by the government. But, Cobbett assured his readers, the Small Note Act could not cure the fundamental disorder in British finance; it could only provide a brief respite before the inevitable collapse. Needless to say, these gloomy predictions of Cobbett's were not accepted by the government. The annual speech of the chancellor of the exchequer (Frederick Robinson), delivered in February 1824, acclaimed the country's "state of content and prosperity" in such glowing terms that he became known to the readers of the *Political Register* as "Prosperity Robinson," a distinction he shortly had reason to regret.[74]

During the last half of 1823 and the first part of 1824, Cobbett kept the currency issue very much in the background, except for an occasional reminder that gold was vastly to be preferred over the "rags" being issued by the 800 country banks in Britain. But it was not necessary for him to wait long before the easy money program began to take its toll.[75] A muted alarm was sounded in April 1825 when William Huskisson, president of the board of trade and a member of the cabinet, warned the House of Commons of "the excessive speculation that was going forward."[76] The speculation took a variety of forms, including investment in foreign securities and heavy purchases abroad of cotton and other raw materials. Two months after the Huskisson warning, Edward Ellice, who had won a seat at Coventry in the 1820 contest with Cobbett, raised the spectre of the need for another government suspension of cash payments – a theme Cobbett had been expounding for some time.[77] Gold had been flowing out of the country at an alarming pace, reducing the holdings of the Bank of England from £12 million at the beginning of 1824 to £4 million by the middle of 1825.[78] The country banks – the "rag rooks" in Cobbett's terms – had so assiduously applied themselves to the printing of paper money that almost all the currency outside of London was made up of their £1 and £2 notes, despite the legislation that had made gold coins the official currency since May 1, 1823.[79] Cobbett, who had been reporting these events with more than usual moderation, moved back into the spotlight in July with a story that reopened the gridiron issue with all its original virulence. It was entitled "Gold and Bank Notes; or, the Rag Rooks in Confusion."[80] Frederick Jones of Bristol had gone to a local bank and asked for gold coins in payment of several of their notes which he tendered. When he was refused he consulted Cobbett. Cobbett promptly took the matter to Joseph Hume, member of parliament for Montrose, who had become the most tenacious and reliable supporter of reform in the House of Commons. Between Hume in parliament and Cobbett in the *Political Register* the story received wide notice. The Bristol bank quickly realized its error, but not before the note-holding public around the country saw the moral. The rag rooks were everywhere requested to take back their rags and provide gold instead. In Bristol, where the problem had first arisen, a broadside was distributed reading "I have the pleasure of being a disciple of Mr. Cobbett . . . as there is no way of knowing what may happen, get Gold, for if Restriction come it will be too late."[81] Within a matter of months, dozens of poorly financed country banks were forced to close their doors, impoverishing thousands of note-holders and depositors in every part of the kingdom.[82] As the crisis mounted, bankers and merchants called on the Bank of England for support. The Bank's problem, as rather inelegantly described by Cobbett, then became "what the farmers call the *wet gripes*; that is, a dreadful pinching accompanied with what they in their homely style call a running out."[83] On December 16 the cabinet was told that the Bank, "completely drained of its specie & . . . reduced to 100,000 sovereigns . . . expects to be obliged to suspend cash payments tomorrow, and they want the Government to step forward to their assistance & order the suspension."[84] That would have rendered the government incapable of paying the interest on the debt, the very event which Cobbett had always predicted would be the signal for the Feast of the Gridiron.[85] Perhaps that thought alone would have been enough to stiffen the resolve of Lord Liverpool (he was also encouraged by the firm stance taken by the Duke of Wellington). The decision was made to try to brave out the storm with the assistance of a loan from the Bank of France.[86] And so the crisis was met; within a week the panic had run its course. Huskisson declared that in another forty-eight hours it would have been necessary to terminate all commercial transactions, except those that could be conducted by barter.[87] He neglected to mention those that could be paid for in gold. As soon as parliament returned for the 1826 session, the ministers added one more patch to England's monetary legislation: the issue of any further banknotes under £5 was prohibited; the notes then outstanding – these had been greatly reduced in number by the notes paid or defaulted during the run on the banks – had to be withdrawn by April 1829.

Events proved that Cobbett's original prediction had been wrong: The government had managed to resume cash payments without defaulting on its debt. But it had done so by the narrowest squeak. To give Cobbett his due, he had been mostly right about his modified prediction: Peel's bill of 1819 had not been fully carried out in the form in which it was passed. Even so, this was not followed by a change in government. The question whether he had been right or wrong was of particular significance to himself. The symbol of the gridiron, which had appeared sporadically on the masthead of the *Political Register* since February 1821, had been made a regular feature at the height of the panic in December 1825, when it appeared almost certain that a collapse was imminent. Undaunted by the turn of events, the gridiron symbol on the masthead was continued without interruption on each weekly issue until Cobbett's death ten years later. Cobbett decided that the Feast of the Gridiron should be held, and it was set for April 6, 1826 at the London Tavern. Tickets for the dinner were 12s. 6d. "including a bottle of wine to each person."[88] And although the announcement had declared that the number of tickets was limited to 500, "as no greater number of persons, can, it is supposed, conveniently dine," only about half that number attended. Cobbett explained that "the room would not have conveniently contained any more than there were." The principal feature was, of course, Cobbett's talk. This was adequate, but added little to what he had been saying during the past several years. And although Cobbett declared that "It was observed by many, that they never heard so many, such long-continued, such loud and such hearty peals of laughter," it actually was not an occasion of natural joy, but rather one of forced gaiety.[89] There would have been reason for real jubilation if what had happened to the system of finance had produced "a revolution in government" (as Paine had predicted) which permitted a more representative House of Commons (as Cobbett had predicted). But the victory, if it can be called that, was a sterile one, since it turned on the interpretation of a jest, rather than on a matter of substance. It is probable that the only reason for holding the celebration was to put an end to, or at least counter, the argument of Cobbett's enemies that he had been proved wrong.

The debate on finances cannot be closed without mentioning two elements which influenced the positions taken by the parties to the dispute – one relating to principles, the other to objectives. The first of these can be put in the form of a question: Is the government responsible to any degree for the state of the national economy? The official answer of the early nineteenth century was no. Lord Liverpool cited the poet:

> Of all the ills that nations can endure
> How few are governments the cause or cure.

In contrast, Cobbett's answer was yes, and this has become the official answer of the twentieth century. The debate today is focused on a

The gridiron in 1833. Cobbett's celebration of the Feast of the Gridiron in 1826 did not prevent his adversaries from renewing the subject in later years. This drawing by John Doyle ("HB") shows Althorp, Peel, and Spring-Rice courteously inviting Cobbett to take his position on the coals. The bearded Althorp exclaims: "Oh positively you must have a broil." Peel on the right says: "You cannot object to so *equitable* an adjustment." Cobbett with equal politeness replies: "Ah mammy dont ask me"

second question, the one that Cobbett posed: What is the correct economic policy to be pursued in order to fulfill that responsibility? It is a question that even now cannot be answered with any certainty. We observe, however, that Cobbett's remedies (cutting government expenditure and reducing taxes) are still seriously considered as candidates for the relief of economic distress.

As to the second element, it is essential to note that Cobbett's objectives were quite different from those of any other participant. The members of the ministry were, of necessity, focusing on what would work: what would keep the government running from one year to the next, and what would keep them in office. Members of the opposition, like those in the cabinet, would surely have named "a sound system" as their first objective, but this was almost certainly colored by what might be helpful in aiding their return to power. Ricardo and McCulloch, as well as the other political economists, were interested in optimizing the total economy of the country over the long run. Bankers, farmers, manufacturers, and merchants were inclined to favor action that was most suitable to the interests of bankers, farmers, manufacturers, and merchants.

In contrast, Cobbett's predominant interest was to improve the lot of the working poor – the great mass of the people – which, he believed, could be done only by drastically changing the system of government, even destroying it if need be. There was no attempt to obscure this bias. "I would bow down every other class," he wrote, "if I could not restore the labourers to their former happy state without bowing down all the rest."[90] To Cobbett, the prosperity of a country was not measured by its exports or imports, by its roads and public buildings, by its palaces and mansions. "If I am asked whether I look upon such and such a nation to be in a state of prosperity; I ask, whether the labouring classes be, out of their honest earnings, well fed and well clad."[91] He was often thought mischievous, or worse, by his contemporaries for urging action such as the hoarding of gold, which endangered the banks and jeopardized the economy of the country.[92] They could not understand a man who, without obvious advantage to himself, could urge a repudiation of the national debt. The clue, however, to this and other positions taken by Cobbett is found in his belief that they would ultimately lead to a government that would be more attentive to the interests of the majority of the people. While in America in 1819 he had written:

Society ought not to exist, if not for the benefit of the whole. It is and must be against the law of nature, if it exist for the benefit of the few and/or the misery of the many. I say, then, distinctly that a society, in which the common labourer, with common health and strength and with economy and sobriety and industry and good morals and good manners, cannot secure a sufficiency of food and raiment, is a society which ought not to exist; a society contrary to the law of nature; a society whose compact is dissolved.[93]

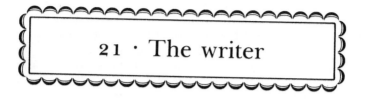

21 · The writer

Of all the authors I ever met with . . . I never yet met with one, who was not smitten with the folly of hoping that all the world would be eager to read what he wrote.

WHEN THE FEAST of the Gridiron was grimly celebrated in 1826, Cobbett was living with his family in Kensington, then a suburb of London, where they had settled five years before. He had been on the move almost constantly between 1816 and 1821. In 1816 the family had been together in Botley, living in the house rented from General Kempt. When the Spa Fields episode occurred in November of that year, Cobbett left for the center of excitement in London, where he stayed for four months.[1] Then from 1817 to 1819 he was in America. From 1819 to 1821 he was in London lodgings. Most of the time since the Botley days the family had been "scattered about like a covey of partridges that had been sprung and shot at."[2] They had no home of their own. The two younger girls, Ellen and Susan, and the youngest son, Richard (eleven, nine, and two years old at the time of Spa Fields), remained with Mrs. Cobbett throughout the period. The eldest daughter, Anne, and the three oldest sons, William, John, and James, were sometimes with one parent, sometimes with the other. James, who had remained in America to tend the seed business Cobbett had established there, did not return to England until 1822. Then, for the first time since 1816, the family was fully reunited in their new Kensington home.

Kensington also saw the temporary repair of their financial stringency, although not before Cobbett had faced several new crises. Shortly after he had been discharged from bankruptcy late in 1820, he was met with two suits for libel as a result of that letter to Wright about Henry Hunt: "Beware of him! He rides about the country with a whore" – the letter that Thomas Cleary had produced at the Westminster hustings in 1818 and which Cobbett, in a typically impetuous moment, had declared to be a forgery perpetrated by Cleary or Wright. To this charge the *Political Register* had added some unpleasant comments about Wright's conduct while working for Cobbett.[3] Both Cleary and Wright brought actions. The two cases were heard in December 1820 by Ellenborough's successor, Chief Justice Abbott. In the first, Cleary claimed damages of £2,000. He was represented by Henry Brougham, whose defense of Queen Caroline had elicited such caustic criticism from Cobbett. Cobbett, flanked by two law student sons, defended himself in the crowded courtroom with the volunteered assistance of lawyers who "kept writing little hints on slips of paper and handing them to the boys for Papa's use, either when he was cross-questioning the witnesses or during his speech." The judge condemned Cleary's breach of confidence in revealing the contents of a private letter, and the outcome was "the most glorious thing that ever happened for Papa": the jury came in with a verdict for nominal damages of 40s.[4] Within a week, however, Cobbett suffered a solid and wholly justified defeat at the hands of Wright, who, represented by James Scarlett, later attorney general, secured a verdict for £1,000. Wright, unlike Cleary, had taken care to have a special jury.[5] "They have now, they say, sunk me in good earnest!" wrote Cobbett following the decision, and well they might say so, since penniless Cobbett was at Wright's mercy, with the debtor's cell as his probable destination. Yet Cobbett was indomitable: "This is no *sinking*. This is what the sailors call merely 'shipping a sea' . . . you will see that this, like every other sinking I have experienced, will be at last a mounting in place of a sinking."[6] Anne was sure Wright would never get a farthing: "we are determined that he shall not have it."[7] But it was not necessary to test that resolution. Cobbett was rescued by an old friend, George Rogers, carter of Southampton, who effected a compromise settlement with Wright for £700, which Rogers paid out of his own pocket.[8]

While Cobbett was thus putting the finishing touches to his relations with one of his earlier publishing associates, problems were brewing between him and his current associate, William Benbow, who became the object of one more of those squabbles with publishers that had begun in Philadelphia more than twenty-five years before. Benbow, a reformer imprisoned when the Habeas Corpus Act was suspended in 1817, appeared in the United States while Cobbett was there, and they became friends. The first edition of Cobbett's *English Grammar,* published in 1818, was dedicated to Benbow, and Benbow was one of Cobbett's accomplices in disinterring the bones of Thomas Paine. He returned to England at about the time Cobbett did and became the publisher of the *Political Register* beginning with the issue of June 3, 1820.[9] Anne, who seems to have had the best business head in the family, became suspicious of Benbow's small remittances, and by January 1821 he had been removed.[10] Anne wrote to James: "Benbow has turned out to be the greatest, ten thousand million times the greatest, villain that Papa ever had to deal with, and that you know is saying a great deal. Wright was an angel in comparison."[11] "Cobbett quarrelled with so many people that it is easy to assume that it was always his fault in one respect or another. In this case, and perhaps in others as well, Cobbett's casual attitude toward money and his failure to require periodic accountings made it easy for the impecunious Benbow to get himself in trouble.

When Benbow went out, John Cobbett, who was twenty-one years old, went in. His first day as publisher confirmed all of Anne's suspicions of Benbow. John came home that night with twenty-five pounds, after paying all expenses. Previously, "we sometimes have not had any money at all from Benbow for several weeks together and then when we did get it, perhaps £5 at a time."[12] This improvement in finances enabled the family to leave the lodgings they were occupying in Brompton and move into the house in Kensington, the first upward turn in their fortunes since the 1810 trial. Anne observed the difference in her father: "It has a happy effect upon his temper. If you were here," she wrote to James, "I am sure Papa would be happier than he ever was in his life."

We have got a piano, and there he sits of an evening and hears the girls play and sing, and very often, with the Roses or the Codds, we make a little dance and Papa will go to bed in the next room and always tells us not to stop on his account, and sometimes we dance or play and sing while he is snoring, and sometimes he will listen for an hour or two after he is in bed to the music, with his door open.[13]

The Kensington house had been selected for the family by one of Cobbett's oldest friends, Major Philip Codd, former adjutant to the Duke of Sussex, who was well acquainted with Cobbett's propensity for expansive projects. Anne noted: "Major Codd found the place and took it. Said, there being only 4 acres, and within walls, Papa could not hurt himself much."[14] The family remained in the Kensington house from 1821 to 1833 – a period in which Cobbett scored his greatest literary and political successes and demonstrated, despite the limitation of four walled acres, his unlimited ability to hurt himself.

He was no sooner established in Kensington than he began to make use of the land, which, at the time the family moved in, was nothing but bad meadow. "Nature made me for a farmer certainly; and that I will be again," he wrote to a friend.[15] He shortly had enough vegetables for two or three families. He added cows, pigs, turkeys, geese, ducks, and chickens. The stables and outbuildings were enlarged. It would be cheaper, Cobbett decided, "to have a carriage and two horses, than to go, as we do now, with stage and hack and post chaise work."[16] A cart was ordered to do local hauling. Several riding horses were added. All this Major Codd may have expected. What may not have been expected was Cobbett's entry into the nursery business on a grand scale. He arranged with his son James while still in America for large shipments of seeds and graffs, and for continuing sources of supply after James's return to England. By 1825 Cobbett had planted a million forest trees and about 10,000 apple trees.[17] His favorite among the imported forest trees was the locust (*Robinia pseudo-acacia*). The wood of this tree, Cobbett asserted, was "absolutely indestructible by the powers of earth, air and water." Locust and white oak (also sold by Cobbett) were used in America to make wagons half the weight and twice the strength of English wagons. The locust was used for the tiller, trunnels, and other critical parts of ships; "if a ship had all its ribs, and beams, and knees of locust, it would be worth two common ships." A Long Island hog-gallows post made of locust wood, which had been standing in the ground for more than eighty years, yet "still as sound as the day it was felled," was displayed at the office of the *Political Register*.[18] The careless villain who broke a locust hop pole after it had been in the ground a mere twenty years "would, if he had the courage, cut any throat without remorse."[19] Cobbett was far more interested in promoting the planting of locust trees than he was in making money from them. He bought a locust from Lord Ranelagh, had it cut up, and gave away blocks of the wood to demonstrate its worth.[20] Strawberry plants were offered, at Cobbett's cost, to those who bought trees.[21] The advantages of the locust and the various other American imports available at the nursery became a regular feature of the weekly paper; readers were invited to come and see for themselves. "Great concourse to see my nursery and garden," wrote Cobbett in September 1825; "everyone calls it the most beautiful thing that eyes were ever fixed on."[22]

The extent of this activity required an expanded organization. At one time the impatient Cobbett had a hundred day laborers digging, sowing, and planting on the four-acre plot. Several regular gardeners were employed under a foreman. To enable the three oldest Cobbett sons to devote their time to the study of law, Cobbett's office at 183 Fleet Street was placed in charge of his former bailiff from Botley days, John Dean, who was provided with a house and promised a clear £100 a year.[23]

By the end of 1826 Cobbett found the four acres with its million young trees too restrictive. He leased three garden plots at Barn Elm on the south side of the Thames, a sixty-minute walk from Kensington over the new Hammersmith bridge. Less than a year later he signed a lease for an eighty-acre farm adjoining the garden plots.[24] The new acquisitions were not for the purpose of growing things for sale, but to conduct experiments in the cultivation of animal food, particularly maize, the rutabaga (Swedish turnips or "swedes"), and mangel-wurzel. It was an expensive undertaking. At one point more than forty men were employed in these projects, although a more normal complement was "eight men and a boy, besides myself and sometimes a helper or two."[25] The rent of the two new properties was more than £600 a year. In America, Cobbett's enthusiastic endorsement of the Swedish turnip had led to its almost immediate acceptance as a major field plant that was cultivated from Canada to the gulf of Mexico in accordance with principles prescribed by Cobbett.[26] He urged its acceptance in England – selling the seed and promoting its usefulness – but after further trials at Barn Elm, Cobbett decided that the mangel-wurzel was a more efficient food for cattle.[27] Cobbett's experiments with maize proved that it could be satisfactorily grown in England, despite predictions to the contrary.[28]

While these results were great victories for Cobbett's ego, financially they meant nothing but heavy cash outlays, with no way of recouping the costs.[29] So too were Cobbett's efforts in other directions. He became interested in the possibility of making straw hats in England in order to provide supplementary income for the wives and daughters of farm laborers, and to eliminate the need for the importation of such hats from Italy. Cobbett discovered that the proper straw could be grown locally (he found a source of the straw and sold it for what it cost him). He learned how to bleach it and how to weave it, which he described in later editions of his book *Cottage Economy*. The result was a new cottage industry. For his services to the country he was awarded a silver medal (he thought it should have been a gold one) by the Society for the Encouragement of Arts, Manufactures, and Commerce, whose president was the Duke of Sussex, sixth son of George III. Satisfaction, but no greater financial reward, was derived from the report of "Mr Muir, who writes to the Society of Arts from Greenock in Scotland, and tells the Society that in his neighbourhood, they owe to Mr Cobbett's little book, that one thousand five hundred women and girls are now in employment, who would, otherwise, have no employment."[30]

Another of Cobbett's projects was his "American stove." When he was living in Philadelphia he had discovered a fireplace made of cast iron that was superior to anything available in England. It would heat a room thirty by twenty feet with one-fourth the fuel required for a "box in the wall." This cast iron fireplace, known in America as the Franklin stove, supposedly an invention of the redoubtable Ben Frank-

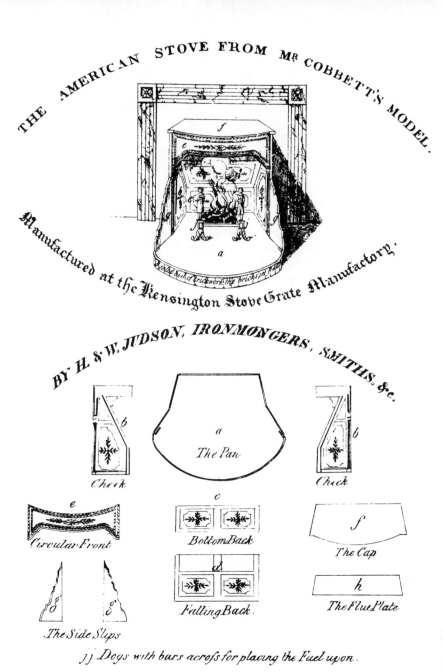

THE AMERICAN STOVE FROM MR COBBETT'S MODEL.

Manufactured at the Kensington Stove Grate Manufactory.

BY H. & W. JUDSON, IRONMONGERS, SMITHS, &c.

b — Cheek

b — Cheek

a The Pan

e Circular Front

c Bottom Back

f The Cap

d Falling Back

h The Flue Plate

g g The Side Slips

j j Dogs with bars across for placing the Fuel upon.

Cobbett's American fireplace. The cast iron stove or fireplace introduced by Cobbett into England was probably derived from what the Americans call the Franklin stove, supposedly the invention of the redoubtable Ben.

One of Cobbett's stoves is still in use today at Hargham Hall, Norfolk, the home of the present Sir Thomas Beevor, descendant of Cobbett's friend and benefactor of the same name lin, was introduced and vigorously promoted in England by Cobbett. He arranged for its production by a Kensington ironmonger, who received whatever profit may have resulted.[31] And there were other good works of a profitless nature. Cobbett and his eldest son, William junior, successfully waged war in the courts and in parliament against unscrupulous turnpike operators who were charging 4½d. for one-horse carts instead of the 3d. prescribed by law. At one point it was found necessary to have three horses and a carriage "in the execution of our turnpike projects."[32] For these services Cobbett was given a handsome silver cup by the grateful people of Kensington. Cobbett also experimented with the roasting of grain to produce a coffee substitute, and with the use of the husks of maize for the manufacture of paper. Nothing came of the coffee project.[33] It proved physically possible (although not financially feasible) to make paper out of corn husks, and Cobbett, with his usual optimism for his ventures, rashly predicted that "in a very few years all paper used by grocers, seedsmen, ironmongers, linendrapers, haberdashers . . . will be made out of the corn-plant."[34] But such, alas, was not the case.

It was Cobbett's writing that kept these projects afloat. By the time of his death in 1835 his works totalled more than 120 volumes, causing *The Times* to declare that "Cobbett was by far the most voluminous writer that has lived for centuries."[35] Most of this writing was accomplished in the fifteen years after he took up residence at Kensington, during the time he was busy planting and grafting trees, experimenting with maize and mangel-wurzel, pursuing coffee substitutes and new ways of making paper, and – of course – taking an active part in the hectic political life of the period. Cobbett simplified his day by rising between four and five in the morning and getting his writing out of the way before going on to other activities.[36] Much of the writing was dictated: originally to his children, later mostly to male secretaries, a succession of whom were in his employ from about 1827 to 1835.[37] He seldom looked at the finished manuscript, so that when his children took dictation they occasionally toned down passages they thought too strong.[38]

Nearly all of Cobbett's writing that was published in book form was for the purpose of instruction, and nearly all the instruction related to four subjects: language, gardening or farming, personal behavior, and government affairs, with a goodly amount of overlap among categories.[39] The language books of this period include a grammar for use by those who wished to learn French, a French – English dictionary, and a spelling book.[40] "For once in my life," wrote Cobbett announcing publication of the grammar, "I have written a book without a word of politics in it . . . while all will agree, that the book cannot be the worse for such exclusion."[41] As Cobbett predicted, the lacuna was no deterrent to the aspiring linguist. The book was printed and reprinted in a large but unknown number of editions – there were at least fifteen by the middle of the century – and Cobbett claimed that "More young men have, I dare say, learned French from it, than from all the other books that have been published in English for the last fifty years."[42]

Cobbett produced five gardening or farming books after the move to Kensington. The contrast between the traditional English kitchen garden ("nicely laid out and the paths bordered with flowers") and the barren farmyards Cobbett saw on Long Island during his 1817–19 stay stimulated him to write *The American Gardener* (1821), which, published in at least a dozen editions, became the vade mecum for several generations of American housewives.[43] In 1828 Cobbett published *The English Gardener*. Superficially, this was a revision and expansion of the earlier work, but the revision and expansion were so extensive as to constitute an entirely new book. The American instructions on how to eat an artichoke, for instance, were deleted, presumably being unnecessary for the more sophisticated English; the bare two pages accorded the cucumber in the American edition became more than a dozen for the English reader; the potato was dismissed in the earlier volume with no more than "Every body knows how to cultivate this plant," while the later book contained eight pages of discussion, starting with the criticism of the potato as a substitute for bread, but with the begrudging admission that "as a mere vegetable, or sauce, as the country people call it, it does well to qualify the effects of fat meat, or to assist in the swallowing of quantities of butter." Cobbett never ate it himself, "finding so many other things far preferable." One is apt to forget, among such endearing marks of eccentricity, Cobbett's real genius for exposition. *The English Gardener,* like all his books of instruction, is a model of good writing: strong, lucid, plain, well ordered. Viewed solely from that point of view, it is a masterpiece. Generations of readers who bought the book without regard to the beauty of the writing have testified to the practical value of its contents. And finally, the book served a further purpose. Cobbett's advertisement describing *The English Gardener* invited the gentlemen of the time, who rarely took spade in hand, to free themselves from the tyranny of their gardeners: "The book, if read with attention, will soon qualify any gentleman for knowing, at least, when his garden is well managed." And so it proved. A few years after it was published, an unidentified correspondent wrote to the horticulturalist John Loudon: "I have reason to believe that Mr. Cobbett's book has been extensively influential among the higher orders of society; and that . . . it has been a means of raising disputes between gardeners and their employers."[44] Whether this stimulated or deterred sales is impossible to say. The book went through a number of editions in the nineteenth century and was reprinted as recently as 1980.

The Woodlands was also published in 1828. "Many years ago," Cobbett explained in the preface, "I wished to know whether I could raise Birch trees from the seed. I looked into two French books and into two English ones without being able to learn a word about the matter. I then looked into the great book of knowledge, the *Encyclopedia Britannica*: there I found in the general dictionary, 'Birch Tree, see Betula: Botany Index'. I hastened to Betula, with great eagerness; and there I found, 'Betula, see Birch Tree'." Cobbett's book, in contrast, told everything "from the gathering of the seed, to the rearing up and the cutting down of the trees" – not only of the birch, but of fifty or so others as well. The locust occupied the center of the stage in *The Woodlands* and in many *Political Register* articles. It was not unknown to English horticulturalists. There were specimens here and there, and the merits of the locust were described in several old books on tree culture. "Notwithstanding this, we never heard of a man in England that ever planted this tree, until I took the matter in hand, except as a thing of mere ornament."[45] Unfortunately for Cobbett's nursery business, the interest he aroused in the locust was in the seedlings he offered, rather than in the young trees which he had gone to the expense of planting a few years earlier. John Loudon, after visiting Kensington in 1828, reported that "while all sorts of trees, with the exception of a few varieties of the apples, are growing old in the nurseries, from being but little asked for, Mr. Cobbett cannot raise a sufficiency of seedlings to supply the demand."[46] He sold over a million locust seedlings. Those that went to Sir Thomas Beevor of Hargham Hall, near Norwich, were still producing valuable timber in the 1970s, more than a hundred and fifty years after they had been planted. In general, however, the wood of the locust had only a brief popularity. Its marine use disappeared with the wooden ship. Another short span of interest occurred during the period when the spokes of motorcar wheels were made of wood. And although as gate and fencing posts the locust is still "unrivalled for strength and durability by any native timber except that of the yew," it is only rarely used for that purpose in England.[47] Cobbett's book *The Woodlands* was not a commercial success and has never been reprinted. Yet an authoritative twentieth-century publication confirms that it "continues to be worth reading."[48]

The other farming text published in 1828 met a similar commercial fate. It was *A Treatise on Cobbett's Corn*, dealing with the cultivation of Indian corn, or maize, which, in the author's egocentric hands, was transmuted into "Cobbett's Corn." The primary purpose of taking the eighty-acre farm at Barn Elm was to determine whether this product could be successfully grown in England. Cobbett succeeded in producing a crop of nearly a hundred bushels an acre, which, with his usual excess of optimism, he figured was worth three times the cash yield of an acre of wheat.[49] Cobbett predicted that "you will see this corn in the field of every farmer, and in the garden of every cottager in England." The results of his experiments were heralded in letters from Cobbett to the editors of London newspapers who were sent ears of corn in the husk and loaves of bread made of two parts maize, one part rye. A continuous flow of "Cobbett's Corn" articles appeared in the *Political Register*. The claims for the product became more and more exaggerated. "In a few years it will put an end to the importation of corn [wheat and other grain] and flour forever." It would assist in making perfect the changes to be brought about by parliamentary reform: "It will prevent the labourers from ever being slaves again; it will inevitably re-produce small farms; it will make the labourers more independent of their employers; it will bring back, it will hasten back, the country towards its former happy state." Barn Elm farm was thrown open to the public so the curious might see for themselves. They came, so Cobbett claimed, by the thousands. Specimens of Cobbett's corn were sent off to agricultural shows, and letters went out to editors of country papers. Cobbett extolled the virtues of beer made from the stalks of the corn. "My men are now drinking this beer, and I taste no other beer myself." Several thousand ears of corn were offered free to laborers in the southern counties of England.[50] In 1831 the *Political Register* publicized the success of a large number of Cobbett fans in growing small patches of maize; one had been able to produce a crop as far north as Paisley in Scotland.[51] But none of this had any long-run impact on the English farming community as a whole, either in the planting of maize or the purchase of Cobbett's book. There was a second edition of the work, and that was all. Yet its relaxed style and amusing digressions make it an entertaining book, even for one whose farming experience has been limited to the care of a single potted geranium. A perceptive contemporary review began:

It is a property of genius, not only to be in love with its chosen pursuit, but at the same time to make others in love with it. Mr. Cobbett writes about his own beloved corn, as he calls it, with an enthusiastic freshness that communicates itself to the most listless reader: it is hardly possible to keep the plough out of the ground as you read his description of the plant and the history of its cultivation.[52]

Despite this appeal, the plough was rather generally kept out of the ground insofar as the cultivation of Cobbett's corn was concerned. More than twenty years elapsed after the book was published before small, but increasing, quantities of maize began to be imported into England. But not until the twentieth century, long after Cobbett's efforts had been forgotten, did the sceptical farmers of England accept the product as a valuable crop for animal feed and begin to reap some of the benefits Cobbett had proclaimed a hundred years earlier.[53] The first edition of *Cobbett's Corn* (but not the second) had its title page and table of contents printed on paper made of maize husks. This, the wrapper covering the early parts of *Advice to Young Men,* and one issue of the *Political Register* are the only known uses of the results of Cobbett's paper experiments.

The most famous of Cobbett's works related to farming was *Cottage Economy* (1822), which dealt to a large extent with life inside the farmhouse itself. It was written for the purpose of showing a farm laborer's family how to get the most out of their small income. They should brew their own beer and drink it instead of tea, which was more expensive, had no strength in it, caused sleeplessness, and weakened the nerves. "Put it to the test with a lean hog: give him the fifteen bushels of malt, and he will repay you in ten score of bacon or thereabouts. But give him the 730 tea messes, or rather, begin to give them to him, and give him nothing else, and he is dead with hunger and bequeaths you his skeleton, at the end of about seven days." The laborer's family should eat bread, baked at home, in preference to the beastly potatoes – bread was more nourishing and was cheaper. They should keep poultry and bees and pigs and a cow (the produce of a cow was equal to half a man's wages), and this could be done on a quarter of an acre. Cobbett's detailed explanation of how to do all these things was accompanied by comments on the education of children and an aesthetic appreciation of the hardworking wife: "Give me for a beautiful sight, a neat and smart woman, heating her oven and setting in her bread!"[54] *Cottage Economy* was an immediate success. The *Edinburgh Review* found it "an excellent little book – written not only with admirable clearness and good sense, but in a very earnest and entertaining manner – and abounding with kind and good feelings as well as most valuable information." It urged "all persons in easy circumstances, who live in the country" to distribute "these little books."[55] Cobbett himself modestly claimed that "every parson ought, upon pain of loss of ears, to present [a copy] to every girl he marries, rich or poor."[56] In the first ten years, 100,000 copies were sold; in all, more than twenty editions were printed, including three in the twentieth century. It is in print today.

Cobbett's contributions to the agricultural field were not limited to his own writing, since in 1822 he resurrected and reprinted a "lost" classic: Jethro Tull's *Horse-Hoeing Husbandry*, originally published in 1731. Tull advocated planting in rows spaced sufficiently far apart to allow easy tillage during the growing period, as contrasted with the ancient practice of sowing seeds broadcast. This method, which had been in large part forgotten, was popularized by Cobbett first in America and then in England.[57] "I have obtained the premium of five guineas from the Wharfedale Agricultural Society for the best crop of Swede Turnips, grown from your seed, and after your plan," read one of the many letters Cobbett received.[58]

Three of Cobbett's books are mainly devoted to instruction on matters of personal behavior: *Cobbett's Sermons* (1822), *The Emigrant's Guide* (1829), and *Advice to Young Men and (Incidentally) to Young Women* (1830). The sermons were first issued in parts beginning in March 1821 and were published in book form in the following year.[59] They had all the outward manifestations of what an intelligent vicar might deliver from the pulpit on a Sunday morning. They discussed such subjects as "Hypocrisy," "Drunkenness," and "Gaming." They were replete with biblical quotations. Yet there is the strong suspicion that they had another purpose: that, for example, the sermon on "Hypocrisy" was directed at Wilberforce; that the sermon on "The Sin of Forbidding Marriage" was for the benefit of Malthus and his followers; and that the sermon entitled "God's Vengeance against Murderers," dealing with the cruelty of a husband toward his wife, was intended for George IV, whose wife had died the month before the sermon appeared. By 1825 they had attained a circulation of 240,000, so that Cobbett was able to declare that more of his sermons had been purchased than those of all the clergy of England combined.[60] He presumably also enjoyed his impish utilization of the legal provision which exempted "religious" tracts from the stamp tax.

The Emigrant's Guide is a charming little book which, regrettably, has been out of print for more than a hundred years. A modern-day reader cannot fail to be entertained by the twenty-odd letters from former Sussex residents in America to their relations in England; by bits of practical information on life aboard ship, including an explanation of how women in the steerage can dress and undress without offense to their sensibilities; and by Cobbett's description of the puritanical ways of the Americans and how newcomers will be expected to behave.[61]

The Emigrant's Guide was closely followed in time, and in style, by *Advice to Young Men and (Incidentally) to Young Women,* which ranks high, perhaps highest, among all of Cobbett's works for amusement and edification. "Happiness ought to be your great object," Cobbett says almost at the outset, and this is what the book was about. It was a healthy and worldly book, possibly intended as an answer to the solemn and otherworldly advice commonly preached to the lower classes. The advice which Cobbett offered was in the form of six letters addressed, successively, to a youth, a young man, a lover, a husband, a father, and a citizen. Much of the material was autobiographical – but, one suspects, slightly romanticized at almost every point, so that the author appears somewhat more heroic, more understanding, more lovable, and more sympathetic than in real life. *Advice* is the source of Cobbett's account of learning grammar in an army barracks and his selection of Nancy Reid as the girl he wanted to marry, as well as most of the description of life at Botley when the children were small. These and other anecdotes were used to illustrate the standards of conduct most likely to produce the greatest happiness. Many of the social customs of 1830 are now archaic, and some of Cobbett's notions were eccentric even then, but the main thrust of the advice is as appropriate today as when it was written. Cobbett's stories frequently have a wider application than the narrow terms in which they were stated. To cite an example: "It was said of a famous French commander, that, in attacking an enemy, he did not say to his men 'go on', but, 'come on'; and whoever have well observed the movements of servants, must know what a prodigious difference there is in the effect of the words *go* and *come.*"[62] The nineteenth century produced a number of books on how to lead a good and happy life, but *Advice to Young Men* is the only one that has survived. Seven new editions have been published in the twentieth century.

The final category of Cobbett's works is those chiefly concerned with the system of government and, in particular, the impact of government on the working man. This single subject was year after year the main burden of the *Political Register,* and it is natural that the theme should predominate in *Rural Rides,* which appeared serially in the current issues of the *Political Register* from 1822 to 1826.[63] Published in book form in 1830, it is the work for which Cobbett is best known today, and it is one of his most enjoyable for the general reader, taking its place, in that respect, with *The Life and Adventures of Peter Porcupine, A Year's Residence in the United States, The Emigrant's Guide,* and *Advice to Young Men and (Incidentally) to Young Women.*

Rural Rides begins in September 1822: "This morning I set off in rather a drizzling rain, from Kensington, on horse-back, accom-

panied by my son James . . . my object was, not to see the inns and
turnpike-roads, but to see the country; to see the farmers at work,
and to see the labourers in the fields."[64] This purpose was amply fulfilled. On each leg of each journey Cobbett described the soil, the
crops, the condition of the farmers and of their laborers. He said in
Advice to Young Men that "To come at the true history of a country you
must read its laws; you must read books treating of its usages and
customs in former times; you must particularly inform yourself of the
prices of labour and of food."[65] In *Rural Rides* Cobbett left, for those
who want to come at the true history of England, an unequalled picture of the early nineteenth century, written by a man well qualified
to observe and to comment. Yet it is not a dull collection of statistics.
We read about the shepherd who knew he had thirteen score and five
sheep, but was unable to say how many hundred; about the belief that
"a great nut year [is] a great bastard year"; about the sign standing in
a garden near a neat little box of a house, reading "PARADISE PLACE.
Spring guns and steel traps are set here." Small episodes yield the full
savor of the country and its people. Many of the incidents involve
Cobbett himself. In October 1825 he and his youngest son, Richard,
rode their horses north from Winchester:

After, however, crossing the village, and beginning again to ascend the
downs, we came to a labourer's (once a farm house), where I asked the man,
whether he had any bread and cheese, and was not a little pleased to hear
him say "Yes". Then I asked him to give us a bit, protesting that we had not
yet broken our fast. He answered in the affirmative, at once, though I did not
talk of payment. His wife brought out the cut loaf, and a piece of Wiltshire
cheese, and I took them in hand, gave Richard a good hunch, and took
another for myself. I verily believe, that all the pleasure of eating enjoyed by
all the feeders in London in a whole year, does not equal that which we
enjoyed in gnawing this bread and cheese, as we rode over this cold down,
whip and bridle-reins in one hand, and the hunch in the other. Richard, who
was purse bearer, gave the woman, by my direction, about enough to buy two
quartern loaves; for she told me, that they had to buy their bread at the mill,
not being able to bake themselves for want of fuel.[66]

Fortunately for us, Cobbett did not stick precisely to his objective of
seeing the country, the farmers, and the laborers. Inevitably, there is
something that sets him off on a digression relating to one of his
favorite topics: himself, his grievances, his theories, and his crotchets.
A small boy wearing a smock frock causes him to recall his own childhood; a plantation of scotch firs and oaks reminds him of the superiority of locust trees; an eighty-year-old laborer cutting grass evokes
Cobbett's self-satisfied comment that the mower does not know how
to hold the scythe properly. Cobbett's long memory for his grievances
produced remarks on the 1810 trial for libel, the suspension of habeas

corpus in 1817, the Coventry election of 1820 – even on the villainy of Judge McKean that had occurred a quarter century before.[67]

Many of the apparent digressions were not that at all; almost all of them relate to subjects which had an impact on the farmers and their workers; subjects such as the enclosures, the game laws, the tithes, the salt tax – a cruel burden to those whose only meat was bacon cured with salt. When Matthew Arnold said that "Cobbett's politics were at bottom always governed by one master-thought – the thought of the evil condition of the English labourer," he was too restrictive.[68] Not simply Cobbett's *politics*, but his idiosyncratic views of social, economic, and religious issues were so governed. He hated the methodists because they taught the poor to be satisfied with their lot in this life, issuing "nonsensical little books . . . to make you believe that it is necessary for you to be starved to death in order to ensure you a place in heaven after you are dead."[69] He hated the middlemen who did not increase the quantity or quality of goods produced, but added to the cost of articles purchased by the working man. Much better than the village stores were the markets and fairs of olden times which brought the producer and consumer face to face without a burdensome intermediary.[70] His dislike of the quakers and Jews stemmed from this objection to nonproducers. The quakers were forestallers, buying from the farmers and holding to sell at the most advantageous prices; they were "jews in grain," and "worse than the Jews."[71] Both quakers and Jews were jobbers and moneylenders. In his campaign against unlawfully charged turnpike tolls, Cobbett discovered that many of the turnpikes around London were farmed by Jews.[72] The word "Jews" as used by Cobbett often referred to those engaged in occupations similar to those of Jews: he spoke of jobbers and moneylenders as "Jews or Jewish Christians," or "Jews and Jew-like Christians."[73] The quakers were "broad-brimmed Jews" or "buttonless Jews."[74] Paper money was a "Scotch, Jew, Quaker trap."[75] Cobbett resented Ricardo's fortune derived from "watching a turn in the market," since the half million gained by Ricardo had to come out of the pockets of those doing productive work.[76] He had no dislike of quakers so long as they were engaged in some productive activity. The quakers of Pennsylvania, mostly farmers, were "the best people in the world."[77] His dislike of Jews was more complicated: It was partly because of occupation, partly because they were "foreigners," and partly because of their blasphemy against Christianity.[78] He specifically disclaimed any intention that the Jews be persecuted, but they were not to be encouraged either, as to do so would "join in the blasphemy."[79]

Cobbett thought that the potato was less nourishing and more expensive than bread, making elaborate computations to show that this was so.[80] However, his principal objection to the potato was based on an issue of human dignity. The English farm worker for generations had been accustomed to eat bread as the chief item of his diet, supplemented, when available, by cheese or bacon.[81] The potato in most English farming communities was boiled up to feed pigs. It was an affront to the laborer to be asked to eat pig food, "and bad pig meat too."[82] The Irish custom of raking potatoes out of the coals and eating them with the fingers without utensils was especially degrading. Cobbett's inveterate habit of gross exaggeration, plus his sense of humor, produced statements like this:

A potato is the worst of all things for man. There needs nothing more to inflict scrofula on a whole nation. It distends the stomach, it swells the heels, and enfeebles the mind. I have no doubt, that a whole people would become ideots in time by feeding *solely* upon potatoes. Like other vegetables, this root, in moderate quantity, is well enough in the way of sauce; but, as the main article of the meal, as the joint to dine on, it is monstrous, or, rather beastly, to think of it.[83]

Another of Cobbett's crotchets that repeatedly appeared in *Rural Rides,* and was only partially explained there, was his view that the population of England was declining, rather than increasing. Everywhere he travelled, he observed large churches and decaying villages. The church at Old Romney, for example, could hold 1,500 persons, and there were only twenty-two or twenty-three houses remaining in the parish.[84] The first census in Britain was taken in 1801. Cobbett was able to point out what he thought were discrepancies between this data and that produced at subsequent ten-year intervals.[85] He had other reasons to disbelieve the objectivity of government reporting, and thought that the claimed increases were part of a propaganda campaign to prove that prosperity existed at a time when the poor of England were suffering great privation. He also suspected that the figures were for the purpose of supporting the claimed need, by Malthus and others, for population control among those receiving parish aid.[86] The "main drift of these writings is to impute all these [the miseries of the country] to the people themselves and not to their rulers; and, at the same time, to find an apology for the rich in suffering the poor to be reduced to starvation."[87] No one suggested controlling the breeding of the clergy, the sinecurists, and the "deadweight," all nonproductive classes supported by public money. "It is the *working* population, those who raise the food and the clothing, that he [Malthus] and Scarlett want to put a stop to the breeding of!"[88]

Cobbett's dislike of London, the "wen," was partly because of the noise, smoke, and crime of the city, but to a greater extent because it represented a parasite whose swelling was at the expense of the impoverished country people.[89] The wen was the residence of the nonproductive class made up of tax-eaters, sinecurists, deadweights, middlemen, "jobbers and Jews" – all depending for their income on the rest of the population and eating the food that had been taken away from the communities where it had been grown: "go to the *villages*," Cobbett wrote in an open letter to Canning, "and see the misery of the labourers; see their misery, compared to the happy state in which they lived before the swellings out of this corrupt and all-devouring wen."[90]

Rural Rides concentrated on one principal aspect of the problem of the laborer: it revealed his poverty, and the reasons for it as seen by Cobbett. Heavy taxes and paper money were at the root, abetted by such ancillary evils as the enclosures, the game laws, the Speenhamland system. The other principal aspect of the laborer's problem with which Cobbett was concerned was the inadequacy of payments under the poor law to those in distress, and the imminent danger that such payments might be further reduced or even eliminated. The complaints of those paying poor rates were made respectable by Malthus's assertion that the poor laws only tended to defeat their own purpose by creating more poverty. Legislation consistent with this view was introduced in parliament by William Sturges Bourne and James Scarlett.[91] The premise underlying Malthus's proposals was his belief that the poor had no right to relief. In Malthus's own words, a laborer out of work "has no claim of right on society for the smallest portion of food," and "the laws of nature, which are the laws of God, had doomed him and his family to suffer for disobeying their repeated admonitions" – that is, had doomed them to starve. It was to this premise that Cobbett directed his attack in two other works: *A History of the Protestant "Reformation"* and the *Poor Man's Friend*.[92] The *History* was originally published in parts from 1824 to 1826, and the *Poor Man's Friend* was published in 1826, while Cobbett was still engaged in the journeys described in *Rural Rides*. Stated briefly, Cobbett argued that the laws of nature ("the principles of society") demand that each person be provided with the necessities of life; that before the Reformation this provision was made by the church, which was required to set aside a third of its revenue for the benefit of the poor and sick; that after the Reformation (the church property having been appropriated by the king and his rich friends), provision for the impoverished was made by the poor law statute enacted during the reign of Queen Elizabeth I; and that, in the event that the poor were not thereby provided with the necessaries of life, they had the right to be maintained "out of the lands, or other property, of the rich." It

443

N⁰. I.

COBBETT'S
POOR MAN'S FRIEND:

OR,

Useful Information and Advice for the Working Classes;
in a Series of Letters, addressed to the Working Classes
of Preston.

LONDON :

Printed and Published by W. COBBETT, No. 183, Fleet-Street.

PRICE TWO-PENCE.

LETTER I.

TO THE

WORKING CLASSES OF PRESTON.

Kensington, 1st August, 1826.

MY EXCELLENT FRIENDS,

1. DURING one of those many speeches, which you have
so recently done me the honour to listen to, I promised to
communicate, in the form of a little book, such information
and advice as I thought might, in the present state of things,
be useful to you. I am now about to fulfil this promise.
The recollection of the misery, in which I found so many
of you; those melancholy effects of poverty produced by
taxation, that I had the sorrow to witness amongst a people
so industrious and so virtuous; the remembrance of these
will not suffer me to be silent on the subject of the means
necessary to the restoration of your happiness, especially
when I think of the boundless kindness which I received at
your hands, and which will live in my memory as long as
memory shall live in me.

2. We are in a very ticklish state of things: the most
sluggish and torpid of men seem to be convinced, that there

B

Title page of *Cobbett's Poor Man's Friend*. Cobbett called this small book "the most
learned book that I ever wrote." Derived in large part from his *History of the Protestant "Reformation"*, it proposed to show "how there came to be so much poverty"
and proclaimed the legal and moral right of those who "do the work and fight the
battles" to a reasonable level of subsistence

was left to Cobbett's speeches, the *Political Register,* and a later book, *Cobbett's Legacy to Labourers* (1835), to declare openly what was so obviously implied:

Well, then, what is the conclusion to which we come at last? Why, that the labourers have a right to subsistence out of the land, in all cases of inability to labour; that all those who are able to labour have a right to subsistence out of the land, in exchange for their labour; and that, if the holders of the land will not give them subsistence, in exchange for their labour, they have a right to the land itself. Thus we come to the conclusion, that, if these new, inhuman and diabolical doctrines were acted upon, instead of giving that "security to property," which is their pretence, there would be an end of all respect for, and of all right to, property of every description![93]

A History of the Protestant "Reformation", using materials derived from a recent book written by the English historian John Lingard, was almost wholly devoted to a demonstration that the so-called Reformation was engendered in the "beastly lust" of Henry VIII and forced on an unwilling people by acts of unprecedented ferocity and greed sanctioned by that monarch and his protestant successors, and that it was not a reformation at all, but a "devastation." ". . . it is my chief business," Cobbett declared, "to show that this devastation impoverished and degraded the main body of the people."[94] Cobbett's enthusiasm for the task led him into a much wider range of controversial subjects relating to the history of the English church (and the sex life of the "virgin queen") than would have been necessary if he had confined himself to proving his ultimate conclusion. The story that he unfolded made the catholic position – "the religion of our forefathers" – far more appealing than most protestants liked to admit. Because of this, the book proved to be the most explosive of all Cobbett's works. It was execrated by church of England clergymen. It was extolled by the Roman catholics. "I have published a book that has exceeded all others in circulation, the Bible only excepted," declared Cobbett.[95] By 1828 the total sale of the sixteen separate numbers, published in book form beginning in 1826, had attained 700,000. This did not include those printed in Ireland, America, France, Spain, Switzerland, Italy, Portugal, Romania, Germany, Holland, Australia, and Venezuela. In America the sale was said to exceed 100,000. In Paris there were "three different booksellers selling three different translations." A stream of irate replies flowed from the printing presses, and Cobbett was forced to defend himself from the charge that he had become a convert to Rome.[96] It is a mere quibble to contend, as some have done, that Cobbett's polemic was erroneous in detail and gave an exaggerated account of the Reformation. If Cobbett too warmly urged that everything in the old religion had been good and that the change was made solely for sordid reasons, this was only a fair counterbalance to three centuries of erroneous and exaggerated propaganda to the opposite effect. John Ruskin put it nicely: "the sum of my forty-four years of thinking on the matter, from an entirely outside standpoint – as nearly as possible that of a Turk – has led me to agree with Cobbett in all his main ideas, and there is no question whatever, that Protestant writers are, as a rule, ignorant and false in what they say of Catholics – while Catholic writers are as a rule both well-informed and fair."[97]

As might be expected, Cobbett revelled in the controversy he had provoked: He enjoyed anything that might be upsetting to the contemporary clergy of the church of England, who often lived in un-Christian splendor, rendered little service, and supported the oppressive measures of the establishment; he disliked the arrogance of the rich whig families who had been among the principal beneficiaries of the Reformation; he had always contended that the poor men of England had been better off in ancient times than they were in the nineteenth century; and he had, for years, been a strong advocate of catholic emancipation. Perhaps, too, the implication that the English might do well to return to catholicism was a humorous reply to Wilberforce's irrational belief that the Irish could be converted to protestantism.[98]

It is amazing, after surveying the mountainous output of writing, to find the quality as good as it is. There are dull passages, plenty of them; there are repetitions, too many of them.[99] But on average the quality was high. Southey's comment that "there never was a better or more forcible writer" is demonstrated by the extent and character of Cobbett's readership. No journalist ever attained such eminence. He was read by all his contemporaries: by the prime ministers of England, by the presidents of the United States, by Napoleon and Talleyrand. As Cobbett himself said, "there is no piece of earth which has any thing worthy of a government, where the *Register* is not read, and that too, by persons composing the government."[100] He was read, during the French wars, on ships at sea and in army mess halls. He was read by Carlyle and Macaulay; by Byron, Shelley, Lamb, Coleridge, Wordsworth, Southey, Hazlitt, Peacock, Tom Moore, Leigh Hunt, Matthew Arnold; by Philip Freneau, Emerson, and James Fenimore Cooper; by the German poet Heine; by Ricardo, Malthus, Bentham, James Mill, John Stuart Mill, and Karl Marx. He is mentioned in novels by George Borrow, George Eliot, and Benjamin Disraeli. He was caricatured by Gillray, Cruikshank, and Doyle. He was the subject of a parody – along with Coleridge, Byron, Sir Walter Scott, and other literary luminaries of the day – in *Rejected Addresses* (1812) by

James and Horace Smith, a work that was reprinted some twenty or thirty times, and he was the subject of an ode in the Smiths' *Horace in London* (1813); he was included with a similarly distinguished group in another volume of parodies called *Rejected Articles* (1826) by P. G. Patmore. The appeal of Cobbett's writing to his contemporaries was described by one of them, Sir Henry Lytton Bulwer:

Whatever a man's talents, whatever a man's opinions, he sought the *Register* on the day of its appearance with eagerness, and read it with amusement, partly, perhaps, if De la Rochefoucauld is right, because, whatever his party, he was sure to see his friends abused. But partly also because he was certain to find, amidst a great many lies and abundance of impudence, some felicitous nickname, some excellent piece of practical-looking argument, some capital expressions, and very often some marvellously-fine writing, all the finer for being carelessly fine, and exhibiting whatever figure or sentiment it set forth in the simplest as well as the most striking dress.[101]

Lies? That there were occasional lies cannot be doubted. Misstatements of fact are inevitable even in a modern newspaper with its superior information-gathering services. And in Cobbett's case his radical opinions and hyperbole were readily translated into lies by his opponents.

Cobbett's hope that the "whole world" would want to read his writing was largely realized. But despite the large numbers sold of many of his books, Cobbett was unable to release himself, except for occasional sunny intervals, from the financial straits that had become a way of life. He seems to have regularly underpriced his publications to get the maximum number of readers, and, to get the unit cost down to where he could justify the low price, frequently ordered more copies than he was able to sell expeditiously, leaving him with a large inventory of unrealizable assets. Two of the bestsellers, *Cottage Economy* and the *Sermons*, were issued in parts at threepence a number, and in bound volumes at only sixpence more than the price of the separate issues. When *Cottage Economy* was enlarged to include instructions on the production of the straw plait, Cobbett stated: "The book is nearly double the bulk that it was at first: but I have never altered the price of it, because I would do nothing to put it beyond the reach of poor people, for whose benefit it was written." The *Poor Man's Friend* was sold at twopence a part; the five parts when bound were offered at a shilling. "This is not the way to get money," wrote Cobbett, "but my object was to put this little book within the reach of almost every body."[102] On occasion his books were pirated and he received nothing for them. When this happened to *The American Gardener*, Cobbett's response was to castigate the pirate (a Baltimore printer) for omitting the dedication to Mrs. Tredwell, Cobbett's neighbor on Long Island.[103] Although we lack precise figures for his publishing business, it is plain that the profits were not enough to support his family and carry on his extraneous ventures.[104] In 1827 we find Cobbett sending John Dean, in charge of the shop in Fleet Street, a message of the sort he once sent to John Wright: "The sum of money that I wrote to you about I *must have*, on the 19th instant. Whether it be yours or mine, it signifies not: that sum I must have, and on that day, which is this day week."[105] As early as 1828 Cobbett was once again compelled to borrow money.[106] And there is a letter from John Cobbett to his father in 1832 urging him to reduce the printing order for the French – English dictionary. He was fearful of "having all this immense stock on our hands . . . when it . . . is not without difficulty that I can meet all the bills now out."[107]

Money, however, was never a major consideration with Cobbett. His passion was for something more honorable or, at least, more difficult to attain. He craved a heroic role in serving the world, and in particular, that part of the world which few cared to serve: the poor and the friendless. The fact that few cared to assume this burden and that it was the heaviest and most difficult of all burdens that could be assumed only made the cause more attractive to him. The reward he sought for this service was not worldly goods, as we have seen; nor was it mere inner satisfaction or recognition in heaven. He openly and unashamedly declared that what he wanted was "fame." "I care not for their money or their estates," he once said of the aristocracy, "but I care for my fame, and that I will not fail to secure."[108]

Although this avowal was made when Cobbett was about sixty years old, the strong aggressive component in his nature, which accounted for his constant striving for superiority, had been manifest since childhood. Later, when entered upon his career, he quickly proved his superiority as a soldier, rising from private to sergeant major in three years and establishing himself, in the process, as a dominant force in the regiment, even among the officers.[109] He just as rapidly proved his superiority as a writer, first in America and then in England. But he was not content to be a superior soldier, or a superior writer; he insisted on his superiority as a husband, as a father, as an employer, as a farmer, as an economist, as a teacher, as a . . . whatever role he was playing at the moment. The introduction of a better fireplace or domestic straw plait, or a demonstration of how the laws should be enforced against wrongdoers, were means of proving his superiority in the same way as were the introduction of a better tree or a better apple or a better method of cultivating turnips, or a sounder system of currency.[110]

This enormous aggressive force had been met, almost at the outset of Cobbett's career, by the first of a series of frustrations that continued for the next twenty-five years. His effort to expose the corruption that existed in the army forced him to flee from England in 1792. His attacks on Rush's false cure for yellow fever stripped him of his earnings and drove him back to England in 1800. His condemnation of flogging put him in prison from 1810 to 1812. His efforts to relieve the distresses of the poor people of England through reform of a corrupt government led to another exile from 1817 to 1819. Not only were good deeds met with punishment, but the punishment was accompanied by vilification from the press and from the establishment to which the press pandered. The vilification did not stop with known facts; outright falsehoods were circulated. While he was in America, the *Courier*, a ministerial paper, claimed that Cobbett had been fined $700 for writing against the American government. This was a complete fabrication; there had never even been a charge lodged against him.[111] Charles Dundas, member of parliament for Berkshire and cousin of Lord Melville, declared that Cobbett had been an associate of Arthur Thistlewood, who had been hanged for high treason in 1820, whereas Cobbett had never seen or corresponded with Thistlewood.[112] The *New Times* and *Courier* falsely claimed that Cobbett, in buying a house, had paid the "required premium of £500 by a check on the Catholic Association" – for which, as Cobbett pointed out, "there is not even the shadow of a pretence."[113] In 1822 *The Times* claimed that Cobbett was in the pay of the English treasury![114] In 1823 the whig papers implied that Cobbett was in the pay of the Bourbon government of France.[115] The allegation that Cobbett had been a British-paid spy in America prior to 1800 and had subsequently been dismissed from that service was a constantly renewed falsehood. The great *Times*, the newspaper that declared on Cobbett's death that he was "in some respects a more extraordinary Englishman than any other of his time," had hardly a civil word to say of him while he was living. The general view taken by that paper and the balance of the "respectable" press, as well as by most of the gentlemen in and out of parliament, was that Cobbett was some kind of renegade, an outlaw, a traitor, a blackguard, a mountebank, whose sole motivation was in the large profits he allegedly derived from his activities.[116]

Cobbett's literary efforts were met by a conspiracy of silence among the leading contemporary newspapers and journals. Neither his *History of the Protestant "Reformation"*, which had an unparalleled sale throughout the western world, nor any of the many other successful books published by him, was ever noticed by a paper or journal, with the single exception of the enthusiastic review of *Cottage Economy* by the *Edinburgh Review*.[117] And his frustrations took one further form: At the same time as he was being denied merit for the views espoused in his writings, these views, often only slightly disguised, frequently reappeared in the rival press, on the floor of parliament, and in the mouths of speakers at public meetings.[118] The snobbery of the period was reluctant to admit much merit in the ideas of a humbly born, uneducated, renegade newspaper editor.[119] William Carpenter, radical reformer and publisher of *Political Letters and Pamphlets*, spoke of the surprising extent to which Cobbett's "views and arguments are made use of by men who never think of avowing to whom they are indebted for their borrowed plumes."[120] William Smart, no admirer of Cobbett, wrote: "it is impossible not to see that his main ideas were taken, without acknowledgement as he complained, by politicians and statesmen, as well as by farmers and landowners."[121] The high tory newspaper, the *Standard*, claimed that speeches of Grey, Brougham, Durham, Graham, and Macaulay, as well as opinions expressed in *The Times* "and other more respectable journals," were derived from Cobbett's writings.[122]

It comes as no surprise, therefore, that when Cobbett later asserted: "I wrote for fame," he immediately added "and was urged forward by ill-treatment and by the desire to triumph over my enemies."[123] The 1810 libel prosecution, in particular, was never far from his thoughts. Mentioned again and again in his writings, often when its relevance is difficult to detect, it became Cobbett's hair shirt.[124] He could not clear his mind of the unfairness of being sent to jail like a common criminal for having condemned the flogging of young boys in the militia who had complained of not being paid what the law required. This incident had taken him away from his family and from the farm that he loved nearly as much as his family, and had precipitated the financial distress from which he had never recovered. No effort was made by the government to right the wrong, even after protests against flogging had become an accepted part of the scene and were no longer prosecuted. Attempts made by Cobbett in 1828 and again in 1832 to have the £1,000 fine remitted, which might have constituted a token admission that a wrong had been done, were peremptorily rejected.[125] After being turned down in 1828, Cobbett wrote: "I had not forgotten, nor have I yet forgotten, nor shall I ever forget or forgive, the treatment which I have received from persons in power in England. But, they are *not England*; they are not *my country*; my country is unhappy, in misery, sinking in character, and it is my duty to endeavour to restore her to her former state . . . but above all things, it is my duty . . . to better the lot of the labouring classes."[126] The injustice from which Cobbett personally suffered he equated with the injustices suffered by the entire class from which he had sprung. They did the work and received a niggardly share of the benefits. Cobbett, harried and persecuted for his efforts to serve the public, saw liberal rewards heaped on those who, in his eyes at least, had added nothing to the well-being of the country.

Cobbett's response to these repeated rebuffs took two predictable courses: praise of himself and abuse of others.[127] Everything Cobbett did, from the most simple to the most elaborate, was heralded by him as of unique importance. "So help me God, I would rather see a full-sized ripe apple from one of these graffs than I would see myself made a knight of the Garter."[128] Indian corn was "the greatest blessing that God gave to man."[129] It was not mere chance that it had been Cobbett, of all the inhabitants of England, who was responsible for this boon: "The truth is, that I know how to make things move. Another man might have written about the thing to all eternity; and his writing might be better than mine; but very few men could, like me, have made the thing move."[130] And so it went. "I have done a great many wonderful things . . . my name will live many score years after me." "When I am asked what books a young man or young woman ought to read, I always answer: Let him or her read all the books that I have written." "Ten thousand times my ears have been saluted, from the lips of men that I have never seen before . . . 'Here's the cleverest man in England'."[131]

To the cries of "egotism" that met this type of effusion Cobbett responded, "mock-modesty . . . is, in fact, only another term for hypocrisy." "A great deal of what passes for 'modesty' ought to pass for cowardice or servility."[132] Cobbett was only saying out loud what "more civilized" men keep to themselves, as we see in the conduct of the small child who is not old enough to have been inhibited by social convention. Cobbett made no secret that he thought himself superior to the public figures of his day.[133] When George Canning became minister for foreign affairs and leader of the House of Commons on Castlereagh's death in 1822, he was taken "regularly to school" by Cobbett in a series of six articles. It was not presumptuous of Cobbett to instruct Canning, because "as to all the chief matters appertaining to your office, I have greater ability than you." And Cobbett proceeded to demonstrate this assertion: Cobbett had more accurately predicted the course of events in the past; Cobbett was Canning's literary superior; Cobbett could write and speak French better than Canning "and, perhaps, better even than any of your interpreters"; Cobbett knew the principles and practice of public law (he had translated Martens's *Law of Nations*) as well as Canning and could write on them more forcibly than Canning; and so on – an extraordinary exercise.[134] Shocking? But who is such a hypocrite as to assert that he has never had similar thoughts in the privacy of his bedroom?

As time passed and frustrations increased, Cobbett's ambition mounted. The fame that Cobbett had in mind was not merely public recognition that he was industrious, virtuous, and able. It was that, but much more besides. He wanted to be called by the nation to a place of power from which he could relieve the poor and administer justice. He was grossly offended by a statement of Castlereagh in 1817 that the petitions for reform that were pouring into parliament were due to "the instigations of men, who, without any pretensions, were aspiring to high office." Cobbett testily replied that while Castlereagh might think he had no pretensions, "there are hundreds of thousands of persons, and sensible persons too, in this kingdom, who think I have."[135] In 1825 Cobbett predicted that the people would soon be saying "how unfortunate for us that Mr. Cobbett had not been the minister of England twenty years ago."[136] Two years later, when it was rumored that Lord Goderich would be succeeded as prime minister by Dudley Ryder (the rumor was wrong; Wellington won the post), Cobbett offered himself in an open letter to the king: "there is not one man in Your Majesty's dominions, who will not unhesitatingly declare, that I am a thousand times as fit to be your minister as he is, and that I am, at this moment, more fit for that office than any other man in the kingdom."[137] Although the offer as worded must be regarded as a bit of Cobbettian humor, he certainly thought himself fully capable of filling the office.

It would hardly be urged that all the abuse that flowed from Cobbett's pen was attributable to the conduct of his adversaries. Much of it was a part of his natural aggression and came effortlessly, almost unconsciously. A man so constituted needed enemies. When accused of having unfairly assaulted others, he declared: "that which is true, though it may be seriously censorious, can never be called abusive."[138] Seriously censorious, indeed, were some of the terms Cobbett applied from time to time to whoever might be his target at the moment. Canning was an "impudent mountebank," a "jack-pudding," a "loathsome dish." Burdett was a "base paltroon." Castlereagh was a "shallow pated ass." Liverpool was a "pick-nose wiseacre." Brougham was "all jaw and no judgement." Wilberforce was "the prince of hypocrites." Bentham was "Old Jerry the Rump Cock." These are only the briefest sample of the hundreds of epithets which Cobbett, presumably, thought not abusive. Nor was he a believer in de mortuis nil nisi bonum: it "is a foolish maxim that says we are not to speak evil of the dead: it is the maxim of knaves imposed on fools. We are to say nothing but the truth of the dead, and the same rule we ought to observe towards

"The Political Bellman." The year 1827 saw rapid changes in government. Liverpool was forced to retire in March. His successor, Canning, died in August. Canning's successor, Goderich, resigned in December. Cobbett promptly offered his services, and others, not so openly forward, hoped to occupy positions of importance in the new government.

The Bellman, Wellington (who was given the task of forming a cabinet), is surrounded by applicants, including Peel, Eldon, and Russell. Russell, the waif at Wellington's right, says: "I wants a job master I'll dust the carpets." Cobbett renews his offer from the window on the right, while George IV, on the left, surveys the crowd and says: "I have seen those faces before, and dont like them, but I sup[p]ose I must take what I can get"

the living."[139] When the recently dead Duke of York, a notorious lecher and coward, was portrayed as a saint and hero by the London newspapers, Cobbett courageously set forth the true facts. "If these praises of the Duke of York be suffered to pass without comment, who shall say that a young man will be wrong if he endeavour, or, permit himself to imitate the life and actions of the Duke of York?"[140] This worshipper of the truth also believed that calling attention to the faults of his friends was as essential as pointing out the virtues of his enemies. "I like the Americans very much; and that, if there were no other, would be a reason for my not hiding their faults."[141] Thus, among his friends, he publicly criticized William Windham for his

453

opposition to a bill allowing distillers to use sugar in place of grain; Lord Cochrane for his stock dealings; Lord Folkestone for his refusal to submit a petition of Cobbett's to the House of Commons (and much more besides); Daniel O'Connell for his mishandling of the Catholic Emancipation Bill in 1825. He occasionally found good things to say about those he did not agree with: Sir Francis Burdett was "an English gentleman . . . wholly beyond the reach of everything that leads to dirty compromises, and of talent . . . equal to this or to any other undertaking." Peel "appears to me to have a solider head than any minister that I have ever yet seen in power." Canning was "a correct, a clear and elegant writer; an acute reasoner; has, in speaking, a perfect command of words, and may be said to be truly eloquent." Wellington was better fitted for prime minister than "any one of the nine who have gone before him." George III, despite his many faults, was no hypocrite.[142]

The secret of this apparent evenhandedness among friends and foes was that Cobbett was attached to causes, not to men. He commended acts that were consistent with the position he espoused, and attacked those he thought were inconsistent with it.[143] He did not hesitate to attack this week a man he had applauded the week before, and vice versa. In this respect he was the opposite of Wilberforce, who sided first with Pitt, then with Perceval, then with Liverpool and his henchmen Sidmouth and Castlereagh – and thus was guilty of supporting one piece of oppressive legislation after another by smugly reposing his confidence in whoever was the prime minister. Cobbett, in contrast, was rarely motivated by personal relationships. He had fixed notions of what was right and wrong, and these rather than friendship governed his conduct. His son James (making notes in preparation for a biography of his father, which he barely started) wrote:

He had but little individual attachment. Liked people's company; & they liked his (when he was agreeable). But he formed very little of *friendship*. And wd. break off with any one, however old an acquaintance, on any affront, or being crossed in his will.

In Rural Rides . . . he speaks of his "ardent friendship and not less ardent enmity". But he was not steady or constant in either; excepting that, as to the enmity, *public* causes were continually arising to keep the enmity renewed, or to revive it . . . He was engrossed with the effect he sought to produce on society at large. So that, after all, there was with him but little banding together with others for a common end, as with many men inspired by the "patriotic" sentiment. He might be sd. to *use* others, rather than to act with them.[144]

James, born in 1803, could have had little recollection of his father before the harrowing Newgate experience of 1810–12, when Cobbett was nearly fifty years old; hence, James's comments cannot be applied unqualifiedly to the earlier years of Cobbett's life, when he seems to have had a fair number of real friends. Cobbett would have claimed that he had a great many friends in his later years; but most of those he included in that category were more properly "devoted admirers": They were delighted to entertain the great man as a guest in their homes or to do the various favors he from time to time asked of them.[145] There rarely was any two-way flow of respect and affection that is characteristic of typical friendships. Cobbett was oblivious of this: "as to my family and friends, I leave them to say whether there is the company of any person on earth, in which they delight more than they do in mine. I do not believe, that I have experienced the breaking off of friendship with ten persons in the whole course of my life ... Why the devil then, am I to suppose myself unamiable?"[146] Cobbett had answered his own question several months earlier when he wrote: "It is, in short, the caring nothing for any body, that has enabled me to obtain something like justice for myself."[147]

That the later Cobbett seldom made an effort to ingratiate himself is reflected in his relations with Francis Douce, former keeper of manuscripts in the British Museum and Cobbett's neighbor in Kensington. To Douce, just around the corner in Kensington Square, Cobbett sent a letter via one of his daughters, complaining that slugs and snails from Douce's garden were invading Cobbett's garden and feeding on his vegetables. Was he joking, or was he serious? – Douce was unable to decide, but his reply covered both eventualities. He pointed out to Cobbett that his own cabbages had been ravaged by "the legions of vermin in question from your premises," while his nerves were being impaired by the howling of Cobbett's dogs, "an infliction worse than the pains of purgatory."[148] To cite another instance, Cobbett told, with obvious amusement, an account of a Scotch pedlar on Long Island,

who, on finding my doors wide open on a summer's day, walked into the hall, and then into the parlour where I was sitting, and, turning round at the end of the table, placed, without saying a word, his pack upon it, pulling his arms out of the straps of the pack, which I, with reciprocal taciturnity, took hold of and tossed out of the window, which, being a free country, was standing wide open, as it were, on purpose to admit of the ejectment. It was not till after this that the Scotchman spoke, which he did in a manner that would certainly have procured him the honour of following the pack, if he had not, upon due notice given, taken the more circuitous route by the door.[149]

No further examples are necessary to show why Cobbett stood alone in the world in his battle for what he thought right. When he was gently chided for being bitter, unforgiving, and uncompromis-

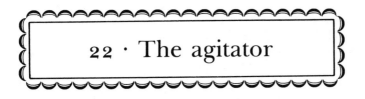

22 · The agitator

How is a man to be a match for the devil, unless he be at least half a devil himself?

COBBETT'S POLITICAL activities continued to occupy the paramount position in his life during the years he was selling trees, growing Swedish turnips, and writing the books for which he is best known today. His weekly stint in the *Political Register* during this period, as before, dealt principally with politics and only incidentally with such things as straw hats, improved fireplaces, and Cobbett's corn. In almost every year from 1821 to the date of his death he took his politics on tour, lecturing as he travelled around the country.[1] And the possibility of becoming even more actively involved in politics as a member of parliament was never far from his mind after his defeat at Coventry in 1820. This hope was stimulated by a young baronet, a man of independent means, whom Cobbett had met in 1823 during the agitation surrounding the Norfolk petition of that year. Sir Thomas Branthwayt Beevor, third baronet, of Hargham Hall, near Norwich, was twenty-five years old when he first heard Cobbett talk, and he became an immediate admirer and disciple. He may have been associated with Cobbett in the short-lived *Norfolk Yeoman's Gazette,* which had been established in 1823 to counter the reactionary *Norwich Mercury.*[2] He bought locust trees from Cobbett and planted them on his estate. In January 1824 the *Morning Chronicle* carried an announcement that Beevor proposed to hold a meeting in London of such gentlemen "as wish to see Mr. Cobbett placed in the House of Commons." Since it was unlikely that there would be a general election in the near future, the meeting was postponed.[3] Beevor renewed his proposal in December 1825, at the peak of the financial panic, and a meeting was scheduled for February 8, 1826 at the Freemason's tavern in London, where a room to accommodate 300 was engaged. Ten times that number attempted to gain admission. They filled the meeting room and another that adjoined, jammed the stairways and passages leading to the meeting place, and overflowed into the street.

They were packed in so tightly that Cobbett and Beevor found it impossible to gain entry, whereupon the meeting, after some confusion, was adjourned to Lincoln's Inn Fields, where an empty coal wagon was impressed into service as a hustings. Once the crowd had been reassembled, a resolution was adopted declaring that it would be "beneficial to the country if Mr. Cobbett were a Member of the Commons' House of Parliament." A subscription committee was appointed with Beevor as treasurer.[4] Cobbett had made it plain at the outset that any effort on his part to gain a seat would have to be financed by others, since on no account would he expend "any portion of those earnings, which, whether great or small, all belong to my wife and children."[5] At the Lincoln's Inn Fields meeting, £600 was raised and another £250 was "promised from the country." Frequent notices regarding the subscription appeared thereafter in the *Political Register* with the names of the agents qualified to accept remittances.[6] When a subscription was opened in Dublin, Lord Cloncurry, known in Ireland as "the poor man's peer" sent in £20 with a message declaring that Cobbett was "the ablest advocate of liberty in his own country and of fair play to mankind in general," and that the catholics of Ireland "owe him more than to any other individual in existence, with the exception, perhaps of the most excellent Earl of Fingall."[7] In all, a total of £1,700 was raised.[8]

Up to this point there had never been a mention of the place where Cobbett proposed to run for parliament. The *Examiner,* friendly with the Westminster incumbents, Burdett and Hobhouse, first declared that Burdett (who had not been on speaking terms with Cobbett since 1817) proposed to contribute to Cobbett's campaign and, three weeks after the carrot had been proffered, warned Cobbett that he would face certain defeat if he should be a candidate for Westminster.[9] In May 1826, when it was still uncertain whether dissolution would be that month or in the autumn or even early the following year, Cobbett declared for Preston, Lancashire.[10] Preston, a cotton manufacturing town with a population of about 25,000, had an illusory attractiveness: It had a wide franchise, one of the widest of any English borough, and an active group of reformers who had sent a delegation to greet Cobbett at Liverpool on his return from America in 1819.[11] The two seats at Preston had been divided in the past between the whig Earls of Derby and the tory "corporation and manufacturing interest." Hence, one seat was filled from 1796 to 1812 by Lord Stanley, son of the twelfth earl, and from 1812 to 1826 by a nephew of the earl, while the other seat had been occupied since 1802 by a member of the Horrocks family, principal owners of a Preston cotton mill employing a large number of those eligible to vote. The two interests had traditionally presented a united front against any third candidate, spending on the election of 1820 more than £11,000, of which £8,000 went to the public houses of Preston. In 1826 the corporation decided it would no longer officially participate in any more expensive elections, and the coalition was dissolved. Cobbett's opponents were the whig E. G. Stanley, grandson of the earl, and John Wood, a barrister on the northern circuit, son of a Liverpool merchant, who ran as an independent.[12]

Cobbett made a preliminary sortie on May 15 when he visited Preston with his twenty-six-year-old son John, Sir Thomas Beevor, and several other friends. John sent home an account of their reception:

We made our triumphal entry at 6 o'clock this evening, in an open barouche from Liverpool. Such an immense, such a dense mass of people you never beheld! The Gr. [governor] was, with difficulty, got into the Inn (the Castle Inn in the market place, a very fine open space.) He took a little wine and water to drive down the dust he had swallowed in the entry, and then stepped up to a window in a bow front of the House. There he was received by really the largest meeting that I ever beheld, and he made a noble, beautiful speech of ¾ of an hour long; pleased them all mightily, and then dismissed them till tomorrow night at the same time, when he and Sir T.B. are to make them grand speeches, developments [?] and their adieu for this time; for we start off Wednesday morning. Since the speech and since tea, Sir T.B. and I have been out a little way on the Manchester road. In our way, we have been assisted by the weavers, and with two in particular we had considerable talk: they tell us coolly that (provided the master-manufacturers remain in their present quiescent state) *we are certain of success*; and they instanced their own dwellings, saying one of them, that, out of seven dwelling in that house, all will vote for us; the men said, that, out of eight, seven would vote for us, and the eighth too, most likely. We are certainly hearing of the ill-success of Wood in the canvass: such as, in a house of 9 voters, yesterday, when he asked for votes, he was told they were all reserved for Cobbett. He said something against the Gr. but was answered, that that was all calumny, etc. etc. etc. Our colour is light green and white. Wood's is green; but there must be green. It is the independent colour.[13]

Cobbett had no sooner returned to London after his three-day exploratory tour of Preston than it became known that parliament would be dissolved almost immediately, with an election to follow in June. Cobbett was back in Preston on May 29. This time he brought his whole roster of sons – all four of them – as well as a small group of friends; Sir Thomas Beevor came directly from Norfolk. As the Cobbett party approached Preston, they were enthusiastically greeted in Chorley, Bolton, and Bamberbridge. At Walton they were met by the procession ("preceded by a band of music") which was to accompany them into the city.

The crowd was much more numerous, and far more excited than it had been

Portrait of Cobbett by Adam Buck. Adam Buck (1759–1833), a skilled portrait painter of the period, painted a number of the notable figures of the time, including Sir Francis Burdett, Mary Anne Clarke, and Henry Hunt

on any former occasions. A greater proportion of the assemblage, too, carried green branches, the size and thickness of which made them, in many instances, to be borne with difficulty. Amongst the flags which decorated this procession, the most remarkable was one of a very considerable size, of a cylindrical shape. On one side was a full length figure of Mr. Cobbett. On another side was seen Britannia weeping, a lion prostrate with a trident through his head. In another compartment, John Bull appeared with the debt on his back, and he was almost sinking under the weight, whilst death was striking at him, and he bleeding at every pore. Hope with her anchor, however, was by. The following verses, from Cowper's "Table Talk," were handsomely written under the several devices: –

And all his country beaming in his face . . .
No sycophant or slave that dared oppose
Her sacred cause, but trembled when he rose;
And ev'ry venal stickler for the yoke,
Felt himself crush'd at the first word he spoke.
Such men are rais'd to station and command.
When Providence means mercy to a land,
He speaks and they appear; to him they owe
Skill to direct, and strength to strike the blow;
To manage with address, to seize with power
The crisis of a dark decisive hour.

When the carriages had arrived at the Castle Inn, the multitude had increased to an extent beyond all power to enumerate them.[14]

That evening Cobbett spoke from the windows of the Castle inn to an audience of several thousand. But his candidature was not a mere local affair; the talk was published in London and appeared in Paris in a French translation.[15] Cobbett was everywhere cordially received as he began a house-to-house canvass of the town in the ten days preceding the commencement of polling.[16] Perhaps things were going too well, for in the next week two negative developments occurred which were hardly the result of coincidence. The tories, who had previously evidenced no interest in the election, suddenly announced a last-minute candidate: Robert Barrie, captain in the royal navy and resident commissioner at Kingston, Ontario. Cobbett's suspicions regarding this action were almost certainly correct: Preston had a large catholic population who would have to disqualify themselves if asked to take the oath of supremacy. Stanley and Wood, who were pledged to catholic emancipation, had agreed with Cobbett not to demand the oath; but Barrie, being a tory, could do so – and he did, thereby eliminating many votes that would have gone to Cobbett.[17] And the master manufacturers did not "remain in their present quiescent state," as John Cobbett had phrased it; they made it clear to their employees that Cobbett was not someone they could tolerate.[18]

When the polling began on June 10 it was apparent that still another obstacle had been created. Barricades had been erected in the streets leading to the polling place so as to create four long chutes or pens – one for the voters of each of the four candidates. Constables with staves were stationed at the point where the voters entered the chutes and at the other end so as to control access to the poll clerk. The constables thus regulated the flow of voters. A system of voting by tallies was followed, which meant that the constables admitted ten voters for one candidate and then ten for another and so on (later changed to four voters, then to one), but the operation of the system depended on the integrity of the constables and those who directed their actions.[19] The voters sometimes stood in the open chutes for as long as an hour waiting their turn. During that period they were subjected to harassment by lawyers for the opposing candidates who attempted by cross-questioning to establish a basis for disqualification.

These arrangements were the responsibility of the mayor, who, in this pre-Pickwickian era, bore the Pickwickian name of Nicholas Grimshaw. To Grimshaw and the other returning officers, Cobbett and his supporters protested against the polling by tallies, "which is unknown to law," the browbeating of the waiting voters by lawyers for opposing candidates, the enforced delays which kept the voters waiting for long periods, the "flagrantly partial" system of admitting voters, and the practice of closing the polls early when Cobbett had rounded up adherents ready to vote for him.[20] At one point Cobbett had 130 voters "actually sworn, and waiting with their certificates in their hands for the purpose of being polled," but only 16 of that number were permitted "to come up to be polled, while you caused the rest to be kept back from the polling bar by the actual force of constables and others, acting under your authority." On the third day a party of the first dragoon guards were brought in, for which Cobbett saw no use "except that of terrifying my voters, and preventing them from exercising their rights."[21] On the ninth day of the election with five more to go and only a third of the electors voted, Cobbett decided it was useless to struggle further against such odds. He ceased bringing voters up to the polls.[22] When they were closed on June 27 the vote stood at Stanley, 3,041; Wood, 1,982; Barrie, 1,657; and Cobbett, 995.[23] Stanley had polled more votes than any candidate in the history of Preston. Cobbett however, had stood first in the number of "plumpers" – voters who, eschewing the right to cast one vote for any two candidates, chose to assert their unadulterated devotion to one candidate only. Thus Cobbett had 451 plumpers; no other candidate had as many as 100. The strength of the other three candidates was in the number of split votes they received: almost every time an elector cast a vote for Wood or Barrie (between whom there was great rivalry) he also cast another for Stanley. Those voting for Stanley cast a second vote for Wood or Barrie. By an arithmetical exercise which reweighted the number of single and split votes cast, Cobbett convinced himself that his "own voters" outnumbered those of any of the other candidates; but he was wrong.[24] However, he was comforted by the assurance he received from counsel in London that the election could be upset on review by the House of Commons special committee dealing with contested elections.[25] And there were other facts that salved Cobbett's ego. During his personal canvass before the polls opened, he had been promised more than 2,000 votes from eligible protestant electors, which would have given him the second seat in preference to Wood; he was therefore confident that the illegal practices complained of were responsible for his defeat.[26] In addition to the incidents cited by Cobbett in the written complaints submitted to the mayor, it was apparent that the other candidates were guilty of illegal treating. A Preston resident writing about the event at a later date declared that "the expenses of some of the candidates were enormous, far exceeding those of any previous contest. Almost during the whole election, the town presented a complete saturnalia."[27]

The continued enthusiasm of the mass of people for Cobbett, even after the election had ended, allowed him to leave Preston as though he had been a victor.[28] The crowds that escorted him out of the city were greater than those that had hailed his entry the month before. Ten to fifteen thousand persons, marching to the music of a volunteer band, accompanied his carriage beyond the boundaries of the town. At Blackburn, ten miles away, he was greeted by a crowd equally large who pressed around his open carriage. "Such huzzaing, such shaking of hands, such congratulation, such praises, such blessings, from hundreds and thousands of lips!" The handshaking there and at Bolton left Cobbett, the next day, unable to tie his own cravat. In Manchester even greater crowds were encountered: "not less than twenty or thirty thousand people," and the local authorities, fearing another Peterloo, forbade a public address. Cobbett, notwithstanding all, returned to London in a good mood, although out of sorts with the editor of the generally friendly *Morning Herald*, who thought Cobbett should have defied the Manchester authorities and, even worse, referred to him (now sixty-three) as "an old man," which Cobbett thought wholly unsuitable for one of his vigor. He put the case with his usual pungency, suggesting that he was young enough to catch the offending editor "by one of those things he calls legs, and toss him over the fence from Piccadilly into the Green Park." Cobbett's protest against the Preston election was not carried through to conclusion. Although it was filed promptly, eventually it had to be dropped because one of Cobbett's sureties failed to come forward with the bond required by the rules of the House of Commons.[29]

The general election of 1826 made no great change in the complexion of the government or in its direction, but such change was not far off. For in 1827 the long, harsh reign of Lord Liverpool came to an end. His administration had suffered substantial losses since the queen's affair in 1820. The principal villains of that piece and of the oppressive legislation that preceded it had dropped off one by one. Sidmouth was the first to go. He retired as home secretary in 1821 and left the cabinet in 1824. The hated Castlereagh took his own life in 1822, and was replaced as foreign secretary by the more flexible

Canning. And finally Liverpool suffered a stroke in 1827 and resigned the premiership, ending one of the longest terms in history as prime minister.[30] As though the nation had had enough of such servitude, Liverpool's unbroken term of fifteen years was followed by seven changes of leadership in eight years. Canning's brief ministry, from April 1827 to his death in August of that year, was followed by the even briefer service of Lord Goderich ("Prosperity" Robinson), who remained in office for four months. Wellington's three-year term from January 1828 to late in 1830 was succeeded by the three-and-a-half-year term of Lord Grey. Melbourne took over in July 1834, Peel in December 1834, Melbourne again in April 1835. Most of these changes reflect the restlessness of the times, which left its permanent mark in the remedial legislation adopted by parliament. The first of these was the grant of catholic emancipation.

The hero of the war for catholic emancipation – a war that was finally won in 1829 – was Daniel O'Connell, the "liberator," whose similarity of temperament to that of Cobbett may explain the alternate bouts of admiration and contempt that characterized their years of association. He was a tall man, "expanded and muscular – precisely such as befits a man of the people" – and portly as he grew older. He had "a strong understanding and stronger feelings"; he had "singular clearness, promptitude, and acuteness," with powers of persuasion that enabled him to "make the worse appear the better reason." His language was "often coarse and seldom elegant." His thoughts had "too much of the impatience of conscious strength to submit to orderly disposition"; it would be utterly unnatural in such a man to be other than violent. While he claimed he was the "best abused" man in the world, one who knew him well suggested he was the "best abusing" man. He was

singular, not merely in the vigour of his faculties, but in their extreme variety and apparent inconsistency; and the same may be said of his character. The elements of both were so many and diverse, that it would seem as if half a dozen varieties of the human species, and those not always on the best of terms with each, had been capriciously huddled together into a single frame to make up his strange and complex identity.

"He" above was O'Connell as described by one of his close associates, but the comments would have been equally applicable to Cobbett.[31]

That O'Connell, as an Irish catholic and a barrister, should be sympathetic with the plight of his country and his religion and should resent the inferior status prescribed for catholic barristers requires no explanation. Cobbett's interest is not so apparent. It began with his concern for the safety of England and the cost of garrisoning Ireland to insure that safety (in 1800 the population of Ireland was more than half that of England), but as he studied the facts this pragmatic concern very early expanded into compassion for the Irish people and indignation at the injustice of their treatment.[32]

O'Connell as a young man in his twenties (he was a dozen years younger than Cobbett) had opposed the union with England that had been agreed upon in 1800, and since that date had been an advocate of catholic emancipation; that is, of the elimination of statutory provisions which prevented catholics from holding certain positions and from exercising certain civil functions. A catholic serving in the army could rise as high as colonel, but was not eligible to become a general or field marshal. A comparable disability existed in the navy. Catholics could not sit in either house of parliament. Catholics in England, but not in Ireland, were disqualified from even voting for a member of the House of Commons. They were also ineligible to become sheriffs or to hold municipal office or to become king's counsel or judges or members of the privy council.[33] Prejudice against the catholics had been so strong, particularly among the older generation of Englishmen, that the proposal to remove only the trifling army and navy disability had led to the downfall of the whig ministry of All the Talents in 1807 and provided the fuel for a tory "no popery" campaign in the parliamentary election that immediately followed. In 1801 Pitt had run afoul of an obdurate George III on a similar issue. Equally strong feelings on the Irish side led O'Connell and his adherents to regard catholic emancipation as a panacea for the woes of Ireland.

Cobbett saw the issue in quite different terms. He readily agreed that it was ludicrous to exclude Irish and English catholics from the highest positions in the military services (particularly while Hanoverian catholics were not excluded).[34] His complaint was not that catholic emancipation did too much, but that it did too little. The cause of disaffection in Ireland – what made that country such a dangerous neighbor – was that the people were year after year living on the edge of starvation while huge quantities of food produced there were being exported to England; they were ruled by a rich, mainly nonresident, protestant aristocracy that owned most of the land; they were forced, through the tithe system, to support a heretical protestant religious establishment of more than a thousand clergymen, many of whom, like the aristocracy, lived outside Ireland. Cobbett's solution was forthright: The protestant hierarchy should be eliminated, both civil and clerical ("unestablishing by law that church which has been by law established"); the tithes should be abolished; a poor law system should be established to provide the necessities of life for the Irish paupers, and it should be supported by rates levied on the landowners as in England.[35] "No efficient measure of defence can be taken without first doing justice, without first giving freedom, to the catholics of Ireland."[36] The mere elimination of the civil disabilities of catholics, allowing them to be generals as well as colonels, allowing them to sit in parliament and to become mayors, would benefit only the upper classes, not their starving countrymen. It was a decent thing to strike down these disabilities, but it was ridiculous, Cobbett saw and said, to claim that this would solve the Irish problem.[37] In April 1826 there were 1,800 individuals in the north parish of Cork who had not more than one meal in forty-eight hours. "The merits of the question itself," Cobbett stated, "lie in a very small compass." What would the "putting of a dozen lords into the House of Peers" do toward putting "meat, bread and beer into the bellies" of the working people of Ireland?[38]

The Irish issue, perpetually bubbling on the back of the stove, was brought to a boil by O'Connell when he created the Catholic Association in 1823 as a political pressure group and provided the sinews of war for the association by creating the "catholic rent" in the following year, to which all good catholics were expected to contribute, if no more than a penny a month. Shortly money was pouring in at the rate of £1,000 a week. The program aroused the religious and social passions of the country, uniting for the first time the catholic aristocracy, the catholic peasantry, and the catholic priesthood.[39] The events that ignited the passions in Ireland did not go unnoticed in London, where the home secretary, Robert Peel, who knew the Irish well as a result of a six-year term there as chief secretary, watched the developments with increasing alarm. When parliament met on February 3, 1825, the king's speech expressed regret that "associations should exist in Ireland, which had adopted proceedings irreconcilable with the spirit of the constitution, and calculated, by exciting alarm, and by exasperating animosities, to endanger the peace of society."[40] This was promptly followed by a bill to outlaw the Catholic Association.

A large deputation of Irish emancipationists headed by O'Connell came to London in February to oppose the bill and to support legislation for catholic emancipation. The day after O'Connell arrived in London, he called on Cobbett, and he, as well as other members of the deputation, consulted with Cobbett from time to time thereafter.[41] The publication of Cobbett's *History of the Protestant "Reformation"* in 1824 had made him, according to a speaker at a Dublin meeting of the Catholic Association, "the most powerful advocate the Catholic cause ever had." The London *Morning Post* expressed the thought somewhat differently: "It is notorious that whenever, during the last twenty years, a political hurricane has swept over England,

Cobbett has uniformly lent himself to widen its range and quicken its fury."[42]

Cobbett warmly supported the strong line taken by the Catholic Association. "They know well that the history of the whole world contains not a single instance of oppression being put an end to by the *humility* of the oppressed." Yet inevitably the bill for putting down the Catholic Association, after parliamentary debates totalling 2,580 inches of newspaper space, or almost 18 square feet ("equal to that of a good large four-post bedstead"), was enacted and became law on March 9.[43]

In the meanwhile, a bill for emancipation had been introduced in the House of Commons by Sir Francis Burdett.[44] *The Times* made it known that two "wings" were to be attached to Burdett's bill: The catholic clergy in Ireland were to be supported by payments from the British government, and the 40-shilling freeholders of Ireland, who now had the right to vote in parliamentary elections, would be disenfranchised; the vote would be allowed only to £10 freeholders – five times the existing qualification.[45] The bill passed in the House of Commons on May 10, but a week later was voted down by the House of Lords. Cobbett had denounced Burdett for his part in the affair as soon as the purport of the legislation had been made public: Burdening the English taxpayer with the cost of supporting Irish clergy was wholly unjustified while Irish tithes were being applied to support the protestant clergy, and the proposed disenfranchisement was abhorrent to the fundamental precept on which the reform movement stood. Cobbett also reproved O'Connell for his participation in a plan which would subject the priests of his own religion to the control of the English government and take away the vote from 300,000 of his countrymen.[46] He gave a full account of O'Connell's several meetings with Cobbett in London when he was warned first against the blandishments and flattery he would receive from the "devils" he would have to deal with, and later against the course he was pursuing in taking Burdett's advice instead of Cobbett's. The cause of the fiasco, Cobbett asserted, had been O'Connell's inordinate vanity and selfish ambition for a silk gown and a seat in parliament; he was the dupe of men far more clever and cunning and of much greater experience than himself; no, on further thought, O'Connell was "not the victim, but the practiser of duplicity."[47] To these charges O'Connell provided a fumbling answer, first claiming that the wings had been justified, since they would benefit rather than injure the catholic interest, then claiming that the wings had been approved by his fellow deputies Bishops Doyle and Murray, then claiming he had been misquoted, and at last acknowledging that he had been wrong and would thereafter oppose the two provisions which Cobbett, joined by leading Irish catholics, found so objectionable.[48]

In the meantime, O'Connell's henchman John Bric launched an ad hominem assault on Cobbett in which many of the past accusations against him (including his borrowing from Burdett a dozen years before) were featured.[49] O'Connell himself, on being confronted with Cobbett's charges, commented: "What a strange creature it is! If I had leisure, I think I would laugh a little at him by way of reply."[50] Cobbett proceeded to make it plain that if any laughing was to be done, it was to be done by him and not by O'Connell. The *Political Register* of September 24, 1825 was devoted wholly to a three-act play written by Cobbett entitled *Big O and Sir Glory: or, "Leisure to Laugh"*. The "Big O" was, of course, O'Connell, and the "Sir Glory" was the baronet who in an exuberant moment had been called "Westminster's pride and England's glory" by one of his admirers, a bit of hyperbole which Cobbett never let him forget. Three days after *Big O and Sir Glory* appeared in London, the first act was reprinted in the *Dublin Morning Post*, where it was in such demand as to enable the vendors to exact "from one to five shillings for each paper remaining in their hands."[51]

The principal characters in Cobbett's play, in addition to the name parts, included Anna Brodie (representing *The Times*) and the editors of several other papers, as well as certain hangers-on of O'Connell and Burdett. Burdett's associate Francis Place, the former tailor, appeared as "Peter Thimble." It was not the sort of play that could be acted, and there was nothing in it that was new. The central theme was the involvement of Burdett and O'Connell in the emancipation bill and the resulting charges and countercharges, in the course of which Cobbett allowed himself the pleasure of working off old and new grievances. Burdett was pilloried for his stinginess, his indolence, and his early relations with Lady Oxford; O'Connell, for his deception, his arrogance, and his vanity. Cobbett himself appeared in the third act of the play as the hero: "A very mild and placid, patiently-enduring 'Old Fellow'." He dealt in high style with some of the retaliatory accusations that had been levelled against him by John Bric, who was unkindly referred to as the "foul discharge from the flatulent bowels of cormorant vanity."[52]

O'Connell's acceptance of the wings had, no doubt, been a serious blunder. For a man of less ability, it might have proved fatal to his career. "Nothing is so unpopular as prudence in Ireland," wrote one of its patriots, suggesting the corollary that nothing in Ireland is so popular as the lack of prudence.[53] In any event, O'Connell pushed on indomitably, forming the New Catholic Association in July 1825 to replace the one that had been banned earlier that year and returning to the collection of the catholic rent just as if nothing had happened in parliament. The catholic rent, flowing in a never ending stream, had far greater significance than would appear on the surface. When the *Morning Chronicle*, which had been "the bitterest enemy" of emancipation in 1824, changed its tune in 1825, Cobbett suggested that the editor of that paper might have been "touched, as it were, with the finger of grace."[54]

The new association demonstrated in the general election of 1826 that it could control the vote of the Irish freeholder even againt those landlords who had traditionally directed their tenants in the ballotting for county members. One antiemancipation candidate after another went down to defeat as the freeholders, marching to the polls under the eye of the village priest, deserted their landlords.[55] In 1827 and 1828 renewed efforts were made by Burdett on behalf of emancipation, despite Cobbett's predictions (which once again proved true) that the ministry would never allow a Burdett-sponsored bill on this subject to get through parliament.[56] The 1827 motion lost by a small margin in the House of Commons; the 1828 motion was decisively defeated in the Lords. It took a series of seemingly unrelated events to get the ministry to bring in a bill that could succeed. The first of these events occurred several days after the House of Lords had turned down the 1828 bill, when a major change took place in Wellington's ministry, a change which was ultimately to lead to both catholic emancipation and passage of an act for parliamentary reform. When Wellington became prime minister in January 1828, he had included in his government some of the more liberal tories – former followers of Canning, who had died the year before. Chief among these was William Huskisson, secretary for war and colonies. As a result of a contretemps with the duke, Huskisson left the cabinet on May 28, 1828. He was followed by Palmerston, Earl Dudley, and Charles Grant.[57] Grant's replacement as president of the board of trade was Vesey Fitzgerald, member of Parliament from county Clare. This meant that Fitzgerald would have to stand again, in accordance with the practice of the time, but there seemed to be no serious problem of reelection. Suddenly came the startling announcement that O'Connell would become a rival candidate. He stoutly asserted his legal opinion (contrary to what had been universally assumed) that if he were elected he would be legally entitled to take a seat in parliament without renouncing his religious beliefs, and would proceed to do so. Cobbett, who instantly forgot all the harsh words exchanged between the two, was delighted by the announcement and by O'Connell's smashing victory, brought about by the Irish priests and

Cobbett and Burdett: "A *Character*-istic Dialogue." It is not likely that Cobbett and Burdett had any conversation after 1817, but Doyle enjoyed portraying this imaginary discussion. Cobbett: "Being much in want of a *Character* I make bold Sir F— to ask you for one – it appearing that your benevolence in this way embraces all sorts of Criminals, you cannot consistently refuse *me*!" Burdett: "I cannot do any thing for you! – Your *Character* is already *Registered*!" The reference to Burdett's benevolence to criminals may relate to his friendship with the Irish nationalist Roger O'Connor

their marching parishioners, who voted for "the cross" in preference to their landlords. When the election ended on July 5, parliament was still in session, and while O'Connell immediately used his franking privilege as a member of parliament to get a letter off to his wife, he remained in Ireland, making no effort to take his seat as he had promised. Once more Cobbett's praise was replaced by gall: O'Connell's sole interest was to get "a share of the common spoil" instead of providing the confrontation that could bring about a downfall of the present government.[58]

But O'Connell did not have to go to London to get what he wanted; his victory, standing alone, had a profound impact on the administration. "The organization exhibited is so complete and so formidable," the defeated Fitzgerald wrote to Peel, "that no man can contemplate without alarm what is to follow in this wretched country."[59] The tension steadily increased as great assemblages of peasants, "organized in semi-military fashion, with banners, music, green sashes, and cockades," gathered throughout the country. Leveson-Gower, the Irish chief secretary, wrote to London recommending military preparations: Ireland should be considered "as on the eve of rebellion or civil war, or both." Although Peel for years had been a leading opponent of emancipation, he now saw that expediency demanded a retreat, and the iron duke, who had demonstrated more than once the wisdom of retreat, agreed. For months, while strict secrecy was maintained, Wellington and Peel tried to convince the king of the need for concession. Not until January 1829 did they get his grudging consent. Thus most members of parliament were taken by surprise when the king's speech at the opening on February 5, 1829 recommended a "review of the laws which impose civil disabilities on his Majesty's Roman Catholic subjects."[60] This signalled the end of the struggle. On April 13, 1829 the bill for catholic emancipation brought in by Peel became law. It was accompanied by legislation incorporating one of the two original wings – that which raised the franchise from 40s. to £10.

"Here then," wrote Harriet Martineau, "we have witnessed the close of one of the most important controversies which ever agitated society in any age or country."[61] O'Connell had secured what he wanted, or what he thought he wanted, and for a time was the hero of Ireland. Irish catholics were now able to serve in parliament – O'Connell eventually commanded forty of the hundred Irish votes in the Commons. And catholics were eligible for appointment as king's counsel. (O'Connell alone, among the prominent Irish barristers, was denied that honor.)[62] For this victory, which Cobbett thought hardly worthy of the name, Cobbett was entitled to a large share of the credit. No one had done more to break down protestant prejudice than had Cobbett in his *History of the Protestant "Reformation"*, in his numerous *Political Register* articles extending over a period of twenty-five years, and in the speeches he had made around the country in which he bravely denounced "no popery" without regard to the impact of this traditionally unpopular issue. He minced no words. In 1826 he had told a Norwich audience that it was disgraceful that "no popery" had been chalked on the doorway of their cathedral; that it was base and cowardly to attack those who professed the religion of their ancestors.[63]

Cobbett was not satisfied with catholic emancipation, because of the conditions which accompanied it and because it had done nothing for the misery of the people. He had fought the disenfranchisement to the last: "I do not wish to see rich catholics let into power, while poor catholics are deprived even of the rights that they now enjoy."[64] One cannot help wondering how much hardship and heartbreak might have been avoided if, at this point, the emancipation had followed Cobbett's solution of ridding the country of protestant domination, of abolishing the tithes used to support the protestant clergy, and of levying on the land to provide relief for the Irish poor.[65] Yet although Cobbett did not get what he wanted, and O'Connell did, they soon agreed to a reconciliation. In May 1829, the month after the bill had been passed, they shook hands to signal the end of their enmity – at least for a time.[66] In this they displayed another similarity: They were quick to fight and quick to forgive; to fight at slight provocation and to forgive without rancor; and so they continued alternately fighting and forgiving until Cobbett's death in 1835.

The catholic emancipation produced some side effects which had important consequences on the issue of parliamentary reform. First, the Irish catholics in parliament under O'Connell's leadership increased the numbers who could be counted on to vote for reform. Second, the Peel–Wellington decision to yield to expediency shook the tory party to its foundations. So bitter were some of the tory reactionaries against this betrayal of the protestant interest that they helped to bring down the Wellington government (already weakened by the loss of Huskisson's followers), and made it possible for the whigs, who were pledged to reform, to return to power after more than twenty years out of office.[67] Symbolically, the owner of a Duke of Wellington public house in Nottinghamshire took down "his sign of the Noble Premier and publicly burnt it."[68] The tory control of parliament, which had continued unbroken since 1807 (and, except for 1806–7, unbroken since 1784), lasted only twenty months after passage of the Emancipation Bill. Entry of the catholics into parliament and the fragmentation of the tory party were not the only events which brought the whigs back into power. George IV died on June 26, 1830 ("I can find no one thing to speak good of, in either the conduct or character of this king," wrote Cobbett) and was succeeded by his steady-going and popular sailor brother, the Duke of Clarence, who took the throne as William IV.[69] July brought the French revolution of 1830, in which the tyrannical Charles X was replaced by Louis Philippe with such appealing restraint and good taste as to cause the *Edinburgh Review* to predict that "the battle of English liberty has really been fought and won at Paris."[70] England itself was ripe for change; it had never recovered from the disruption that had followed the end of the Napoleonic wars. "The period from 1815 to 1830 was one of deep depression," wrote the economic historian L. C. A. Knowles. Even as late as 1835 exports from the United Kingdom were still below the level of 1815, and "it was not until the early years of the second half of the nineteenth century that agriculture experienced once again what might be called prosperous times."[71] In Cobbett's practical terms, "cauliflowers last June, were sold at two-pence each, which used to sell for nine-pence or one shilling at the same time of the year. No wonder that we see, all round London, market-garden land covered with dark thistles and couch grass."[72] After two bad harvests, the English countryside was in a state of near-rebellion. In June 1830 hungry laborers in Kent started burning barns and ricks; by August they were breaking threshing machines; by September the turbulent reign of Captain Swing was well under way.[73] "Revenge for thee is on the Wing / From thy determined Capt. Swing," read one of the more cheerful of the many threatening notes received by farmers and landowners.[74] Thus, the admission of catholics to parliament, the breakup of the tory party, the death of George IV and the succession of William IV, the French revolution of 1830 and the spread of the spirit of rebellion into Belgium, the distress in the British economy, and the rural uprising all combined to create an atmosphere that made the return of the whigs inevitable.

On October 26, 1830, the day of the opening of parliament, Wellington was pelted by the London mob. When reform was mentioned as a means of redressing the grievances of the people, Wellington stiffly replied that he saw no way to create a legislature "equal in excellence to the present," and that no measure of reform would be proposed by the government so long as he was prime minister. Two weeks after he had delivered this death warrant, Wellington was out of office.[75] His tory administration was succeeded by a whig government under the leadership of Lord Grey, whose open advocacy of reform dated back to 1792.

Within a few hours after Grey assumed office, he announced that efforts would immediately be made to "relieve the distress which now so unhappily exists in different parts of the country"; that outrages and excesses wherever perpetrated would be suppressed with "severity and vigour"; and that a measure for reforming "the representation" in parliament would be submitted, the king having given his permission, but that it would not include "any of those fanciful and extensive plans which would lead, not to reform, but to confusion."[76]

The distress mentioned by Lord Grey had been well documented in the *Political Register*. For a year prior to the start of the incendiarism Cobbett had been calling attention to a new cycle of increasing hardship. "The state of the country is this," he wrote in May 1829:

The labouring people, whether in agriculture, handicraft, or manufactures, are in a state of half-starvation, from one end of England to the other; farmers cannot pay, have not paid, more than sixty per cent., on an average, of their Lady-day rents; corn (taking the six sorts together) is now, notwithstanding the last short crop and bad harvest, seven per cent. cheaper than it was last year at this time, after a good crop and good harvest; foreign commerce is in so wretched a state, that freights are at about a fourth of what they have been on an average of the last ten years.[77]

Throughout the balance of 1829 and on into 1830, issue after issue of the *Political Register* reported growing suffering and distress. Cobbett warned that while soldiers might restrain the soft people of the towns, they could not keep order among the hungry rural laborers:

The country people, less intelligent and less talkative, are accustomed to all that hardens man; their hands are hard as sticks; they bear cold like cattle; they live detached in lanes or amongst woods; they are accustomed to move about in the dark, and are not easily frightened at the approach of danger; they have been used to eat meat, they are thoughtful, and are rendered resolute by suffering. Each man lives near about where his grandfather lived; every one hears of the change that has taken place; and, above all things, every man and woman and child old enough to understand any thing, looks upon his parish as being partly his; and a sufficiency of food and raiment he looks upon as his inheritance. Never, let what will happen, will these people lie down and starve quietly.[78]

The wave of machine breaking and burnings of ricks and barns that began in east Kent in the summer of 1830 spread westward into Sussex and Surrey. By the time Lord Grey took office as prime minister in November, Cobbett reported that fires were "now blazing in twenty six counties out of forty England contains." A few days later he reported that a great part of parliament had "gone home to look after their houses and farms."[79] The disturbances were accompanied by demands for better administration of the poor laws in the case of those who were unemployed, and for higher wages in the case of those who were working. Both objectives were accomplished on a wide basis. The farmer employers often displayed sympathy for the plight of their workers; acting together, they successfully forced reductions in tithes from both clerical and lay tithe owners, making it easier for the farmer to pay a decent wage.[80]

Lord Grey's promise that any "outrages" would be put down "with severity and vigour" was more than adequately fulfilled. Men convicted of acts of violence were hanged in twelve counties. Another 500 or so were sentenced to transportation. In Hampshire alone over 100 were sent off on prison ships bound for Australia and a life of exile from their homes and families.[81]

A commonly held view among members of the establishment, both whig and tory, was that the fires did not originate with the distress of the farm laborers, but were being instigated by "persons whom that distress did not affect." First Peel and then Grey made this claim late in November 1830.[82] In at least one instance fires were reported after "two respectably dressed men who were travelling in a barouche" had passed by. Another claim was that "foreigners" were at the bottom of the trouble.[83] It did not take long – only a matter of weeks after the assertions of Peel and Grey – before Cobbett was named as instigator of the troubles. On December 16, Arthur Trevor, member of parliament for the rotten borough of New Romney in Kent, a violent opponent of reform, asked Sir Thomas Denman, the new attorney general, whether a certain diabolical publication had come under his notice, and whether he intended doing anything about it. The diabolical publication was identified as "Cobbett's Register." A week later Trevor moved that the attorney general be ordered to proceed against Cobbett, who was accused of "exciting the population to disturbance and discontent . . . it was to such publications that the first French revolution might be mainly attributed."[84] Several days later "the bloody Old *Times*" reported that a farm laborer, Thomas Goodman, sentenced to death for having set five fires near Battle in Sussex, had "made a full confession of his guilt, and attributes his untimely end to that notorious demagogue, William Cobbett." Cobbett had lectured in Battle a fortnight before Goodman's first fire. The words of the confession read: "I, Thomas Goodman, never should af thought of douing aney sutch thing if Mr. Cobbet Cobet had never given aney lactures i believe that their never would bean any fires or mob in Battle nor maney other places if he never had given aney lactures at all." Cobbett lost not a moment of denouncing the "pretended statement" of Goodman as a fraud: The confession had been taken down by "a parson, and that is quite enough with regard to the truth of the report." The parson, moreover, lived in Crowhurst, twenty miles from Lewes, where Goodman was imprisoned, suggesting that he had gone to Lewes for the purpose of soliciting a statement that might implicate Cobbett. The *Times* story accompanying the "confession" stated that the first fire destroyed the property of the landlord of the George inn at Battle, "who had refused Cobbett the use of his principal room for the purpose of delivering his lecture." To this Cobbett retorted that the "story about the room at the inn at Battle having been refused me, is sheer falsehood"; that he had never applied for it or any other place there. Then, in quick order, Cobbett pointed out that the fires began in east Kent, where Cobbett had not been for years; that they began three months before he visited west Kent; that the fires in west Kent started before Cobbett had gone there.[85]

The week after Cobbett published this convincing reply, *The Times* reported a second "confession" from Goodman, who had been transferred from Lewes to the jail at Horsham. There Goodman stated to three magistrates that Cobbett had said: "it would be very proper for every man to keep gun in his house . . . that they might prepare themselves in readyness to go with him when he called on them." Cobbett answered this new accusation by showing that at his trial Goodman said that "he could not account for the feeling that prompted" his acts, "except that he was goaded to their commission by an irresistible impulse." The gun story seems to have been an evolutionary development from Cobbett's statement at Battle that every man capable of bearing arms was entitled to have a vote.[86]

The declarations of Peel and Grey that "instigators" were behind the violence had been made late in November 1830. Trevor's charges against Cobbett came in the middle of December; the confessions of Goodman were made late in December and in the first week of January 1831. In the midst of these, word came from Sir Thomas Beevor that a Norfolk vicar had been going about with a story that Cobbett's connection with the fires had been established, and that he had absconded. When this was traced, it turned out that it had originated with the Marquis of Blandford, who, obviously embarrassed by the disclosure, explained that he had only repeated the gossip that "was very general in the House of Commons and in the different Club Houses." At the same time, John Benett, member of parliament for Wiltshire, a confirmed enemy of Cobbett, accused him on the floor of parliament of being "at the bottom of the commotions."[87]

On February 17, 1831 the grand jury at the Old Bailey, at the instance of the attorney general, returned an indictment charging Cobbett with seditious libel. The charge was based on language in the article singled out by Trevor from the *Political Register* for December 11, 1830:

But without entering at present into the *motives* of the working people, it is unquestionable that their acts have produced good, and great good too. They have been always told, and they are told now, and by the very parson that I have quoted above, that their acts of violence, and particularly the burnings, *can do them no good*, but *add to their wants*, by destroying the food that *they would have to eat.* Alas! they know better: they know that one thrashing-machine takes wages from ten men; and they also know that *they* should have none of this food; and that *potatoes and salt* do not burn! Therefore, this argument is not worth a straw. Besides, they see and feel *that the good comes,* and comes *instantly* too. They see that they *do* get *some* bread, in consequence of the destruction of part of the corn; and while they see this, you attempt in vain to persuade them, that that which they have done is *wrong.* And as to one effect, that of *making the parsons reduce their tithes,* it is hailed as *a good* by ninety-nine-hundredths even of men of considerable property; while there is not a single man in the country who does not clearly trace the reduction to the acts of the labourers, and especially *to the fires;* for it is the terror of these, and not the bodily force, that has prevailed.[88]

The article itself, some twenty pages long, was headed "RURAL WAR."

The trial was held at the Guildhall on July 7, 1831 before Lord Tenterden and a special jury requested by the crown.[89] Despite the special jury, the scene was more encouraging than it had been in 1810. The former Chief Justice Ellenborough, the offspring of a bishop, was overbearing; Tenterden, the son of a hairdresser, was mild-mannered.[90] Similarly, the present attorney general, Sir Thomas Denman, was universally regarded as more agreeable than Sir Vicary Gibbs. He described Cobbett as "one of the greatest masters of the English language who has ever composed in it," but Cobbett, who refused to exchange compliments, claimed that he had "never met with any thing so insufferably stupid as the document [the indictment] . . . drawn up by a Whig Attorney-General."[91]

Cobbett had decided to defend himself once more, although he was attended by his solicitor, E. C. Faithfull of Staple Inn, and accompanied by three of his sons and three close friends: Sir Thomas Beevor, William Palmer of Bollitree, Herefordshire, and Joseph Blount of Hurstbourne Tarrant, Hampshire. The moment Cobbett entered the court, crowded to suffocation with two to three thousand spectators, "there was a great and general clapping and cheering for some time." Cobbett, turning around and addressing himself to the audience, said: "Be patient, gentlemen, for if truth prevail, we shall beat them."[92]

Cobbett's victory, for such it turned out to be, was one of the high points of his career. The *Star,* an evening paper of small circulation, captured the spirit of the occasion: "The proceedings at Guildhall may be regarded either as a trial of Mr. Cobbett, instituted by the Whig Administration, or as a trial of the Whig Administration, conducted by Mr. Cobbett. In this respect it will be ever-memorable."[93] Cobbett's attack on the whigs was delivered under nearly ideal conditions. Lord Tenterden, a confirmed tory, was not likely to be offended, and Cobbett had a unique audience. He had subpoenaed as witnesses the chief ministers of the whig cabinet: the prime minister, Lord Grey; the lord chancellor, Henry Brougham; the home secretary, Lord Melbourne; the privy seal, Lord Durham; the foreign secretary, Lord Palmerston; the secretary for war and colonies, Lord Goderich – who were required to listen while Cobbett lectured them on their shortcomings.[94] The whigs, he charged, claimed affection for the liberty of the press, but in the seven months they had been in office they had carried on more state prosecutions than had the tories in the preceding seven years. The whigs gained great credit for patriotism and for being lovers of freedom of the press by voting against the 1819 acts imposing restrictions on publications, but when they came into office they made no effort to repeal the acts; instead, they made use of them: "He's no traitor," quoted Cobbett, "he has committed no treason, but treason lay in his way and he picked it up." The whigs had not brought actions for libel against their "desperate defender," *The Times,* although that paper had called borough members of parliament the "hired lacqueys of public delinquents," nor against "the other dead tools of the Whig Government," the *Morning Chronicle* and the *Courier,* which in May 1831 had described the judges opposing the whig reform proposals as "degraded," acting "in disregard of decency," and improperly interfering in politics in a manner that would justify impeachment.[95]

The Goodman case was skillfully used to support Cobbett's claim of a "whig conspiracy" against him. With the help of a declaration signed by 103 persons who had heard him talk at Battle, including a farmer whose barn had been burned by Goodman, Cobbett established that he had not advised anybody "to have a gun, and to be prepared to go with him: that he did not utter any words having a tendency to urge people to set fire to property." When he called Lord Melbourne to the witness stand, Cobbett asked him why the government had pardoned Goodman. Denman objected, and the judge agreed, that the question was "irregular and illegal," thereby creating the exact impression that Cobbett wished to create: that Goodman had been saved from the gallows in return for his "confession" implicating Cobbett.[96]

As to the language of the indictment, Cobbett claimed that the quotation from the *Political Register* had been taken out of context, pointing with glee to the attorney general's use of a fragment beginning with the word "But":

I now come to the garbling of the Attorney-General: but I may be wrong; it might not be his garbling; it may be the learned gentleman's ordinary mode of writing. I am sure, gentlemen, that *you* have never seen a letter beginning with the word "But." "But" is a word which grammarians call a conjunction, and it is used for the purpose of joining words or sentences to one another. The Attorney-General, however, has chosen to begin his extract with a "but."

The language immediately preceding that selected by the attorney general had expressed Cobbett's disapproval of the use of violence: "Out of evil comes good," Cobbett had written, following this with the sentence "We are not, indeed, upon that mere maxim, 'to do evil that good may come from it'." Cobbett could not have intended the laborers to destroy the property of the farmers for whom they worked, as he had stated in the article that the farmers were not the cause of their distress – the fault lay in the tithes and heavy taxes. The issue of the *Political Register* on which the charge of libel was based included a letter from Lord Sydney in which he implored the laborers to join heart and hand in suppressing the fires. And finally, Cobbett blasted the prosecution's case out of the water when he put Brougham, the lord chancellor, on the stand to prove that as recently as December he had asked for the right to publish Cobbett's 1817 "Letter to the Luddites" on behalf of the Society for the Diffusion of Useful Knowledge "for the purpose of putting an end to the riots and fires." Denman as a leading member of that society almost surely winced when Cobbett declaimed: "My learned friend has called my writings 'false, scandalous, and seditious' and a Society of which he is a member has borrowed my book with a view to publishing it!"[97]

Thus Cobbett's character witnesses came as an anticlimax. His old friend the Earl of Radnor, who had voluntarily appeared without Cobbett's request, to provide him moral and practical support, testified that Cobbett was not a person likely to excite the working classes to outrages against their masters or anyone else, and similar conclusions were voiced by several other friends of Cobbett's who had accompanied him to court.[98]

Cobbett's speech had lasted more than four hours. It ended with a final blast of eloquence directed at the whigs. They had always been tyrannical; "they were always the most severe, the most grasping, the most greedy, the most tyrannical faction whose proceedings are recorded in history."[99] They hated Cobbett because for twenty years he had "insisted upon the sort of reform that we must have; and they are compelled already to adopt a large part of my suggestions, and avowedly against their will."

It is their fears which make them attack me, and it is my death they intend. In that object they will be defeated for, thank Heaven, you stand between me and destruction. If, however, your verdict should be – which I do not anticipate – one that will consign me to death, by sending me to a loathsome dun-

479

Cobbett in 1830–1. This lithograph of a rather amateurish painting attributed to George Cooke, an American artist, was the one Cobbett described as representing him "in the dress that I wore at the 1831 trial." It seems possible that the clothes are those which Cobbett wore when he called on Queen Caroline in 1821: "A claret coloured coat, white waistcoat, and silk stockings, dancing pumps and a powdered head." Anne to James, Jan. 17, 1821 (Nuffield)

geon, I will with my last breath pray to God to bless my country and curse the Whigs, and I bequeath my revenge to my children and the labourers of England.[100]

The trial ended shortly after six in the evening, when the jury was sent out to deliberate. As the hours passed, the majority of the spectators left for home, but several hundred waited in the courtroom all night long. At a little before nine in the morning the weary jury sent the judge a message saying that they could not agree on a verdict, "six being of one opinion, and six of another." They were, accordingly, discharged, and Cobbett walked away a free man.[101]

Charles Cavendish Fulke Greville noted in his diary:

They have made a fine business of Cobbett's trial; his insolence and violence were past endurance, but he made an able speech. The Chief Justice was very timid, and favoured and complimented him throughout; very unlike what Ellenborough would have done. The jury were shut up the whole night, and in the morning the Chief Justice, without consulting either party, discharged them, which was probably on the whole the best that could be done. Denman told me that he expected they would have acquitted him without leaving the box, and this principally on account of Brougham's evidence.[102]

The victory was commemorated in a manner of Cobbett's own design. Below an engraving of himself "eighteen inches long by thirteen inches wide and which is sold for ten shillings," he inscribed in his own fine handwriting (also engraved) the story of the prosecution, giving the names of the judge, the attorneys, the members of the whig cabinet, and the jurors, together with the principal facts of the case – all in one sentence about 400 words long. Suitable for carving on an obelisk, it began: "This portrait represents me in the dress that I wore at the Trial, before the Lord Chief Justice, Lord Tenterden, and a Special Jury, in the Guildhall of the City of London, on the 7th day of July, 1831, in the second year of the reign of King William the Fourth."[103]

23 · The Reform Act

It is unquestionably true, that the mind of the whole country, the tax eaters excepted, is fast coming round to the cause of reform. Misery is a great teacher.

IN NOVEMBER 1830, when a whig administration pledged to reform took office under the leadership of Lord Grey, it was far from clear that it would be able to redeem that pledge to any substantial degree. There was no agreement even among the leaders of the party, much less the rank and file, on what reforms should be made. Grey himself was a question mark; after his abortive attempts at reform thirty years before, he had "kept public expression of his views to very general terms."[1]

The indecision among the whigs was characteristic of the entire reform movement. The quadrumvirate of 1807, Cartwright, Burdett, Cobbett, and Place, had been split up by the quarrels between Burdett and Place in 1810, between Burdett and Cobbett in 1817–18, and between Burdett and Cartwright in 1819. The Burdett–Place breach was healed sometime between 1817 and 1819, but Place simultaneously rendered himself persona non grata to Cobbett. Whatever unifying force existed among the four leaders was extinguished when the old major died in 1824. With him also died the *Black Dwarf*, which he may have subsidized.[2] Place, never a figure of public importance, had quietly allied himself with the philosophical radicals led by Jeremy Bentham, whose views and those of his followers were being elucidated by the *Westminster Review* founded by Bentham in 1824.[3] There were changes too among those who had been fringe figures in the past. Cobbett's disciple, Hunt, who had only been in the background in the earlier years, had become a major independent force as a result of the Peterloo affair of 1819. William Hone, after delighting half the nation and enraging the other half from 1815 to 1821 with his political lampoons, had been lost to the reform cause when he took to less controversial subjects following the death of Queen Caroline. Richard Carlile ceased to publish his paper the *Republican* in

1826 after extended disagreement with Cobbett about religion (Carlile was an atheist), about government (Carlile was a republican), and about sexual relations (Carlile had published an account of contraception as practiced in France, and had endorsed sexual intercourse for unmarried females).[4] While continuing to issue publications objectionable to the government, Carlile undertook a new role in the reform movement in 1830 when he rented the Rotunda, Blackfriars Road, which he made available, for a fee, to various reformers and reform associations. Cobbett, Hunt, Carlile, and others spoke there to large audiences.

The supporters of reform were commonly described, and commonly described themselves, as either moderate reformers or radical reformers.[5] A moderate reformer, very roughly, was one who was not opposed to some type of change in parliamentary representation so long as it was not extensive; it might be nothing more than the elimination of one corrupt borough. He was opposed to any large expansion of the franchise and almost certainly to the secret ballot, which was regarded as a particularly iniquitous innovation.[6] A radical reformer usually favored, as a minimum, universal manhood suffrage, annual parliaments, and the secret ballot.[7] The wholesale elimination of rotten boroughs was taken for granted and often not specifically mentioned in reform programs. But some radical reformers favored far more drastic changes, such as suffrage for women as well as for men, the abolition of the peerage, the elimination of the monarchy, and the redistribution of property.

Cobbett called himself a radical reformer.[8] He believed in annual parliaments, universal manhood suffrage, and the secret ballot, but made no secret of his willingness to accept something less.[9] He did not favor giving the vote to women.[10] He did not desire to do away with the peerage or the monarchy.[11] He did not favor a redistribution of property.[12] The structure or machinery of reform was of less concern to Cobbett than its product: He wanted a legislature that would deal equitably with the people, removing all existing laws that discriminated against or were unduly burdensome to the poor:

It is a reformation of abuses that is wanted; a real reformation; a reformation that we can *feel*. We want to be able to say, "such and such an abuse *has been reformed*; such or such a robber *has been made to disgorge*, or has been punished; such or such sinecures or unmerited pensions *have been abolished*; such or such taxes *have been repealed*".[13]

The abuses that particularly rankled were those that discriminated against the poor: for example, the tax system which raised most of the government revenues through levies on consumer goods; the game laws which deprived the poor of a source of food in order to preserve the sport of the rich; and the recent changes in poor laws which permitted the employment of assistant overseers with compensation contingent on the savings they could accomplish.[14] "The work of grinding down the people to a state of starvation is too powerful for the delicate nerves of the rich, and is, therefore, delegated to an agent of this description."[15]

The distinction that Cobbett drew was not between radical and moderate reformers, but between true and sham reformers. A true reformer was one whose ultimate goal was the creation of a system that dealt more fairly with the underprivileged on such practical subjects as the taxes, the game laws, and the poor laws. A moderate reformer was no reformer at all, because the changes he was willing to accept in the legislature could not possibly be sufficient to readjust the balance between the powerful and the weak. Even one who professed devotion to annual parliaments, universal suffrage, and the secret ballot could be a sham reformer, or, to use a term which Cobbett often preferred, a "shoy-hoy," the Hampshire name for scarecrow. A sham reformer was one who, regardless of verbal declarations, demonstrated by his actions that he was not wholeheartedly interested in redressing the wrongs that existed in society. He might, perhaps, have joined the cause to gain personal popularity, or to advance the interests of his party, or simply to demonstrate his independence, but whatever the reason it was not the right one unless it was for the purpose of striking down the wrongs suffered by the poor. Accordingly, Cobbett was suspicious of the motives of the whigs in the House of Commons who were most vocal about the need for reform: the "Lord Johns and Lord Charleses" – aristocrats who professed belief in the cause, but whose actions often belied such professions. If Lord John Russell was a true reformer, how could he declare in 1827 that there was "great lukewarmness throughout the country" towards reform owing to the "satisfactory manner" in which the government was conducted?[16] If John Lambton, later Lord Durham, had a genuine interest in reform, why did he fail to evince any interest in the subject between 1821 and 1831?[17]

The new lord chancellor in Grey's cabinet, Henry Brougham, was among those in Cobbett's long list of sham reformers. How else could one view a man who had made a declaration in writing in favor of radical reform in 1814 when he had hoped to become a successful candidate for Westminster, and then a few years later tried to shuffle it off as "a few words spoken at a tavern"?[18] Cobbett had great admiration for Brougham's talents: his industry, his intelligence, his oratorical skills; but he had supreme contempt for Brougham's pandering to the press, his erratic behavior, and his irresponsible tongue:[19]

"It is all flight with him: all hop, skip and jump."[20] Or, in more sober terms, "In this gentleman it is impossible to discover any thing but great ability, without any fixed principle."[21] The whigs Cobbett most consistently admired – a notably small and exclusive group – included Lord Grey, Lord Holland, Lord King, and Lord Folkestone (Earl Radnor).[22] He was ambivalent about Joseph Hume, whom he praised most of the time, but frequently found lacking in the necessary zeal.[23]

Cobbett had more respect for the out-and-out opponents of reform – the Duke of Wellington, for example – than for those he thought were sham reformers, of whom Burdett was Cobbett's prime example. Burdett had voted for the Corn Bill in 1815, although the bill was introduced at the behest of the landowners for the purpose of raising the price of wheat, which necessarily meant increasing the cost of food for the poor. He sat through the 1817 attacks on reformers in the House of Commons and did not speak a word in their defense. He cast his lot with Canning, "sitting with his knees in Canning's back" when the latter became prime minister in 1827, despite Canning's unequivocal declaration that he was opposed to reform and would oppose it to the end of his life "under whatever shape it may appear."[24] Cobbett's conclusion that Burdett had other interests that had a stronger pull on him than the desire to help the poor people of England was amply justified by events. Burdett ended his parliamentary career by relinquishing his Westminster seat in 1837 and reappearing as a tory representing north Wiltshire. Burdett's fellow member for Westminster since 1820, John Cam Hobhouse, dubbed "Sancho" by Cobbett for his adherence to the tall, thin knight (the "Don"), was another sham reformer. During the Westminster election of 1819 he day by day became increasingly expansive in his reform philosophy in order to gain votes.[25] More recently he had voted in parliament for the Dead Body Bill (Cobbett claimed to have scotched it in the Lords), by which the bodies of paupers would be turned over to medical students for dissection – still another example of discrimination against the poor.[26]

Although Westminster was publicly regarded as the hotbed of the radicals, Cobbett claimed that it had become a rotten borough controlled by Burdett and the Rump.[27] Exposing the Rump became as popular a pastime with Cobbett as exposing Burdett. Each year since the historic Westminster election of 1807 in which Sheridan, the whig candidate, had gone down in defeat before the combined forces of Cobbett, Burdett, and Place, the Rump had mounted a "triumph of purity of election" dinner at the Crown and Anchor tavern in honor of Burdett, and, since 1820, in honor of Hobhouse as well. The twentieth anniversary of the event was scheduled for May 23, 1827, less than a month after Burdett had indicated his support for Canning, the avowed opponent of reform. On May 8 the *Morning Herald* carried a notice signed by Cobbett and Hunt announcing their intention to be present at the dinner "in the hope of obtaining an explanation of circumstances, which, in our opinion, indicate . . . a settled design to betray the cause of the people, and to barter the remnant of their liberties for the gratification of the vanity, or pecuniary interest, of those, who have heretofore professed themselves to be the most zealous defenders of those rights."[28]

The joint signature was as surprising as the proclamation itself. Cobbett and Hunt had not been "on terms" since 1822, when they had a public falling out as the result of Hunt's comment about Mrs. Cobbett's inability to keep servants, a comment that appeared in the memoirs Hunt was publishing serially while serving a two-and-a-half-year prison sentence in Ilchester prison for his part in the Peterloo affair.[29] Bitter words were exchanged between the two men. In February 1825, Hunt had sued Cobbett (and lost) in an extremely silly action for libel arising out of an unrelated incident.[30] After this six-year war, the patching up of matters between the belligerents, coupled with a threat of hostile cooperative action against one or both of the Westminster members of parliament, brought a large crowd to the Crown and Anchor tavern on the appointed evening in May 1827: "nearly twice as many as had ever been seen at one of these dinners before." Burdett and Hobhouse with a number of their friends sat at the head table across the top of the room, while Cobbett, Hunt, and their friends sat at a long table next to the right-hand wall. When the health of Sir Francis Burdett was proposed, Cobbett suggested a long (and not too coherent) amendment which related to Burdett's recently announced support of Canning. This was followed by "a yelling, a noise, a hurly-burly" that made it impossible to hear what anyone was saying. When the health of Hobhouse was offered, Cobbett proposed an amendment referring to incriminatory language Hobhouse had used at the anniversary dinner of 1818. This brought another huge uproar and an exchange of words in which Cobbett referred to Hobhouse as "little Sancho." An aroused Hobhouse seized one of the "wands" carried by the stewards at the dinner – "good stout sticks about seven feet long" – and threatened to knock Cobbett down. When this attempt was frustrated, a dozen or more stewards armed with wands and egged on by shouts of "throw him out" advanced on Cobbett. Cobbett's friends met the charge and repulsed the stewards.

Mr Hunt made a *chevaux de frieze* with the chairs turned upside down on that side; and, though, at the beginning of the battle, I had been (not being on my guard) torn off the table with the loss of part of my waistcoat, I was soon surrounded by a body of men, who, if I had pressed it, I verily believe, would have gone and plucked the Baronet from his chair, and tossed him out into the street.

When Cobbett remounted the table to address the crowd following the defeat of the stewards, a new battle took place there, "and down came the table with us all, the crash keeping time with another crash that was going on in the vicinage of the Baronet, just by whose head a butt end of one of his steward's wands had passed, and smashed a pane of glass in the window behind his back."

The baronet left the meeting, and T. J. Wooler took the chair. Hunt had refused to do so, saying that "he would never disgrace himself by sitting in a chair that had been sitten in by Sir Francis Burdett."[31] Then Cobbett left. According to the *Morning Chronicle*, he "was not treated with all the kindness he could wish, but he and his friends bore the pushes and elbows which they received, with comparative meekness. The noise (we cannot say the hilarity) of the evening was kept up to a late hour."[32]

The restoration of good relations between Cobbett and Hunt did not last long. In 1829 they had another falling out, again on a personal matter. But in 1830 the old association was tentatively renewed when Hunt, with Cobbett's support, stood for Preston at a by-election and managed to defeat the incumbent, E. G. Stanley, grandson of the Earl of Derby and future prime minister.[33] By 1831, however, they were again at war.

It was a new generation of agitators outside parliament that came closest to meeting Cobbett's conception of true reformers. As early as 1822, Cobbett came to recognize the need to gain a following of younger men. "Those that are my age will be mere twattlers in eight or ten years' time."[34] As a result, he had increasingly directed his remarks to a younger audience "because it is, it must be, on you, on your opinions, on your resolutions, on your courage, that the result will depend" – "for as to the OLD ones, as to those who have during the last thirty-eight years been bribed, or menaced, or scourged into habitual abjectness, they are, in a moral and political point of view, of no more consequence than the beasts of the field."[35]

By 1830, when Cobbett was sixty-seven (Bentham eighty-two, Burdett sixty, Place fifty-nine, and Hunt fifty-seven), a fresh generation of radical reformers had made its appearance. Most significantly, they, like Cobbett himself, were from and for the lower classes. William Lovett, James Watson, John Cleave, William Carpenter, and Henry Hetherington were among the leaders. All five were still in their thirties. They had mostly grown up on a diet of Cobbett's *Political Register*, and thus were indoctrinated with the history of the reform movement. They were far from bribed or scourged into "habitual abject-ness." All five became leaders in the war of the unstamped press that was waged between 1830 and 1836.[36] All five were active in the char-tist movement that began in 1836. All five, as fighters for freedom, were prosecuted by the government and served prison sentences. Four out of five became editors or publishers of radical newspapers, following in the footsteps of Cobbett.[37]

In keeping with the rising demand for reform, Cobbett established a new publication in July 1830. It was a monthly paper (thereby avoid-ing the stamp tax on newspapers) priced at twopence.[38] Cobbett called it *Cobbett's Two-Penny Trash,* the term which his enemies had contemptuously applied to his cheap publication of 1817. The first issue stated that the purpose of the new paper was to "explain to the people of this kingdom what it is that, in spite of all the industry and frugality they can practise, keeps them poor." The second issue declared: "again and again, I say *reform, reform,* as the sure, and, per-haps the only, means of preserving the institutions and the tranquil-lity, and restoring the happiness, of England." In December 1830 it was reported that "the miscreant Cobbett is read in every cottage where the march of intellect has enabled them so to do."[39] Three months after the first issue of *Two-Penny Trash,* two of the younger reformers began cheap papers of their own which were specifically designed to challenge the stamp tax, as they were published more often than monthly. These were *Political Letters and Pamphlets* at two-pence, published by Carpenter, and *Penny Papers for the People,* pub-lished by Hetherington.[40] Carpenter openly demonstrated his debt to Cobbett by automatically assuming all of Cobbett's pet hates including *The Times,* the whigs, the national debt, flogging, Pitt, Castlereagh, and Arthur Trevor. Cobbett demonstrated his sympathy with Car-penter by accepting advertisements for his publications, and Carpen-ter reciprocated. Hetherington, although a republican who did not acquiesce in all of Cobbett's views, was a confessed admirer. He fre-quently reprinted Cobbett's articles, and endorsed him for parliament as "labourers' best friend – the unrivalled advocate of useful reforms and equal rights for all classes."[41] Following close on the heels of these efforts by Carpenter and Hetherington came a spate of other reform publications, issued both in London and in other large cities, that swept the country like a tidal wave. More than 500 illegal journals were published between 1830 and 1836.[42]

This new wave of cheap reform newspapers led by Cobbett's exam-ple was paralleled by a widespread movement for the establishment of reform societies. In July 1829 Cobbett and Hunt had launched an organization variously called the "Association of Friends of Radical

Reform," the "Radical Reform Association," and the "Radical Reform Society."[43] At a meeting held on September 7, 1829 Cobbett seconded a motion in favor of presenting an address to the people of England "calling upon them to join this Society in its endeavours to obtain a Radical Reform." In "taking the lead in this affair," Cobbett stated that it was important that all who favored the cause should recognize that their enemies were those who wished for a total change in the form of government – that is, the republicans, who could ruin the cause by offending the middle class. He called, therefore, for "an explicit declaration that we do not wish for any government other than that of King, Lords and Commons. Real Commons, of course."[44] While the enemies were not specifically named, it is plain that Cobbett was referring to Carlile and his followers.

Two months after this plea for local support, Thomas Attwood, a Birmingham banker and a paper money man (whom Cobbett nevertheless admired), organized a "General Political Union of the Industrious Classes, for the Protection of Public Rights," more commonly known as the Birmingham Political Union.[45] The organization held its first public meeting in January 1830, at which it set forth its objects and operating regulations. The Cobbett formula was followed. A demand for reform was accompanied by a specific disclaimer of any intention to change the monarchy or the House of Lords.[46] Cobbett heralded the event as an epochal step: "We see, at last, then, the middle class uniting with the working classes. Everywhere . . . I have endeavoured to show the necessity of such union."[47] By the end of 1830 political unions of much the same character had been formed in more than fifteen towns.[48] Political societies, cooperative societies, trade union societies sprang up everywhere. Two of these whose interest was primarily in reform were formed in 1831: the National Union of the Working Classes, in which Hetherington, Lovett, Watson, Cleave, and Carpenter played leading parts, and the National Political Union founded by Thomas Erskine Perry, in which Place was an active participant.[49]

The reform societies served a double purpose. They provided an efficient mechanism for community action, and they channelled local requests for relief of various sorts into a national campaign for parliamentary reform. Thus, in May 1829, eight months before the Birmingham Political Union had made its first public appearance, the people of Birmingham, meeting in response to the call of Thomas Attwood and his associates, had adopted twenty-five resolutions describing the cause of the current economic distress and proposing certain economic remedies.[50] All but one of the twenty-five resolutions expressed views Cobbett had been promoting over the past fifteen years.[51] But the resolutions said nothing about the need for parliamentary reform.[52] When the Birmingham Political Union was created in January 1830, it adopted a resolution in favor of reform as a means of obtaining the economic relief previously demanded.[53] Until that time, Attwood had not placed a high priority on parliamentary reform, but had contended that the currency issue must be settled first.[54]

To the reform newspapers and reform societies as means of keeping the issue alive must be added a third force: the lecture platform. Until 1829 almost all of Cobbett's talks, except those associated with elections, had been in rural communities and addressed to farmers and farm laborers. In October 1829 he announced his intention of delivering a series of lectures to the people of London, although he added that he had no "ambition to shine as what the Irish call an *orator*. I have the most thorough contempt for speech-making, having observed throughout my life that the most voluble speech-makers are the greatest fools."[55] The talks would be made at irregular intervals – three were to be given in late November and December, and others, after parliament had convened, as the need developed. "In short, I mean, during the ensuing campaign, to carry on a constant rivalship with the Collective" – Cobbett's cynical name for parliament since the time that James Perry, editor of the *Morning Chronicle,* had soberly declared that body to be the "collective wisdom of the nation."[56]

The first three talks were delivered on November 26, December 10, and December 17, 1829 in the theater of the Mechanics' Institute. An admission charge of a shilling was made. The lectures were to begin at eight o'clock "precisely"; those expecting to attend were requested to be punctual. All three lectures were well attended and enthusiastically received; although the second, delivered before a packed house of people "in the middling ranks of society" including many ladies, was rudely interrupted by a rowdy group of about forty Irish hecklers whose leaders had to be forcibly ejected – two were lifted up and thrown through the window into the adjoining room – before Cobbett could resume. "The monsters were hired and paid: no doubt of that," wrote Cobbett.[57]

The day following the last of the three 1829 London lectures, Cobbett headed for the industrial midlands accompanied by a daughter and two sons. He spoke in such towns as Derby, Manchester, Liverpool, Stockport, Todmorden, Huddersfield, Oldham, Preston, Leeds, and Sheffield.[58] At Todmorden he for the first time entered a factory. By the end of January 1830 he had travelled nearly 700 miles, and in fifty-three days had made twenty-seven speeches for a total of some sixty-one hours.[59] What seems to have surprised Cobbett more than anything was the respectability that reform had suddenly assumed. His talk at Liverpool was attended by the principal people of the city, and Cobbett modestly declared that the applause he received was "beyond the merits of any man." At Stockport the stage box was occupied by the town's magistrates. At Oldham the audience included the "most opulent people." At Leeds "even the Tory *Intelligencer* gave him six columns." Cobbett was back in London for the opening of parliament in February 1830. He delivered two more lectures there, and, seeing no sign of softening in the Wellington government, immediately took to the road once more. He began by revisiting friends in Norfolk, then went on to Cambridgeshire, to Hull, Lincoln, Leicester, Wolverhampton, and Shrewsbury, for what he called his eastern and midland tours.[60]

It is easy to fall into the error of believing that with all this restless campaigning, Cobbett was the typical hardened politician, enjoying the admiration of the crowds, thinking of nothing but swaying his audience. But about the time one is ready to conclude that Cobbett was like other men, he demonstrates that he was not. From Horncastle, in Lincolnshire, in the midst of his eastern tour, Cobbett sent back this report for insertion in the *Political Register* of April 17, 1830:

There is *one deficiency*, and, that, with me, a great one, throughout this country of corn and grass and oxen and sheep, that I have come over during the last three weeks; namely, the want of *singing birds*. We are now just in that season when they sing most. Here, in all this country, I have seen and heard only about four sky-larks, and not one other singing bird of any description, and, of the small birds that do not sing, I have seen only one yellow-hammer, and it was perched on the rail of a pound between Boston and Sibsey. Oh! the thousands of linnets all singing together on one tree, in the sand-hills of Surrey! Oh! the carolling in the coppices and dingles of Hampshire and Sussex and Kent! At this moment (5 o'clock in the morning) the groves at Barn-Elm are echoing with the warblings of thousands upon thousands of birds. The thrush begins a little before it is light; next the black-bird; next the larks begin to rise; all the rest begin the moment the sun gives the signal; and, from the hedges, the bushes, from the middle and the top-most twigs of the trees, comes the singing of endless variety; from the long dead grass comes the sound of the sweet and soft voice of the white-throat, or nettle-tom, while the loud and merry song of the lark (the songster himself out of sight) seems to descend from the skies. Milton, in his description of paradise, has not omitted "song of earliest birds." However, every thing taken together, here, in Lincolnshire, are more good things than man could have the conscience to ask of God.[61]

Cobbett returned to the groves at Barn Elm in time to receive, almost simultaneously, the exciting news of the French uprisings of July 1830 and the equally exciting news ("all England is stirring") of the heavy losses suffered by the intransigent tories in the English general election.[62] The news from France, he wrote his solicitor, "makes me glad that no boroughmonger would let me have a seat. I shall now have one in a reasonable time, or there will be *no seats for anybody*."[63] So sure was Cobbett of this result that he cancelled, forthwith, a campaign commenced four months earlier for the raising of a £10,000 fund to enable him to buy a seat.[64] To make certain that others were aware of the significance of what had occurred across the channel, he arranged for a dinner at the London Tavern on August 16 to honor the French patriots who had overthrown their tyrannical government. Under his aegis funds were raised for the benefit of the widows and children of those who had died in the Paris street fighting.[65] The day after the dinner, Sir Thomas Beevor and James Cobbett set off for Paris with a letter of introduction from Cobbett to the aged Lafayette, a key figure (as he had been for over fifty years) in one more stirring episode in French history.[66]

As so often was the case, Cobbett set the pace for the reformers. The benefit dinner at which he presided, held on August 16, was followed by similar dinners on the two succeeding nights: one on August 17 chaired by Henry Warburton and one on August 18 chaired by Sir Francis Burdett.[67] On August 23 the Beevor–Cobbett delegation was received at the *hôtel de ville* by the prefect of Paris, attended by Lafayette, representatives of the national guard, and municipal officers. Entertained at dinner by the prefect, they were seated as *corps diplomatique* when they visited the Chamber of Deputies.[68] Five days later a deputation headed by John Bowring, editor of Bentham's *Westminster Review*, presented addresses to the prefect from the London reformers who had met on August 18.[69] Other English liberals, including J. S. Mill, John Roebuck, John Austin, and Thomas Macaulay were not far behind.[70] Cobbett expressed the hope that deputations would be sent to Paris from all the large cities in England where public meetings were held. Even the small town of Lewes in Sussex adopted a resolution extolling the "magnanimous conduct of the brave Parisians," and sent off a delegation to Paris.[71] The author of *The Passing of the Great Reform Bill* wrote: "The feeling of boundless exultation which sprang up in the vast majority of Englishmen is hardly conceivable to us who have known nothing like it. It created a new world. Every class thrilled to it."[72]

Responding to this burst of enthusiasm for freedom, Cobbett announced a proposal to "address the working classes on the subject of the recent events in France and to offer them my advice as to the conduct which they themselves ought to pursue, in order to assist in obtaining a just reform in the Commons' House of Parliament." Eleven lectures were given between August 30 and October 7, 1830 at the theater of the Rotunda. Admission was twopence; the proceeds, after deducting expenses, were for the benefit of the widows and orphans of Paris.[73]

The lectures were taken down by a shorthand reporter – among the few talks of Cobbett that were so recorded. They are remarkable for their clarity and for their use of homely illustration and cynical humor which brought alternate bursts of applause, laughter, and cries of "shame" from his audience. In the eleven lectures, Cobbett managed to cover most of the principal points that made up his philosophy of reform, with particular emphasis on the many examples of legislative discrimination in favor of the landed aristocracy who controlled both houses of parliament: nine-tenths of the total government revenues were derived from excise and customs, and only one-tenth from landed property.[74] A tax was levied on the auction of personal property, none on landed property. No death duties were imposed on landed property, but they were on a merchant's stock and trade. The aristocracy paid nothing for postal services. The revenues to which the lower classes contributed so much were largely expended for the benefit of the aristocracy and their dependants in the form of pensions, sinecures, clerical livings, army and navy commissions, and other government emoluments: the 113 members of the privy council received £650,000 a year of the public money. The public property known as crown lands was leased to the aristocracy at nominal rates: That for which the Duke of Marlborough paid a mere £62 a year was relet by him at £3,000. The privileges of the rich were not, however, limited to tapping the public purse. A law enacted by them in 1820 permitted a landowner to seize a trespasser without a warrant and immediately bring him before a magistrate (a fellow landowner) for summary punishment, but a £100 freeholder was exempted from the law and could gallop horses and hounds through the property of a small farmer unmolested; the farmer's sole remedy was an action for civil damages. The poor law system, originally adopted for the benevolent protection of the poor, had been converted by recent legislation into one designed to save the expenses of the rich, and so on, in a list that stands as a shocking commentary on the concept of noblesse oblige. To the charge of the Earl of Wilton that "the people were beginning to treat the aristocracy with disrespect," Cobbett replied:

What! treat with disrespect those that gave us two admirals for every ship of the line, and one commissioned officer for every five private men? What! treat them with disrespect, two families of whom have received in sinecures, during 40 years, as much as has carried on the whole government of the United States? Treat them with disrespect? That would, indeed, be monstrous![75]

As Cobbett talked to his working-class audiences at the Rotunda, the fires burning in Kent, for which he was shortly to be blamed, were spreading across the county into Sussex and from there to adjoining counties. It was widely believed – and Cobbett believed – that at the opening of the new parliament in October 1830, the duke would come forward with his own reform program to forestall the return of the whigs, as he had done on the issue of catholic emancipation.[76] Hence, the duke's stark rejection of any degree of reform came as a surprise.[77] But once this statement had escaped his lips, it came as no surprise that the tories found themselves out of office in a matter of two weeks. The Rotunda lecturers, led by Cobbett and Hunt, had left little to chance. They maintained constant pressure on the tories by scheduling a new series of radical reform talks nearly every weekday night from the opening of parliament on October 26 until Wellington tendered his resignation on November 16.[78] During this period Wellington was jeered and pelted by the mob, and was forced to seek refuge at Lord Bathurst's house in Downing Street. The king's visit to the City for the lord mayor's dinner on November 9 had to be cancelled. "The Duke was scarcely safe in the streets, and the King's popularity was evidently on the wane," wrote Hobhouse of the situation on November 4. "Sir James Graham," Hobhouse added "thinks a revolution almost inevitable." By the time Grey was installed as Wellington's successor, the principal Rotunda talks had stopped, and so had the street disorders. The rick burning continued in the country, but in London Hobhouse stated that by November 22 "the course of life . . . ran pretty much as usual."[79]

On taking office, Grey immediately appointed a four-man committee to draft a reform bill, which, he specified, should be "of such a scope and description as to satisfy all reasonable demands, and remove, at once, and for ever, all rational grounds for complaint from the minds of the intelligent and independent portion of the community."[80] It was, in brief, to be a permanent solution. The committee consisted of Lord Durham, Grey's son-in-law, as chairman, and Lord John Russell, James Graham, and J. W. Ponsonby (later Lord Duncannon). The bill they prepared was introduced in the House of Commons by Russell on March 1, 1831. It exceeded the expectations of everyone – radical reformers, moderate reformers, and anti-reformers – in its draconian treatment of the rotten boroughs. Brougham had once proposed that five of such boroughs be disenfranchised. A whig lawyer of prominence said that the disenfranchisement of fifteen would be as good as a republic. Russell's bill disenfranchised, wholly or in part, 107 of the boroughs, which returned a total of 168 members. The seats thus taken away were principally to expand the county membership, while a smaller number were assigned to the unrepresented or underrepresented towns.[81] In the boroughs, every occupier (owner or leaseholder) of a house worth £10 a year was to have the franchise.[82] On the second reading in the House of Commons, the bill passed by a single vote (302 to 301), and would have been lost if it had not been for the Irish contingent. Grey induced a reluctant William IV to dissolve parliament, and in the general election that followed in late April and May, many of those who had voted against the bill lost their seats. General Gascoyne, who had represented Liverpool for more than thirty years, was rejected there after only ten hours of polling. "Nothing could go on worse than the elections," moaned the tory Charles Greville on May 7. "Reformers returned everywhere, so much so that ... we have only to await the event and see what the House of Lords will do."[83]

A second reform bill, much like the first, was approved late in September by a majority of 109. The House of Lords, however, vetoed it. Cobbett expressed the commonly held view that the bishops (who had voted 21 to 2 against the legislation) "were the cause of the loss of the bill."[84]

The action of the Lords was the signal for an explosion. A riot at Derby was not quelled until several persons were killed by the soldiers called in to restore order. The royal castle at Nottingham owned by the Duke of Newcastle was burned out. Three weeks later a Bristol mob went mad, pillaging and burning the bishop's palace, the mansion house, the customs house, the excise office, all three town prisons, four toll houses, and forty-two dwelling places and warehouses. The disorders were put down by military force at an estimated cost of 400 persons in civilian dead and wounded.[85] In October and November 1831, the fires that had burned so fiercely in the countryside during the autumn of 1830 as a prelude to Wellington's departure from the government reappeared. Country papers reported 143 fires in the thirty days prior to mid November.[86] In London, shops were closed and all business was suspended in a large part of the city. Handbills fringed in black and listing the names of the peers who had voted against the bill appeared on the streets. The Marquis of Londonderry was struck off his horse and so badly injured that he had to be taken home by hackney coach. Windows of the Duke of Wellington and Earl of Bristol were broken.[87]

The bishops bore their full share of the odium. In Bristol, as we have seen, the palace was destroyed. The bishop of London discreetly cancelled a scheduled attendance at the rededication of a parish church when it was learned that the entire congregation intended to have "instantly quitted the church" when he reached the pulpit. The bishop of Winchester was hanged in effigy at the top of the market house opposite the palace at Farnham. In Exeter and other places the bishop's effigy was disposed of in a more conventional manner: "Instead of Guy Fawkes, who has for more than 200 years been burned in effigy on the 5th of November, the Bishops have been burnt this year!"[88]

Cobbett and the other radical reformers were made uneasy by the rumors that parliament, which had been prorogued until November 22, would be deferred to a much later date; that Grey was prepared to make substantial concessions to gain approval of the upper house; that he was losing the support of his followers; that he might resign.[89] But none of these proved true. Parliament met early in December, a third bill still in satisfactory form was introduced in the Commons by Russell, and on December 18, 1831 it passed on the second reading with an even larger majority than the time before.[90] With this attended to, parliament adjourned over the holidays. The action of the Commons was the signal for Cobbett to begin another lecture tour of the midlands, thus making sure that there would be no letup in pressure. Between mid December 1831 and the end of March 1832, when he returned home, Cobbett travelled "nine hundred and eighty odd miles. Altogether, I stood upon my legs, speaking, upwards of a hundred and thirty hours; that is to say, more than five days and five nights."[91] Back in London, Cobbett recorded the introduction of the bill in the House of Lords and its slow progress there. Grey himself became the cause of alarm on April 14 when he stated to the Lords that "although he thought fifty-six boroughs were not too many to disenfranchise, and that ten pounds was not too small a sum to which to extend the suffrage, these propositions were no part of the principle of the Bill; and both of them might be altered with perfect consistency with that principle."[92] Cobbett, deeply disturbed by this invitation to water down the bill, immediately printed a letter expressing his concern and sent it off the same night to leading reformers in "every considerable town in England." He urged them to act. "Now, if petitions from *public Meetings* do not instantly *pour in*," ended Cobbett's letter, "I am convinced that Ministers mean *to raise the suffrage*. I have thus *warned you*: I have done my duty, and I hope you will do yours." Petitions did immediately pour in, making Grey more aware than he might have been of the strong feelings against amendment.[93] The opposition in the Lords, which had allowed the bill its second reading by a narrow margin, fell on it in committee. At the first test, on May 7, the government was outvoted on an opposition motion to postpone consideration of the disenfranchisement clauses. Grey and his cabinet played the only card they had left: They advised the king

"Lineal Descent of the Crown." The conservatives were convinced that expanding the franchise and reducing the number of rotten boroughs meant the end of the monarchy. Here Lord Grey uses a "bill" (billhook) to hack away at the timber supporting himself and the crown, while Cobbett (left), Joseph Hume (center), and Daniel O'Connell (right) assist Grey by pulling on the rope, which will bring down both Grey and the crown that they would be compelled to resign unless he would agree to the creation of the number of new peers necessary to carry the bill, perhaps as many as fifty. The king hardly hesitated; he accepted the resignations and called on Wellington to form a new cabinet:

To describe the agitation in London, and the anger of the people against the Lords, the Bishops, Wellington, and particularly against the King, is a task that no tongue or pen can perform . . . to refuse to pay taxes was amongst the mildest of the measures that were proposed at the several meetings . . . A cry for a republic was pretty nearly general; and an emigration to Hanover formed the subject of a popular and widely-circulated caricature.[94]

Placards were posted all over London reading "To stop the duke, go for gold" – an application of Cobbett's long-favored device for bringing down the government by causing a run on the Bank – and on a single day, May 14, the Bank of England paid out nearly a half million pounds in gold. The bishop of Lichfield, who preached at the parish church of St. Bride in the heart of London on Sunday, May 13, had to be spirited away in order to avoid the hostility of the mob.[95] The people of Manchester, in a petition signed by thirty to forty thousand, urged the House of Commons to stop all supplies. "The history of this one week will for ever serve as an answer to those insolent beasts who talk of the people as being nothing," wrote Cobbett. In face of the strong feelings so visibly expressed, Wellington could not get others to join him in forming a tory ministry. The king had no alternative but to recall Grey and yield to his terms.[96] The episode had a chastening effect on the peers; Wellington and his closest followers absented themselves on the final vote so that no new creations were necessary. Thus the bill passed the House of Lords with a substantial majority and became law on June 7.[97] A total of 475 days had elapsed since the date it had been first introduced; throughout that period the country had been in almost constant turmoil. The bill had been watered down in the legislative process, but it still disenfranchised, wholly or in part, eighty-five rotten boroughs.[98]

From the outset of the bill's parliamentary career, the reformers themselves had sharply disagreed on whether it should be supported or opposed. Although the whigs had gone far beyond expectations in the elimination of the small boroughs, they offered nothing on two of the three other most important aims of the reformers, and very little on the third. The duration of parliaments (maximum of seven years) was left untouched; voting was still to be conducted openly rather than by ballot; and suffrage was hardly universal. In the boroughs, the franchise was given to £10 householders, that is, to those paying rent of at least £10 a year, and in the counties there was a moderate expansion beyond the traditional 40-shilling freeholders by extending the vote to the larger tenant farmers.[99] The total number of voters was increased, perhaps by three-quarters, but still only about 635,000 persons in England now had the right to vote, out of an estimated adult male population of roughly 3½ to 4 million.[100]

Cobbett was quite willing to accept Russell's bill despite these shortcomings. "It does not extend so far as my wishes would go; but, as I have always said . . . every sensible man takes what he can get."[101] Hunt, however, belittled the bill when he discussed it in parliament as a member for Preston, a seat which he held from December 1830 to December 1832. Thus, although Hunt had played a conspicuous part in agitating for reform up to the time the bill was introduced in March 1831, his role after that date was a negative one. Hunt's statements in opposition to the bill were seized upon by the anti-reformers in parliament, and he rapidly lost his following in the reform movement, disappearing from the political scene soon after the general election of 1832, when he failed to be reelected at Preston.[102] A final breach between Hunt and Cobbett had occurred early in 1831, ending the off-and-on relationship that had begun more than twenty years before.[103]

John Plamenatz, Chichele Professor of Social and Political Theory at Oxford, concluded that the passage of the bill was due to the efforts of three sets of persons "none of whom liked the others": the whigs who saw the measure through parliament, the Benthamites (contributing the least) who irritated and stimulated the whigs, and the radical agitators who "frightened their opponents into acquiescence." Cobbett and Hunt, Professor Plamenatz added, "did more than any other men to frighten the ruling oligarchy."[104] The credit that Plamenatz accorded to Cobbett and Hunt would have been difficult for any respectable nineteenth-century contemporary, to whom it would have been accepted doctrine that parliament acted only on "rational grounds" as conceived by "the intelligent and independent portion of the community."

The conclusions of Professor Plamenatz contain the following three separate elements, all of which are true, but which require glosses to present the whole truth: that fear carried the Reform Bill, that the fear was experienced by the "whig oligarchy," and that Cobbett and Hunt did more than anyone else to create this fear.

First, fear worked as it did because of twenty-five years of education on the need for reform and its inevitability, creating on the one hand a sense of urgency and on the other a feeling of guilt at the wickedness of the existing system.

Second, the fear experienced was general, affecting not only the

whig oligarchy, but also the tory oligarchy, the lesser members of parliament, the monarch, the farmers, the bankers, the merchants, the
lawyers, even some of the reformers. This generality is illustrated in
many ways. The 1831 election which provided the whigs with such a
large majority is one example, but an even more telling one was the
part played by the Rotunda lectures of Cobbett and Hunt between
October 26 and November 16, 1830 which accompanied the fall of
the Wellington ministry and the return of the whigs after a lapse of
more than twenty years.[105] The leading whig newspaper, the *Morning
Chronicle,* in a surprising article condemning the 1831 libel action
brought against Cobbett by Grey's government, remarked: "we certainly think Ministers are not a little beholden to him for his services
at a very critical time."[106] And is not the same thought expressed in
these cynical lines of W. M. Praed published on December 9, 1830,
shortly after the new cabinet was announced?

> If Cobbett is the first of men,
> The second is Lord Grey;
> Oh must we not be happy, when
> The Whigs are in to-day![107]

Third, the fears arose from the coincidence of many separate
forces: the severe economic distress, the riots and fires, the radical
newspapers, the radical societies, the radical speeches, the uprisings
in France and Belgium, the threatened run on the Bank of England,
the cholera epidemic that swept England in the winter of 1831–2.
One of the major practical contributions of Cobbett and Hunt, and
particularly of Cobbett, who did the thinking for the two, was the
channelling of the responses to all these events into a single avenue –
a campaign for reform – instead of allowing the energies to be dissi-
pated into a dozen separate campaigns relating to the corn laws, taxation, tithes, currency, free trade, poor laws, game laws, and so on.[108]
Credit must also be given to Cobbett and Hunt for excluding from
the mainstream of the movement those who favored the overthrow of
the monarchy and its replacement with a republican form of government. Neither of these contributions increased fear, and both made it
easier to get the legislation accepted.

Turning to the agitation for reform, many individuals in addition
to Cobbett and Hunt are entitled to a share of the credit, and none
have been more generally acclaimed than Thomas Attwood, the Birmingham banker who founded the Birmingham Political Union, and
Francis Place, the man behind the scene in London. Attwood's role
was a peculiar one that invites further study. The tories in the House
of Commons accused the whig government of sanctioning his pressure tactics.[109] These, when examined, suggest that at the Birming-

ham end of the axis, Attwood was astutely stoking the discontent that existed there, and at the London end (with Place's help) was trying to convey the impression that he might not be able to restrain much longer the forces he was attempting to provoke.[110] Place is reported as saying in private that when the Lords threw out the bill in October 1831, there was little real feeling or spirit in the people and the Birmingham Political Union was kept alive only by the subscription of three men who sent £50 apiece and saved it.[111] The protest there against the action of the House of Lords, registered in a huge town meeting held on October 20, "was largely a whig affair and Attwood played no part in it."[112] Further Birmingham meetings were coupled with various rumors: Taxes were not going to be paid; there was going to be a run on the Bank; men were going to be armed by subscription; a national guard (French style) of seven divisions, with officers and colors, was going to be created.[113] These all, from beginning to end, remained rumors. Nothing happened in Birmingham like the machine breaking, the burning, the pillaging, the rioting, the assaults that were happening nearly every day in other parts of the country. Thus, if events in Birmingham played a decisive part in the passage of the Reform Bill, it was a tribute either to Attwood's dramatic abilities or to the imagination of the lawmakers. "The cabinet feared, not what Attwood would do with his army, but that he might lose command of it," commented Michael Brock, and Attwood was sedulous in implanting this view.[114] While Place was telling those in the government that he and Attwood were trying to keep things "as quiet as possible," he was getting out placards which he hoped would cause a run on the Bank of England. Place's account of the incident, in which he gives himself a major share of the credit not only for the placard but also for destroying the duke's chances of returning to office, casually mentions that "some one" (who, he does not identify) had suggested the placard. The "some one," it now appears, was John Fielden, the Todmorden cotton manufacturer, a longtime admirer of Cobbett who was almost certainly aware of Cobbett's numerous articles on how a government could be brought down by a run on the Bank.[115]

To return to Attwood, he came to the reform cause late, and may have been given too large a share of the credit for the passage of the bill by Francis Place and others writing from the middle- and upper-class point of view – and, in one instance at least, for the wrong reasons.[116] When Attwood was honored by a dinner at the Guildhall, George Grote, a fellow banker, praised him for having "divested the physical force of the country of its terrors and lawlessness"! – an appealing image to a banker, but hardly the one that had won the day.[117] Far closer to the truth was the egocentric claim of Cobbett: "I sowed the thoughts; but it was the operations of poor Swing that made those thoughts spring up into action."[118]

Cobbett did not wait for anyone to honor him at a banquet. As soon as the passage of the Reform Bill was assured, he made arrangements to celebrate his triumph, for so he deemed it, at his own party. He announced a "Chopstick Festival" to be held on July 7, 1832 at Sutton Scotney, a small village in Hampshire. "Chopstick" was Cobbett's word for farm laborers. ". . . if they had not resolved not to be reduced to potatoes, and if they had not acted *as they did,* in order to preserve themselves from this state of horrible degradation, Wellington would not have been turned out, Grey would not have come in, the Parliament would have acted upon Wellington's insolent declaration, and we should have had no Reform Bill at all."[119] Sutton Scotney was selected because it was the place where 155 farm laborers had signed a petition to the king in the autumn of 1830 describing the misery of the people in their part of the country and calling for a radical reform. One of the signers, who had walked sixty miles to deliver the petition to the king in Brighton (but there was told to take it to the home secretary), and his brother were subsequently transported for life for allegedly being part of a hungry mob that went from place to place in search of relief, and had accepted or taken money.[120] The festival was to honor these men and the other signers of the petition. The date, July 7, was selected because it was the anniversary of Cobbett's victory in the 1831 libel trial. On the day appointed, some six or seven thousand persons joined the celebration, including "the petitioner chopsticks, all in white smock-frocks, and blue ribbons in their hats."[121] Cobbett contributed three capital rounds of beef weighing 40 lb each, 141 loaves of bread, and a 72 lb ham which Cobbett had bought in Nottinghamshire and which Mrs. Cobbett had cooked. Huge quantities of mutton, beef, and bacon were contributed by others. There were 250 lb of puddings.[122]

Cobbett did not return to London after leaving Sutton Scotney. Instead, he travelled around Hampshire and into Sussex, staying with friends, talking everywhere, and everywhere basking in the glory of his achievement among the country people eager to pay homage to the man who had "done more" – he had said so himself – "in making a reform than any other thousand men in England."[123] Cobbett's exuberance was almost certainly enhanced by the decision he had made to remove his main residence from the despised wen. For at the time the Reform Bill was passing in the House of Lords, he had agreed to rent a farm of 160 acres at Normandy near Ash, Surrey, only seven or eight miles from his birthplace at Farnham.[124] The lease at Barn Elm farm had expired in 1830, while that at Kensington would run out in March 1833, and its four walled acres had never been much more than a toy to Cobbett. Normandy farm became the last of Cobbett's farming adventures. It was where he died in 1835.

Two-Penny Trash, which had served its purpose, was terminated with the issue of July 1832, and Cobbett turned his attention to the task of being elected to parliament under the new act. He had already acquired two solid prospects. In August 1831 a committee of prominent reformers of Manchester had invited him to become a candidate for that city.[125] He had gone there in December 1831 and given six talks in which he had stressed the long hard road that still lay ahead: The bill would accomplish nothing of itself; it only "furnishes the means of making the reform" through the enactment of further legislation.[126] These further changes were embodied in fourteen propositions which Cobbett submitted to his audience.[127] If the electorate did not believe in these changes, they should not vote for him.

The Manchester talks were followed by a dinner held on January 30, 1832 presided over by John Fielden of Todmorden, "one of the greatest of the great manufacturers in this country" and one of the most progressive.[128] Six months later Cobbett received a second flattering offer. He was invited to become a candidate for the borough of Oldham (six or seven miles north of Manchester) under unusual circumstances: Fielden, who had been first approached, had stated that he would allow himself to be nominated "on the condition, which he made very binding," that Cobbett should be his colleague, or, if not, that Cobbett should be in parliament for some other place. Of the 1,200 to 1,500 electors at Oldham, 500 had signed a requisition on the first day it was open for signature, declaring in favor of Cobbett and Fielden.[129] Oldham had been allocated two members of the House of Commons under the new law, the same number as Manchester, although it was one-sixth the size of Manchester. Cobbett accepted the invitation. But he would also, he disarmingly explained, continue his candidacy at Manchester, which was his first preference.[130]

Thus, in August 1832, with the Chopstick Festival and triumphant tour of Hampshire and Sussex behind him, Cobbett proceeded to Manchester and Oldham to solidify his status as candidate. En route he stopped off at Birmingham to debate the currency issue with Attwood before a public audience.[131] Then he spent two weeks in Manchester and Oldham canvassing the electors. In mid September he went on to Newcastle, Durham, and Hexham and a few points in between, speaking almost every evening to large audiences. He reached Edinburgh on October 14 and allowed nearly a month to tour southern Scotland. It was his first visit, and despite his long abuse of the Scots, the bluff old reformer was received with banners and bands and public dinners, ending with the one in Glasgow where he was hailed as "the most extraordinary man of any age, or of any country."[132] By the time he returned to London at the end of November, he had been away eighty-seven days, had travelled 1,464 miles, and had delivered seventy-eight speeches.[133] Those who heard Cobbett for the first time were surprised to observe his geniality and mild manner: "The most sarcastic and provoking things oozed out at his lips like milk or honey."[134]

Two weeks later Cobbett was headed back to Manchester and Oldham for the first elections under the new Reform Act. The polling at Manchester and Oldham began on the same day – December 13, 1832. At each place there were five candidates for the two vacancies. In Oldham it became apparent at the outset that the electors for Cobbett and Fielden numbered four times those for the nearest rival, and they were officially declared victors at the end of the first day. In Manchester the polling continued for at least three days. At noon on the first day it became known that Cobbett had won at Oldham, "so that," Cobbett explained, "it was naturally to be expected that the electors of Manchester who intended to vote for me, would either transfer their votes to the candidate that they liked next best, or that they would not vote at all." At the end of the second day, Cobbett stood last among the five candidates, and he withdrew. Forgetful of what he had said five months before, Cobbett declared that he had only accepted the Manchester invitation because it had come first. "Had the invitation come first from Oldham, I should certainly have declined that for Manchester."[135]

When Cobbett returned to London at the end of December, he rented a house suitable for the member of parliament for Oldham at 21 Crown Street, 400 yards from Westminster Hall. The family moved there from Kensington by January 29, 1833, the date of the opening of parliament.[136] The problem of suitable attire for Cobbett's debut was turned over to a tailor who plied his trade a few doors from Cobbett's current office at 11 Bolt Court, Fleet Street. The tailor, J. Swain, a regular advertiser in the *Political Register*, was given five days' notice of Cobbett's requirements:

As you are disposed to have the goodness to clothe me for the perilous undertaking; and, as you wish to know what sort of dress I shall like to have; my decision is as follows; to wit:
1. A *black* coat, made *full*, and like a black coat that I have at home; or like the blue coat that I *wear now*, and not like the more fashionable ones.
2. A white washing waistcoat, of which, I suppose, I have enough.

Cobbett on the treasury bench. "You may know a man by the company he keeps."
John Doyle, one of the master artists of the day, drew this sketch of Cobbett sitting
on the treasury bench, consciously unconscious of the ferocious stares of those who
regarded him as an interloper. Cobbett sits next to Althorp, and Stanley (Cobbett's
opponent at Preston and future prime minister) glares at the Poor Man's Friend.
Burdett is at the rear

3. *Black pantaloons,* made not very, very long and big.
In that dress, I shall, I think, *be able to fight the devil, if he should come to meet
me.*[137]

On the first day of the meeting of the reformed parliament, the *Morning Chronicle* reported that "the members assembled here in great
numbers as early as half-past one o'clock. By two o'clock we should

Sketch of Cobbett by Daniel Maclise. Daniel Maclise (1806–70), close friend of Charles Dickens, painted and sketched many of the famous names of the middle nineteenth century – Dickens, Thackeray, and Disraeli, among others

suppose that there were at least three hundred present, which is a much greater number that we ever remember to have seen on the first day at the opening of any former parliament."[138] Cobbett was one of the first to arrive. He asserted himself by doing what no other new member was known to do: He sat down on the treasury bench, traditionally reserved (as Cobbett well knew) for the leader of the house – in this instance Lord Althorp, who, when he arrived, accepted the seat next to Cobbett.[139] The self-educated man who had raised himself from ploughboy to member of parliament, the first ever to do so, sat with one leg crossed over the other, his high hat pulled well down on his head, oblivious of angry stares and as unconcerned as he would have been at his own fireplace.

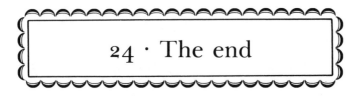

24 · The end

No man has a right to pry into his neighbour's private concerns ... but ... when he once comes forward as a candidate for public admiration, esteem, or compassion, his opinions, his principles, his motives, every action of his life, public or private, become the fair subject of public discussion.

COBBETT HAD extravagant hopes for the reformed parliament of 1833. He thought that the great towns of the north, beginning at Birmingham and ending at Paisley and Glasgow, "will send one hundred men, at any rate, willing and able to plead the cause of the working millions."[1] He looked for solid and serious new men from the lower and middle classes, for "A man with turtle-soup in his belly, and with French wine exhilarating his brain, never yet did his duty towards the people."[2]

A hundred such determined men, or even fifty, could be a decisive factor between the fairly evenly divided whigs and tories. The unreasonableness of Cobbett's hopes was demonstrated as soon as parliament convened. The whigs and tories had a common interest in uniting against the reformers, and those reformers who shared Cobbett's objectives, far from amounting to a hundred or fifty, were never more than a gallant handful.[3] The architects of the Reform Bill had combined a semblance of liberality with carefully thought-out constraints: "the supremacy of the governing class was preserved and was intended to be preserved."[4] Wholly apart from the electoral system itself, an unpaid parliament that remained in session for as long as half the year almost necessarily produced a body of men of financial independence whose first interest was in the preservation of their property. The parliament of 1833 was no exception. It contained 217 sons of peers or baronets, and 500 out of the 658 members could be regarded as representatives of the landed interest.[5] The balance was made up chiefly of merchants, manufacturers, bankers, and lawyers who were opposed on principle to any drastic change in the social or economic system. Under these circumstances, harassment was the only tactic open to the radical reformers.

Cobbett's principal objective on entering parliament was to reduce taxes, and particularly those imposed on the working people: "if a reformed parliament do not reduce taxes before it has sitten a year; and that, too, to very great amount, if nobody else will take the trouble to hang me, I will hang myself, if I belong to that parliament."[6] The battle for tax reduction was fought by the radicals on two fronts: Efforts were made to cut government expenditures of all sorts, including the pensions and sinecures which Cobbett had been condemning most of his adult life, and those efforts were speedily voted down by huge majorities;[7] and efforts were made to effect a more equitable distribution of the tax burden.[8] The landed interests which had been in control of parliament for many generations had seen to it that the bulk of the taxes came from levies on articles of consumption. Where that was not the case, care had been taken to exact as little as possible from the rich. The assessments of large country houses were routinely understated, so that Stowe, the magnificent mansion of the Duke of Buckingham, a palace more than 900 feet long, was assessed an annual house tax of £42 10s. – an amount paid on houses of London merchants worth one-twentieth of Stowe.[9] The freehold property of the landed proprietors was wholly exempted from duties on both legacies and probate, whereas the livestock and equipment of the farmer and the inventory of a merchant were taxed as high as 10 percent, and probate duties had to be paid.[10] When the Duke of Sutherland died, his annual income of £240,000 was passed on to his heirs without a farthing of tax, while the widow of a poor man who left £51 in a savings bank would have to pay £6 or £7 in probate and administration duties.[11] The taxes on leases, mortgages, annuities, promissory notes, receipts, appraisals, deeds, and assignments were all graduated downward, so that the larger the amount the lower the tax rate. The first tax to come off after the end of the Napoleonic wars was the income tax. It took another fourteen years before the tax on beer was removed. During that period the tax on the poor man's beer was 200 percent, while the tax on the rich man's wine was 20 percent. Cobbett's cynically worded motion to alter the stamp tax laws as to "cause, in all cases, the rich to pay . . . duties in the same proportion as the poor" was defeated by a vote of 26 to 250.[12]

The malt tax was a favorite target for Cobbett. It brought approximately £6 million into the treasury, but, according to his computations, the monopoly which the method of tax collection gave rise to resulted in a total cost to the public of about £14 million annually. Despite strong demand for repeal of the malt tax from agricultural communities, it was defeated by a vote of 59 to 142.[13]

Although Cobbett's interest was primarily in farm laborers, he was not indifferent to the growing problems of workers in industry, and strongly supported a bill, introduced by Michael Sadler in 1832 and carried on in 1833 by Lord Ashley, to limit factory work to ten hours a day for all under eighteen years.[14] The claim of the millowners that such limitations would jeopardize the national economy was scoffed at by Cobbett:

Heretofore, we have sometimes been told that our ships, our mercantile traffic with foreign nations by means of those ships, together with our body of rich merchants; we have sometimes been told that these form the source of our wealth, power, and security. At other times, the land has stepped forward, and bid us look to it, and its yeomanry, as the sure and solid foundation of our greatness and our safety. At other times, the Bank has pushed forward with her claims, and has told us, that great as the others were, they were nothing without "PUBLIC CREDIT", upon which, not only the prosperity and happiness, but the very independence of the country depended. But, Sir, we have this night discovered, that the shipping, the land, and the Bank and its credit, are all nothing worth compared with the labour of three hundred thousand little girls in Lancashire! Aye, when compared with only an eighth part of the labour of those three hundred thousand little girls, from whose labour, if we only deduct two hours a day, away goes the wealth, away goes the capital, away go the resources, the power, and the glory of England![15]

Ashley's bill was voted down by a large majority, and those interested in protecting the health of children had to be content with a compromise bill which placed a twelve-hour limit with a sixty-nine-hour week on children under eighteen years. It did, however, provide for a nine-hour limit with a forty-eight-hour week on those under fourteen years. Employment of those under ten years was prohibited, except in silk mills.[16]

The whigs were able to provide further proof that parliamentary reform was meant to stop where it began – with the redistribution of parliamentary seats – and that no general improvement in the lot of the lower classes was intended. In 1833 they introduced, and carried by the usual large majority, the Irish Coercion Bill, "conceived in the spirit of the most absolute government," which attempted to resolve Irish discontent and violence by suspending the Habeas Corpus Act and by providing for trial by martial law rather than before judge and jury.[17] Although fought to the last by Cobbett and other radicals, including, of course, the Irish catholic members of the House of Commons, the government steamroller crushed the opposition. The moguls of the whig and tory parties, those great men who established the policies of the government, were unable to see the wisdom of Cobbett's frequently reiterated advice that the problem would not be solved until parliament decided that Ireland should no longer be ruled by a small protestant minority.

The most hateful of all whig legislation was the Poor Law Amendment Act of 1834, which combined a cold-blooded desire to cut the cost of poor relief with the convenient Malthusian precept that in the long run it was in the interest of the poor that the receipt of relief be made as disagreeable as possible. Under the new law no relief was to be granted to ablebodied persons and their families except in "well-regulated workhouses" to be established throughout England on a regional basis.[18] This was to be the home of those thrown out of work through lack of employment. It was also to be the retirement home of the hand weaver who earned 3s. 9d. a week – less than £10 a year – unless he was able to save enough out of this munificent sum to support himself and his wife in their old age.[19] In the workhouses, distinctive uniforms were to be worn, as in prison; and husband and wife, and parents and children, were to be separated. A spartan diet was to be enforced.[20] The age-old system of local administration of relief by neighbors was to be replaced by a central committee of three men sitting in London. It was an efficient and inhuman bit of legislation designed by well-meaning and insensitive theorists like Edwin Chadwick, and enthusiastically supported by the large ratepayers. It brought down the cost of poor relief by imposing unspeakable hardship on the poor. Cobbett fought the bill during its passage in parliament, and from that time until the date of his death attempted to secure its repeal.[21] The injustice and cruelty of the act were described by Cobbett in a little book published early in 1835: *Cobbett's Legacy to Labourers,* which attributed a large part of the blame for the legislation to Henry Brougham, lord chancellor in Grey's ministry. The book was intended to support Cobbett's efforts to secure a repeal of the new laws, but repeal had to await the action of future generations.[22] The book's title was explained in these words:

I call it a LEGACY, because I am sure, that, not only long after I shall be laid under the turf; but after you shall be laid there also, this little book will be an inmate of the cottages of England, and will remind the working people, whenever they shall read it, or see it, or hear of it, that they once had a friend, whom neither the love of gain, on the one hand, nor the fear of loss, on the other, could seduce from his duty towards God, towards his country, and towards them; will remind [them that] that friend was born in a cottage and bred to the plough; that men in mighty power were thirty-four *years* endeavouring to destroy him; that, in spite of this, he became a Member of Parliament, freely chosen by the sensible and virtuous and spirited people of Oldham; and that his name was

Wm. COBBETT.[23]

Those writing about Cobbett's parliamentary career have declared that he was ineffectual, that the last endeavor of his life ended in failure.[24] In a sense this is true, but it is not the whole truth. It is true that despite his egocentric predictions of what he would accomplish, he was unable to perform the impossible: that of defeating the combined whig–tory majority. It is true also that his speeches were not greeted by cheers. But cheers are hardly a good measure of success: The average whig or tory member of the House spoke to an audience of brothers, brothers-in-law, cousins, ex-schoolmates, boozing pals, hunting companions, fellow club members, and political allies, and was cheered when he said something his friends liked to hear. When something was said that they did not like to hear, the gentlemen of the House utilized the yawn, the cough, the sneeze, the ironical cheer, and other marks of disrespect to make it almost impossible for the speaker to proceed.[25] After Cobbett witnessed the struggles of some of his less hardy colleagues during the first three months of the 1833 session, he wrote:

What is wanted in the House is this: ten men, who care not a single straw for all the noises that can possibly be raised against them; who would be just as insensible to the roarings and the scoffings as they would to the noise of a parcel of dogs howling at the moon . . . The reader is not aware, nor can he have an idea, of . . . what it is to get up in the face of three or four hundred men, nineteen twentieths of whom are anxiously watching for an opportunity of picking some little hole or another in the coat of him who so rises up; while every one of those same men begins cheering the moment a Minister begins speaking against him.[26]

Cobbett himself was not outwardly flustered by the heckling. He spoke slowly and distinctly. "Every word was in its proper place; and there were no disjointed sentences."[27] He made some speeches in the House of Commons which, to a twentieth-century reader, seem as good as those made by men with more experience in parliamentary debate whose utterances were greeted with applause.[28] The value of Cobbett's contribution was not, however, in his oratory, but in having the courage to pry into subjects not ordinarily explored, and to question matters that had ordinarily not been questioned. Thus, his role as a member of parliament was no different from what it had been as editor of the *Political Register,* except that he now had access to more information, he could speak directly to the legislators whose conduct he was criticizing, and he had a potentially wider audience through the medium of the newspapers reporting parliamentary debates. Cobbett's years of probing into pensions and sinecures, which involved naming men and women in high society – an "ungentlemanly" probing, Lord Althorp would have it – was sufficiently embarrassing to both grantors and grantees to cause the eventual discontinuance of the practice of making grants except in return for proved services.[29] There was no magic in the method; it worked only through ceaseless repetition until a firm public opinion was formed. Cobbett made what seems like an exceedingly foolish attack on Peel, moving that the king be asked to remove Peel as a privy councillor for his part in the deflationary legislation of 1819. After an irate response from Peel, Cobbett's motion was defeated by a vote of 298 to 6, and the motion itself, at the instance of Lord Althorp, was expunged from the records of the House.[30] Unlike the Knight of the Mournful Countenance who assaulted a windmill in the belief that it was a giant, Cobbett assaulted a windmill knowing that it was a windmill, and probably did so not because he thought he could win, but because he wanted to demonstrate to the forelock-pulling class from which he sprang that if they were to exercise power they must learn to overcome their deferential attitude toward those in authority. It was "the base part of the people" Cobbett wrote, that looked upon the upper classes as better than themselves. "Now unless this feeling be changed: unless the people be cured of this baseness, nothing that can be done by men, even the most able and industrious and zealous, will ever render them better off than they now are." The great families of England could no longer be accepted as leaders as they had been in the past; they had become nothing more than "a prodigious band of spungers, living upon the labour of the industrious part of the community."[31]

Thus Cobbett's parliamentary career cannot be summarily dismissed as a failure because of the large majorities against him or the lack of cheers accorded to his speeches. More relevant is the extent to which his attacks on the sacred precincts of the ruling classes encouraged those who came after him to throw off their traditional inhibitions, and discouraged ministers from introducing proposals which would be subject to the criticisms expressed by Cobbett. We must credit Cobbett for his influence on future generations or for his percipience, or both, because most of the major remedial legislation relating to state and church urged by Cobbett and opposed by the ministers of the day, except his proposals relating to the debt, were eventually enacted into law by parliament.[32]

Regardless of what Cobbett was able to do in parliament, it is plain that it was less than he had hoped to do. Almost certainly he could have been more effective if he had been well. He had become heavy, and in 1833 experienced a "dreadful short breathing," obliging him "to stop, and to stand still in the street, ten times in going from Crown Street to the House of Commons." His heels "were always swelling in the most odious manner."[33] He was seventy years old when he entered parliament, possibly the most advanced age of anyone entering the Commons for the first time with the object of playing an active part there. The initial session was one of the longest and hardest on record: Night after night the debates continued until three or four in the morning.[34] Many of the money bills in which Cobbett was interested were introduced after midnight: On the evening of April 30, 1833, twenty-four money bills were passed after 3 A.M.[35] To a man in the habit of going to bed at eight or nine o'clock in the evening and rising at four or five in the morning, the burden imposed by the hours maintained in the House of Commons and by the close atmosphere of the old chamber was certain to have its impact on his health. In April 1833, three months after the session began, Cobbett was unable to attend because of influenza. At the end of May he still suffered from a violent cold and hoarseness accompanied by a cough. "I have at times, especially in November and April," he had written a few years earlier, "a constitutional and hereditary cough, which I have had every year that I can remember of my life, and which is always more violent and of longer duration in London than any where else."[36] During April and May 1833 he had to struggle to get himself out of bed and into his seat at Westminster. Petitions poured in to him for presentation to parliament. He conscientiously read pending bills and official reports. For a man who properly performed his duties, parliament was a full-time job, albeit without pay. For a man who was ill, who had obligated himself for the cost of three establishments (a residence in Crown Street, a house in Bolt Court used as an office, and a farm in Surrey), and who had no source of income apart from what he could make by his writing, the demands made by parliament and his other commitments could have been close to torture.

On July 2, 1833, Cobbett was made a member of a select committee to investigate the activities of William Popay, a police spy and provocateur.[37] He arrived home from parliament at two o'clock in the morning. What happened then was enough, coming on top of his other concerns, to precipitate what seems to have been a serious mental breakdown:

I . . . had to creep to my bed without a bowl of warm milk and a little tea in it, which I always wish for in such a case. I found neither bowl nor fire, and nobody but the man to let me in, though there was wife, three daughters, two sons, and two maid servants in the house, all in good beds of my providing. Too happy should I have been, however, if this had been *all*. But, when I got into that bed which I so much needed for rest as well as for sleep, that *tongue*, which, for more than 20 years has been my great curse, and which would have worried any other man to death, suffered me not to have one moment's sleep, after my long fatigues and anxious labours; and, as I saw that this was a mere *beginning* of a month of it, she breakfasting in bed every day, and having the sofa to lounge on, and the park to take exercise in, to provide strength of lungs and the power of sustaining wakefulness at night, I also

saw, that I must give up the affair of Popay, or get out of my house. Therefore as soon as it was light, I called up my man, and decamped to Bolt Court;
and there I remained 'till the day when the king prorogued us.[38]

The family at Crown Street was "wife, three daughters, two sons."
The other two sons were elsewhere: William junior probably at Normandy farm, caring for it in his father's absence, and James living by
himself in London following a falling out with his father in 1831 over
an episode connected with the trial in which Cobbett had scored such
a satisfactory victory over the whig prosecution.[39]

Cobbett refused to return to his family at Crown Street, although
urged to do so. He discharged Mary Ann Blundell, the girl in charge
of the Bolt Court shop, alleging that she was a "vile instrument in the
hands of the Westminster parties" (the family at Crown Street) who
had encouraged her "to be a spy upon me, to insult me and all those
whom I employed."[40] Holed up in Bolt Court, Cobbett was reluctant
to leave, even to visit his farm. This isolation continued long after
parliament had been prorogued in August. At the end of October,
Cobbett wrote a letter in the *Political Register* addressed to his Oldham
constituents stating that he was "a self-devoted martyr to the filth and
stink of this wen," and it was "absolutely impossible" for him to get
away for five days, or ten days, or even for two days, in order to visit
them.[41]

Cobbett's suspicions of a conspiracy against him were heightened
by an especially vitriolic attack on him by the *Morning Chronicle* of
September 21. The article stated that Cobbett's *Political Register* had
deteriorated, lacking "even that raciness and shrewdness which used
sometimes to redeem his malignity and abuse." It claimed that Cobbett had been maintaining himself "by much bad 'book-making'," and
warned him that "his exit from public life is nigh at hand."[42] Cobbett
quickly demonstrated that, whatever else he may have lost, his "raciness" was still intact. Thirty-seven pages of the *Political Register* were
devoted to a saucy reply.[43]

Three months later, in December 1833, Cobbett became convinced
that "the lawyers . . . in their dens called inns of court" (John and
James Cobbett were barristers with chambers in Clifford's Inn) were
saying that the books bearing Cobbett's name were written by his children; that he was an impostor. In an article entitled "The Monsters,"
written on Christmas day, Cobbett made a lengthy denial, relating in
detail the conditions under which he had written each of his publications. How did Cobbett know that the Monsters were spreading this
unbelievable story? He had seen it in "the writing of an eminent lawyer."

Nancy Cobbett in about 1830

However, it is not now that I have discovered the schemes to which I have alluded before. The spreading of this story is only the beginning of an intended execution of the scheme. I cannot swear that my opinion is correct; but it is my firm belief that a scheme has been on foot for a considerable time, by a crafty, round-about, hidden, damnable process, to crush the *Political Register,* and to drive me from my seat in Parliament! . . . The scheme became apparent to me so long ago as about the first of July last; and, from that day to this, to defeat the scheme and blow the conspirators to atoms, has been almost my sole occupation. My constituents of Oldham . . . will now see why it is that I do not budge from Bolt-court.

Continuing, Cobbett asserted that his reply to the attack that had been made on him by the *Morning Chronicle* had been "a flogging by proxy" – it was intended for backs other than that of the editor of the *Morning Chronicle,* "but it served both." These unnamed covert enemies were challenged by Cobbett "to come on to the open assault."[44]

The clue to this world of conspiracy lies in two tangled threads of personal history concerning Cobbett's deteriorating relations with his wife and the perilous state of his finances. Nancy Cobbett, as far as we know, was everything a loving wife should be, except that she was not completely compatible with her difficult husband. She had far more reverence for rank and royalty, once even saying that she thought it would be an honor to be trampled to death by the horses drawing the coach of George III as she saw him ride off to prorogue parliament.[45] She was far more conventional, and wished the children to be sent to schools for their education.[46] She was far more conservative, and seems to have heartily disapproved of Cobbett's tree farming, his way of life on Long Island, and his various experimental projects. She disliked many of Cobbett's rough-hewn friends, and none more than that rascally Henry Hunt who had been so openly critical of her housekeeping.

In May 1827, when Nancy Cobbett was fifty-three years old and possibly subject to menopausal depression, she attempted to cut her throat. The gossip around London was that she had "been on bad terms with her husband for some time, and told him if he went to the Westminster meeting on May 14 [the dinner honoring Burdett and Hobhouse which had been disrupted by the rowdy conduct of Cobbett and Hunt] she would destroy herself. On reading the account of that meeting in the *Herald* she tried to commit suicide."[47] This version was largely confirmed in an unpublished memorandum written by Cobbett in the following year in which he stated that Nancy had committed this "most violent and . . . tragical deed" solely because she had just read in the newspapers that her husband had walked away from the meeting arm in arm with Hunt. Cobbett added that shortly prior to this incident "there was, that which had never happened before under my roof, a family quarrel, not between husband and wife, but between the children, the wife taking the part on one side and the husband on the other." As a consequence of this quarrel, Cobbett had engaged in what he called "a contest for mastership" in which, for a period of seventy-five days, he lived in his study during the day and at night in a room at the back of the Kensington house which he locked off from the rest of the building. He was visited by his amanuensis, Charles Riley, who occasionally spent the night, but refused to communicate with any member of the family except in writing. "What I had to guard against, was, being in the presence of my wife, and hearing her plaintive voice and seeing her tears, so that this locking up made a necessary part of the plan."[48]

The suicide attempt did nothing to draw the couple closer together. From the middle of 1827 to 1830 Cobbett lived mostly at Barn Elm farm when he was in the London area, spending some Saturday nights and Sundays at Kensington. On Nancy's birthday and on wedding anniversaries Cobbett often sent his greetings along with an explanation of why he could not be with her. In 1830, while he and his family were steadily growing more estranged, Cobbett wrote *Advice to Young Men,* which portrayed not his actual home life, but his myth of the perfect life of an ever loving couple and their devoted children – part of a larger myth that exalted everything in Cobbett's life, beginning with that perfect childhood in Farnham from which he had run away four times.[49] Cobbett's travels in 1830 and 1832, after he had given up Barn Elm farm, took him away from home more than half the time. By the end of 1832 he had acquired Normandy farm, which he occupied alone, and sometimes with his eldest son, William, but never with any other member of the family. William junior was living there in July 1833 when the family breakup at Crown Street had occurred. He had assisted his father in the acquisition of the farm, although he did so reluctantly, since he thought that it was wholly unsuitable and tried to persuade his obdurate parent to take another and somewhat smaller property in the same area.[50] When that effort failed, William settled down at Normandy farm at the end of 1832, presumably for the purpose of running it in conjunction with John Dean, Cobbett's faithful employee from Botley days. Thus from July 1833 to Cobbett's death in 1835 the family was split in two. Cobbett lived at Bolt Court and Normandy farm. After he left Crown Street, Nancy and the children stayed on for a short time, then moved into a house at 10 Red Lion Court, where, presumably, they were joined by James.[51]

The split in the family brought to a head a crisis in Cobbett's financial affairs. The *Morning Chronicle* quite rightly noticed the deterioration in the *Political Register,* a deterioration which had set in before 1833. The account of Cobbett's tour of Scotland in 1832 had little of the sparkle of the accounts of the rural rides made in the 1820s and few of the shrewd observations characteristic of his earlier writings. After Cobbett entered parliament in 1833, his newspaper became mainly a repository for letters from readers, articles that had appeared in other papers, and accounts of parliamentary proceedings, with short, pedestrian articles by Cobbett containing only occasional flashes of his old brilliance.[52] There were far too many articles about paper money, and about how the American president, Andrew Jackson, was driving that iniquitous commodity out of the United States.[53] He was too busy and too tired and too ill to rise to his former heights. Not surprisingly, circulation of the *Political Register* fell off. Nor did the new books published in the years 1831–4 sell well. In his effort to expand their distribution, they were, as before, priced too close to their cost; and Cobbett, as before, often printed more copies than were needed.[54] Matters were further complicated by the drain on his resources caused by his activities at Normandy farm. He bought livestock, including ten Ayrshire cows purchased on his trip to Scotland. He built a stable, cattle shed, kiln, and privies, and installed a new floor in the barn. He hired a large staff and paid them well. He could not resist experimentation of a type that had no prospect of immediate financial return. In 1834, for example, he undertook a study to determine "the relative produce of 26 sorts of grass, sowed at the same time in the same field."[55] That part of the farm not set aside for experimental projects was principally devoted to growing seed to be retailed through the shop in Bolt Court, instead of producing crops that would have a ready market at the time of harvest. At one time the unsold stock of seed carried over from Barn Elm and Kensington days exceeded 8,000 pounds in weight.

In the nine years immediately following the bankruptcy in 1820, Cobbett managed to become indebted to Sir Thomas Beevor in the amount of £6,000.[56] It seems possible that half that amount was borrowed by Cobbett in 1829 to make good a deficiency in his accounts as executor under the will of a Miss Boxall, a friend of the Cobbett family who had died in 1825.[57] Much of this indebtedness to Beevor was paid off between 1829 and 1834, some of it, presumably, as a result of the success of Cobbett's *Advice to Young Men,* published in 1830, his last great book. One of the reasons for Cobbett's lecture tours beginning late in 1831 and extending through most of 1832 had been to raise money. In Edinburgh his talks had brought in "more than sixty pounds a night."[58] There is no available evidence as to how much of this was applied to a reduction of debt and how much was invested in Normandy farm. In September 1832, two months after a petition to William IV for the return of the £1,000 fine of 1810 had been rejected, Cobbett made an appeal to the public for reimbursement, explaining his need for funds to acquire the farm, but this appeal brought him something less than £300.[59]

When Cobbett broke with his family in 1833, his money matters became a part of the controversy. This was almost inevitable, because the inventory of books held in Cobbett's fortress at Bolt Court was partly owned by the "Westminster parties" – some had been written by them, and some were Cobbett's own works which he had given to members of the family in the past. These, presumably, had created much of the problem which faced the embattled Cobbett when he first took himself off to Bolt Court in July 1833, a problem from which he had freed himself two months later by turning the books over to their owners.[60] The remaining books which Cobbett owned himself were mortgaged to Sir Thomas Beevor for the £1,900 still due him.[61] And adding to the complications, Cobbett claimed that the £3,000 deficiency in the Boxall estate had been spent on his children, which they stoutly denied.[62] By March 1834 a compromise had been worked out: Cobbett would immediately pay £350 of the debt owed to Beevor, and another £260 in installments of £5 a week; the balance would be paid by John and James with money they borrowed from John Fielden. Cobbett assigned to John and James the stock of books which he owned, out of the sale of which they would reimburse themselves. When this had been accomplished, the balance of the stock would be returned to Cobbett. Cobbett would pay £4 a week for the support of his wife and three daughters.[63] Contemporaneously with the financial settlement, John and James announced their withdrawal from any participation in a monthly publication called *Cobbett's Magazine* which they had started in February 1833.[64]

The settlement with John and James had disposed of the obligation to Beevor but left Cobbett with other debts in unstated amounts. It also left him with limited sources of income. The *Political Register,* at best, could be only narrowly profitable. This could not be said of Normandy farm, which, despite Cobbett's sanguine expectation, needed continued inputs of funds to pay rent, tithes, rates, and the wages of farm laborers.[65] The money to support Normandy farm and to meet Cobbett's other obligations had come, therefore, mainly from the sale of books published by Cobbett after the 1834 assignment to John and James, from the sale of seeds, and from further borrowings. Lecturing for money was ruled out as undignified for a member of parliament.[66]

The handling of Cobbett's complicated financial problems was simplified (although not necessarily to Cobbett's advantage) by the appearance on the scene sometime late in 1833 of an individual we know relatively little about, one Jesse Oldfield, former ivory dealer at Sheffield. Oldfield moved into Bolt Court and, acting sometimes as agent for Cobbett and at other times on his own account, sold books and seeds, served as intermediary between Cobbett and his family, managed the office, and advanced Cobbett money as he needed it – which was frequently.

The family controversy had gone on from the first week in July 1833, when Cobbett left Crown Street, until the end of March 1834, when the compromise settlement was reached by which Sir Thomas Beevor was paid off. This almost certainly accounts in part for Cobbett's declining activity in parliament during the closing days of the 1833 session (which ended August 29) and during the first two months of the 1834 session (which began on February 4). By the time the compromise settlement had been reached, Cobbett was once more incapacitated by the hoarseness and cough that had afflicted him the year before. He left Bolt Court for Normandy farm, where from time to time he issued bulletins on his health.[67] The experience of fifty years, he reported, assured him that the cough "will not quit me until the wind shift from the east to the south and south-west." Because of the cough, Cobbett could get no sleep lying down; he managed "to get a little sleep sitting up in bed & laying his head on his knees. This he used to call 'dog sleep'."[68]

Thomas Macaulay, who had been a fellow member of the House of Commons in 1833 (and had later read many of Cobbett's works), made this diary entry in 1855:

In truth his [Cobbett's] faculties were impaired by age; and the late hours of the House probably assisted to enfeeble his body & consequently his mind. His egotism & his suspicion that everybody was in a plot against him increased and at last attained such a height that he was really as mad as Rousseau. Poor creature! I could write a very curious & entertaining article on him, if I chose.[69]

Unfortunately, Macaulay did not choose.

The twentieth century has tended to replace the word "mad" with terms that are more precise to the scientist and more puzzling to the layman.[70] The story of Cobbett's life has inevitably brought to light symptoms that are significant in classifying mental disorders: his great egotism, his suspicious nature, his readiness to see conspiracies against him, his extreme aggressiveness, his desire for revenge, his lack of emotional attachment to others, and his strong sense of unrivalled power and superiority which produced such a violent reaction when there was any suggestion that he was lacking in either. "I . . . have never been thwarted in my will by any body," he stated in 1831. "I never had a *rival* in my life, in anything," he declared in 1833.[71] All these characteristics, observable in some degree from Cobbett's youth, grew steadily with the years, and reached a new level in 1833, when – as we have seen – he began to find conspiracies against him among members of his own family. Even this episode did not dampen his ego. So too, when William junior, who had watched over Normandy farm since its acquisition in 1832, who had stood loyally by his father during the family quarrel, and who had tended him during his illnesses, left him in April 1834, declaring that he "would not live under such tyranny," Cobbett was able to write Oldfield with surprising calmness: "Thus, you will see *the last child* goes!"[72]

The difficult old man was left with a team of four worshipful stalwarts: Jesse Oldfield, Cobbett's principal man of affairs and source of funds; James Gutsell, Cobbett's secretary for the past several years; John Dean of Botley days, who had returned to Cobbett's service in 1825 and who was called on to perform tasks of infinite variety; and, the most recent addition, the tailor Benjamin Tilly, foreman of Swain and Co., Cobbett's neighbors on Fleet Street, who beginning in about 1833 acted as Cobbett's secretary when Gutsell was not available. Dean and Gutsell were shuttled back and forth between Bolt Court and Normandy farm; one of the two was left in charge of the farm whenever Cobbett was absent.

By the end of May 1834, when the wind had, apparently, shifted out of the east, Cobbett was able to return to his duties in the House of Commons. By then, wearied with illness and family problems, he had little of his old fire. He spoke a number of times in the first half of June, but what he had to say was almost wholly limited to comments two or three sentences long, as though it was too much effort to say more. From July 18 until parliament adjourned two weeks later he made only three short statements. Two of these related to criticism of the hated poor law bill of 1834.[73]

Within a month after parliament had been prorogued, Cobbett was off on a long-planned tour of Ireland with money borrowed from Oldfield.[74] Normandy farm was left in charge of Dean. Passing through Birmingham on his way to the Holyhead ferry, Cobbett bought a large number of locks which he sent back to Dean with instructions for their installation. They were "for front house-door, back-kitchen door, new brew-house door, stable door, and others. And padlocks for barn, outer yard gate, coach-house, and fine *chest-locks* for the three chests. All good and strong." Three more bars were to be added to the bars in the front windows; all three outer doors were to be locked when Dean went to bed, taking the keys with him. Dean was told to "Collect together all pots, pans, especially cookery-ware and *pewter*, not absolutely wanted for *daily* use, and lock it all up, either in my room, or in the coach-house, when you have the coach-house locked up." The letter continued for another seven pages with minutely detailed instructions, like those which Cobbett had sent from Newgate to Botley twenty-odd years earlier, on what should be done with the laborers, the cows, and the crops – and containing a few cynical comments regarding Oldfield and Gutsell.[75] Gutsell, who was to have accompanied Cobbett, had been left behind to demonstrate that Cobbett could get along without him.[76]

In Ireland Cobbett was wildly acclaimed by high and low. He stayed with General Sir George Cockburn at Shangana castle on arrival, and again before leaving despite his advance declaration that he would refuse all invitations to be a guest at country houses. He was entertained at several public dinners despite his advance resolution to attend none. He was greeted by 80,000 persons and a twenty-one-gun salute at Cork. He arrived in Limerick in a carriage drawn by four horses with two postillions wearing white hats and gold bands. He was hailed as a preeminent "statesman, politician, moralist, political economist, grammarian, historian, gardener and farmer" and as a writer surpassing Swift in "purity, simplicity, in clearness and cogency."[77] His Irish trip, including visits to homes of the poor, was described in ten letters published in the *Political Register* addressed to Charles Marshall, one of Cobbett's illiterate farm workers at Normandy farm.[78] The conditions he described among the poor were shocking; but the letters were otherwise dull. After several weeks of travel alone, Cobbett relented on his earlier decision and summoned Gutsell to join him in Dublin.[79] They returned to England late in November. There had been a change in government – the administration of Lord Melbourne had ended after only five months – and an election had been called for the first week of January. Cobbett directed his steps, therefore, to Oldham, where he and Fielden were reelected without opposition.[80]

The new parliament met on February 19, 1835. Cobbett was present but once more plagued by that irritating cough. He made a brave attempt to speak on March 10 on a subject very close to his heart: the repeal of the malt tax. So hoarse that he could not be heard across the table at which he was standing, he had to sit down after croaking out a few inaudible sentences.[81] At the end of March, although still unwell and still unable to speak, he sat in the House for three days from 4:30 in the afternoon until after midnight to hear the debate on Lord John Russell's bill which would take away from the protestant church of Ireland all tithes in excess of the amount strictly necessary to minister to the needs of the communicants of that church, and to apply the surplus to nonecclesiastical purposes, a first step, Cobbett hoped, in reforming what he called the church "temporalities" in England as well as in Ireland.[82] His final book, *Cobbett's Legacy to Parsons*, published in April 1835, was devoted to church reform. It became an immediate bestseller.[83] According to the *Legacy to Parsons,* the church of England, where "the poorer part of the people see the rich seated in pews, while they are compelled to stand about in the aisles," was the only church in the world in which the poor were "treated in a manner different from the rich."[84]

Cobbett's periodic attempts to attend sessions of parliament involving issues of peculiar concern to him – leaving the clean air of the country for the noxious air of the wen – made it difficult for him to rid himself of the cough. He was harassed, too, by his worsening financial condition, which resulted from the continuing demands for cash to sustain Normandy farm. In April 1835 he disposed of much of his livestock and a month later entered into an agreement with Oldfield by which he sold for £1,000 virtually all Cobbett's remaining assets, namely (1) the copyrights to all the books he still owned – nineteen titles published prior to March 1834 and three published since that time – and (2) all of his residual interest in the book stock held by John and James as security for whatever was still due them.[85] Cobbett apparently received no cash out of this transaction: the amount agreed upon seems to have been credited against his indebtedness to Oldfield for advances previously made to him.[86]

A week after Cobbett had stripped himself clean of nearly all his worldly goods, he made his last appearance in parliament, spoke a few words about the inadequate diet provided by the Duke of Richmond for the paupers of southwest Sussex, and then crept back to Normandy farm.[87] He had managed to attend fewer than half the sessions of the new parliament, and had become increasingly feeble. On June 10, in the little garden in front of the farmhouse, he wrote his last article for the *Political Register,* attacking once again the changes which had been made in the poor laws the year before. Brougham, constantly on Cobbett's mind as the primary force behind the hateful new laws, appears in this article as "Lord Crackskull," a very clever man, "though addicted to laudanum and brandy, and . . . with features none of the most human."[88] In the next few days Cobbett had alternating spells of delirium and clarity.[89] In his delirium he dictated, as though Tilly were sitting at his side, an attack on Brougham, complete with punctuation, just as he always did, ending with the sentence: "I shall say no more on this subject, (comma), for the present, (comma), for all ascends into the clouds (full point.)" On other occasions he "talked a good deal of the cruelty of his family towards him."

The family was admitted to his presence by degrees. First William was notified and came. When Nancy and the others asked to visit him, Cobbett dictated a letter declaring that he had no "insuperable objec-

Cobbett's house at Normandy farm, Ash

tion" to seeing any of them, but none should even attempt to sleep there or give an order of any sort to his servants. His ego, even on his deathbed, allowed of no relenting. The thought of sharing authority was intolerable. There was never any suggestion from him that he was in the slightest degree responsible for the breach. It was their fault; they had been cruel to him. He declared to his daughter Anne (presumably because she had stayed with her mother) that he "no longer considered her *his daughter*."

While Cobbett's mind wandered, there was no wandering in his character: He maintained to the end not only his egotism but also his humor and his values. On the day of his death, when Cobbett had become extremely weak,

the doctor, seeing that life would soon close, began very cautiously, and in a manner that to Mr. Cobbett, seemed rather affected, to enquire whether he wished to draw up any "testamentary document", observing that, if he did, "he might as well do it *now* as at *any other time*." "Not," continued he, "that there is any *dainja*," – (danger). To which Mr. Cobbett immediately replied – "I have done every thing that is necessary in that respect . . .". Before the doctor had quitted the room, Mr. Cobbett happening to hear him cough, and not being disinclined to a little sarcastic jocularity, spoke to him with much apparent gravity, and in the same affected drawl, saying – "Doctor, do you take anything for that cough?" "No! Sir," replied Esculapius. "Then," continued Mr. Cobbett, "I think that you should;" and, looking very archly, he added – "not that I think there is any *dainja*." The doctor looked rather blank at this humourous sally; and as he was leaving the bed-side, Mr. Cobbett added, with one of [his] arch and laughing winks of the eye – "There, take that, my buck!"

The day before this, Cobbett had performed his last rites to the land – the true love of his life. Placed in an easy chair, the chair "fixed in a sort of hand-barrow," he was carried outside by his chopsticks like some ancient warrior chief surveying the site of the battle in which he had been mortally wounded. Across the common and around his fields they carried him, "there to behold, for the last time" the beauty of the growing crops and to give his orders to the men working there. On his return to the house he asked for a load of grass to lay on the tiles to cool off his room. Cobbett had created a myth of a William Cobbett who was greater than himself. The man in the myth was a benign sovereign: wise, gentle, just, brave . . . the lover of all that was good, the enemy of all that was bad, the idol of his people. It was a myth Cobbett himself believed in, and according to this myth he lived and died.

Nancy Cobbett was not admitted to the house guarded by the stalwarts until her Billy had lost consciousness. She bathed his temples and moistened his lips, but he was not able "to show either joy or displeasure at her presence." At one o'clock that afternoon – it was June 18, 1835 – his breathing became more difficult. Ten minutes later, "he stretched forth one of his hands, as if bidding farewell; and then leaning back, and closing his eyes as if to sleep, he died without a gasp! Thus terminated the life of 'William Cobbett, the *poor-man's friend.*' "

Epilogue

WILLIAM COBBETT was buried on June 27, 1835 in the graveyard of St. Andrew's Church in Farnham alongside the bones of his parents and grandfather, three hundred yards from where he was born. His funeral was attended by about 8,000 persons, some 3,000 more than the population of Farnham. Among the mourners were several of the radical members of parliament including D. W. Harvey, John Fielden, Thomas Wakley, and Daniel O'Connell.

The newspapers and journals dutifully reported the death of a man whose strange mixture of virtues and human weaknesses made him so difficult to classify. The *Standard*, organ of the high tory party, pronounced Cobbett "one of the greatest men whom England has ever produced" and "the man who, after Mr. Burke, had done incomparably the most for preserving the institutions and honour of England." The *Morning Post*, another conservative paper, more cautiously declared: "we are proud of the name Cobbett as that of a writer and man whom it is impossible that any other country than England could have produced." Cobbett's "Englishness" was also stressed by *The Times*: "But take this self-taught peasant for all in all, he was perhaps in some respects a more extraordinary Englishmen than any other of his time", and it went on to state that "He was an English episode, and nothing more, as greater men have been; for what is Napoleon while we write, but an *episode?*" *Tait's Edinburgh Magazine*, in a eulogistic article of thirty pages in successive issues, called Cobbett "The Last Saxon" and "a standard English classic." *Fraser's Magazine* asserted that although "we differed from him on points of vital importance, we had no hesitation in saying that he with whom we differed was a great man." The *Morning Chronicle* agreed that Cobbett was "an extraordinary man" and "one of the most powerful writers that England has ever produced," but questioned whether "he ever set himself seriously down to discover the truth." The *Westminster Review*, beginning with the words "Mr. Cobbett was undoubtedly one of the remarkable men of the age," proceeded to relate a history of his life remarkable for its inaccuracies. Shortly before the end of this twenty-page article the author turned to "some of the favourable traits" of Cobbett: He was self-reliant, no trifler, cheerful, and not selfish. "His last days were his best . . . He died as men ought to die, resignedly and tranquil." These selections provide a good notion of polite contemporary comment ranging from the surprising eulogy of the tory to the thinly veiled hatred of the whig. Many of the obituaries mentioned the unusually fine family relations of the deceased; in none of them was there a suggestion of any rupture in those relations.[1]

A small group of Cobbett's admirers, including Oldfield and Tilly, made an effort to raise money for a monument honoring Cobbett, but the total amount raised, including £40 from John Fielden and £10 from Daniel O'Connell, never reached £100. Sir Francis Burdett sardonically contributed the bonds evidencing Cobbett's unpaid debts to him, which had been extinguished by Cobbett's bankruptcy in 1820. Fielden arranged for his own tribute by erecting a tablet in the interior of Farnham church. Under Tilly's leadership, a Cobbett Club was formed in 1838, which, for a time, met monthly at Dr. Johnson's tavern in Bolt Court.[2] Much later, Cobbett monuments were erected in Botley near the site of the Cobbett house and in Farnham on the banks of the Wey, only a short distance from his birthplace, the Jolly Farmer, now the William Cobbett. The houses at Botley, Normandy, Barn Elm, and Kensington have all disappeared. Cobbett's farms at the last two places have been taken over principally by the Barn Elm Allotment Society and the Kensington High Street underground station.

Cobbett's influence beyond his lifetime was quite possibly the greatest of any private individual of the period, but it was an influence that quickly lost its identity as it literally and figuratively merged with the landscape. The gardens of England and America for a hundred years, and perhaps more, bore his imprint. Trees were grown, crops were cultivated, lives were shaped, by Cobbett's enthusiasms.

In journalism, Cobbett played a part along with many others in establishing the freedom of the press, and had a distinctive part in the development of the editorial or leading article. He was among the first of the prominent journalists to sign his articles with his own name. He was responsible for a revolution in press history which at least one competent observer has hailed as comparable with the innovation of printing: the publication of a newspaper within the reach of everyone. He seems also to have been the first to succeed in producing an unsubsidized newspaper over any extended period, and took the lead in the fight for a press free from corruption – the corruption of sycophancy as well as that of money.

Cobbett's principal impact was in the field of government. His innovation in reporting parliamentary debates, still an essential part of British political life, has lost all identification with its originator, and now is simply taken for granted as "Hansard". Cobbett's attack on abuses led eventually to greater responsibility among officials, to the selection of public servants on the basis of merit rather than family, and to the more equitable distribution of political power among the people. But ranking first among his achievements must be his special contribution to the cause of the working classes, whom he made aware of their rights and of the necessity of thinking and acting for themselves. If he was not the originator, he was at least the chief protagonist for the view that improvement in the economic conditions of the poor depended largely on parliamentary reform, and that parliamentary reform should be attained by constitutional means. His continuing influence, moreover, was not limited to the economic and political status of the poor; he was the champion of human dignity among the poor, a concept far more elusive than economic or political rights, and one that has become a dominant force in the twentieth century.

Reform activity in the years immediately after Cobbett's death was centered in the chartists, where his influence was evident. Tilly was a chartist, and so was George Rogers, treasurer of the Cobbett Club, and so was James Cobbett, as well as Lovett, Cleave, Watson, Carpenter, and Hetherington, all of whom at one time or another had acknowledged Cobbett's leadership.[3] Yet the chartists without Cobbett were able to accomplish little in actual reform. For after the expiration of the *Political Register* there was no single, continuous voice (as there had been for more than thirty years) marshalling facts, developing arguments, alerting its readers to grievances, and expressing reform objectives. In 1840 Henry Warburton wrote to Sir William Molesworth: "The Radicals in parliament have, at this time, no public out of doors of sufficient influence to fall back upon; no quantity of matter which they can set in motion, and which united to vigour in themselves, would give momentum to what they say and do."[4] The plain fact is that effective reform ceased shortly after Cobbett's efforts ceased. Although further parliamentary changes were needed, it was not until 1862 that such changes were made.

Cobbett's personal affairs became the primary concern of William junior, his eldest son, sole beneficiary and executor under the will which Cobbett signed after the family quarrel.[5] William made an attempt to carry on the *Political Register*, but that publication expired with the issue of September 12, 1835, and a move to revive it the

531

following year was unsuccessful. William wished to continue at Normandy farm, but the lease, by its terms, expired with the death of Cobbett. When William proposed to take over his father's book and seed business he found, to his surprise, that Oldfield claimed the right to all the copyrights and all the stock of books, except the eight titles which Cobbett had conveyed to his family in 1828. William's claim that the assignment to Oldfield was a forgery was rejected by the courts. Cobbett's estate was bankrupt. When Cobbett's effects were put up to auction in January 1836, the auctioneer, a Mr. Piggott of Guildford, refused to offer for sale a box "found to contain human bones, wrapped up in separate papers," presumed to be those of Thomas Paine. There were numerous legends concerning the history of the bones thereafter, but their present whereabouts is a mystery.[6]

Nancy Cobbett outlived her husband by thirteen years, dying in 1848 when she was seventy-four years old. Her remains were deposited with those of her husband in the tomb which had been raised by the family on the site of Cobbett's grave.

The three daughters of William and Nancy Cobbett, Anne, Eleanor (Ellen), and Susan, who were forty, thirty, and twenty-eight years old at the time of Cobbett's death, never married. It is difficult to imagine a suitor calling at the Cobbett home. Anne (1795–1877) became a publisher of her father's books, first operating from the house at Red Lion Court, and after 1837 from 137 Strand, bringing out new editions of several of the eight titles that had been assigned to members of the family and republishing others when Oldfield's copyrights expired. She also was an author, writing the type of practical works that her father would have approved of: *The English Housekeeper* (1835) and *Plain Instructions for Using the Meal and Flour of Indian Corn* (1846). Susan (1807–89) seems to have become a teacher of young children, and translated from French to English a tale by Amalie Schoppe, *Henry and Mary* (1860). We know little about Eleanor except the dates of her birth and death (1805–1900).

The four Cobbett sons were lawyers, all barristers except the youngest son, Richard, who was a solicitor. The influence of the strong-willed father, who gave his own name to his first son and names of friends to the three others, is evident. William (1798–1878), whose life had been dominated by his father and who had his father's predilection for minority causes but little of his father's intelligence, found himself heir to perpetual misadventure. His problems began as a young man: He had been ill much of the time from 1819 to 1821; in 1825 he went to France and in the following year was brought home by his father's threats of disfavor; from 1830 to 1832 he was back in France to escape some unexplained embarrassment. Cobbett's death was followed by the already described efforts of William to continue the *Political Register* and Normandy farm, and to take over the book and seed business, which led to a series of unsuccessful suits against Oldfield from 1835 to 1838, and further suits against Oldfield's widow and executrix in 1853. There was also an unsuccessful petition in 1837 to recover the £1,000 fine imposed on Cobbett for his flogging article. Later William brought unsuccessful suits against the trustees of the Winchester–Botley turnpike for their alleged indebtedness to his father, a promoter of the turnpike in the Botley days.[7] In the course of these proceedings, William was imprisoned for contempt of court as well as for debt; he became bankrupt; and died in 1878 in the lobby of the House of Lords on his way to the court of appeals, where he was pursuing the interest of the unsuccessful claimant in the Tichborne case.[8] He was married, but had no offspring. In 1824, while a student of Lincoln's Inn, William had published *The Law of Turnpikes*, a compilation of the acts of parliament relating to that subject. Two months before Cobbett died he proposed writing a *Legacy to Lords*. In 1863 William junior published a book having that title, which purported to be a work of the father "edited" by the son, but which appears to be largely the work of the latter.

John Morgan Cobbett (1800–77), who had been a candidate in name only for Coventry in 1833 (he had been nominated at the last minute, and because of illness did not attend the election), attempted, without success, to succeed his father as member for Oldham at the by-election held in July 1835. He lost again in 1847. He did gain the seat in 1852 and held it until 1865. In 1872 he was again returned for Oldham, this time as a conservative, and retained the seat until his death in 1877.[9] In 1851, when John was fifty-one years old, he married Mary Fielden, daughter of John Fielden, Cobbett's fellow member for Oldham.

In 1825, John had written an account of a long trip he had made in France, published in book form that year as *Letters from France*. In November 1835, six months after the death of their father, John and his younger brother, James Paul Cobbett (1803–81), began to edit selections from their father's political writings. These were published by Anne Cobbett in weekly parts from 1835 to 1837, when they were bound into six large volumes of more than 3,000 pages. As a young man, James had written five books and translated one other: *A Ride of Eight Hundred Miles in France* (1824); *A Journal of a Tour in Italy* (1830); *A Sketch of the Life of General Lafayette*, a translation (1830); *A Grammar of the Italian Language* (1830); *Practical Exercises to Cobbett's French Grammar* (1834); and *A Latin Grammar for the Use of English Boys* (1835). As a practicing lawyer he wrote *The Law of Pawns and Pledges* (1841).[10]

In 1855 James began in earnest to collect materials for a life of his father, and at that time Anne and Susan wrote out their reminiscences, presumably to assist James in the work he had undertaken.[11] He started to write the life in October 1862, but did not get far.[12] It seems likely that he stopped in the following year when, at the age of sixty, he was married for the first time. He had no children.

Richard Baverstock Brown Cobbett (1814–75) as a small boy made several rural rides with his domineering father but during his adolescence saw less of his father than any of the other children at the same period of life. In an exuberant letter to his sister written in 1840, expressing his preference for the company of young people when their fathers and mothers were out of the way, he adds: "People talk of teaching the young idea [?] how to shoot – I wish they would teach children to shoot their Fathers & Mothers."[13]

Richard married when he was twenty-seven years old (as contrasted with the advanced years of his older brothers), selecting as his bride Jane Palmer, the daughter of Samuel Palmer, prosperous farmer of Bollitree Castle, near Ross, Herefordshire, a longtime friend of Richard's father. Before his marriage, Richard had edited and published a radical paper, *The Champion and Weekly Herald*. He later founded a firm of solicitors in Manchester which continues to this day under the name of "Cobbetts," although no one of that name is now associated with the firm. He also was the founder of a distinguished line of Cobbett heirs, having a son, a grandson, and a great-grandson who were successively knighted for meritorious services to their country.[14] The last of these, General Sir Gerald Lathbury, G.C.B., D.S.O., M.B.E., was posthumously installed as Knight Grand Cross of the Order of the Bath in May 1978. The armorial bearings he chose would have pleased his great-great-grandfather: The shield was supported on one side by a winged horse, to represent General Lathbury's distinguished service as commander of a parachute brigade, and on the other by a porcupine, in honor of that very English ancestor who fought against injustice wherever he found it.

There are, at this date, no living descendants of William Cobbett who bear the family name. Nevertheless, it is a name that will survive in the volumes of his works as long as the language in which they were written survives. They will be read not only for their style, for the picture they give of long ago, and for their saucy humor, but also because they contain messages such as this, that are worthy of the attention of posterity:

Happiness, or misery, is in the mind. It is the mind that lives; and the length of life ought to be measured by the number and importance of our ideas, and not by the number of our days. Never, therefore, esteem men merely on account of their riches, or their station. Respect goodness, find it where you may. Honour talent wherever you behold it unassociated with vice; but honour it most when accompanied with exertion, and especially when exerted in the cause of truth and justice; and, above all things, hold it in honour, when it steps forward to protect defenceless innocence against the attacks of powerful guilt.[15]

Appendix 1 · Some more crotchets

In 1827 an irritated Cobbett wrote to his wife: "the presumptuous talk about my 'crotchets' has become so habitual, that it seems to be almost impossible to eradicate the idea, or to prevent it from breaking forth into sarcastic criticism." Many of Cobbett's alleged crotchets – his odd, whimsical, or stubborn notions – appear in the main body of the text, but others which did not seem to fit neatly into the story are included in this appendix, since they assist in understanding the strange man who nourished them.

Cobbett's son James noted that his father liked to "get into difficulties, to enjoy the pleasure of fighting his way out." Cobbett himself declared, with apparent pride, that "opinions of the *many* have hitherto seldom corresponded with my opinions, and, I am afraid, this will always be the case." A favorite Cobbett exercise was to demonstrate that the popularly held view of a subject was the wrong one.

References: Letter to Nancy, Apr. 16, 1827 (Nuffield); JPC, p. 57; 25 *PR* 534.

Shakespeare, Milton, and potatoes

Among Cobbett's more notorious attacks was that on the talents of Shakespeare and Milton, which, surprising as it may seem, arose out of a diatribe against potatoes: "I regard the praises of this root . . . to have arisen from a sort of monkey-like imitation. It has become, of late years, *the fashion* to extol the virtues of potatoes, as it has been to admire the writings of Milton and Shakespear." Milton's *Paradise Lost,* Cobbett asserted, was "so outrageously offensive to reason and to common sense, that one is naturally led to wonder how it can have been tolerated by a people, amongst whom astronomy, navigation, and chemistry are understood," and then added this clinching argument: "if one of your relations were to write a letter in the same strain, you would send him to a mad-house."

Cobbett always stood with his feet firmly on the ground. He would have no fanciful creations, either the devils or angels of Milton, or the "ghosts, witches, sorcerers, fairies and monsters" of Shakespeare. He objected also to the "bombast and puns and smut" of Shakespeare. His most telling blow against blind worship of the "Divine Bard" was the fraud practiced on the public by the youthful William Henry Ireland (late in the eighteenth century), who wrote two plays which "a majority of the learned and critical classes of this nation" accepted as written by Shakespeare. It was fashion alone, claimed Cobbett, that caused people to applaud "under the name of Shakespear, what they would hoot off the stage in a moment, if it came forth under any other name." He provided his readers with a list of passages in Shakespeare's plays to illustrate what he had in mind.

The essay is an amusing one, and might provide an ideal exercise for a university seminar studying Shakespeare. Yet while Cobbett was a great polemicist, he also had a taste for good writing. He knew much of Shakespeare by heart: "I found, here and there, passages . . . which delighted me very much," and throughout his lifetime Cobbett quoted Shakespeare more often than any other work except the Bible.

References: 29 *PR* 193–7 (repr. in *Year's Residence*, paras. 269–71); 88 *PR* 520–6. See also 16 *PR* 971; 50 *PR* 797; *Advice*, paras. 77–9, 311.

The universities and the learned languages

In 1806, following Nelson's victory at Trafalgar, the French proposed a peace treaty by which Britain would retain all her conquests on the basis of *uti possidetis*. These two words, Cobbett claimed, "have been repeated three hundred and eighty times during the debate in both Houses." Why, he asked, did they not use the English equivalent: "actual possession"?

Do those who make use of such phrases, which the stupidest wretch upon earth might learn to use as well as they, in a few hours; nay, which a parrot would learn, or which a high-dutch bird-catcher would teach to a bull-finch or a tom-tit, in the space of a month; and do they think, in good earnest, that this last relick of the mummery of monkery, this playing off upon us of a few gallipot words, will make us believe that they are *learned*? Learning, truly so called, consists in the possession of knowledge and in the capacity of communicating that knowledge to others; and, as far as my observation will enable me to speak, what are called the *learned* languages, operate as a bar to the acquirement of real learning.

Cobbett challenged the gentlemen of the two universities to debate his claim that the learned languages were worse than useless as a part of general education. In the next six months he received and published thirty-seven responses – mostly anonymous – some attacking, some defending, Cobbett's position. Although Cobbett promised to address himself to the responses, he never did so directly. Ten years later he stated that he had not because he had been distracted by the Duke of York–Mrs. Clarke affair which quickly followed. There is no doubt, however, what he had in mind, as he made clear at another point:

One main thing to insist upon, was, that these great secrets, the Greek and Latin languages, were of *no use*; that they had not the smallest tendency to communicate knowledge; that they had not the smallest tendency to enlarge the mind; that they had not the smallest tendency to enable men to write English correctly; that they were of no sort of use except to impose upon the people in general, and to appropriate to a certain class of individuals, the enjoyment of large masses of public property, which might be otherwise much better employed.

Cobbett called the colleges and universities "dens of dunces," claimed that they were the mortal enemies of youth, the great destroyers of time and talent, and detrimental to the independence of mind in political matters, and that those they purported to educate were unfit to be clerks in grocers' or mercers' shops. The universities, too, were the bastions of religious intolerance, the strongholds of "no popery" propaganda.

The specimens of university education which Cobbett saw all around him were not impressive, and there is much objective evidence to confirm that the educational establishments of the time had fallen to a low state. Adam Smith wrote, near the end of the eighteenth century, that the majority of Oxford professors had "given up altogether even the pretence" of teaching, and Jeffrey in 1792 had declared: "Except for praying and drinking, I see nothing else that it is possible to acquire in this place." While reforms had since been undertaken at Oxford (they had begun earlier at Cambridge), Cobbett's comments were not as frivolous as they might appear on the surface.

References: 11 *PR* 36, 117–18, 236–7, 871; 12 *PR* 225–7, 751; 13 *PR* 401; 16 *PR* 968; 32 *PR* 1067; 34 *PR* 257, 452–5; 40 *PR* 1385; 44 *PR* 21, 718; 66 *PR* 453; Mathieson, *England in Transition*, pp. 119–21. Paine, in Part One of the *Age of Reason* (1794), claimed that learning Latin and Greek was a waste of time, and that a child's genius was "killed by the barren study of a dead language."

Education of the poor

In 1833 Cobbett wrote an article entitled "Education and Heddekashen," the last word being his version of the Scottish pronunciation of the first. It was in response to the assertion of Lord Althorp, chancellor of the exchequer, that Cobbett was "an enemy to the education

of the people." The incident that gave rise to the accusation was Cobbett's opposition in parliament to a grant for the British Museum.
Cobbett's objection stemmed from the prevailing system of taxation,
by which government funds were raised principally by levies on con-
sumable goods; hence, a grant to the British Museum, no matter how
small, meant burdening the working people with a major part of the
cost of a facility which was open between the hours of ten and three,
and closed on Sundays, the only day the industrious classes might
have time to use it.

Cobbett's ideas on education in general were considerably more
complicated. People should be educated for what they were called on
to do in society. Since "It is necessary to the existence of mankind,
that a very large portion of every people should live by manual
labour," those who were to perform such labor should learn their jobs
as children, working with their parents, rather than being cooped up
in schools where they would learn laziness. Their parents should not
be taxed to pay for the schooling of those entering professions which
required book learning. In America, Cobbett pointed out, the schools
were supported by a tax levied on the land; hence, the working people paid no part of it. Cobbett by no means believed that those who
were laborers should always remain in that class; he thought that a
gradual rise over several generations, by which "the descendents of
the present labourer become gentlemen," a more realistic ambition
than "attempting to reach the top at a single leap."

Cobbett feared a government-controlled educational system which
would provide an additional source of patronage (as well as an opportunity to place spies in every community) and be a means of "gaining
the minds of youth"; that is, of teaching them to be blindly submissive
to their masters, to accept abject poverty, and to seek their reward in
the next world:

And with regard to the *blessedness* of ragged backs and empty bellies, and the
great efficacy of these in promoting happiness in a future state, they look at
the big-wigged, long robed, rosy-gilled persons who preach up this doctrine,
who can hardly see out of their eyes, or utter their words, for fat, and who
are much more likely to burst than to starve. "What!" say the people, "is to
become of these ghostly persons and of their wives and families, if ragged
backs and hungry bellies are to be the titles to ever-lasting happiness?" In
short, they see the cheat.

Finally, Cobbett detected fraud in the commonly expressed view of
the upper classes that education would reduce poverty and crime.
Cobbett believed that the way to reduce poverty and crime was to
increase the earnings of the poor through higher pay and lower taxes,
remedies which the upper classes, naturally, disliked. The educational

schemes they proposed were, in Cobbett's view, designed to divert the attention of the working classes from the cause of their poverty and misery. "The 'expansion of the mind' is very well; but, really, the thing which presses most, at this time, is, the getting of something to expand the body a little more: a little more bread, bacon, and beer; and, when these are secured, a little 'expansion of the mind' may do *vary weele*."

Near the end of his life, Cobbett was comforted by an American study which confirmed his opinion, "originating in that of a very sensible father, that early teaching of book-learning had a tendency to enfeeble, if not destroy the mind."

References: 12 *PR* 331; 24 *PR* 747; 30 *PR* 614, 721; 31 *PR* 307; 33 *PR* 296–7, 299; 34 *PR* 242–6, 841; 35 *PR* 522; 48 *PR* 438; 69 *PR* 707, 710; 72 *PR* 307, 477; 73 *PR* 520, 559; 74 *PR* 332; 79 *PR* 787; 80 *PR* 139; 81 *PR* 453, 726; 82 *PR* 40, 577; 83 *PR* 771; 84 *PR* 589; 88 *PR* 322, 515–16, 587; *Cottage Economy*, paras. 11–14.

The industrial worker

Cobbett had little knowledge of the industrial world that was rapidly changing the life of England. He had never been inside a factory until 1830 when he visited Fielden's model plant at Todmorden. The only other factories he was known to enter were one at Paisley engaged in the manufacture of silk cloth and another at Mauchline producing snuffboxes. He had a whimsical explanation for his lack of curiosity about the manufacturing process: "I never like to see these machines, lest I should be tempted to endeavour to understand them."

Yet Cobbett was not indifferent to the problems of the industrial worker. As early as 1810 he argued that the factory hands who had been thrown out of work due to war embargoes should be supported by their former employers. He urged the repeal of the Combination Acts. He condemned the working conditions that existed in most of the factories of the time, and the truck system [paying workmen in goods instead of money] common to many of them. He strongly favored legislation limiting the hours of children and young people. He supported the right to strike.

In Cobbett's "Letter to the Luddites" written in 1816, he took the position that workers were not harmed by the introduction of new machinery, and must be injured by its destruction. By 1826 he had changed his views as the result of observation: "The principles were all correct enough; but their application cannot be universal ... mechanic inventions, pushed to the extent they have been, have been productive of great calamity to this country and ... will be productive of still greater calamity." He saw the advantage of the lower costs attainable through machine production, but thought that this was more than offset by the decline of work in the cottage, which had formerly provided supplemental income for the laborer's family.

References: 12 *PR* 358; 13 *PR* 107; 31 *PR* 687–8; 34 *PR* 387–91; 39 *PR* 76, 342; 40 *PR* 1360; 46 *PR* 436, 523–5; 47 *PR* 119, 358, 542; 56 *PR* 425; 59 *PR* 387, 738–40; 60 *PR* 131–2, 154; 69 *PR* 104; 78 *PR* 273, 389, 410; 80 *PR* 21; 82 *PR* 624, 641; 84 *PR* 196; *Rural Rides*, pp. 127, 272, 317–19, 394, 406.

The Times and the *Morning Chronicle*

"For years," wrote *The Times* immediately following Cobbett's death, "this journal was the favourite weekly victim of an animosity which we suspect to have been on his part more affected than real."

The Times was, without doubt, a favorite Cobbett target. It is less easy to assess the relative portions of affected versus real animosity in his attacks. Occasionally, but not very often, Cobbett had a good word to say about *The Times*. His attitude toward that newspaper changed somewhat after the great Thomas Barnes became editor in 1817. Cobbett's assessment of the pre-Barnes *Times* is summed up in the statement (made in 1816) that it was the "most corrupt of prints . . . conceived in sin and brought forth in iniquity." Cobbett's criticism of *The Times* under Barnes fell into two main categories: he claimed that the *Times* policy was dictated by considerations of circulation; that the paper was always waiting to see "which way the cat jumps" before it took a position on any subject; and he claimed (somewhat inconsistently) that *The Times* "uniformly advocated punishment, cruelty, proscription and blood, against all those, in whatever country, who were striving for freedom." Hence he called it "The Bloody Old Times." In cataloguing all the incidents which justified this title, Cobbett listed deeds which antedated Barnes, but the "Bloody" title seems to have been bestowed after Barnes became editor.

Cobbett did not attack Barnes personally; his invective was reserved for the paper itself and members of the Walter family who were the owners of the paper. When the proprietor, John Walter, died in 1812, his interest was divided among a number of individuals, including two married daughters, Mrs. Anna Brodie and Mrs. Mary Carden, and a son, John, who managed the paper. The battle of personalities began in November 1821 when *The Times* ran a story stating that "Mr. Cobbett has thrown open the front of his house at Kensington, where he proposes to sell meat at a reduced price." The presumed factual basis for this statement was that Cobbett had killed two of his calves for his own consumption and sold what he did not want to neighbors.

Thereafter the manager of *The Times* was referred to in the *Political Register* as "Walter the base." *The Times* became more personal, referring on one occasion to Cobbett's "paunch." Cobbett then began calling *The Times* "Anna Brodie." She and her sister were "foul-tongued hags" for the "slanders" put forth against Cobbett, and he promised to be by no means sparing of the paunches of the two ladies or of such "other parts belonging to them that I may think worthy of description."

The name "Bloody Old Times," or simply "The Bloody," lasted for Cobbett's lifetime, and "Anna Brodie" for nearly as long. Surely the lady of that name and her husband, the Reverend Alexander Brodie of Eastbourne, Sussex, were weary of Cobbett's name-calling long before he discontinued the practice.

In 1833 Cobbett violated his long-standing rule against suing for libel and collected £100 from *The Times* for its reference to him as "an uncertificated bankrupt." If, as *The Times* suggested, Cobbett had little real animosity against that paper, he had a more generous character than he ordinarily evinced.

In contrast to Cobbett's contests with *The Times*, his gibes at John Black, editor of the *Morning Chronicle*, the leading whig newspaper, seem completely devoid of venom, and displayed the high good humor of which he was capable. One reason, perhaps, was that Black usually agreed with Cobbett on the issues of the day, the whigs being out of power from the time Black became editor in 1817 to the end of 1830, when Grey became the reform prime minister with Cobbett's enthusiastic endorsement. Much of Cobbett's humor related to Black's Scottish ancestry. He spoke, for example, of Black's love of justice and liberty that were evinced "when his Scotch prejudices are asleep." In the midst of the 1825 monetary crisis Cobbett began calling him *"Doctor* Black," along with two other followers of Ricardo: "Doctor" J. R. McCulloch and "Doctor" Thomas Tooke. Thereafter Cobbett had great fun with the degree he had bestowed on Black:

It was I that made this gentleman a *Doctor*. A thousand times have I repented of it, and a thousand times have I congratulated myself on the subject. When he runs after Wilmot Horton and Malthus and Brougham, I really am so enraged with him that I could break his bones, and certainly should if he were within my reach; then again, in a day or two, he does something to make me so proud of him, that, though a Scotchman, I almost wish him to be my own son.

At another point, when Black disagreed with Cobbett, the latter wrote: "It was not for *this* that I made you a Doctor; and, by — if you go on at this rate, I will un-doctor you, and reduce you again to your very kilt."

Cobbett could be tart with the Doctor and with the *Morning Chronicle* when he thought they deserved it; there is no sign that he ever pulled his punches in the case of one or the other, but overall he maintained a creditable relationship with both editor and newspaper for approximately fifteen years (up to the time of his breakdown in 1833), demonstrating that Cobbett was able to agree and disagree, when he chose to do so, without resorting to objectionable abuse.

References: *The Times*: *Times*, June 20, 1835; 31 *PR* 467–8; 40 *PR* 1146, 1277, 1566, 1593; 41 *PR* 252, 813; 42 *PR* 445; 43 *PR* 293, 494; 45 *PR* 347, 371–81; 46 *PR* 679–89; 63 *PR* 665; 70 *PR* 507; 78 *PR* 236, 421; 81 *PR* 12; 87 *PR* 341. *Morning Chronicle*: 53 *PR* 94; 55 *PR* 645; 63 *PR* 389–97; 69 *PR* 691; 76 *PR* 2, 556; 77 *PR* 221.

Music

Among Cobbett's shortcomings was his dislike of puns and music; music, we quickly add, of the ordinary sort, for Cobbett found his music in the farm and field: "A hundred sheep eating corn, is, I think, the most pleasant music that ever met the ear of man. An old farmer in Hampshire, who was very rich, and whose silly neighbours were persuading him to have the daughter taught music, said 'Na! talk of muzic indeed; gi' me two flails and a cuckoo'!" The sweetest music, he wrote at other times, is "the ploughman's whistle and the jingle of the traces," or "when it comes from the trees and the bushes."

Psalms sung by the choristers in the church gallery in accordance with ancient custom were perfectly acceptable, and Cobbett approved of the vocal music in the methodist meeting houses: "A number of women and girls singing together make very sweet sounds," adding, by way of explanation: "Young girls like to sing; and young men like to hear them. Nay, old ones too." But he disliked the new practice, introduced by the church of England, of having the congregation sing hymns to the accompaniment of the organ. The only good use of an organ, Cobbett claimed, was that made by Tull when he converted one to a seed drill.

The piano in the farmer's home was a symbol of slothfulness, while the Italian singers who flooded Cobbett's London were symbols of effeminacy.

References: 6 *PR* 617; 12 *PR* 425, 848, 879; 13 *PR* 393, 679; 40 *PR* 1014; 47 *PR* 621; 77 *PR* 264; 82 *PR* 81; 86 *PR* 89; 88 *PR* 205; *Cobbett's Corn*, para. 152; *Rural Rides*, p. 188.

Religion

In 1815 that great defender of established religion, the prince regent, during a conversation with Wilberforce "spoke strongly of the blasphemy" of Cobbett's writings, perhaps having in mind Cobbett's essay cynically contrasting the British government with that in America, where they were "destitute of the honour of being governed by some illustrious family." Possibly, though, the prince regent's remark was evidence of perception in another direction.

Cobbett was outwardly more conventional about religion than he was about most subjects. He was church of England – "the good old Church of England as by act of parliament made and established" – and on more than one occasion stated that he was resolved to stick to it "just as I received it from my father, and as he received it from my grandfather." He attended church services on Sunday, making a point of doing so when he was travelling about the country.

It is difficult to say precisely what this outward conformity meant in terms of belief. In 1813, when he was asked directly whether he was a "Churchman, believing the religion of that Church, as expressed in her Creeds, Articles, and Prayer Book; or, are you a disbeliever of that religion, and belong to her from *political* motives?" he refused to answer on the ground that the questioner had no right to put the question to him – "No man has a right to rummage into another man's heart." And then he added, "Our Church calls upon nobody to make confessions of their belief. The law only requires us to be *silent,* where we do not agree with her." Almost certainly, Cobbett did not accept in full the creeds, articles, and prayer book, and was hardly able to suppress a laugh at the thought of divine revelation being prescribed by an act of parliament and "rendered plain and tangible by a good clear 'Whereas' at the out-set."

Without ever saying flatly what he had in mind, Cobbett wrote enough about religious "superstitions" and "falsehoods" to make it obvious that he rejected the miraculous incidents in the Bible as thoroughly as he rejected them in Milton and Shakespeare: "Credulity is the offspring of ignorance, and superstition is the child of credulity." Taking what was almost certainly a tongue-in-cheek attitude, he enjoyed twitting those who believed in some miracles, but not in others; the unitarians, for example, who rejected the incarnation but accepted the resurrection. He wrote: "I cannot, and I will not, separate the Scripture into *false* and *true.* It is, and it must be, all of a piece. If the miracles took place, so did the incarnation. We are told of both in the same book, and we have no other authority for either. – To deny, therefore, the fact of the divinity of Christ, is, I repeat it again, to deny the truth of the Christian system." Cobbett asserted that "as a Churchman" (an important qualifying phrase) he believed the Bible was "all of divine origin; but, my belief has nothing to do with the *proof* of the truth of the thing believed."

There are some areas in which Cobbett's stand was less ambiguous.

He was for the right of everyone to say and write just what he thought about religion. This issue was raised early in 1812 (Cobbett was still in Newgate), when Daniel Eaton was sentenced to prison for eighteen months and to stand in the pillory for an hour, for publishing Part Three of Paine's *Age of Reason,* a treatise purporting to demonstrate that the Old Testament contained no prophecies of the coming of Christ, and that the account of Christ in the New Testament was "a fabulous invention." Cobbett reported that when Eaton stood in the pillory he was cheered by the thousands who had gathered at the Old Bailey, but not because of any attachment to deism: "it was their attachment to the liberty of the press, to which they know well that they owe whatever of freedom they enjoy." Cobbett claimed that as a result of the trial he had read all three parts of Paine's work,* "and I really do not find in them any of that ribaldry or mockery that have been so much talked of. They are sober, argumentative essays ... though the author may be wrong." He urged Baker, the hated Botley parson, to come forward with a rebuttal to Paine, offering to publish the rebuttal at his expense. Baker at first accepted but then backed out, and no one else took up Cobbett's offer.

In 1813 Cobbett involved himself in the controversy evoked by parliamentary legislation removing the civil disabilities of the unitarians, who disbelieved in the doctrine of the Trinity. The Trinity, he pointed out, was an essential part of the Christian faith; denying the Trinity is denying the divinity of Christ: "what did Mr. Paine, or Mr. Eaton, or any body else ever do, or attempt to do, more than this?" Cobbett argued that it was wrong to exempt any one sect from a part of church faith. "I am for no partial repeals. I am for a general act, permitting every man to say or write what he pleases upon the subject of religion." A few months later the *Freethinking Christians' Magazine* described Cobbett as one "who opposes Christianity under the pretence of being a Christian."

The issue of religious freedom was raised once again in 1813 by Daniel Eaton's publication of *Ecce Homo,* a translation of a work by the French philosopher d'Holbach, a vigorous opponent of Christianity. Although Cobbett stated that he did not agree with the writer "in all his opinions," he praised *Ecce Homo* as "possessing great *literary* merit," and he expressed the wish that it be answered. The same issue of the *Political Register* contained a letter from "Observator" commending Cobbett for his warm advocacy of the "cause of Mother Church," and defending him against the charge that he favored the

---

*In 1820 Cobbett claimed that he had not read the *Age of Reason* until then, and had done so only because of an attack by the bishop of Llandaff on Paine's book. 35 *PR* 724.

doctrines of Thomas Paine. "Observator" commended the newly published *Ecce Homo* as tending to "unfetter the human mind." Cobbett ran three other letters from "Observator," and had more to say about *Ecce Homo*. A careful reading of it had "given rise to difficulties" in Cobbett's mind. "There are parts of that work, which, I confess, I am quite unable to answer; and which, nevertheless, I must see answered before my mind can be settled upon the subject." Cobbett promised to state these difficulties in detail, but never did. Papers discovered in 1977 reveal that "Observator" was George Houston, a journalist and freethinker who had arranged the translation of *Ecce Homo* for Eaton. Houston was an acquaintance of Timothy Brown, banker, brewer, radical, and freethinker, one of Cobbett's closest friends, who had interested himself in seeing that Cobbett would bring *Ecce Homo* "into notice." A letter from Brown to Houston assured him that Cobbett "enters fully into your views."

There is nothing in what Cobbett said about *Ecce Homo* either in the *Political Register* or in the recently discovered letters from Cobbett to Houston that alters, in any respect, the position that Cobbett had previously taken on the subject of religion: He was for free discussion of religion, and he continued his policy of focusing attention on the series of miracles on which church doctrine was founded.

In November 1814 Houston was sentenced to two years' imprisonment for his part in publishing *Ecce Homo*, and for twelve months of that time (issue of January 21, 1815 to issue of January 20, 1816) was nominally printer and publisher of the *Political Register*. It is not possible to say what that may have signified, since the names of printer and publisher were changed more than twenty times during the thirty-odd years of the life of the paper. Thereafter Houston seems to have disappeared from Cobbett's life. The files of the privy council indicate that he sought employment as a government informer in 1816 shortly after he ceased to be publisher of the *Political Register*. Hence not much weight can be given to his statement to the government that Cobbett had developed a plan to massacre the House of Commons; or that Cobbett had opened his mind to Houston on the subject of religion and was "even a more decided enemy than Mr. Brown"; or that after the *Ecce Homo* episode, Cobbett's friends in London let it be known that the position he had taken "was not altogether agreeable" to them. Cobbett had better reasons to be circumspect in expressing his opinions on religious subjects. He was under bond to maintain good behavior for seven years from 1812. The strong feeling against deism evinced by the public reaction after Cobbett returned to England in 1819 with Paine's bones may be an explanation of why Cobbett had relatively little to say about miracles after that date. But another possible element was the decline in incidents which made the issue relevant: "I never meddle with religion, except when religion meddles with politics," he wrote in 1820.

Cobbett's final letter to Houston has been properly described by its discoverer as more "anti-clerical than . . . anti-religious." But Cobbett had never made a secret of the fact that he was against luxurious living by church dignitaries; that he opposed plural appointments, clerical nonresidency, and the grant of livings to army officers on half pay; that he disliked the political activities of the clergy, particularly their hostility to parliamentary reform and their participation as magistrates in suppressing the poor. He criticized members of the cloth engaged in business as wine merchants and bankers. He wished to strip the church of its "temporalities." He did not like the principle of a church established by law; he thought the American system of free choice, voluntary support, and the prohibition of any tie between church and state a far better one. And to avoid the impression that he was against all clergy, it should be added that Cobbett thought that the working clergy, those serving the parishes, were outrageously maltreated and underpaid. He favored a legislative minimum pay for curates.

To sum up, Cobbett was emotionally attached to the church of England all his life, although he doubted those aspects of doctrine derived from miraculous incidents. He liked a morality that emphasized good works, and in a sense, his adherence to the church of England was cemented by his dislike of what he saw elsewhere: He disliked what he thought was the hypocrisy of those who left the church of England for reasons of doctrine and established their own doctrine on no more supportable grounds. He hated the sects that believed in predestination or in the efficacy of faith as contrasted with works, or those that "condemned the rest of the world to eternal flames," or those that taught that salvation was attainable only through servility and discomfort in this life. He liked the concept of uniformity of religion, since it would prevent bickering over differences in creed. He once wrote: "Without, therefore, attempting any defence of the Church, her rites, ceremonies, or doctrines, I have no hesitation to say, that as far as my experience enables me to speak, her followers are the best sort of people." To the charge that church of England adherents went to church from habit, to sleep, and to show off their clothes, he replied:

For my part, I see no harm in people dressing themselves once a week, and meeting together at a certain place to show off; and if some of them, more advanced in years, or too young to see the advantage of beauty, do chance to take a nap, it only shows, that, as Rousseau observes, "sermons are always good for something".

References: First para.: Coupland, *Wilberforce*, p. 413; 27 *PR* 72.
  Second para.: 32 *PR* 912; 33 *PR* 301; 38 *PR* 70; 67 *PR* 805.
  Third para.: 24 *PR* 4–5; 33 *PR* 301; 82 *PR* 705.
  Fourth para.: 23 *PR* 709–14, 809, 833; 24 *PR* 7, 70, 549, 582–3, 617; 25 *PR* 602; 26 *PR* 348; 29 *PR* 71, 153; 38 *PR* 93. But cf. 56 *PR* 282–4.
  Fifth para.: 21 *PR* 689, 747, 750–1, 790, 814; 22 *PR* 52; 23 *PR* 712–14; 24 *PR* 5, 66, 68, 227, 778–9.
  Sixth para.: 23 *PR* 710, 714, 833; 24 *PR* 2–9, 227; *Freethinking Christians' Magazine*, Aug. 1813, p. 347.
  Seventh to tenth paras.: 13 *PR* 597, 862; 24 *PR* 516, 521–5, 549, 586, 616, 716–17, 724; 25 *PR* 602; 35 *PR* 742–69; 45 *PR* 507, 546–7; 47 *PR* 359; 48 *PR* 377; 52 *PR* 353–6; 82 *PR* 705; 84 *PR* 519; *Legacy to Parsons*, letters v, vi. And see note on *Ecce Homo* below.
  Eleventh para.: 24 *PR* 226; 82 *PR* 705.
  Ecce Homo and Houston: I am indebted to the article of J. R. Dinwiddy in *Notes & Queries* ccxxii (July–Aug. 1977), 325 for information regarding the privy council papers (PRO pc 1/4032), which include four letters from Cobbett to Houston as well as other papers relating to the *Ecce Homo* episode; for facts concerning Houston and his relations with Timothy Brown; and for the reference to Cobbett in the *Freethinking Christians' Magazine* of August 1813.

Coffee, tea, and tobacco

Cobbett condemned coffee and tea – "slops," he called them –because of the cost, because of their effect on health, and because of the way the users became enslaved by the habit.

He estimated the cost of a year's tea drinking at £11 7s. 2d. This included the obvious items: the tea, sugar, and milk, constituting three-quarters of the total. It also included some not so obvious items: 5s. for one set of tea tackle on the assumption that at least one set was demolished each year; 16s. and some odd pence for the cost of the fires; another 15s. for the time required to make the tea, drink it, wash up, sweep the fireplace, and put things to rights again; and a final £1 19s. for the extra cost of beer consumed at a public house which would have been saved if the family brewed beer instead of making tea.

There was no "useful strength" in tea, nothing nutritious in it; it produced want of sleep, and it shook the nerves. "It is in fact, a weaker kind of laudanum, which enlivens for the moment and deadens afterwards." The three scourges of England, Cobbett thought in 1815, were tea, potatoes, and pedlars.

Coffee was very nearly as bad. If taken strong, both tea and coffee produced heartburn. "The writers all agree" that coffee "produces griping . . . I have not the smallest doubt that coffee might be taken in such a degree of strength, as for a quart of the liquor actually to kill, in a few hours, the stoutest man." Noting that coffee was a bean, Cobbett cited the case of a man from Tilford in Surrey who killed himself by making a heavy meal of broad beans, and another at Cobbett's sheepshearing in Botley who killed himself by eating kidney beans "cooked in the manner the French cook them." Women, in particular, were warned against tea and coffee. "Their never ceasing astringent effects produce costiveness; and that, too, till it becomes *habitual,* than which there is not a greater destroyer of beauty and of health, and particularly of the former, which it assails first, and which, having robbed of its rose colour, it substitutes a tawney in its place."

When Cobbett was living at Botley, he replaced tea and coffee with a drink made of roasted wheat, "And I positively assert, that it would be impossible for me to distinguish the beverage made from the wheat, from that made with coffee, except that the former has a rather milder and pleasanter taste than the latter."

As to tobacco, if Cobbett had been a female "the lips that held a quid, or touched a pipe or segar, should never touch my lips." At another point he classified smokers with "singers" and "ringers."

One must not assume that Cobbett always lived by his precepts. His pronouncements on these and other subjects were always well intended and were usually good rules: good for himself as well as for his readers; but they were not always followed. The man who advised others to "keep their expenses within the bounds of their income," who urged that goods be purchased with ready money rather than on credit, and who declared that the man in debt was a slave, lived beyond his means most of his life, regularly purchased on credit, and was perpetually in debt. The man who inveighed against the evils of the piano had one in his house at Kensington. Cobbett had learned the habit of taking snuff from the French, but, he wrote in 1820, "it has required only a very little effort to get rid of the filthy encumbrance." However, a letter written by daughter Anne in December 1821 implies that he was still using snuff at that date. Something he wrote in 1830 makes it plain that he occasionally smoked a pipe. And it is not at all improbable that Cobbett enjoyed a cup of tea or coffee at various times. One must take care to distinguish the myth Cobbett had created of himself from the fact. He was by no means a saint; in many respects he was like the rest of us.

References: 29 *PR* 168; 35 *PR* 524–7, 656, 661–2, 670, 693–5; 44 *PR* 759; 69 *PR* 421, 527; 82 *PR* 345–9; *Advice*, paras. 27, 60; *Cottage Economy*, paras. 23–4, 29–30; Anne to James, Dec. 27, 1821 (Nuffield).

Appendix 2 · Cobbett and Malthusianism

〰〰〰〰〰〰〰〰〰〰〰〰〰〰〰〰〰〰〰〰〰

"PARSON MALTHUS" – the Reverend Thomas Robert Malthus, holder of the first professorship of political economy in Britain – was a recurring theme in Cobbett's writings. His debate with Malthus was not, as some simplifiers have implied, over the single issue of Malthus's "principle of population," but was related to six different contentions of Malthus and his followers, which are described below.

1 *Population is proportioned to subsistence.*

In the preface to the first edition of *An Essay on the Principle of Population* (1798) Malthus declared: "It is an obvious truth . . . that population must always be kept down to the level of the means of subsistence," and this thought appears again and again in the body of the *Essay.* Cobbett agreed with the principle from the first time he mentioned it (1804) until the last time he mentioned it (1824).

References: 6 *PR* 869, 874; 7 *PR* 230; 13 *PR* 646; 51 *PR* 15.

2 *Population tends to increase faster than subsistence.*

Malthus stated in Chapter 1 of the 1798 edition that "the power of population is indefinitely greater than the power in the earth to produce subsistence for man."

This principle was accepted by Cobbett in 1804, but what he wrote later suggests that he no longer agreed with it: (1) In 1824 he asserted that since one man could raise enough food for twenty men, an increase in numbers could do no harm "so long as you do not augment the numbers that do not work"; (2) in 1826 he pointed to the valley of Avon, where the people raised nearly twenty times as much food and clothing as they consumed, as proof that there was no natural tendency to increase beyond the means of sustenance; and (3) in 1831 he referred with approval to "the answer which Mr. Godwin

551

gave to the book of Malthus." Godwin's answer, published in 1820, included various suggested methods of augmenting food production.

References: 6 *PR* 869; 52 *PR* 143–4; 59 *PR* 738 (*Rural Rides*, p. 317); 72 *PR* 70.

3 *Distress among the English poor was due to the increase in population.*

In later editions of the *Essay* Malthus urged that it be brought home to the comprehension of the common people that "they are themselves the cause of their own poverty; that the means of redress are in their own hands, and in the hands of no other persons whatever; that the society in which they live, and the government which presides over it, are without any direct power in this respect." (Bk. IV, ch. 3)

Cobbett disagreed, claiming that (1) there had been no increase in population in recent centuries, (2) the distress was due to taxes and other factors controlled by the government, and (3) the problem was one of food distribution, not food production: Each laborer, Charles Hall had pointed out, produced six to eight times as much as his family required; the poor were being starved in the midst of plenty.

References: *PR* 1044; 41 *PR* 285, 548; 42 *PR* 615; 46 *PR* 65; 49 *PR* 337, 398; 52 *PR* 131; 72 *PR* 71. The basis for Cobbett's disbelief in the census figures is discussed in Chapter 21, and was almost certainly colored by the widely accepted view that "everywhere towns and cities were drawing away the peasantry" and by the statistics produced in the latter part of the eighteenth century showing that in the towns and cities of the Old World, as contrasted with those of America, deaths outnumbered births. See H. S. Commager, *The Empire of Reason* (New York 1977), pp. 96–103.

4 *The increase in population was due to financial assistance provided by the poor laws.*

The "first obvious tendency" of the English poor laws, wrote Malthus, "is to increase population without increasing the food for its support." (Ch. 5, 1798 ed.)

Cobbett disagreed with this conclusion, pointing to the rapid increase of population in Ireland, where there were no poor laws.

References: 50 *PR* 799; 51 *PR* 15.

5 *The growth in population should be checked by "moral restraint."*

Malthus claimed in later editions of the *Essay* that the poor were "obligated" to practice moral restraint, by which he meant late marriage or no marriage at all, and that these must not be accompanied by "irregular gratifications." (Bk. I, ch. 2; Bk. IV, ch. 1). Neo-Malthusians like Francis Place thought that contraception, rather than late marriage, was the only feasible check. Others proposed emigration.

Cobbett disagreed with all the proposals: moral restraint, contraception, and enforced emigration.

References: 13 *PR* 646; 31 *PR* 564; 32 *PR* 25; 34 *PR* 1019; 69 *PR* 351. The subject of contraception is referred to in Ch. 23, n. 4. The issue of "moral restraint" was involved in Cobbett's play *Surplus Population*, mentioned in the same note.

6 *Poor relief should be denied in order to check population.*

In the later editions of the *Essay* Malthus proposed that a "regulation" be made eliminating public assistance in respect of children born after the issue of the regulation; and that the poor man should be taught that the "laws of nature, which are the laws of God, had doomed him and his family to suffer for disobeying their repeated admonitions, that he had no claim of right on society for the smallest portion of food beyond that which his labour would fairly purchase." (Bk. IV, ch. 7)

This was the principal ground for Cobbett's disagreement with the Malthusians. He claimed that (1) it was illegal to deny relief to the poor; (2) it was unjust to compel the poor to bear the burdens of society (producing the food and clothes, paying taxes, rendering military service) and to deny them any benefits, while tax money was being splurged on the parasites of society: the sinecurists, the clergy, the "dead-weight"; and (3) it was unwise to put the poor "on the footing of the law of nature," in which they would be justified in using force to take what they wanted.

The Malthusian concept involved in this paragraph was incorporated into the poor law amendments of 1834, creating the cruelty that Cobbett warned against, and which later was so bitterly attacked by Charles Dickens in such novels as *Oliver Twist* and *Our Mutual Friend*.

References: 31 *PR* 562; 32 *PR* 25; 34 *PR* 853, 1019; 35 *PR* 99; 39 *PR* 436; 46 *PR* 65; 47 *PR* 427. Cobbett's attack on the poor law amendments is discussed in Chapter 24. Cobbett also ran four articles by William Hazlitt ("A.O." and "The Author of a reply to the essay on population") attacking Malthus because of his proposed denial of poor relief. 11 *PR* 397, 882, 935; 18 *PR* 1014.

Two confusing articles entitled "Cobbett and Malthusianism" have appeared in the *Journal of the History of Ideas*, XIII (1952), 250 and XIX (1958), 348.

Notes

Abbreviations

Add. MSS. – British Library, Additional Manuscripts

Anne – "Account of the Family" by Anne Cobbett (Nuffield xv)

DNB – *Dictionary of National Biography*

ER – *Edinburgh Review*

JPC – Recently discovered notebook entitled "Memoranda relating to Life & Times of Cobbett" dated "Manchester, July 6, 1855. J.P.C." (estate of General Sir Gerald Lathbury)

JPC Memoir – "A Memoir of William Cobbett by James Paul Cobbett" (70-page manuscript) with introduction dated "Manchester October 1, 1862" (Nuffield xiv)

No. 1 Correspondence – Recently discovered notebook entitled "No. 1 Correspondence from 14 Jany. 92 to 24 Sepr. 1793" containing copies of Cobbett's correspondence relating to the 1792 court-martial and the original of his discharge from the army. At some point, pp. 69–74 of the notebook were removed, and thus all correspondence after March 1792 is missing

PRO – Public Record Office

QR – *Quarterly Review*

Susan – "Additional Notes" written by Susan Cobbett relating to family affairs (Nuffield xvii)

WR – *Westminster Review*

Various other documents held in the Nuffield College library are identified by the numbers assigned to them in M. L. Pearl, *William Cobbett: A Bibliographical Account of His Life and Times* (London 1953), pp. 223f.

The Cobbett children are identified in the notes by their Christian names alone: Anne, William junior, John, James, Ellen, Susan, and Richard. Their mother, Anne Reid Cobbett, is referred to as Nancy.

The writings of Cobbett are referred to in the notes by short titles alone. Their full titles and information about their publication are given in the Cobbett portion of Sources.

16. Out of Newgate

Motto: 18 *PR* 615.

1 Hazlitt, *The Spirit of the Age,* p. 333.

2 Roberts, *Whig Party,* pp. 272, 294; 17 *PR* 801; 21 *PR* 774.

3 16 *PR* 11, 920. The second action was a criminal indictment against Mrs. Clarke and two others for conspiracy, in which Vicary Gibbs, the attorney general, represented the defendants!

4 Huch, *Lord Radnor,* pp. 56–69.

5 In July 1811 Burdett sued William Scott, brother of Lady Oxford, over £5,000 which Burdett claimed he had given Scott because he believed that Lady Oxford and her husband were going to separate.

6 Hannah More wrote to Lord Barham, former first lord of the admiralty and cousin of Gambier: "Yet terrible as Bonaparte is in every point of view, I do not fear him so much as those domestic mischiefs – Burdett, Cochrane, Wardle and Cobbett. I hope, however, that the mortification Cochrane, etc. have lately experienced in their base and impotent endeavours to pull down reputations which they found unassailable, will keep them down a little." Lloyd, *Lord Cochrane,* p. 75.

7 18 *PR* 458.

8 William Smart, *Economic Annals of the Nineteenth Century* (New York 1964 repr.) 1:227.

9 "The Decline and Fall of the English System of Finance" in Paine, *Political Works,* p. 497. In the quoted language Paine was mimicking Pitt, who had used these words to refer to the French condition.

10 32 *PR* 1030; 20 *PR* 10.

11 35 *PR* 222.

12 Hansard, 1st ser. xxvii: App., cclx. The report was not available to the public until August 1810.

13 18 *PR* 66, 97, 129, 205.

14 18 *PR* 258. C described the origin of the paper at 43 *PR* 145.

15 32 *PR* 512. In 1819 C seemed to claim that 300,000 had been sold as of December 1816, but he may have been referring to the number as of the date he was writing. 34 *PR* 1055. In 1824 he gave 40,000 as the "whole" number that had been sold, but he may have been referring only to the quantity of the stereotype edition. 49 *PR* 809. In 1828 C stated that 30,000 copies had been printed and circulated in the "two penny trash" form in 1817. 65 *PR* 115. Later in the same year, he claimed that more than 100,000 copies had been sold. 65 *PR* 608.

16 *Paper against Gold* was also issued in a series of fifteen twopenny parts.

17 20 *PR* 9–10, letter xxv.

18 C had frequently recommended repudiation in earlier articles. He did not do so in *Paper against Gold,* although he stated that the paper money could be lessened only by "the destruction of the whole mass." 18 *PR* 260, letter 1. He believed that "the day is, probably, not far distant, when a guinea, a real *golden* guinea, will buy a hundred pound's worth of three per cents." 20 *PR* 130, letter xxix. Even more, he foresaw "paper-money tending to total annihilation." 23 *PR* 166.

19 20 *PR* 12, letter xxv.

20 These figures are for 1809, when taxes amounted to £70 million. 18 *PR* 328, letter iii. In 1977–8, by way of contrast, interest on the debt in Britain was approximately 15 percent of tax revenues.

   The distinguished economist J. R. McCulloch in 1816 joined C in urging a reduction in interest on the debt as the only way to relieve the distresses of commercial and agricultural interests. Smart, *Economic Annals* 1:510.

21 20 *PR* 131, letter xxix.

22 In a letter to Croker of November 11, 1810 Perceval wrote: "I should consider the measure proposed as tantamount to a parliamentary declaration that we must submit to any terms of peace rather than continue the war." Quoted in Smart 1:255. See also Arthur D. Gayer, W. W. Rostow and A. J. Schwartz, *The Growth and Fluctuation of the British Economy* (Oxford 1953) 1:107.

23 Bryant, *Years of Victory,* p. 440.

24 19 *PR* 1409.

25 ". . . who is there mad enough to expect, that we shall be able to put the French

out of the Peninsula ...?" 19 *PR* 68. In October 1811 C suggested a British withdrawal. 20 *PR* 524.

26 Charles Grant Robertson, *England under the Hanoverians* (London 1953 repr.), p. 450.

27 18 *PR* 873.

28 Aspinall (ed.), *Correspondence* v:439.

29 18 *PR* 1136.

30 18 *PR* 1233. One wonders to what extent C was relying on the widespread belief that the prince was for anything his father was against.

   C's defense of the prince appears at 18 *PR* 1036, 1318; 19 *PR* 1. The prince was politically "a sheet of unsoiled paper." 19 *PR* 202.

31 One cannot exclude the possibility that C believed that the prince regent might mitigate his sentence. Anne claimed that C rejected an offer to be let out in return for a promise that he "would be silent on the subject of the princess." Anne, p. 28. Leigh Hunt reported a similar offer to himself if he would abstain from commenting on the prince. J. E. Morpurgo (ed.), *The Autobiography of Leigh Hunt* (London 1959), p. 233.

32 19 *PR* 17.

33 19 *PR* 432. In March 1812 C hinted that Perceval had been kept in office because, as former attorney for Princess Caroline, he was in possession of "The Book" (published in 1813 as *An Inquiry, or Delicate Investigation into the Conduct of Her Royal Highness the Princess of Wales* ...) and other unpublished material pertaining to the relations between the prince and his estranged wife. 21 *PR* 400–11. The hint was enlarged to an unequivocal claim in *George IV*, paras. 100, 110. The story is branded "absurd" by Gray (*Perceval*, p. 90n).

34 19 *PR* 353. C's gradual disillusionment with the prince is summarized at 20 *PR* 388–90. One of his earliest acts was the restoration of the Duke of York as commander-in-chief of the army, although the prince's advisers were apprehensive about C's response. Aspinall (ed.), *Correspondence* VII:337.

35 18 *PR* 1214. It shortly appeared that the French notice of renunciation was deceitful, but the Americans had gone too far to back down. Morison, *Oxford History* II:106; Morris, *Encyclopedia of American History*, p. 138.

36 12 *PR* 678–9. See also 12 *PR* 245, 266, 365.

37 10 *PR* 973; 12 *PR* 262, 266; 13 *PR* 423, 481; 14 *PR* 5.

38 18 *PR* 1185; 19 *PR* 458, 555, 577, 935; 20 *PR* 257, 289, 321, 545, 649, 717, 737, 813; 21 *PR* 12, 65, 129, 193, 624, 781.

39 12 *PR* 981.

40 H. Adams, *History of the United States* VII:356.

41 18 *PR* 1195; 19 *PR* 556.

42 20 *PR* 550, 650; 22 *PR* 812.

43 10 *PR* 973; 12 *PR* 268, 645, 963–4; 13 *PR* 425, 489, 977. C made many other assertions in 1807–8 that were inconsistent with his views in 1811–12, particularly concerning the ability of the Americans to conduct a war against Britain. 12 *PR* 238, 682; 13 *PR* 19, 41, 54, 200. Cf. 21 *PR* 195; 23 *PR* 2–5.

44 13 *PR* 468–7.

45 20 *PR* 334. Yet in 1823 C claimed that no one but Canning could possibly believe that Britain and America could "cordially co-operate with one another for their mutual good." 47 *PR* 719.

46 C's concern over British objectives in Europe as they affected the American issue is expressed at 20 *PR* 743–56.

47 In a letter to Mathew Carey of Philadelphia, July 16, 1815 (Historical Society of Pennsylvania), C attributed his earlier attitude toward America as due, in part, to "that *legal persecution* ... I endured in America" and suggested that he had been "brought round by the feeling of greater persecution." Place had once accused C

of "carrying his personal feelings [against the Americans] into a national dispute." C attempted to justify himself "on the ground of taking revenge." Add. MSS. 35145, fol. 8.

48 C's hard-line position in the earlier period had been formulated in 1806 when the conciliatory ministry of All the Talents was still in office. 10 *PR* 970. Hence in both 1807 and 1811 his stance, at conception, was antigovernment. "I have never, in any case, been in favour with those who were in power." 31 *PR* 640.

49 21 *PR* 649.

50 The assassination and resulting trial are reported in detail in Mollie Gillen, *Assassination of the Prime Minister: The Shocking Death of Spencer Perceval* (London 1972).

51 Romilly, *Memoirs* III:35.

52 Earl Leslie Griggs (ed.), *Collected Letters of Samuel Taylor Coleridge* (Oxford 1956–71) III:410.

53 21 *PR* 682. That there was considerable rejoicing at Nottingham is unquestioned, but the *Nottingham Journal* contended that the bellringing was inadvertent: that it happened to be practice night for the ringers. Gillen, pp. 33–4.

54 21 *PR* 660–1. It is not clear whether the charges against Bellingham were false, as he alleged. The British ambassador to Russia claimed that Bellingham had been given all possible assistance. 22 *PR* 674; Gillen, pp. 135–8.

55 21 *PR* 671.

56 21 *PR* 683.

57 21 *PR* 688.

58 21 *PR* 719.

59 21 *PR* 722–3.

60 21 *PR* 723. "In all there were twelve judgeships between the three Common Law courts – the King's Bench, Common Pleas and Exchequer. Each of these courts had a president, the Chief Justice or Chief Baron and three 'Puisne' judges." Halévy, *History* 1:26.

61 Letter to the Rev. Richard Polwhele, Oct. 10, 1800 (Nuffield).

62 Simond, *An American in Regency England,* pp. 33, 159.

63 See, for example, 15 *PR* 911–17; 16 *PR* 110.

64 Anne, p. 22.

65 Shortly after his release, C was determined to print a one-page summary of the prosecution in every issue of the *PR* "as long as I shall live." 22 *PR* 110. This was discontinued after about six months (23 *PR* 31), but thereafter the incident was constantly referred to. In *Advice,* written eighteen years afterwards, there are three references to the jail sentence.

66 Anne, pp. 31, 34.

67 Peter Walker visited C every day he was in prison. 53 *PR* 267. Other visitors included Sailor Jeffries and Councilman Favell. 33 *PR* 578; 52 *PR* 406, 420.

68 22 *PR* 91. See Simond, p. 161. The number of such visitors, according to C, was more than a thousand. 53 *PR* 486.

69 *Diary, Reminiscences, and Correspondence of Henry Crabb Robinson,* ed. Thomas Sadler (London 1872) I:210.

70 22 *PR* 55. C's two sureties were Timothy Brown and Peter Walker. 22 *PR* 112.

71 22 *PR* 92. C declined an invitation to a public dinner in Norwich. 22 *PR* 113. Meetings were held at Paisley and Oxford to celebrate C's release. 22 *PR* 147.

72 *Times,* July 9, 1812. The writer of the letter might have been John Wright or Henry White, editor of the *Independent Whig.* C's proposal that his well-wishers purchase the back numbers of the *PR* is at 18 *PR* 182–4.

73 22 *PR* 92–3. The denial was not quite "once for all"; it was repeated in 1817. 32 *PR* 12–13.

C's proposed advertisement did not use the words "softening my tone," but said that the *Register* must "take quite a new tone and manner, nay, that its matter must also be changed; that, in short, it must be nearly, if not quite, the exact opposite of what it has hitherto been." *Courier*, Dec. 31, 1819. The text as quoted in *The Times* of July 9, 1812 is not complete, and in the portion cited above uses the words "totally different to [from]" instead of "the exact opposite of."

74 An even less favorable account of C's conduct was given by Wright in 1820. *Republican* XIII:596–602.

75 C's pride did not prevent him from denying Gibbs's allegation. Ch. 15, n. 52.

76 Susan's gloss on letter of Anne (Melville, *Cobbett* II:73) referred to in n. 77 below.

77 Anne to Frederick Reid, July 13, 1812 (Melville II:72; present location unknown).

78 22 *PR* 93–4.

79 Letter of Anne; see n. 77 above.

80 22 *PR* 94.

81 Letter of Anne; see n. 77 above.

17. Peace

Motto: 18 *PR* 782.

1 Brougham, *Historical Sketches* II:171. Keith Feiling credits Lord Liverpool with four "primarily ministerial powers": he was a candid, businesslike speaker; had a stout heart; was a peacemaker and a patriot; and was loyal to his colleagues. *Sketches in Nineteenth Century Biography* (London 1930), pp. 21–3. He was educated at Charterhouse; his first cabinet was chiefly distinguished by having what was probably the largest number of Carthusians (four) and the smallest number of Etonians (one) of any cabinet of the nineteenth century.

2 34 *PR* 1048. "Never was there people satisfied with a smaller portion of talent in its prime minister." 46 *PR* 153.

3 ". . . the aptest of all Pitt's disciples." 27 *PR* 689.

4 Ibid.

5 23 *PR* 817. C was not the only Englishman who admired Napoleon. Some of the more prominent are discussed in a strange book by E. Tangye Lean, *The Napoleonists* (London 1970).

6 25 *PR* 88–9; 26 *PR* 235.

7 26 *PR* 236.

8 25 *PR* 90.

9 26 *PR* 234–5.

10 25 *PR* 94; 24 *PR* 326.

11 24 *PR* 329.

12 24 *PR* 328.

13 25 *PR* 94; 26 *PR* 237.

14 25 *PR* 648, 784.

15 26 *PR* 289–90.

16 26 *PR* 231.

17 24 *PR* 386–7, 514, 577; 25 *PR* 481–3, 515, 606.

18 24 *PR* 387–8, 578; 25 *PR* 461.

19 25 *PR* 515. On Napoleon's death, C scorned the suggestion that he be called "a great man." 39 *PR* 1051. C warmly espoused the cause of republicanism in France and the United States (27 *PR* 325), but declared that he was not a republican and never wished for republican government in England. *Year's Residence*, pp. 558–9. It is not clear whether he used "republican" in its two different meanings or favored a republic for other countries but not for England or favored a republic for England but thought it indiscreet to say so. In 1821 C said flatly: "I do not like republican government." 40 *PR* 1546. See also 42 *PR* 125–6.

20 25 *PR* 791. "He was a despot humbling despots." 32 *PR* 1055.

21   27 *PR* 360. In 1802 C had declared that in certain cases one nation has the "undoubted" right to interfere in the domestic concerns of another. 2 *PR* 442.

22   In July 1815, after Louis XVIII had been installed a second time, C wrote: "No, no, Louis: you are restored, as you were last year, by foreign bayonets ... You have a stormy time to pass. The battle between light and liberty, on the one side, and darkness and despotism, on the other; that battle which began in 1789, is still going on. It may rage fiercely for a time; but, it will not be put an end to unless by the triumph of the former." 28 *PR* 4. See also 25 *PR* 547: "sooner or not, those principles must triumph."

23   20 *PR* 585–7. See also 22 *PR* 264.

24   25 *PR* 642.

25   "In May and June [1814] no one in England, unless it were Cobbett, entertained more than a passing doubt of British success on land and water." Henry Adams, *The Formative Years*, condensed and ed. Herbert Agar (London 1948) II:961. According to C, "one man in authority actually said: 'We shall now beat those Americans: and that will destroy Cobbett's credit forever'." 36 *PR* 62.

26   25 *PR* 519.

27   Hansard, 1st ser. XXVII:1045 (June 1, 1814).

28   26 *PR* 356. See also 26 *PR* 610. The Serpentine demonstration began with Nelson's victory at the battle of the Nile; the staged victory over the Americans came later in the program and is not so dramatically described by *The Times* for August 2, 1814.

29   The British government's intention to punish the Americans by burning their coastal towns was known to C shortly after Bonaparte's surrender in April 1814, and was relayed by him to an American official in London. 47 *PR* 726–7.

     To the complaint that the British had burned "scarce books" in the Library of Congress, *The Times* of November 1, 1814 declared that "a single shelf in the Spencerian library would purchase all the scarce books that ever found their way across the Atlantic since the United States have had to boast an existence; and sure we are, that if there were any scarce books at Washington, the 'readers, that *could* read them' were much scarcer."

30   C contended that the British public was never told about the New Orleans disaster, and in 1833 he rehearsed the events for the benefit of the uninformed. 80 *PR* 771.

31   Morison, *Oxford History* II:129. Cobbett had earlier made much the same observation. 26 *PR* 581.

32   On January 3, 1815, ten days after the treaty of Ghent had been signed, Castlereagh agreed to a secret triple alliance with Austria and France, by which Britain was obligated to put 150,000 men in the field in the event of war with Russia and Prussia.

     The whig opposition in the House of Commons supported the war against America to the very last. In November 1814 only Samuel Whitbread and Sir Gilbert Heathcote favored a peaceful settlement. 26 *PR* 623–7. In December 1814 Sir William Curtis, speaking in the London Common Council, "agreed ... that a peace with the Americans was extremely desirable, but he trusted he should see them confoundedly flogged first." *Times*, Dec. 10, 1814; 26 *PR* 771.

33   50 *PR* 226: The American sailors "were not fighting against me and against my neighbours, but against Gatton." 32 *PR* 1056: "The struggle in England ... is the struggle of oppressed Europe." At a later point C said he had been for the Americans because the English boroughmongers were against them. 77 *PR* 3.

34   26 *PR* 449.

35   26 *PR* 546; 26 *PR* 837.

36   26 *PR* 546; *Times*, Oct. 19, 1814. C believed that the earlier outpourings of *The Times* had been a cause of the war. 26 *PR* 833.

37   On June 5, 1815, two weeks before Waterloo, *The Times* asserted: "The revolution-

ary ideas of France have already made but too great a progress in the hearts of men in all countries, and even in the very centre of every capital ... It is not Buonaparte that at present forms the danger of Europe: he is unmasked. It is the new opinions ... This is the true hydra which must be destroyed."

38   26 *PR* 454–5. According to C, the federalist papers had prolonged the war by convincing the British government that the Americans were about to overturn Madison. 28 *PR* 139–40.

39   27 *PR* 72. Hippisley, while admitting that he had spoken "in terms of strong reprobation," denied using the words reported by *The Times*. 27 *PR* 148.

40   27 *PR* 325.

41   27 *PR* 518–19. These principles reflect rights which the English nobility and landed gentry had already won from the monarch through the reforms that culminated with the 1689 Act of Settlement. By their control of parliament they could make or unmake the sovereign; they had, among themselves, political and legal equality; they made the decisions concerning taxes and passed the laws concerning punishment. They had asked for and been given the assurance that freedom of speech, and of debates or proceedings in parliament, ought not to be impeached or questioned in any court. The freedom of the press was quite a different affair, for the press was distinctly and exclusively a lower-class profession. Hence, the constraints on a free press were of little significance to the ruling classes, who had won the right to say in parliament whatever they wanted to say.

42   Of course C also regarded the peace as another personal triumph. 27 *PR* 325, 577.

43   C later asserted that the intrigue of the British ministry had brought Napoleon back. 33 *PR* 18.

44   31 *PR* 420. See also 30 *PR* 129.

45   28 *PR* 106–7.

46   Crop failures had occurred in 1809, 1810, 1811, and 1812. Frank O. Darvall, *Popular Disturbances and Public Order in Regency England* ... (London 1934), p. 21. C reported riots over food shortages and high prices during 1811–12 in Cornwall and Devon and at Carlisle and Bristol. 21 *PR* 492, 531. See Darvall, pp. 95–6.

47   Darvall, p. 55. One of C's correspondents provided a scale of pay for weaving from 1792 to 1815 showing that there had been a steady decline, with bottom prices in 1811–12, a substantial upturn in 1814, and a sharp drop in 1815. 29 *PR* 307.

48   Darvall, pp. 53–4. The figures given by B. R. Mitchell and Phyllis Deane (*Abstract of British Historical Statistics* (Cambridge 1971), p. 187) for numbers employed in the cotton industry during these years are subject to question, since they show a 5 percent increase in employment between 1810 and 1812 while also showing (p. 179) that cotton consumption declined by more than one-third.

49   21 *PR* 545.

50   22 *PR* 23. C's credibility as to the deteriorating condition of the farm laborer is enhanced by his recognition that in certain parts of England (for example in West Sussex, where good landlords existed) the workers were well fed and comfortably housed as compared with those in the north of Wiltshire, in Somerset, and in eastern Kent. 47 *PR* 356, 452, 660–1.

The complex causes of Luddism are discussed in E. P. Thompson, *English Working Class*, pp. 593f: Hunger "may help to explain its occasion, but not its character."

51   31 *PR* 733.

52   32 *PR* 25.

53   22 *PR* 14.

54   22 *PR* 24.

55   Darvall, *Popular Disturbances*, pp. 259, 263.

56 Ibid. p. 102.
57 Ibid. pp. 124, 260, 263.
58 Ibid. pp. 104, 130-1.
59 *Year's Residence*, p. 502.
60 H. W. C. Davis, *The Age of Grey and Peel* (Oxford 1967 repr.), p. 169.
61 Consumption of raw cotton in millions of pounds fell from 124 in 1810 to 73 in 1812. The 1810 level of production was not regained until 1820-1. Mitchell and Deane, *Statistics*, p. 179.
62 Darvall, pp. 144-9.
63 Smart, *Economic Annals* 1:516n.
64 There was no objective measure of harvests, and agreement occurs only when one was extremely good or extremely bad. Even a single source provides conflicting conclusions. See, for example, reports for 1810, 1812, and 1814 in Smart 1:225, 332, 396, 528.
65 27 *PR* 161.
66 30 *PR* 421.
67 28 *PR* 142.
68 Gayer et al., *British Economy* 1:115. A contemporary, Matthias Attwood, said: "In the years 1815 and 1816 this country was involved in calamities and sufferings as great and severe as . . . have been ever endured by any civilized community." Hansard, 2nd ser. v:102 (Apr. 9, 1821).
69 28 *PR* 140.
70 30 *PR* 175.
71 Smart 1:529.
72 30 *PR* 770, quoting the *Morning Chronicle*.
73 Smart 1:492.
74 31 *PR* 12-14.
75 32 *PR* 405-8.
76 Gayer et al., 1:121.
77 Smart 1:493n.
78 31 *PR* 765. The prince's pleasure dome in Brighton, dubbed the Kremlin, reminded C of a square box decorated with the tops of turnips and flower bulbs of various types. 41 *PR* 180.
79 30 *PR* 455.
80 Smart 1:540.
81 30 *PR* 369-73.
82 30 *PR* 801, 808.
83 There was virtually no reform activity in parliament between Brand's motion for reform in 1812 (Hansard, 1st ser. XXIII:99 (May 8, 1812)) and Burdett's motion for the appointment of a committee to inquire into the state of representation in 1817 (ibid. XXXVI:704 (May 20, 1817)). In the debate on the latter, J. W. Ward declared "that a motion for reform in Parliament produces upon my mind the same effect as a motion for a democracy, a motion for a revolution, a motion that the form of government should now cease and determine" (758).
84 In February 1814, stock prices rose on the London exchange on false news of the death of Napoleon. Lord Cochrane, his uncle Andrew Cochrane Johnstone, and another were found guilty of this hoax in a trial before a special jury presided over by Lord Ellenborough. The latter sentenced Cochrane to pay a fine of £1,000, to stand in the pillory for one hour, and to be imprisoned for a year. Cochrane was struck off the list of navy post captains and expelled from parliament and from the order of the Bath. He admitted that he had made a small profit from the rise, but denied any part in the hoax. He was immediately reelected to parliament by the voters of Westminster and was warmly defended by C, although C openly expressed his regret that Cochrane should have speculated in the shares. See 25 *PR* 353, 385, 602, 769, 810; 26 *PR* 1, 33, 65, 129, 210, 257, 384, 412. In 1832

Cochrane was reinstated in the navy with the rank of rear admiral. The court case led to a century-long enmity between the descendants of Cochrane and Ellenborough.

85 Huch, *Lord Radnor*, pp. 84–8, 94.

86 E. P. Thompson, *English Working Class*, pp. 665–8; Davis, *Age of Grey and Peel*, pp. 167–87. Under the Seditious Societies Act of 1799 it was unlawful to organize branches of a society; hence, each Hampden Club was a separate unit.

87 In 1810 C wrote of "those political hot-beds, called clubs and societies, which never did yet, in any part of the world, produce good and wholesome and lasting fruit." 17 *PR* 570. His dislike for such organizations began with his earliest writings and continued throughout his life. See *Works* 11:13; 3 *PR* 34–5; 15 *PR* 524, 556; 30 *PR* 535–6; 31 *PR* 289, 734; 32 *PR* 220, 263, 1166; 58 *PR* 326; 62 *PR* 606–7.

However, C seems to have been a member (along with his friends Bosville, Hallett, and Timothy Brown) of the London Union Society that lasted from 1812 to 1814, which may not have been much more than a discussion group. 32 *PR* 266; 34 *PR* 406.

88 Letters to Hunt (Adelphi). After C and Hunt had a final falling out, C spitefully provided some notion of Hunt's rustic style of speaking in these two sentences: "I have lautely bin in Normany, Genmun; a great forrren country in Vrance, Genmun" and "the ministers would have been adeluden ov the peepul." 76 *PR* 95, 484.

89 30 *PR* 272.

90 Petition of the Inhabitant Householders of the City and Liberties of Westminster to the Regent, September 1816. 31 *PR* 365, 367.

91 31 *PR* 658. C and Cartwright favored the vote for those aged twenty-one or more. When Hunt announced that he favored eighteen, C agreed. 34 *PR* 356. By 1818 Bentham and Burdett were supporting universal suffrage. Halévy, *History* 11:31n. C probably never felt strongly about the need for complete universality, but only that "the people were in any way honestly represented." *Times*, Jan. 20, 1823.

At this point female suffrage does not seem to have been an issue. When the question was raised in 1831, C stated that he did not intend to include the vote for women. See ch. 23, n. 10.

92 At this time C was so insistent about the importance of annual parliaments that he bitterly attacked Robert Waithman, a prominent London merchant and reformer, as a traitor to the cause for favoring triennial elections. 32 *PR* 122–8. See also 34 *PR* 292: "I have no fears for his bottom, but great fears for his top." There had, however, been some falling out over other issues before this. 23 *PR* 563; 25 *PR* 707, 720, 723.

93 31 *PR* 365, 366.

94 31 *PR* 449–78.

95 34 *PR* 113–16. C was badly off in his estimates. He believed that tax revenues in 1817 would not "yield a clear amount of more than 35 millions" (32 *PR* 137), later raised to £37 million (32 *PR* 593), whereas gross income for that year was more than £65 million, and the cost of collection was about £5 million. One of the major differences was that the treasury received about £12 million in 1817 from arrearages in income tax, which had been repealed the year before. C also substantially underestimated tax revenues for 1816. 29 *PR* 396.

96 30 *PR* 307–8.

97 30 *PR* 369. See also 30 *PR* 649.

98 Smart, *Economic Annals* 1:489; 30 *PR* 623, 707–19.

99 Letter to Henry Hunt, June 5, 1816 (Adelphi). A letter to Hunt from William junior in mid September reads: "We have housed no wheat, nor any thing else, except a few peas." Sept. 13, 1816 (Adelphi).

100 John D. Post, *The Last Great Subsistence Crisis in the Western World* (Baltimore and

London 1977), pp. 14, 16, 27. The 300-year period 1550–1850 is recognized today as the "little ice age." Post, p. xii.

101 31 *PR* 595. Early in January 1817 he wrote: "Do you not think, that the drama is drawing towards a close?" 32 *PR* 2.

102 "The Decline and Fall of the English System of Finance" in Paine, *Political Works*, p. 487.

103 31 *PR* 626; 35 *PR* 409; 36 *PR* 174, 177, 280; 38 *PR* 128–9. At times C suggested that reform might come before the collapse. 44 *PR* 662.

104 Other changes that took place at about this time include C's move to London for the winter of 1815–16, when he stayed much of the time at the home of his friend Timothy Brown at Peckham Lodge, and again for the winter of 1816–17, when he was "in and near London." From December 1816 or thereabouts C lived in the house he had rented at 8 Catherine Street.

The January 27, 1816 issue of the *PR* stated that it was "printed and published by and for William Cobbett Jun," who was then eighteen years old. 30 *PR* 127–8. See also 32 *PR* 450, where William junior is referred to as "proprietor."

105 31 *PR* 545.

106 C claimed that there were 100 clubs at which the *PR* was read aloud. 29 *PR* 355.

107 A claim that a tax was payable on the single sheet was later asserted by the stamp office for an aggregate of £80,000, but it does not seem to have been pressed. 32 *PR* 872; 53 *PR* 5.

108 31 *PR* 613, 673; 32 *PR* 551. C claimed that the total sale of this one issue was more than 200,000. 33 *PR* 425.

The circulation of all newspapers had declined markedly after the end of the war with France. Before the cheap edition was inaugurated, "more than 1600" copies of the *PR* were being sold (32 *PR* 566), as contrasted with the 4,750 copies being printed in 1806, the last date for which we have a specific figure.

109 31 *PR* 545, 547, 576. After C's manuscript had gone off to London, he had serious misgivings about the cheap edition and sent his son John to stop it, but by the time John arrived in London 6,000 copies had been sold. 32 *PR* 550–1.

110 C gave Paine credit for awakening "the spirit of enquiry" in the common people. 44 *PR* 707.

111 William H. Wickwar, *The Struggle for the Freedom of the Press 1819–1832* (London 1928), pp. 52–3. Compare the view of Coleridge: "it is the duty of the enlightened Philanthropist to plead *for* the poor and ignorant, not *to* them." *Collected Works of Coleridge* 4: vol. II:137.

112 *Times*, Nov. 14, 1816. Because of the "unprecedented demand" for this article, it was republished. *Times*, Nov. 20, 1816.

113 31 *PR* 639–40.

114 The cost per copy was 1½d. when 100 copies were purchased. 31 *PR* 641. The broadsheet was replaced by a pamphlet on December 21, 1816, it having been noticed that the tax on pamphlets containing news was only 3s. per issue, regardless of the number printed. 32 *PR* 453. On such payment, it became "licensed by authority" and, according to C, could be distributed anywhere by persons who had no license. In 1818 the price was reduced to 11s. per 100. 34 *PR* 57.

115 32 *PR* 46. C later stated that the name had been coined by his erstwhile colleague William Gifford (now a government sinecurist). 62 *PR* 26. In 1830 C gave credit to Gifford, Walter (*The Times*), Stuart (*Courier*), and "other hack-supporters of the system." *Two-Penny Trash* 1:5.

C's first use of the term seems to have been in 1820. 35 *PR* 576.

116 *QR* xvi (Oct. 1816), 275.

117 32 *PR* 94.

118 31 *PR* 610, 705, 769; 32 *PR* 109, 129; E. P. Thompson, *English Working Class*, p. 801; Aspinall, *Politics and the Press*, pp. 46–9.

119 32 *PR* 94. *Two-Penny Trash* 1:2: "the sale rose to sixty or seventy thousand" a week.

120 32 *PR* 256. C claimed the sale of 20,000 on a single day in London. 32 *PR* 567. Presumably this was the issue of April 5, 1817, "Mr. Cobbett's Taking Leave of His Countrymen." By mid 1818 C was claiming that "two millions of Registers are in the hands of the people." 33 *PR* 615.

121 Richard Rush to James Madison, Apr. 18, 1817 (Historical Society of Pennsylvania).

122 31 *PR* 799; 32 *PR* 39, 626. 32 *PR* 612: "I did more in the space of a month to prevent depredations of this sort, than all the new penal laws, all the magistrates, and all the troops had been able to do in seven years; and to prove this there were fifty magistrates ready and willing to come to the Bar of the Parliament." C stated that from the first appearance of the cheap *Register* to the suspension of the Habeas Corpus Act "not a riot took place in any part of the kingdom, except at one place in Scotland where the people had been *too loyal* to permit any meeting for reform." 33 *PR* 420.

123 31 *PR* 688. Although Ricardo praised C's letter to the Luddites, he later believed that C "underestimated the effect of machinery in throwing men out of work." *Letters of David Ricardo to Thomas Robert Malthus*, ed. James Bonar (Oxford 1887), p. xv.

124 Darvall, *Popular Disturbances*, p. 134n, quoting Frank Peel, *The Rising of the Luddites, Chartists and Plug-Drawers* (1888). Samuel Bamford (*Passages in the Life of a Radical*, ed. Henry Dunckley (London 1893) 1:6–7), speaking of C's influence, said: "Riots soon became scarce, and from that time they have never obtained their ancient vogue with the labourers of this country."

125 31 *PR* 650.

126 The society, founded in 1814, took its name from Thomas Spence, who had died earlier that year. Spence believed that land should be public property to which all persons had an equal share.

  C thought Spence "a most virtuous man." *Collective Commentaries*, p. 221. According to the ultraconservative *Quarterly Review*, Spence "was honest; he was not one of those demagogues who, like Cobbett, make mischief their trade because they find it a gainful one." XVI (Oct. 1816), 267. A handbill of the society published in 1816 or thereabouts stated that the misery of the people was not due to the expenses of the government (C's position) but to the unjust exactions of the landowners. Francis Place claimed that the Spenceans had "some forty or fifty followers." Wallas, *Francis Place*, p. 122; but see E. P. Thompson, *English Working Class*, pp. 672–5.

  A quite different account of these Spa Fields meetings and the Spencean involvement in them is given in Halévy, *History* II:16–18.

127 32 *PR* 875.

128 31 *PR* 651.

129 A third meeting, held on December 10, 1816, created no public attention, and further meetings seem to have been contemplated. 32 *PR* 806; E. P. Thompson, pp. 695–6.

130 32 *PR* 906. C had reason to believe that the handbill was issued from one of the police offices. 33 *PR* 627. He also claimed that, prior to the third Spa Fields meeting, a bill directly traceable to Lord Sidmouth's office had been stuck up exciting the people to riot. On being good-naturedly twitted regarding his desire to be king, C replied in the same mood: "Oh, no! a king's office is too little power for me." In response to the further question whether he wished to be the greatest person in the nation in point of power, C stated that this was far beyond his wishes, but he added: "But I am by no means aware, that such a wish would be criminal; and, perhaps, it might even be meritorious." 35 *PR* 219.

131   32 *PR* 884. The "damn'd scoundrel" was later identified as John Castle, who C claimed was a government informer and provocateur. David Johnson (*Regency Revolution: The Case of Arthur Thistlewood* (Salisbury 1974), p. 38) states that that Castle was not employed by the government as a spy until 1817. At another point C claimed that Castle tried to induce Hunt to "join the mob in taking the Tower." 32 *PR* 858.

132   32 *PR* 273. A large part of the crowd involved in the rioting had attended a hanging at the Old Bailey in the morning, then walked north to Spa Fields, leaving there before Hunt arrived. However, the group also included some genuine Spenceans, who seem a disorganized, harebrained lot. One of these, T. J. Evans, secretary of the society, was later convicted of libeling the army in the *Manchester Observer*, which he published. 39 *PR* 200; 40 *PR* 200. A third (and perhaps fourth) component was represented by Arthur Thistlewood, a professional revolutionary, and John Castle, government informer. See n. 131 above.

133   Davis, *Age of Grey and Peel*, p. 184.

134   Undated letter from Robert Peel in Dublin to J. W. Croker in London in *The Croker Papers: The Correspondence and Diaries of the Late Honourable John Wilson Croker, LL.D., F.R.S.* . . . ed. Louis J. Jennings (2nd ed. rev., London 1885) 1:100. Croker's reply suggests that Peel's letter had been written on December 3 or 4; hence, the rumor may have been based on information disseminated before the Spa Fields meeting of December 2.

135   31 *PR* 750.

136   The sole victim singled out for punishment was John Cashman, a drunken sailor recently discharged from the navy, who had engaged in a scuffle at one of the gunshops that had been robbed. Cashman was hanged on a specially constructed gallows outside the shop. Cashman admitted that he had assisted in the escape of one of the Spencean leaders, young James Watson, who had shot the spectator and fled to America. See Henry B. Fearon, *Sketches of America* . . . (2nd ed., London 1818), pp. 211–13.

137   31 *PR* 738.

138   31 *PR* 739; 32 *PR* 887. Lord Cochrane was in King's Bench prison serving an additional sentence for escaping (to go to the House of Commons for the purpose of launching an attack against Ellenborough). See n. 84 above.

139   C later claimed that there had been nearly 2 million signatures (32 *PR* 500), and later still that there had been 1.5 million. 37 *PR* 222; 48 *PR* 386; *Two-Penny Trash* 1:2.

140   In October 1816 C had unsuccessfully tried to dissuade Burdett from calling the meeting. 33 *PR* 433. When Burdett failed to appear, Cartwright acted as chairman. To put Burdett's views to the meeting, C proposed household suffrage (32 *PR* 556–7), although several months earlier C had publicly announced his own acceptance of universal suffrage. 31 *PR* 658. The meeting voted for universal suffrage and annual parliaments. Bamford, *Life of a Radical* 1: 17–19; 32 *PR* 235–6. For C's appointment as delegate to the meeting, see H. Hunt, *Memoirs* III: 413–16.

141   32 *PR* 619–20. The petitions filled three coaches. 34 *PR* 1104.

142   Hansard, 1st ser. xxxv:78 (Jan. 29, 1817); 32 *PR* 299.

143   Hansard xxxv:4, 34–6. The assailant was never identified. C claimed that there had been no bullet and implied (later alleged) that the attack had been instigated by a government agent to create a provocation. 32 *PR* 621-4, 1017. Cochrane, Hunt, and C applied to the Hampshire undersheriff to call a meeting "to address the prince regent on the insults offered him on the returning from the parliament." *Report on the Manuscripts of Earl Bathurst Preserved at Cirencester Park* (London 1923), p. 432 (cited hereafter as *Bathurst Papers*).

144   32 *PR* 620. C claimed 27,000 signatures.

145 There were 527 petitions, of which 468 were printed. Smart, *Economic Annals* I:547n. That a petition extended "through several sheets of paper" was one of the other "usual" grounds for rejection. 33 *PR* 161. A petition referring to other documents accompanying it was also not acceptable. 33 *PR* 552n.

The prevailing view of parliament seems to have been that expressed by Lord Castlereagh in 1813: "individuals should not be encouraged to organize statements for the signatures of others." Hansard, 1st ser. XXVI:994-5 (June 30, 1813).

146 Ibid. XXXV:411 (Feb. 18, 1817); 32 *PR* 301-7. The committee report implicated the London Union Society, which, according to the petition of Thomas Cleary, had been extinct for three years. 32 *PR* 267. Cleary's petition was prepared by C. 34 *PR* 303.

147 Hansard, 1st ser. XXXV:438 (Feb. 19, 1817); 32 *PR* 307-20.

148 Hansard XXXV:554 (Feb. 24, 1817). Sidmouth said that some "noble lords" had complained that prosecution had not been instituted. The tory *Quarterly Review* for October 1816 (presumably published in December) wrote of C: "Why is it that this convicted incendiary, and others of the same stamp, are permitted week after week to sow the seeds of rebellion, insulting the government, and defying the laws of the country?" XVI:275. See also C's description of Sidmouth's presentation. *American P.R.*, May 15, 1817.

149 57 George III c. 3; 32 *PR* 289-300. Five days elapsed between the date the bill was introduced in the Lords and the date it passed in the Commons. Three other related bills were under way in parliament, the most important of which, the Seditious Meetings Act, became effective on March 31. 57 Geo. III cc. 6, 7, 19. On March 27, Sidmouth sent a circular to the lords lieutenant of the counties declaring that the justices of the peace were empowered to apprehend any person charged with the publication of blasphemous or seditious libel. In the following year, parliament passed an outrageous law indemnifying persons who, since January 26, 1817, "have acted in apprehending, imprisoning or detaining in custody persons suspected of high treason or treasonable practices, and in the suppression of tumultuous and unlawful assemblies," whether or not their actions were legal, and depriving persons unlawfully detained of the right to damages. 58 Geo. III c. 6. Yet J. E. Cookson (*Lord Liverpool's Administration: The Crucial Years 1815-1822* (Edinburgh 1958), p. 114) declares that the government was "in an astonishingly feeble position."

150 C. D. Yonge, *Life and Administration of Robert Banks Jenkinson, 2d Earl of Liverpool* (London 1868) II:298-9. C, Hone, and the *Examiner* (Leigh Hunt and his brother John) were specifically named by Southey, who, as regular contributor to the *Quarterly Review*, was possibly author of the article cited in n. 148 above. Eight days before Southey's letter to Liverpool, Southey had received a letter from John Rickman stating: "They have passed a law for the safe custody of Cobbett, and Hunt, and are now afraid to act at all." Orlo Williams, *Life and Letters of John Rickman* (London 1911), p. 192. The Duke of Sussex, sixth son of George III, told his adjutant, Major Codd, that C was to be imprisoned. Anne, p. 35.

151 32 *PR* 456. In 1830 C claimed that the amount had been £10,000. 69 *PR* 458.

152 32 *PR* 462, 465; Anne, p. 35. See also 88 *PR* 771. According to C, John Quincy Adams, ambassador to Britain and later president of the United States, said that C's flight from England was regarded as a "great triumph" by the ministers. 44 *PR* 353; 65 *PR* 51.

18. America again

Motto: 32 *PR* 523-4.

1 32 *PR* 465, 910-16. See also 52 *PR* 332.

2　32 *PR* 911.

3　William junior to John Morgan, May 7, 1817 (Historical Society of Pennsylvania). Rousseau lived with C on Long Island for a time. 67 *PR* 794.

4　32 *PR* 909, 918–20. C's quarrelling with Ogden is explained in greater detail, but with no greater credit to C, at 40 *PR* 595.

5　Letter to Jackson, June 7, 1817 (Rutgers); letter to Nancy, May 19, 1817 (Nuffield); James to Anne, June 6, 1817 (Nuffield); Chester L. Barrows, "William Cobbett and Long Island," *Journal of Long Island History* VI (1965); *Year's Residence*, para. 1067.

　　C recalled Judge Ludlow as "a learned and most excellent man." 33 *PR* 282.

6　For imprisonments during the 1798–1800 period see E. P. Thompson, *English Working Class*, p. 161n. Persons confined for treason following the 1817 suspension were estimated at 133, "most of whom were subsequently discharged without trial" (p. 700n). Even the local magistrates were forbidden to visit the prisoners. 32 *PR* 708.

　　C left manuscripts for two issues of the *PR*. Letter to Dickins, May 12, 1817 (Boston Public Library). The first was dated "Botley 26th March" – presumably to forestall any premature alarm. The second was "Mr. Cobbett's Taking Leave of His Countrymen." The quotation is from the latter, p. 27.

7　"Mr. Cobbett's Taking Leave of His Countrymen" [no. 14 of 32 *PR*], pp. 2, 25, 30–1.

8　*Black Dwarf*, Apr. 2 and 16, 1817. Wooler assumed that C was "rich." Ibid. Oct. 8, 1817. The name of Wooler's paper was probably derived from Scott's novel *The Black Dwarf*, published in 1816.

　　Harriet Martineau, *The History of England during the Thirty Years' Peace 1816–1846* (London 1849) I:144: "It may be easy to call this apprehension cowardice; but there can be no doubt that Cobbett was the most dreaded of all the political writers of that time . . . Cobbett went unscathed. The terrors of the law were reserved for more incautious and feebler delinquents."

9　*QR* XXI (Jan. 1819), 135. The *Courier* falsely asserted that C had "lately been fined $700 for writing against the American government." 34 *PR* 307. Another claim was that £80,000 was due the government for stamps not paid on the cheap *Register*. 32 *PR* 451.

10　C claimed that "upon making up the accounts and disposing of the stock" of the *Parliamentary Debates, Parliamentary History*, and *State Trials* "it appeared I had cleared by these a sum not exceeding one thousand pounds." Statement of 1820 (Illinois). This implies that there was some profit, but if so (and no detail is available to check the accuracy of the implication) the profit probably was small.

11　C later said that he had borrowed £5,000 while he was in prison. This could have been made up of the £2,000 from Burdett and, possibly, the £3,000 from Reeves secured by a second mortgage on C's Botley property.

12　32 *PR* 459–60; letter to Hunt, Jan. 14, 1814 (Adelphi). According to the *DNB*, Kempt's house was called "Botley Hill." It is difficult to understand the economy of moving out of Botley House, where no rent was payable, into Kempt's house, leased for fourteen years at £300 a year. While C was in America he rented his Botley farm. *Year's Residence*, para. 1035.

13　Much of what C wrote was dictated by him, and not read afterwards, which may partly explain the difficulty in reconciling the figures he used for his debt to Burdett. In 1822 he said that he had borrowed £2,000 from Burdett in 1812 and another £300 in 1816. 42 *PR* 491. Three years later he stated that he had borrowed £2,000 in 1812 and £700 more in 1816, "making the whole debt two thousand seven hundred pounds." 55 *PR* 798–9. This apparently did not include the £300 which Wright had received from Burdett and which C had voluntarily assumed as his own liability (see ch. 15, n. 64). To complicate matters further,

Burdett's biographer claimed that the amount C had borrowed from Burdett was £4,000 and that this had occurred in 1811. Patterson, *Burdett* 11:475. An unidentified news clipping of June 1836 states that the bonds then held by Burdett were as follows: one bond dated June 20, 1811 for the sum of £2,000, with interest thereon, and another dated Feb. 29, 1816 for £1,445, which latter amount, by a memorandum on the face thereof, appears to have been the aggregate of interest on former bond, £370; Wright's bill with interest, £375; and "cash then had," £700.

In the lengthy explanation of 1825, C asserted that Burdett had made him a gift of the £2,300, but that C had insisted on treating it as a debt; that Burdett had solemnly promised to keep its existence secret; and that before leaving for America C had urged Burdett to take all his property to satisfy the debt, but Burdett had refused, saying that he did not want the money. 55 *PR* 798–9. See also 42 *PR* 491; 69 *PR* 468–71.

14 According to C, the weekly circulation of the *PR* prior to the cheap edition was more than 1,600, which "yielded a profit of £1,500 a year or more." 32 *PR* 566. It is doubtful whether this would have covered C's interest, taxes, rents, and living costs.

15 C first claimed profits of £200 a week or £10,000 a year. 32 *PR* 459, 526. Later he stated that for a period of something over four months (presumably November 1816 to February 1817, when the cheap edition scored its great success) his net profit had been £1,800 "not counting paper." Statement of 1820 (Illinois). This is roughly £100 a week in profits before the unknown cost of the paper. (In 1830 C renewed the claim that his profit "clear of all expenses" had been £200 a week. 69 *PR* 465.)

16 Baker served as vicar from 1803 to 1854. Until 1836 the parish used the old church, which was about a mile from C's house along a country footpath. Long after C left Botley, he continued to flail at Baker. See e.g. 76 *PR* 151.

17 11 *PR* 105; 14 *PR* 720.

18 Anne to Wright, Oct. 2, 1808, Add. MSS. 22907, fol. 59.

19 Anne, pp. 31–2. Nancy's beautiful younger sister, Eleanor, married James Warner of Steeple Court, Botley, member of a leading family of the area.

20 When the family returned to Botley for a few months in 1819–20, they found living there very disagreeable. Anne to James, Dec. 6, 1820 (Nuffield).

21 33 *PR* 710, 717; 34 *PR* 571, 592; H. Hunt, *Memoirs* 111:476. Possibly the family lived at 8 Catherine Street, London, which C had leased in 1816.

22 Statement of 1820 (Illinois).

23 Since the Jan. 27, 1816 issue of the *PR* it had been "printed and published for Wm. Cobbett Jun."

24 Letter to Jackson, June 7, 1817 (Rutgers). Jackson received a third of the profits. 37 *PR* 1442.

25 Letter to Jackson, June 27, 1818 (Yale).

26 Jackson ceased acting as publisher in January or February 1819, when William junior returned to England from the United States. Jackson had quarrelled with Hunt (34 *PR* 490) and was succeeded as publisher by Hunt's friend Thomas Dolby. Dolby lasted for less than a year.

27 The money was borrowed from Thomas Hulme, master bleacher of Lancashire, who was repaid by C's publisher, William Clement, out of the proceeds of C's works. 69 *PR* 468. At other points C asserted that the money had been borrowed from Clement. Statement of 1820 (Illinois); 78 *PR* 326; entry for William Clement in *DNB*. Hulme's history after C met him in 1816 (*Year's Residence*, para. 861) is outlined at 68 *PR* 56.

28 Early in 1818 C claimed weekly sales of 25,000. Letter to Dickins, Jan. 20, 1818 (New York Historical Society). According to a report in the Home Office files, the circulation was 8,000 in October 1819. HO 42/170. The twopence price was con-

tinued, and if one assumes a 15 percent return on sales of 8,000, the profit would have been £10 per issue. An average of thirty-eight issues a year was published during 1817–19.

29   29 *PR* 1, 289; 30 *PR* 97; *American PR*, XXXIII:1.
     In the first several issues of the American publication, C introduced some sensitive subjects: the corruption of the English press by the government; the corruption of parliament through its method of election; and the domination of the monarch by the boroughmongers. The royal family, C wrote, were despised rather than hated by the common people; not one of them "since their being pitched upon to fill the throne of England, has ever discovered symptoms of a mind much more than sufficient to qualify the possessors for the post of exciseman." *American PR*, xxx:161, 172.

30   Pearl, *Cobbett*, p. 93; Gaines, *Cobbett*, pp. 123–4. The *American PR* was published in New York May–September 1816 and May 1817–January 1818, with two "extra sheets" in March 1817.

31   32 *PR* 540. Henry Cobbett (son of C's brother George) had been a midshipman along with the novelist Frederick Marryat on Lord Cochrane's ship, the *Imperieuse*. Oliver Warner, *Captain Marryat* (London 1953), p. 29, where he is incorrectly described as C's son. After leaving New York, Henry rejoined Cochrane in Chile and on July 1, 1819 was reported to be first officer on Cochrane's flagship, the *O'Higgins*. *National Advocate*, New York, Nov. 3, 1819. By 1821 he was in command of the 44-gun ship *Esmeralda*.

32   For twenty years prior to the Spa Fields episode, "popular political meetings had been largely in abeyance." E. P. Thompson, *English Working Class*, p. 744.

33   Bamford, *Life of a Radical* 1:16. C paraphrased what the ministerial papers said about Hunt: "But, you are a 'violent man and the *respectable* people are afraid of you'." 34 *PR* 204–5. See also 34 *PR* 304, in which C praised Hunt for his decency, disinterestedness, and bravery.

34   32 *PR* 741. Brougham to Lansdowne, Feb. 8, 1817: "Even Burdett has become moderate and reasonable." Quoted in Aspinall, *Brougham and the Whig Party*, p. 74.

35   32 *PR* 750, 849. 32 *PR* 754: "he did oppose the bill *afterwards*."
36   32 *PR* 751–2. Burdett claimed that he had advised Cochrane against bringing the motion forward "at that time"; that it was made at 3:30 A.M., when he and the greater part of the members had left the house. Patterson, *Burdett* II:420.

37   32 *PR* 513, 545, 609, 737, 833, 865. The first three of these articles were directed at the ministers. The attack on Burdett included general charges of indecision, inconsistency, and jealousy, and specific charges that he had failed to bring in a bill for reform during the 1817 session of parliament, but instead had asked parliament to appoint a committee to investigate the need for reform; and that Sir Francis was so vain that he could not tolerate rivals such as James Paull and Henry Hunt. 32 *PR* 740–3, 755–64, 851–3.

38   C claimed, first, that Burdett had been "bound in honour to keep secret" C's debt (39 *PR* 482); second, that Burdett's reply was never sent to him, but was a "show-answer" and the "basest perversion of the meaning of my letter" intended to create the impression that C had contended "that no man was bound to pay, or ought to pay, any debt of any sort, if he wanted the money for other purposes." 41 *PR* 211; 42 *PR* 503. See also 37 *PR* 1503; 55 *PR* 799.
     The letters first appeared in the *Examiner* on January 3, 1819, where C's letter to Tipper was given in truncated form (with no indication that there had been deletions) so as to omit C's statement that he waived the principle of nonpayment. The account in *The Times* on the following day included the statement, however.
     In the newspaper accounts C's letter to Burdett is shown as June 20, 1817, but Burdett's reply indicates that the correct date was November 20, 1817, the same as C's letter to Tipper.

C's assertion that Burdett's reply was not published in the newspapers presumably referred to an immediate publication, since the article in the *Examiner* did not appear until nearly a year after the reply had been privately circulated. For years C's enemies continued to reprint the letters as evidence of his dishonesty. See e.g. *Blackwood's Magazine* XIV (Sept. 1823), 314–17.

39 E. P. Thompson, *English Working Class*, pp. 715–34; William Thomas, *The Philosophic Radicals: Nine Studies in Theory and Practice 1817–1821* (Oxford 1979), pp. 46–61; Halévy, *History* II:28; 33 *PR* 418–19.

40 34 *PR* 420; Thomas Cleary, *A Letter to Major Cartwright in Justification of the Writer's Conduct at the Late Elections for Westminster; and in Answer to the Calumnies Spoke and Published Against Him by Cobbett, Hunt and Thelwall, and Certain Members of Mr Hobhouse's Committee* (London 1819) in Add. MSS. 27809, fol. 180.

41 33 *PR* 248, 428. Burdett's biographer explains that Sir Francis went to Ireland to appear as a defense witness for his friend, the "utter imposter" Roger O'Connor. But the O'Connor trial was over on August 5, whereas the Derby trial and Brandreth's execution were in November. Burdett stayed on in Ireland until December. Patterson, *Burdett* II:428, 429, 439, 454.

According to the *DNB*, O'Connor was charged with having raided the Galway coach, allegedly for the purpose of rescuing a packet of love letters that would have implicated Burdett in an adulterous affair with a nobleman's wife.

42 33 *PR* 6.

43 33 *PR* 33–4. The Rump's technique in controlling the Westminster electorate is described at 39 *PR* 914. W. Thomas (*Philosophic Radicals*, pp. 60–2) claims that the Rump, rather than Burdett, chose his running mate, but the choice was invariably one of Burdett's close friends.

44 33 *PR* 71–7.

45 33 *PR* 122. C claimed that Burdett failed to oppose the Corn Bill in 1815; that his son had recently enrolled in the army although a standing army in time of peace was "the most hideous amongst all the hideous features of despotism"; and that Burdett should have arranged for proper counsel for the Derbyshire rioters. 33 *PR* 337, 348, 415, 426. Although Burdett objected to his son joining the army, he felt that this was a family matter, whereas C thought that Burdett, as representative of the reform movement, had an obligation to declare himself on this point. Patterson, *Burdett* II:386, 409–10, 427; 33 *PR* 348–54.

46 Bentham claimed that Romilly was not a true reformer. W. Thomas, *Philosophic Radicals*, p. 44.

47 The original of this letter is in Add. MSS. 22907, fol. 372, where the date is shown as April 10. In 34 *PR* 300 the date is given as April 20.

48 Peacock to Shelley, July 5, 1818 in *Thomas Love Peacock Letters to Edward Hookham and Percy B. Shelley* . . . ed. Richard Garrett (Boston 1910), p. 69.

49 The vote was Romilly, 5,339; Burdett, 5,238; Maxwell, 4,808; Hunt, 84; Kinnaird, 65; Cartwright, 23. Although Burdett claimed that he stood completely aloof from the election, Greville thought that he had spent £10,000: "the open houses, cockades, and bands of music . . . were not procured for nothing." *Greville Memoirs* I:3. C put Burdett's cost at £20,000. 34 *PR* 336, 424.

50 34 *PR* 298.

51 C reiterated his forgery claim several times, although with decreasing assurance. 34 *PR* 301, 336, 413, 432 ("no recollection"). But see 34 *PR* 747.

52 34 *PR* 404. C blamed Burdett, however, for the use Cleary made of the letter, and never ceased to tax Burdett with the charge of this impropriety. See e.g. *Collective Commentaries*, pp. 97–8; 37 *PR* 1508.

53 When the letter was written in 1808, C had seen Hunt only two or three times and had never met Mrs. Vince, so it is possible that C did not associate the gossip of 1808 with the man he came to know so well a year or so later. 37 *PR* 1509; H.

Hunt, *Memoirs* II:168, 257, 357. When C said in 1818 that he had known Hunt "intimately" for fourteen years, he was clearly wrong. 33 *PR* 16.

54 Letter to Cleary, Jan. 15, 1819 (Haverford). During the 1820 trial it was revealed that Cleary had refused to show the letter to C's son. 37 *PR* 1441.

55 Wallas, *Francis Place*, p. 117. The bad feelings between Place and Burdett that had existed since 1810 were now patched up (Patterson, *Burdett* II:426; cf. Wallas, pp. 56–7), whereas those between Hunt and Burdett created in 1817 were not healed until 1822, and the Cobbett–Burdett feud went on until C's death.

56 C, through friends in England, had made an unsuccessful bid for candidacy at Coventry prior to the 1818 general election. 33 *PR* 379, 443, 507, 667, 727; 34 *PR* 295. Originally he had intended to offer for Worcester, but for unknown reasons this was changed. Letter to Hunt, Feb. 7, 1818 (Illinois); letter to Freemen of Worcester, Feb. 15, 1818 (Huntington).

57 34 *PR* 364, 414. See also 69 *PR* 471–2 for C's claim that "for seven long years I was his sole prop."

58 34 *PR* 436. Burdett's adulterous relations with Lady Oxford had allegedly ended long before 1811. Patterson, *Burdett* I:247. For other semiveiled references by C to Lady Oxford and Sir Francis's illegitimate child by her, see 34 *PR* 342, 416, 734; 55 *PR* 795, 797. C's letters to Hunt of Oct. 17, 1817 (Adelphi) and Feb. 7, 1818 (Illinois) also contain facetious references to the attractive lady.

59 34 *PR* 1091. Cartwright himself declared that he had been "unceremoniously dropped." Cartwright (ed.), *Life* II:147.

60 Wallas, *Francis Place*, p. 138. The 1819 election, including the mishandling of Hobhouse's candidacy by Place, is related by W. Thomas (*Philosophic Radicals*, pp. 66–89).

61 Anne to James, June 16, 1819 (Nuffield).

62 33 *PR* 55.

63 32 *PR* 768; 33 *PR* 631; Smart, *Economic Annals* I:610n. In 1832 C claimed that Hone had been jailed for publishing a parody for Burdett. 78 *PR* 572. I have been unable to identify the incident. In May–June 1817 Hone was imprisoned after suspension of the Habeas Corpus Act. He was imprisoned again later in the year pending the December 1818 trials, in which he was acquitted.

64 33 *PR* 242.

65 34 *PR* 909.

66 C was convinced that the national debt was greater than the value of all the houses, lands, canals, and mines of England. 33 *PR* 516.

67 35 *PR* 65, 170; Smart I:614–24.

68 35 *PR* 364. See also 34 *PR* 7, 1050; 35 *PR* 170. Canning, an inveterate joke maker, had entertained the House of Commons by his amusing account of a hernia caused to a seventy-four-year-old man, William Ogden, weighted with a thirty-pound manacle after arrest pursuant to one of Sidmouth's warrants. 33 *PR* 565–8; 35 *PR* 247.

69 34 *PR* 222, 225. See also 34 *PR* 16–30, 217, 469, 487, 678, 699, 785, 823, 882, 989, 1074; 35 *PR* 48, 83, 95, 158, 189, 288, 302, 372. At several points C suggested that he himself might arrange for the counterfeiting, and that it was an imminent threat. 34 *PR* 679, 996.

70 Richard Holmes, *Shelley: The Pursuit* (New York 1975), p. 522.

71 Guy A. Aldred, *Richard Carlile, Agitator: His Life and Times* (London 1923), p. 27.

72 33 *PR* 222; 32 *PR* 1185; 33 *PR* 123, 193. See also letter to Dickins, Jan. 20, 1818 (New York Historical Society). Yet in 1828 C said: "as we had missed the opportunity of freeing those countries, and getting a firm hold of them, in 1817, when our troops were yet in France, the best way would have been, to favour Old Spain in recovering her authority, on condition of commercial advantages for ourselves." 65 *PR* 824.

73 34 *PR* 1014. See also 33 *PR* 448; 34 *PR* 30; 35 *PR* 92–6. This, however, was well within English tradition. During the Wilkes agitation of 1770, Lord Chatham declared that it was better for the people "to perish in a glorious contention for their rights than to purchase a slavish tranquillity at the expense of a single iota of the Constitution." Quoted in Henry Jephson, *The Platform: Its Rise and Progress* (London 1892) 1:59.

74 See, for example, 30 *PR* 301; 33 *PR* 53, 397–405, 573, 576; 34 *PR* 120, 151, 161, 180, 283, 448, 466, 533, 694, 746, 772, 829, 840–1, 921, 1069; 35 *PR* 2, 7; 59 *PR* 274; 62 *PR* 28; 65 *PR* 51; 67 *PR* 546 ("vengeance" does not mean "bodily punishment"); 70 *PR* 530, 1039; JPC, p. 13. E. P. Thompson, *English Working Class*, p. 685: "The national leaders Cobbett and Wooler with their pens, Hunt with his voice – were adept at pitching their rhetoric just on the right side of treason."

75 According to C, the crown had no part in the oppression practiced by the boroughmongers, who had systematically attempted to degrade the royal family as well as the people, and tried to keep the king and the people apart. 33 *PR* 355–78; 34 *PR* 710–24.

76 Additional evidence implicating Oliver as provocateur in the Pentrich rising was provided by the sworn statements of William Stevens and Charles Pendrill, which, through C's efforts, were taken in Philadelphia in March 1818. 33 *PR* 539–64.

77 34 *PR* 216. *The Times* is notably absent from C's list; early in 1817 the reactionary John Stoddart ("Doctor Slop") left *The Times*, and Thomas Barnes became editor. C referred (but not for long) to the resulting change in policy as a "defection from the cause of tyranny." 32 *PR* 1132.

78 See 32 *PR* 994; 36 *PR* 1105. In Wilberforce's *A Practical View* (1797), he had defined the role of Christianity as instructing the "lower orders . . . to be diligent, humble, patient: reminding them that their more lowly path has been allotted to them by the hand of God." Quoted by Coupland, *Wilberforce*, p. 240. Place claimed that Wilberforce had been opposed to the rights and liberties of the people "on most if indeed not on all occasions" and "the decided supporter of every measure calculated to debase and enslave them." Add. MSS. 27809, fol. 123. See also Ford K. Brown, *Fathers of the Victorians* (Cambridge 1961), pp. 112–13. A more sympathetic treatment of Wilberforce's conservatism can be found in Coupland, pp. 264–7, 406–46.

79 34 *PR* 213, 372.

80 34 *PR* 438.

81 *Year's Residence*, para. 20 (Mar. 11, 1818).
   C gave his children the English copyright to *Year's Residence*: Part I to John, Part II to William junior, and Part III to Anne. Letter to Nancrede, Jan. 4, 1819 (Haverford), in which Cobbett claimed that he wrote "the book" (presumably Part I) in seven days.

82 *Year's Residence*, para. 308. Elsewhere C expressed his "delight in the society of hogs," claiming that they were more discriminating than lawyers or parsons. 39 *PR* 587–8.

83 19 *QR* XIX (April 1818), 77 declared that Cobbett and Birbeck were "equally disinterested": Cobbett sold patriotism, whereas Birbeck sold land.

84 The postscript relating to Birbeck was reprinted at 34 *PR* 603, 635. "Romantic chaff": letter to Nancrede, Jan. 4, 1819 (Haverford). See also Richard Flower, *Letters from Lexington and the Illinois, Containing a Brief Account of the English Settlement in the Latter Territory, and a Refutation of the Misrepresentations of Mr. Cobbett* (London 1819).

85 Fearon, *Sketches of America*, pp. 64–5, 68–9. Fearon's quotation is a truncated version of Shakespeare's *Third Part of Henry VI* v.6.80–4. Other references to C are at pp. 61, 89, 111, 292–5, 425.

86 *Year's Residence*, paras. 1056–67. See also 65 *PR* 52. C attacked Fearon again in

1821 for his assertion that C had "said something . . . against republican government." 40 *PR* 1544. Presumably this referred to an alleged statement by C that there was much more corruption in Pennsylvania than there was in London, and that his Pennsylvania petition would have been successful if he had resorted to bribery. Fearon, p. 295. Fearon as chairman of a meeting of the Livery reform committee ran afoul of C once more in 1832. 76 *PR* 780.

87 Pearl, *Cobbett*, p. 106. In addition to the [1923?] edition mentioned by Pearl, there was a 1906 edition edited by H. L. Stephen.

In some English local schools, C's grammar was used surreptitiously because of the author's unpopularity with constituted authority. 72 *PR* 776.

88 *English Grammar*, Introduction, paras. 1, 90, 181. The word "Regiment" did not refer to a military unit, but to the two major parties in parliament, which, despite avowed hostility to each other, stood together in opposition to all outsiders – i.e. all those not in "the Regiment."

89 66 *PR* 154.

90 Judge Spencer of New York had "looked into the law of the case, as he had found it reported by Dallas; and . . . he had no hesitation to say, that the proceedings were illegal from the beginning to the end." Letter to Nancrede, Dec. 20, 1818 (Haverford).

91 Petition by C "To the Honourable the Senators and Representatives of the State of Pennsylvania in General Assembly Met" dated Feb. 19, 1818 (Historical Society of Pennsylvania). The amount of the claim was stated as $6,373.

Other references to C's petition of 1818 appear in his letters to Hulme, Dec. 5, 1817 (New York Public Library), Dickins, Jan. 20, 1818 (New York Historical Society), Morgan, Feb. 10, 1818 (Historical Society of Pennsylvania), Nancrede, Apr. 12, 1818 (Haverford).

92 Breck's Recollections 41 (American Philosophical Society). The vote in the Senate was 20 to 9. Fearon, *Sketches of America*, p. 293.

93 Unidentified news clipping "Harrisburgh, Feb. 21, 1818" (Historical Society of Pennsylvania).

94 Letter from Nancrede, Nov. 16, 1818 (Haverford). C later claimed that he had never seen so much political corruption as he witnessed at Harrisburg. 49 *PR* 285, 307.

95 Letter to Nancrede, Nov. 11, 1818 (Haverford).

96 Ibid., Dec. 20, 1818 (Haverford).

97 It is uncertain exactly what was filed with the legislature, although C's letter to Nancrede of Jan. 4, 1819 (Haverford) says: "I am for *disarming* the opposers of the weapon of complaint of indecorous language, without prejudice to my cause or my duty." See appointment of Nancrede, Dec. 20, 1818 (Illinois); letters of C to Nancrede, Nov. 11, 1818, Dec. 20, 1818, Jan. 4, 1819, and Feb. 24, 1819 and undated 21-page petition signed by Nancrede as C's attorney (Haverford); one-page petition dated Jan. 2, 1819 signed by C (Historical Society of Pennsylvania).

98 Early in the contest, C had written to John Morgan saying that their common friend Buck Severne should "keep the turkey for us to celebrate our triumph over Old Tom [McKean]." Feb. 10, 1818 (Historical Society of Pennsylvania).

99 JPC, p. 81.

100 Nancy left Liverpool on [Sept.?] 16, 1817, arriving in New York sometime in November. Fearon, *Sketches of America*, p. 230; Anne, p. 35. She and all the children but William junior and James seem to have left New York by June 1818. Letter to Anne, June 19, 1818 (Nuffield). On their return to England, they rented a small furnished house on King's Road, Chelsea.

101 Letter to Anne, June 19, 1818 (Nuffield), in which C referred obliquely to a domestic row as a "memorable thunderstorm." See also *Emigrant's Guide*, p. 33: "Women, and especially English women, transplant very badly."

102 35 *PR* 12; 38 *PR* 434–5; JPC, p. 80. Apparently C left his tent on Long Island at the end of August 1819. By September, C and James were living in a house at "Kip's Bay Hill, opposite the three mile stone, on the old Harlem road" – in current terms, near 36th Street and Third Avenue. *New-York Columbian,* Oct. 6, 1819; letter to William junior, Sept. 20, 1819 (Nuffield).
103 35 *PR* 121.
104 Gaines, *Cobbett,* p. 128; Grant Thorburn, *Forty Years' Residence in America* (London 1834), p. 227. James was left with 150 pigs. The stock was disposed of at an immense loss. JPC, p. 23. The goods sold in the New York store were apparently purchased in England on credit guaranteed by John Hinxman, who held the manuscript and copyrights of *English Grammar* as security. Faithfull MSS. 1 (Nuffield). See also 79 *PR* 822.
105 Letters to William junior, Sept. 20, 1819, and John, Oct. 9, 1819 (Nuffield). The announcement of C's intention to sail on the *Amity* appears at 35 *PR* 320. Wright's position was that if he took C seven of the other passengers would refuse to travel on the vessel. *Liverpool Mercury,* Nov. 19 and 26, 1819. When C retold the story, he suggested that Wright might not have secured a letter of health from the British consul if C had been on board. 40 *PR* 605–14; 64 *PR* 157–8.
106 Conway, *Life of Thomas Paine,* pp. 322–3.
107 Letter to Hulme, Dec. 5, 1817 (New York Public Library).
108 Letter from Henry, Apr. 2, 1818 (Rutgers); Conway, pp. 323–5; 36 *PR* 46–52.
109 Letter to Hulme, Dec. 5, 1817, loc. cit. The life of Paine and C's participation in its preparation are given in Conway, pp. 328–39. In 1826 Richard Carlile claimed that in exchange for the manuscript C had given Mme Bonneville a note for $1,000 and promised to secure the copyright in England for her benefit, and that Mme Bonneville took back the work when she failed to get the $1,000. *Republican* XIII (May 12, 1826), 607–8.
110 34 *PR* 992. C's view of Paine was colored by his own feeling of indebtedness to him: "At his expiring flambeau I lighted my taper." 35 *PR* 472.
111 35 *PR* 131–2.
112 35 *PR* 383. See also 40 *PR* 594, in which C claimed that before he disinterred Paine's bones there had been negotiations to move the bones to a New York churchyard, where they would be placed "in a refuse place where . . . friendless persons were usually buried." A similar version was given in C's Address to the Electors of Preston in 1826 (Fitzwilliam).

C's helpers at New Rochelle included his son James (40 *PR* 561) and the reformer William Benbow, shoemaker of Manchester, to whom C dedicated his *English Grammar* in 1819. Benbow, a deputy at the January 1817 meeting held at the Crown and Anchor, was imprisoned during the suspension of the Habeas Corpus Act, and came to America after his release. *National Advocate,* New York, Oct. 30, 1819. See 32 *PR* 1060, 1089.

19. Back in England

Motto: *English Grammar* (1820 and subsequent eds.), para. 90.
1 Cobbett's poem "The Monk and the Rabbi," dated New York, Oct. 18, 1819 (Nuffield), was a gibe at the criticism of John Binns, editor of the *Democratic Press* of Philadelphia, and Mordecai Noah, editor of the *National Advocate* of New York. *New-York Columbian,* Nov. 9, 1819. Paine had written a quite different poem entitled "The Monk and the Jew."
2 The great mass of the material relating to this event is reviewed by Robert Walmsley in *Peterloo: The Case Reopened* (Manchester 1969). A good short account is found in Joyce Marlow, *The Peterloo Massacre* (London 1969).
3 Eleven deaths is the usual number. Marlow (pp. 150–1) lists a maximum of fifteen.

4 Bamford, *Life of a Radical* 11:156–7.
5 Martineau, *Thirty Years' Peace* 1:237–8; Wallas, *Francis Place*, pp. 143–4.
6 Cartwright (ed.), *Life* 11:168; Halévy, *History* 11:62–4.
  Hunt, Burdett, Cartwright, Wooler, and Wolseley were convicted by provincial juries, and all (except the seventy-nine-year-old Cartwright, who was fined £100) were sentenced to imprisonment: Hunt, thirty months; Burdett, three months; Wooler, fifteen months; Wolseley, eighteen months. Hobhouse was jailed for two months by action of the House of Commons.
  In the course of his defense, Burdett aimed a below-the-belt blow at C, stating that the communication for which Burdett was being tried was "not addressed, as some had done, 'to the weaver-boys of Coventry,' but to the enlightened electors of Westminster, whose representative he had been." C replied to this "Pharisaical contrast" in an angry article. 36 *PR* 153.
7 Marlow, *Peterloo*, pp. 158–60; Holmes, *Shelley*, p. 537n.
8 Marlow, pp. 182–3; Jephson, *The Platform* 1:484–96.
9 Holmes, p. 532.
10 Letter to James, Nov. 22, 1819 (Nuffield). 36 *PR* 82: "it was, at New York, a common observation, that the Parliament would *be sitting to receive me with new laws against the press!*" See also 69 *PR* 264–5.
11 *Liverpool Mercury*, Nov. 26, 1819; *Evening Post*, Jan. 29, 1820; 36 *PR* 470; 39 *PR* 433. When, in 1830, C visited Bolton, he arranged for periodic payments totalling £5 to be made to the town crier, "John Hayes, who is a poor, but very industrious man." 69 *PR* 98–9.
12 *Times*, Nov. 27, 1819. The *Liverpool Mercury* for November 26, 1819 added C's remark "great indeed must that man have been, whose very bones attract such attention." See also *Courier*, Nov. 29, 1819.
  C's account of his reception at Liverpool is given at 35 *PR* 389. He was visited by delegations from Manchester, Bolton, Blackburn, Preston, and Warrington, and during the next several weeks received addresses from Lancashire (signed by nearly 50,000 names), Leeds (names closely written, in six columns, each being thirty-seven feet long), and a number of others, together with a silver writing stand and pen from the Female Reformers of Manchester. 35 *PR* 399, 445, 476, 482, 516, 542, 546.
13 35 *PR* 391–5.
14 *Times*, Dec. 3, 1819, an article abridged from the *Star*.
15 35 *PR* 407.
16 *Black Dwarf*, Dec. 8, 1819.
17 The overtures seem to have been initiated by C's friends and rejected by Burdett. C claimed that an oral condition to reconciliation had been his demand that Burdett "out of his own purse, furnish the means of facilitating, as soon as the occasion should offer, the entrance of Mr. Hunt and myself into the House of Commons." 35 *PR* 497.
18 *Black Dwarf*, Dec. 8, 1819.
19 Several weeks later C wrote: "it is the politics and political economy of Paine that I admire" (35 *PR* 779), although he made it clear at the Crown and Anchor dinner of December 4 that he rejected Paine's republicanism: "could he displace the kingly government to-morrow and establish a republic, he would not do it." See also 35 *PR* 384, 403–5.
20 Aldred, *Carlile*, pp. 78–97.
21 *Black Dwarf*, Dec. 8, 1819. *Times*, Dec. 4, 1819: "It was really astonishing to hear Hunt express his abhorrence of Carlile's blasphemies, to whom he had served up foaming pots of porter, while he uttered them in court. Here, then, is a proof that irreligion has made no great progress among us."
  After reading the *Age of Reason*, C claimed that while Paine was no Christian,

and his views were as inconsistent and ridiculous as those of the unitarians, he was not blasphemous, since he said nothing in derogation of God. 35 *PR* 717f.

22 Halévy, *History* 1:387.

23 35 *PR* 635, 709, 775, 781, 783.

24 In his argument against the bill on blasphemous and seditious libels, Earl Grosvenor suggested that "there never was any subject treated with more laughter, contempt and derision than the introduction of those miserable bones whether the bones of Tom Paine, or not, he would not undertake to decide." *Times*, Dec. 18, 1819. For C's comments see 35 *PR* 779.

25 Thomas Moore, *The Life, Letters and Journals of Lord Byron* (London 1860), p. 432.

26 *Gentleman's Magazine*, suppl. to LXXXIX pt. II:632; Robert Huish, *Memoirs of the Late William Cobbett, Esqr. M.P. for Oldham from Private and Confidential Sources* (London 1836) II:297. The *Courier* of December 30, 1819 contained an amusing story (obviously fabricated) of the substitution of the Negro's bones for those of Paine.

27 35 *PR* 777–8. To the taunts of those who called him "resurrection man," "bone-grubber," and "grave robber," C was able to point out that in 1821 the Duke of York had ordered that the bones of Major André (who had been executed as a spy by the Americans) be disinterred in New York and sent to England in a man-of-war. 40 *PR* 545, 560, 833, 936, 1404.

28 35 *PR* 780–1 (on "envy"); Anne to James, Dec. 24, 1819 (Nuffield). "Mons. Chasse" (Hunt) was "a fellow whom *we always hated*." Anne to James, Apr. 20, 1820 (Nuffield).

Hunt had not met C at Liverpool.

29 35 *PR* 503; Anne to James, Dec. 24, 1819 (Nuffield).

30 Susan (Nuffield XVII:5).

31 Anne to James, Dec. 24, 1819 (Nuffield). After C returned to London on January 2, 1820, Nancy and the younger children stayed on until May. C visited Botley, probably for the last time, between March 23 and 28.

32 "At the time of my coming away, I owed Mr. Morgan more money than all that I possessed amounted to. An account was, therefore, taken of all my property, and a sale of it was made to Mr. Morgan, I still owing him a balance of 600 dollars." Statement of 1820 (Illinois).

33 Letter to Tubb, Nov. 22, 1819 (Bodleian). Lord George Lennox was gazetted on Nov. 27, 1819 as already returned for Chichester. *Courier*, Nov. 29, 1819. C claimed that the only object in endeavoring to obtain a seat in parliament was to lay before the country a bill to reduce the interest on the debt. 37 *PR* 1598.

34 36 *PR* 29; Anne, p. 36. It seems possible that the arrest occurred on December 13 following a second Crown and Anchor dinner held to promote sobriety among the reformers. The incident was related in dramatic but questionable detail by Carlile in 1826 after a falling out with C. *Republican* XIII:608.

35 The *Political Register* of sixteen pages, two columns to the page, was produced on one sheet, roughly 17 by 21 inches, printed on both sides.

Some of the other burdensome features of this and the other acts are discussed at 36 *PR* 36–46.

36 35 *PR* 385–6. The last 2d. edition was issued on January 6, 1820. Rather than selling the standard sixteen-page edition for 6d. (of which 4d. would be tax), the subsequent issues were lengthened (usually to thirty-six pages) so as to require more than two sheets. These were sold at 6d., thereby avoiding the tax and at the same time giving the reader more for his money. On numerous occasions C reprinted an earlier article in order to exceed the two-sheet minimum. C claimed average sales of 4,000 copies for the first several 6d. issues. *Evening Post*, Feb. 3, 1820. In April 1821 C began issuing a stamped version (in addition to the unstamped one) so that it could be sent by post.

37 Canning, a member of Liverpool's cabinet, described the conditions that gave rise

to this legislation: "What was the situation of the country in November 1819? – Do I exaggerate when I say, there was not a man of property who did not tremble for his possessions? that there was not a man of retired and peaceable habits who did not tremble for the tranquillity and security of his home?" 36 *PR* 228.

38 The attitude of those in power was expressed by the seventy-one-year-old Lord Redesdale in a letter to Sidmouth written three days after Peterloo: "every meeting for radical reform was not merely a seditious attempt to undermine the existing constitution of government by bringing it into hatred and contempt, but was an overt act of treasonable conspiracy against that constitution of government, including the King as its head." Quoted in Martineau, *Thirty Years' Peace* 1:239.

For the youth of England, however, Peterloo was a turning point. Macaulay at Cambridge wrote that the "Manchester business has . . . drawn philippics against the powers that be from lips which I never heard opened before but to speak on university contests or university scandal." George Otto Trevelyan, *The Life and Letters of Lord Macaulay* (London 1959), p. 68.

39 35 *PR* 567, 574. C initially proposed to publish the *PR* once a month without a stamp, but eventually decided to retain the weekly format.

40 Namier, *Structure of Politics*, p. 102.

41 Anne, p. 18; Anne to James, Dec. 16, 1821 (Nuffield).

42 C seems to have written nothing for either the *PR* or the *Evening Post* between February 9 and March 23. In 1821 he proposed to revive the paper "if suitable arrangements can be made," but nothing came of the proposal. 40 *PR* 1533.

43 12 *PR* 283.

44 Halévy, *History* 1:141. 36 *PR* 85: "these out-living freemen require not only to be taken to Coventry, but to be entertained there, and on the road, and to be paid for their time into the bargain!"

45 *Black Dwarf*, Feb. 18, 1820. In the *Evening Post* of February 22 C indicated that £2,000 would be needed "to carry in the out-lying voters and defray other lawful expenses."

46 *Black Dwarf*, Feb. 18, 1820.

47 35 *PR* 501.

48 35 *PR* 545, 568–9. The "fund" has its puzzling aspects; why was C so coy about its intended use in his initial plea? In 1833 he claimed that the original intent had been "for the purpose of making a small publication to be given away"; that £67 had been raised; that he had expended more than £100 on this project. 82 *PR* 13. It is suspected that by 1833 C's memory was extremely unreliable.

49 35 *PR* 642, 707, 785.

50 *Evening Post*, Feb. 5, 1820; *Black Dwarf*, Feb. 18, 1820.

51 Copies of the circular letter are held by the American Philosophical Society, the Bodleian, Duke University, and the Huddersfield Public Library.

52 82 *PR* 14.

53 36 *PR* 23.

54 36 *PR* 34.

55 Letter to Nancy, Feb. 21, 1820 (Nuffield); *Evening Post*, Feb. 15, 1820.

56 36 *PR* 87–9; *Evening Post*, Mar. 1, 1820.

57 The gang was headed by Arthur Thistlewood, who had been involved in the Spa Fields riot of 1816. As a result of the Cato Street episode, in which one of the police was killed, Thistlewood and four of his accomplices were executed on May 1, 1820. At the trial, the chief justice claimed that the defendants' minds had been corrupted by seditious publications, of which there was nothing worse than "Cobbett's Register." 36 *PR* 576–7, 587. Although Harriet Martineau declared that Thistlewood was "too vindictive about his private wrongs to make much pretence of patriotism" (*Thirty Years' Peace* 1:242), he became something of a hero, along

with Cobbett, Paine, and the American Andrew Jackson, to a later generation of radicals. See Disraeli's *Sybil* (Oxford 1975), p. 316.

58 36 *PR* 90, 91.

59 36 *PR* 98–103; *Evening Post,* Mar. 14, 1820.

60 36 *PR* 106–7.

61 To add to the terror, the Savages held up poles "with sheep and bullock heads on them streaming with blood." Susan (Nuffield).

62 36 *PR* 114–15; *Evening Post,* Mar. 14, 1820.

63 In 1835 C asserted that the corporation of Coventry had "expended a sum of money for the purpose of preventing my election for that city in 1820." 88 *PR* 598.

64 36 *PR* 109, 130–2. C had affidavits from a number of persons who had been prevented from voting, but was forced to abandon his petition for parliamentary scrutiny because he was unable to obtain the necessary sureties. 36 *PR* 133–52, 824.

65 36 *PR* 197–205; 40 *PR* 653–6. C suggested that the animosity of the earl was attributable to C's exposure of the sinecures held by the earl's family. 36 *PR* 207–8.

66 36 *PR* 307. C later claimed that his loss at Coventry was due to the nonresident freemen sent down from London for Ellice and Moore. 74 *PR* 748; 81 *PR* 755.

67 Anne, pp. 37–9. C was listed as a bankrupt in *The Times* for July 19, 1820. Apart from this, "not one of the London papers have taken any notice of it from the first to the last." Anne to James, Oct. 13, 1820 (Nuffield). The "Rules" consisted of a prescribed area adjacent to the prison where certain prisoners were allowed to live in lodging houses in accordance with specified rules of conduct.

68 A £13,000 first mortgage was held by John Tunno, and a £3,000 second mortgage was held by John Reeves. In June 1820 C petitioned parliament for relief from the hardship created by the change in the value of money arising from the 1819 bill (the "Peel Bill") for the resumption of cash payments, which required him to pay, in terms of farm produce, "double the sum borrowed" on the first mortgage. The petition introduced by Thomas Coke in the Commons and by Lord Holland in the Lords was ordered to "lie on the table." *Journals of the House of Commons* LXXV:272; *Journals of the House of Lords* LIII:105; 42 *PR* 183, 403; 44 *PR* 354, 406–7.

69 In the petition referred to in n. 68, C stated that the cost of the property and improvements was £30,000 "and upwards." See also 41 *PR* 538. An example of a 50 percent fall in land value is given at 44 *PR* 87.

70 Statement of 1820 (Illinois); 69 *PR* 473. 36 *PR* 375: "in 1812 . . . property was worth nearly, if not quite, twice as much nominally, as it is now." Unsecured creditors filing claims totalled about £5,000. Burdett was listed by C as a creditor in the amount of £2,300 but filed no claim. 78 *PR* 326, 360.

71 69 *PR* 473–4; Anne, pp. 40–1. Anne to James, Oct. 13, 1820 (Nuffield): "yesterday the certificate was signed." In 1833, when *The Times* called C an "uncertificated bankrupt," C retold the story of his bankruptcy and declared that Eldon signed the discharge on November 28, 1820. 79 *PR* 134. The October action presumably was a provisional release, with the final action occurring six weeks later.

72 Martineau, *Thirty Years' Peace* 1:249–50. C later admitted that Caroline was deficient in "sober reason." *George IV,* para. 424. In 1824 C wrote that Caroline was beautiful and everything that a reasonable husband might want: "prone to crum, rather than crust, as she increases in years." 38 *PR* 229–31. The upper classes found her ugly and coarse. Creevey thought she looked like a Dutch doll with a lead-weighted bottom. The ladies criticized her heavy eyebrows, blatant display of bosom, and extravagant use of rouge. *Creevey Papers,* p. 307; Peter Quennell (ed.), *The Private Letters of Princess Lieven to Prince Metternich 1820–1826* (London n.d.), p. 91; Frances Hawes, *Henry Brougham* (New York n.d.), p. 123.

73 23 *PR* 322; *George IV*, para. 58.

74 23 *PR* 372–3; *George IV*, para. 66.

75 Spencer Perceval, Caroline's attorney in 1806, had prepared a volume containing the evidence ("The Book"), which he threatened to publish unless Caroline was reinstated at court. When Perceval became a member of the cabinet in 1807, "The Book" was hushed up. C's story of its publication in 1813 is told at 38 *PR* 238–44; *George IV*, para. 188.

76 36 *PR* 894, 938–60.

77 Anne, p. 40; 37 *PR* 428, 1291; 38 *PR* 230.

78 *Times*, June 7, 1820.

79 After the trial Brougham solemnly proclaimed his faith in the innocence of his client. Hawes, p. 159. C seemed to believe during the trial that she was innocent, for otherwise he could hardly have urged that Bergami be called for the defense, and he roundly asserted her innocence at the time of her death. 40 *PR* 326. But by 1830 he may have had some doubts. Writing of the attitude of the English people, he said: "They compared what they had heard of the wife with what they had *seen* of the husband . . . As far as related to the question of guilt or innocence they cared not a straw." *George IV*, para. 425.

80 Anne to James, Jan. 17, 1821 (Nuffield). On Caroline's death later in 1821, Anne became so ill that it became necessary for C to take her off for a week's convalescence. Letter to Clarke, Aug. 17, 1821 (Nuffield).

Anne's attitude probably reflected the views of many lower- and middle-class women, hundreds of whom "were seen crying in the streets" in sympathy for the queen (36 *PR* 298), as contrasted with the cynical upper-class attitude disclosed in n. 72.

81 Princess Charlotte, daughter of Caroline and George IV, died in childbirth in 1817, a year after she was married to Prince Leopold of Saxe-Coburg. See 37 *PR* 58, 326 for some of Caroline's complaints regarding separation of mother and daughter. One of the grounds for the later stages of this harsh treatment had been Caroline's complicity in arranging a bedroom rendezvous between Charlotte, aged sixteen, and a handsome young officer. Hawes, *Brougham*, p. 126.

82 37 *PR* 32. The reformers' view appears at 36 *PR* 889, 1284; 37 *PR* 77, 146, 227, 270, 636, 753, 762, 796, 1171, 1199, 1225, 1294, 1697; 38 *PR* 192, 271.

83 36 *PR* 994–5.

84 36 *PR* 1203; *George IV*, para. 436.

85 Letters to queen, June 8, 10, 12, 15, 20, 23, 25, and 29, 1820 (Nuffield). Several of the letters are reproduced in *George IV*, paras. 428–32.

86 C later stated that "vindictive feeling" had played a part in his conduct. *George IV*, para. 434.

87 "Cold calculation actuated Brougham's championship of the Princess [of Wales]." New, *Brougham*, p. 85. Wellington thought that Brougham betrayed everybody, including Caroline. Aspinall, *Brougham and the Whig Party*, p. 110. See also Hawes, *Brougham*, pp. 147–8.

88 36 *PR* 1116; *George IV*, para 432. She also proclaimed her intention to remain in England. 36 *PR* 1080, 1240; *George IV*, para. 437. See also 54 *PR* 146–7.

89 37 *PR* 313. Parliamentary criticism of the letter and C's defense appear at 38 *PR* 299–328.

90 The letter appeared in every newspaper. It was reprinted as a pamphlet, of which, according to C, two million were sold in the United Kingdom and a half million in the United States.

91 37 *PR* 328.

92 37 *PR* 326, 331. The *New Times* suspected that C had "given at least the sketch of this most detestable letter," that C's vulgarity had been polished off by "a more

classical pen." 37 *PR* 327. The *Courier* thought the authors might have been the distinguished Dr. Parr and Dr. Reynolds. 37 *PR* 331.

93 Anne, pp. 40–1; *Selections* VI:32n; John to James, Sept. 14, 1820 (Nuffield). The painting still hangs in the Guildhall, London. See also 38 PR 304.

94 37 *PR* 1071, 1134–42; letter to Alderman Wood, Oct. 31, 1820 (Nuffield).

95 37 *PR* 385.

96 37 *PR* 841.

97 C's attacks on Brougham appear at 36 *PR* 894, 986–92, 1033; 37 *PR* 769, 1005, 1023, 1044, 1066, 1071, 1173; *George IV*, para. 444. Some of C's objections were naive, particularly his assertion that Brougham should have called Bergami as a witness. But others were valid. Brougham courteously allowed his colleague Denman to sum up, although Brougham was a far more effective advocate, and Denman was guilty of a silly peroration. 37 *PR* 1050. More serious was the state of the record concerning the "tent" or "awning" under which Caroline and Bergami slept while on board a ship in the Mediterranean. 37 *PR* 1008–17.

98 Hone produced an amusing pamphlet entitled *Non Mi Ricordi* which went into many editions.

99 37 *PR* 1210.

100 37 *PR* 1210–14; Anne to James, Nov. 15, 1820 (Nuffield).

101 The *Courier*, however, was able to find such a justification; it declared that the queen had assumed "the office of first revolutionary leader." 37 *PR* 754.

102 37 *PR* 796. The queen "gave the fire-shovels [C's name for the clergy] a good pull downwards; or rather, their conduct with regard to her placed them in a proper light before the people." 52 *PR* 517.

103 *George IV*, para. 421: "all the foibles, all the vices, of all our rulers, of every description, became intimately known in every cottage in the kingdom." Place, who was very little involved, put the whole blame on the conduct of the queen and her court. Wallas, *Francis Place*, p. 151.

104 37 *PR* 558, 1082. Anne was sure that C would be brought into parliament. Anne to James, Nov. 15, 1820 (Nuffield).

105 37 *PR* 1375; Anne to James, Dec. 6, 1820 (Nuffield).

106 According to C, Caroline's repulse at the coronation was due to her abandonment of the people on the "fatal advice of the Whigs and their tools." *George IV*, para. 457. Although C had warned her beforehand of the "gulph opening before her" (38 *PR* 46), she failed to make use of the public opinion on which her position depended. 40 *PR* 65–89, 219–22.

107 40 *PR* 217–30, 289–423. The instruction in Caroline's will that her coffin was to bear the inscription "Here lies Caroline of Brunswick, Injured Queen of England" was not carried out until the funeral procession reached Colchester (on its way to Harwich). Before the coffin left Colchester, the plaque was removed by order of Lord Liverpool. 40 *PR* 401–4.

108 40 *PR* 435.

109 Manchester Cobbett papers 95, 96 (Nuffield).

110 Letters to Wood, Oct. 29 and 31, 1820 (Nuffield); Anne, p. 41.

The queen paid for the cost of the handbills and placards and gave C £50 for one complete copy of the *PR*, but C was otherwise not compensated. *Selections* I: Addendum and Errata; James to Brougham, Apr. 24, 1860 (JPC). In answer to a charge by *The Times* in July 1820 that he had espoused the cause of the queen for gain, C made a broad disavowal of receiving any money directly or indirectly from her, adding that in 1812 he had been offered £1,000 if he would cease writing on her side. 36 *PR* 1261. See also 37 *PR* 1130.

111 *A Peep at the Peers* showed, for each individual, "all the sums of money which they and the several branches of their family received out of the taxes." C claimed that

100,000 copies were sold at twopence. The pamphlet was underpriced and was raised to fourpence five days after it was issued. 37 *PR* 312, 424.

112 Anne to James, Nov. 15, 1820 (Nuffield); Griggs (ed.), *Letters of Coleridge* v:115.
Many persons were entitled to share in the queen's victory. Burdett, for example, was frequently commended by C for his services. 36 *PR* 1123, 1126, 1137, 1166; 37 *PR* 82, 168, 266.

113 Anne to James, Oct. 26, 1820 (Nuffield). C's visit was made on October 18, six days following his discharge from bankruptcy. He had not presented earlier addresses, as he was "otherwise engaged." 37 *PR* 1130. In November 1820, C wrote a new dedication to his *English Grammar* extolling the queen and declaring that the "haughty and insolent few who have been your enemies, have on all occasions, exhibited . . . a feebleness of intellect, which nothing but a constant association with malevolence and perfidy could prevent from being ascribed to dotage or idiocy."

114 Anne to James, Jan. 17, 1821 (Nuffield). At this later visit by C to the queen's court, C wore a claret-colored coat, a white waistcoat, silk stockings, and dancing pumps.

20. Agricultural distress

Motto: Letter to Wright, June 19, 1809, Add. MSS. 22907, fol. 171.

1 The average price of bread in London per four-pound loaf was 5.9d. in 1792 and 15.3d. in 1800. Mitchell and Deane, *Statistics*, p. 498.

2 C frequently claimed that as much as half a laborer's wages went in taxes. See ch. 12, nn. 60–1.

3 39 *PR* 458. See also 44 *PR* 822.

4 Mitchell and Deane, p. 488.

5 In Hampshire, weekly wages rose from 7s. to 10s. between 1760 and 1809 while unweighted food prices more than doubled. 39 *PR* 450. See also 39 *PR* 496; 42 *PR* 66; 43 *PR* 715; Arthur J. Taylor (ed.), *The Standard of Living in Britain in the Industrial Revolution* (London 1975), pp. 28–9, 53, 74. A Sussex farmer reported daily wages of 1s. 6d. in 1788–90 as compared with 2s. 0½d. in 1791–1819. 43 *PR* 519. In 1822–3 C cited weekly wage rates ranging from 6s. to 12s. 42 *PR* 822; 44 *PR* 581; 46 *PR* 653. At 1826 prices, the weekly allowance for a man, wife, and three children, calculated by Arthur Young in 1771, was 13s. 1d.; calculated by the Berkshire magistrates, it was 11s. 4d. in 1795 and 8s. in 1826. 60 *PR* 179. In contrast, the Guy's hospital allowance for a single patient's food and drink was equal to 6s. 9d. a week. *Poor Man's Friend*, p. 61.

6 29 *PR* 330.

7 Travis L. Crosby, *English Farmers and the Politics of Protection 1815–1892* (Hassocks 1977), p. 21. In 1873 53.5 percent of the land was held by owners of a thousand or more acres. F. M. L. Thompson, *Landed Society*, pp. 32, 113.

8 In the period 1814–16, 1 out of every 7.5 country banks in England failed. 55 *PR* 461. See Fetter, *British Monetary Orthodoxy*, p. 67.

9 The 1816 harvest was one of the worst in history, not only in Britain, but throughout Europe and much of the rest of the world, a condition that was reflected in 1817 prices. Post, *Subsistence Crisis*, p. 37.

10 36 *PR* 285, 299, 372; 37 *PR* 220; 41 *PR* 175. 36 *PR* 298: "if . . . those wars were just and necessary we really have nothing to find fault with." War had been declared by the French, but after Pitt had refused to recognize the French republic or to treat with that government officially. Although C had originally been an enthusiastic supporter of the war, this was before his eyes had been fully opened about the English ruling class. C now claimed that the war had been opposed "by

the reformers, many of whom were most severely punished for that opposition."
36 *PR* 712.

11   To the common argument that the war had been fought to put down Bonaparte, C responded that Bonaparte had not been heard of until seven years after the war had started. 45 *PR* 328. "We had a Devil to beat down, after having raised the Devil up." 65 *PR* 278. One whose outlook was as far removed from C's as Wilberforce claimed that the war with France (1) need not have taken place, (2) was due to Dundas's influence with Pitt and his persuasion that the English could easily take the rich French West Indies, and (3) should have been terminated in 1794 after the death of Robespierre. Coupland, *Wilberforce,* pp. 188, 190.

12   41 *PR* 306. Some of the more notorious sinecures were listed by C at 45 *PR* 107–12. The two brothers of the Earl of Egremont at ages six and three were given colonial appointments that produced income of more than £1 million over the succeeding fifty-nine years.

13   46 *PR* 600.

14   39 *PR* 1054.

15   44 *PR* 168. Cf. John H. Clapham, *An Economic History of Modern Britain* 1: *The Early Railway Age 1820–1850* (Cambridge 1926), p. vii: "after the price fall of 1820–1 the purchasing power of wages in general – not, of course, everyone's wages – was definitely greater than it had been just before the revolutionary and Napoleonic wars."

16   The farm associations' request for a duty on agricultural imports was rejected by the report of a parliamentary committee made in June 1821.

17   Matthias Attwood claimed that between 1817 and 1822 there had been a 25 percent reduction in the circulation of banknotes. Barry Gordon, *Political Economy in Parliament 1819–1823* (London 1976), p. 147.

18   The 1819 bill gave the Bank of England the *option* to pay in gold coin beginning in May 1822; this date was moved forward one year as a result of supplementary legislation in 1821.

19   The hard currency program *was* continued with relatively minor changes, and the purchasing power of the capital value of the consols increased nearly fourfold between 1815 and 1896. John Maynard Keynes, *A Tract on Monetary Reform* (London 1923), p. 15.

20   The three solutions described in the text represent an oversimplification of the proposals. The Attwoods, Charles Western, and several other members of the House of Commons (including Burdett and Graham) supported a reduction in the value of the pound. 42 *PR* 193–230; 66 *PR* 323–5; Gordon, *Political Economy,* pp. 143–51; Smart, *Economic Annals* 11:96–100. C's objections to what he called the "little shilling" project are stated at 60 *PR* 94–5, and the objections of the little-shilling proponents to equitable adjustment are given at 66 *PR* 333.

21   C's proposal required that adjustments in contracts be varied according to the periods at which they were made. 58 *PR* 33. The strongest argument against C's proposal, apart from its complication, was that it represented a candid breach of faith with creditors (although actually no more harmful to creditors than a corresponding amount of inflation) which might impair future borrowing ability. C's proposal, while helpful to debtors in general, also offered the greatest protection to the farm laborer.

22   The iron gridiron: 42 *PR* 293, 380; 44 *PR* 826. The gridiron in the masthead: 38 *PR* 425. This became a permanent fixture in 1826. The Feast of the Gridiron: 39 *PR* 298.

23   C's conclusion that it would be impossible to meet the interest payments was, he believed, supported by two simple sets of figures. (1) Taxes in 1821 were 3.5 times those in 1790; farm rentals had more than doubled; prices and wages were roughly the same; the population, according to C, had not increased; after rentals

and wages were paid, there could not be enough left to cover taxes. (2) The amount of the debt was twice the value of all the real property in England. 42 *PR* 723.

C was not the only one who doubted the ability of the country to pay the debt. In 1821 Earl Grey declared: "we had contracted in depreciated paper an immense debt, which we were unable to pay in our restored currency." Hansard, 2nd ser. IV:835 (Feb. 21, 1821), quoted by Gordon, *Political Economy*, p. 98.

24 Paine, *Political Works*, p. 491.

25 39 *PR* 331. See also 39 *PR* 452, 456. Even after prices began to fall, C talked about "squeezing rents out of the bones of the labourer." 44 *PR* 35, 598.

26 39 *PR* 456. C estimated the underpayment to laborers as £80 million annually. 39 *PR* 453. See also 30 *PR* 427; 38 *PR* 751; 39 *PR* 670, 681, 695, 697, 738.

Three years later C was claiming that "the farmers cannot be *gainers* (any more than other people) by the oppression of the labourers." According to C, the farmer was forced to pay low wages because of the heavy taxes imposed by the government. 51 *PR* 390–3. Thus, in order to be consistent in his claim that the government was the ultimate cause of the distress, he had to be inconsistent in his charge that the farmers oppressed their laborers. Yet C did not relinquish his earlier claim that the distress of the laborer was due to his hardhearted employer. See 51 *PR* 671–3; 56 *PR* 260–2 (but cf. 263!), 422, 518; 57 *PR* 720.

27 "You so gallantly drew your swords on St. Peter's-field at Manchester" in defense of Castlereagh's system. 38 *PR* 15.

28 "I do not, in addressing you upon the cause of your ruin, act from a hope or even a desire to relieve you, or render you assistance in any way." 38 *PR* 5–6.

29 38 *PR* 1.

30 Major articles on agricultural problems during 1821 appear at 38 *PR* 1 ("A New Year's Gift to the Farmers"), 569, 641 ("To Farmers Wives"); 39 *PR* 1, 289, 361, 505, 577, 793, 865, 937; 40 *PR* 230, 505 (this and nine following citations refer to C's article "To Landlords on the Agricultural Report"), 641, 705, 769, 897, 961, 1025, 1089, 1153, 1217, 1281, 1409, 1473, 1641, 1661.

31 38 *PR* 727. According to Charles Western, member of parliament for Essex, two-thirds of the farmers in that county were insolvent in 1822. 42 *PR* 16. Of the 260 held for debt in the Fleet prison in 1823, 120 were farmers. 46 *PR* 661.

32 Anne to James, Dec. 27, 1821 (Nuffield).

33 Battle, Jan. 3, 1822: 41 *PR* 97.

34 Lewes, Jan. 9, 1822: 41 *PR* 164–7.

35 Anne to James, Jan. 23, 1822 (Nuffield).

36 Huntingdon, Jan. 22, 1822: 41 *PR* 265.

37 King's Lynn, Jan. 29, 1822: 41 *PR* 291; Epsom, Feb. 18: 41 *PR* 469; Chichester, Feb. 20: 41 *PR* 484; Brighton, Feb. 25: 41 *PR* 531; Norwich, Mar. 29: 42 *PR* 32; Farnham, May 30: 42 *PR* 514.

38 Smart, *Economic Annals* II:57. Parliament received 1,200 petitions on agricultural distress in the period 1819–21. Gordon, *Political Economy*, p. 80.

39 The economist David Ricardo, member of parliament from 1819 to 1823, had supported Peel's bill of 1819, predicting a price decline of 5 percent, later increased to 10 percent. But "Ricardo had no conception of the degree of deflation he was striving to have parliament impose on the British economy." The estimate of Alexander Baring that the fall would be considerably greater "was to prove far nearer the mark." Gordon, *Political Economy*, pp. 38–9. Ricardo claimed that the disparity was due to the action of the Bank of England in foolishly accumulating gold too quickly and too long in advance of the 1823 conversion date. David Ricardo, *The Works and Correspondence of David Ricardo*, ed. Piero Straffa (Cambridge 1951–73) IX:140.

40 Ricardo, who also thought the national debt had a debilitating effect on the econ-

omy, made what was an equally unpopular suggestion that it be paid off by a one-time capital levy. Gordon, *Political Economy*, pp. 22, 66, 82, 157, 158. Other areas of agreement between C and Ricardo were the need for parliamentary reform and the absurdity of Pitt's sinking fund. Ricardo, *Works* VIII:77, 314; IX:266.

41 Halévy, *History* I: 156: "consecration of custom."
42 Maidstone, June 11, 1822: 42 *PR* 673–4.
43 42 *PR* 681. When challenged, C asserted that he was a freeholder of Kent. Presumably someone had made a grant to C of a small piece of land, as was the common practice. 42 *PR* 690.
44 42 *PR* 698. For press comments on C's victory at Maidstone see Crosby, *English Farmers*, p. 67.
45 Hansard, 2nd ser. VII: 1080, 1087 (June 14, 1822). The exchange as given by C differs somewhat from Hansard, suggesting that C took his account from one of the newspapers. 42 *PR* 712. Hansard was still notoriously inaccurate at this stage.
46 42 *PR* 712, 761. This is C's account, which disagrees in certain respects from that in Hansard (1083).
47 Hansard, 1086. See also 42 *PR* 756. Peel claimed that C had not been "manfully resisted" at Maidstone.
48 *Creevey Papers*, p. 443.
49 The 1822 act did not become operative until the home price of wheat reached 80s., which never happened. Smart, *Economic Annals* II:117.
50 Smart II:95; Hansard, 2nd ser. VI:715 (Feb. 26, 1822).
51 Winchester, Sept. 28, 1822: 44 *PR* 31; Andover, Oct. 12: 44 *PR* 171; Salisbury, Oct. 22: 44 *PR* 217; Newbury, Oct. 17: 44 *PR* 237; Reading, Nov. 9: 44 *PR* 401; Guildford, Dec. 14: 44 *PR* 743.
52 44 *PR* 756. "I want to see some fresh faces." 44 *PR* 663.
53 44 *PR* 252–3. See also 44 *PR* 590.
54 44 *PR* 423, 435. C later claimed that a plea by Kent magistrates asking farmers to keep up the wages paid to their laborers "will produce little effect." 52 *PR* 239.
55 Norwich, Jan. 3, 1823: 45 *PR* 68.
56 Of Coke's claim that no man had done more than he had for the soil, C asked: "May it not be said, with full as much truth, that the soil has done more for no man than it has for you?" 46 *PR* 277.
57 Coke had roguishly declared: "it was so teasing to Ministers to have petition after petition presented"; it was "his great object to plague the Ministers from morning to night." Crosby, *English Farmers*, p. 62.
58 45 *PR* 295.
59 45 *PR* 80. C claimed that only forty persons voted against his proposal (45 *PR* 85), whereas Crosby states that the vote was three to one in C's favor. The phrase "equitable adjustment" was one that Wodehouse had coined in November 1822. 54 *PR* 267; Smart, *Economic Annals* II:136n.
60 The vote on the second ballot was twenty to one in favor of C's proposal. Crosby, p. 69. The two quotations that follow are taken from the same source.
61 45 *PR* 178.
62 45 *PR* 257, 312, 537.
63 Crosby, p. 69.
64 T. Wemyss Reid (ed.), *The Life, Letters and Friendships of Richard Monckton Milnes, First Lord Houghton* (New York 1891) I:94; the talk attended by Milnes was in 1830. H. Hunt (*Memoirs* II:308) states that C "was also a very eloquent speaker." Hazlitt said: "Mr. Cobbett speaks almost as well as he writes." *The Spirit of the Age*, p. 351. See also *Tait's Edinburgh Magazine*, Nov. 1831.
65 Hereford, Jan. 17, 1823: 45 *PR* 230; Epsom, Feb. 11: 45 *PR* 427.
66 *Times*, Jan. 20, 1823. The article, entitled "Signal Defeat and Disgrace of Cobbett," covering more than a page, was devoted largely to a report of the personal attacks

on C, including the false accusation that he had been in "the servile pay of the government," from which he had been dismissed.

C, who was prevented from answering by the uproar of the crowd, claimed that the London papers had misrepresented the affair; that he had actually scored a victory. But his agonized account discloses that he did not like the way he had been treated. 45 *PR* 247, 316; 48 *PR* 749; 57 *PR* 769.

67 45 *PR* 236–8.

68 See e.g. 54 *PR* 202.

69 45 *PR* 420–4, 442. Crosby (*English Farmers,* p. 73) refers to a Hampshire county meeting held in March 1823 attended by both C and Hunt which rejected C's petition but endorsed the appropriation of church property and crown lands.

70 The survival of many farmers was due to the remarkable willingness of the landlords to accept substantial rent reductions. See e.g. 41 *PR* 276. In 1823 four-fifths of the land in Herefordshire was "at present yielding no rent at all." 45 *PR* 234, 248. This factor, unforeseen by C, caused him to overestimate the impact of the fall in prices on the ability of the government to collect taxes. "But neither of us," wrote C in an open letter to Huskisson, "whatever else we might think of the landlords, ever dreamed, that they would be content to give up their rents!" 41 *PR* 589.

71 The *Courier* claimed that wheat would be near 70s. "towards November." C thought it would be 40s. or less. 47 *PR* 679–95. Actually it was 43s. 8d. for the six weeks ended November 15, 1823 (48 *PR* 567) and around 50s. for most of the final quarter of 1823.

72 47 *PR* 686. The crowing of the opposition began even before May 1823, since payment in gold coins by the Bank of England became optional in 1821 and the Bank elected to pay in gold, when requested, at this advance date. *The Times* did its crowing in a four-column article (Feb. 15, 1822).

73 51 *PR* 652, 655. See Clapham, *Early Railway Age,* p. 264: "The country gentlemen were scared at the crack in the corn markets and anxious to slow down deflation; so the banks were authorized to go on with their £1 notes until 1833." C estimated that the Small Note Act added as much as 12s. per quarter (18d. a bushel) to the market price of wheat. See 48 *PR* 244 (10s.); 49 *PR* 412 (8s.); 49 *PR* 482 (12s.).

74 49 *PR* 521; Hansard, 2nd ser. x:304 (Feb. 23, 1824). Robinson later admitted that he had been rather too warm in describing the condition of the nation. 57 *PR* 713.

75 Bank of England credit increased from £17 million to £25 million between August 1823 and August 1825. Fetter, *British Monetary Orthodoxy,* p. 111.

76 54 *PR* 337; Hansard, 2nd ser. XIII:288 (Apr. 28, 1825).

77 Fetter, p. 112; Hansard, 2nd ser. XIII:1387 (June 27, 1825).

78 55 *PR* 454.

79 55 *PR* 25, 77.

80 55 *PR* 9; 57 *PR* 513.

81 Add. MSS. 40385, fol. 123, quoted in Fetter, pp. 112–13.

82 C estimated that one hundred country banks had failed. 57 *PR* 134. Other estimates ranged from thirty-six to eighty. Clapham, *Early Railway Age,* p. 273.

83 55 *PR* 608.

84 *Journal of Mrs. Arbuthnot: 1820–1832,* ed. Francis Bamford and the Duke of Wellington (London 1850) I:426–8, 431, quoted in Fetter, pp. 116–17.

85 C's original proposition was made in 1818, when he said that he would suffer himself to be broiled alive if "the Bank ever paid in coin, and the government continued, at the same time, to pay the interest of the debt in full." 34 *PR* 7–8. The substance of this was repeated several times without change in sense. 34 *PR* 1050 (May 1819) and 35 *PR* 170 (Sept. 1819). It was slightly modified on its next appearance to say that the condition would be fulfilled if the ministry carried out "their resolution" to return to cash payments. 35 *PR* 364 (Nov. 1819). This was

again amended so that the promise to deliver himself up for broiling was conditional on carrying the Peel bill "into full effect." 38 *PR* 425 (Feb. 1821). In this last form it was continuously repeated by C, set off in quotation marks with a citation suggesting that it was copied from the 1819 declaration, which was not the case.

It seems unlikely that C realized in 1821 that he was changing the proposition in substance, but it is a good illustration of the liberty that C often took with language.

To carry the jest to its final conclusion: As the original proposition was stated, C should have been broiled. As reworded in 1821, he had a fairly good argument that he was entitled to stay off the gridiron. New broiling rules were proposed by C in 1829. 68 *PR* 450. In 1835 he reverted to the phraseology of 1821. 88 *PR* 513.

86   Smart, *Economic Annals* II:299.
87   57 *PR* 451.
88   57 *PR* 820. Other gridiron dinners were held at Bolton and Norwich. 58 *PR* 67, 245. A mock Feast of the Gridiron at which C was broiled until the "fat was exhausted" appeared in the *Reading Mercury. Times,* June 23, 1823.
89   58 *PR* 131–2, 142.
90   44 *PR* 823.
91   35 *PR* 114–15. See also 46 *PR* 514.
92   *Letters of David Ricardo to Hutches Trower and Others,* ed. James Bonar and J. H. Hollander (Oxford 1899), p. 176.
93   35 *PR* 115. See also 74 *PR* 327.

21. The writer

Motto: 19 *PR* 493.
1   C was in London from the end of November 1816 to late in March 1817. The year before (1815–16), he had been in and around London from late in December to early in March.
2   69 *PR* 476.
3   The alleged libels are referred to at 32 *PR* 11–21; 34 *PR* 737–48; 35 *PR* 572.
4   Anne to James, Dec. 6, 1820 (Nuffield); 37 *PR* 1417–71. The case was heard on Dec. 5, 1820. In Wright's action against C that followed, evidence was produced to show that it was not a "private letter" but had been used in 1808 to discredit Hunt with the Westminster committee. *The Book of Wonders: Part the Second* (London 1821), pp. 26, 45.
5   37 *PR* 1489–554. The case was heard on Dec. 11, 1820 and is reported in full in *The Book of Wonders: Part the Second.* Scarlett's scathing attack on C in that case may explain, in part, C's bitter denunciation of Scarlett at frequent intervals thereafter.
     In December 1819 Wright had also been awarded £500 in a suit against William Clement, printer and publisher of the *PR* in 1817 and in 1819. Wright had commenced suit against Dolby, publisher in 1819 and 1820, but withdrew this action after C's return and initiated suit against him.
6   37 *PR* 1490.
7   Anne to James, Dec. 16, 1820 (Nuffield).
8   Anne, p. 42. The suggestion of the *Edinburgh Review* for April 1838, p. 57, that this had been paid by Queen Caroline was denied by John in "Addendum and Errata" to *Selections,* who confirmed that the money came from Rogers.
9   Five open letters from C to Benbow and several other reformers imprisoned in 1817 are at 32 *PR* 1060, 1089; 33 *PR* 699; 34 *PR* 1, 33. The month before Benbow was removed as publisher, C publicly declared his complete confidence in him. 37 *PR* 1552. Benbow's career after 1820 is outlined in Patricia Hollis, *The Pauper Press: A Study in Working-Class Radicalism in the 1830s* (London 1970), p. 307.
10   Anne to James, Dec. 6, 1820 (Nuffield).

11 Anne to James, Jan. 17, 1821 (Nuffield).
12 Ibid.
13 Jan. 23, 1822 (Nuffield). The Cobbetts stayed in furnished rooms with a Mrs. Williams at 11 Michaels Place, Brompton from October 1820 to April 1821, when they moved to Kensington.
14 Anne, p. 43. Major Codd was one of C's oldest friends and a subscriber to C's *Works*.
15 Letter to Clarke, Apr. 30, 1821 (Nuffield).
16 Letter to Palmer, Jan. 24, 1825 (Nuffield).
17 Letter to Clarke, Aug. 20, 1825 (Nuffield).
18 48 *PR* 545–7, 555–6.
19 84 *PR* 75.
20 *Woodlands*, para. 362.
21 56 *PR* 501.
22 Letter to Nancy, Sept. 9, 1825 (Nuffield).
23 Susan (Nuffield xvii:3); letter to Dean, Jan. 27, 1825 (Illinois). C's office was moved from 183 Fleet Street to 11 Bolt Court in 1830.
24 At the outset, C's older brother, Thomas, and C's niece were installed at Barn Elm. 66 *PR* 510. C himself spent the greater part of the week there, returning to Kensington for Saturday night and Sunday. 70 *PR* 1107. During C's travels about England in 1830, Nancy stayed at Barn Elm, where she directed the farming. 70 *PR* 1033. When the lease expired in September 1830, the live and dead farming stock, including seven working oxen and a working bull, were sold at auction. 70 *PR* 412. A marked catalogue showing the prices brought for the 157 lots auctioned and the final settlement of accounts is included in the Nuffield collection: Faithfull MSS., no. 8.
25 64 *PR* 745; *Corn*, para. 155. During the peak period of winter employment, C paid each worker 2 lb of bread, ½ lb of cheese, and 2 lb of meat per day. 64 *PR* 584. He later eliminated the cheese and gave 2 lb of bread, 1½ lb of meat, and 6d. in cash. 67 *PR* 116. Hunt, after a falling out with C, claimed that the food was not fit to eat. 72 *PR* 20.
26 47 *PR* 51, 821; 49 *PR* 243. The Swedish turnip had been known in America before C became its champion, but he popularized it as a field crop and food for cattle. C also claimed credit for introduction of the mangel-wurzel for the same use. 75 *PR* 780.
27 Later editions of *Cottage Economy* contain a note dated November 14, 1831 which begins: "This last summer, I have proved that, as keep for cows, Mangel Wurzel is preferable to Swedish Turnips, whether as to quantity or quality."
28 *Corn*, para. 172. The seed used by C for his maize was not imported from America but had been grown in northern France or the Netherlands. 68 *PR* 724.
29 Typically, in August 1828, C sent a cartload of squashes to Covent Garden market, not for profit "but, merely to prove how easily they may be raised." 66 *PR* 192.
30 49 *PR* 810–11. William Lovett, *The Life and Struggles of William Lovett* . . . with a preface by R. H. Tawney (London 1967), p. 12: "at that period straw-hat making was a female mania in our neighbourhood," although Lovett (probably incorrectly) fixes the period as sometime prior to C's promotion. The tory papers of Scotland did their best to deny C the credit for his contribution, although the increased revenues to the Orkney islands alone amounted to not less than £20,000 per annum. 63 *PR* 708–12, 79 *PR* 729. C's unreimbursed cost of the straw hat promotion was £300. 78 *PR* 269.
31 53 *PR* 146–7.
32 Letter to Anne, Sept. 17, 1827 (Nuffield). References to the turnpike war are at 48 *PR* 193, 430; 49 *PR* 300, 358, 803; 50 *PR* 36, 227, 302, 321, 385, 449, 549; 51 *PR* 513; 52 *PR* 116; 53 *PR* 55, 303. The ninety-seven informations of C regarding

Surrey turnpikes where hackney coaches were overcharged produced a recovery of £200, which, after deducting expenses, was divided equally between the person who provided the facts on which C proceeded and the trustees of the roads. 63 *PR* 438, 480.

33 38 *PR* 676; 48 *PR* 822.

34 67 *PR* 36–8.

35 *Times,* June 20, 1835. The 120 volumes do not include C's speeches, the five works he translated, or the four volumes he edited.

36 *Corn,* para. 155; 60 *PR* 261–2; 73 *PR* 140; JPC, p. 25.

37 The secretaries, or those who sometimes acted as such, include C. M. Riley (1827?–1829?), John Y. Akerman (1827?–1832?), James Gutsell (1832?–1835), and Benjamin Tilly (1834?–1835).

38 40 *PR* 826; 42 *PR* 234; JPC, pp. 26–7.

39 C is also shown as author of *A Geographical Dictionary of England and Wales* (1832), most of which was the work of Riley, John Cobbett, and one of the Cobbett daughters. 82 *PR* 782.

40 *A French Grammar* (1824); *A Spelling Book* (1831); *A New French and English Dictionary* (1833). The compilation of the last was "the work of a very clever Frenchman of the name of Aliva." 82 *PR* 781. The spelling book, in its fourth edition by 1834, was attacked by Carlile for its use of fables. Joel H. Wiener, *The War of the Unstamped* (Ithaca and London 1969), p. 160.

41 51 *PR* 262.

42 *The Cobbett-Library* [1835], a catalogue periodically published by C.

43 *Year's Residence,* para. 18; Van Wyck Brooks, *The World of Washington Irving* (New York 1944), p. 293.

44 *Huntia: A Yearbook of Botanical and Horticultural Bibliography* II (Pittsburgh 1965), 86.

45 *Woodlands,* para. 326. *The Woodlands* was issued in parts: the first in 1825, but Parts II–VII not until 1828, when the completed volume was published.

46 *Gardener's Magazine,* 1828, p. 363.

47 H. J. and Henry A. Elwes, *Trees of Great Britain and Ireland* (Edinburgh 1912), pp. 1502–5: "It has always been obnoxious to the British woodsman, partly on account of its thorns, which tore his clothes and hands, partly on account of the hardness of the wood which blunted his tools, and partly because of its liability to be broken by the wind and to reproduce suckers when cut."

An extended discussion of the history and properties of the locust, with a critical analysis of C's claims ("quackery" and "absurdity"), appears in J. C. Loudon, *Arboretum et Fructicetum Britannicum* (London 1830) II:612–24.

48 *Huntia* II:105.

49 *Corn,* paras. 164, 177; 66 *PR* 645. The maize grown by C was a dwarf variety which C had not seen in America. 66 *PR* 255; see n. 28 above. Allegedly, it was called "Cobbett's corn" "not from any vain glory about the thing; but because I have no other way of designating it properly." 68 *PR* 287.

50 66 *PR* 467, 524; 67 *PR* 135; 68 *PR* 479, 545, 625–6, 635.

C had produced enough seed from his Barn Elm experiment to plant 4,000 acres. 66 *PR* 350. In 1831 he announced that his corn could be sold at 50 percent more than American or French. 74 *PR* 380.

51 74 *PR* 589. See also 74 *PR* 377, 699, 824. C claimed to have received letters extolling his corn from 2,043 farmers and farm laborers. 76 *PR* 95.

52 *WR* XI (July 1829), 54.

53 The acreage planted in maize in England increased tenfold between 1971 and 1975. *Agricultural Statistics: England and Wales* (London: HMSO 1975).

54 *Cottage Economy,* paras. 23, 34, 106, 134.

55 *ER* XXXVIII (Feb. 1823), 105, 119.

56 71 *PR* 173.

57 "From this famous book I learned all my principles relative to farming, gardening and planting . . . It contains the foundation of all knowledge in the cultivation of the earth." *The Cobbett-Library* [1835]. C began using Tull's system in 1814. 67 *PR* 125.

C also edited, for the American reader, William Forsyth's *A Treatise on the Cultivation and Management of Fruit Trees* (1802).

58 54 *PR* 240.

59 The first three numbers were called "Cobbett's Monthly Religious Tracts," while the succeeding nine numbers were entitled "Cobbett's Monthly Sermons." These made up the book published in 1822. In 1830 C published, as a thirteenth sermon, a pamphlet entitled *Good Friday; or, The Murder of Jesus Christ by the Jews*, a shamefully antisemitic attack on the pending legislation for relief of the Jews from certain civil disabilities, for which he was soundly spanked by the *Westminster Review* of July 1830 (XIII:188). John Cobbett's *Journal of a Tour in Italy* published in 1831 was criticized for displaying the "cloven hoof" on the same subject. *WR* XIV (January 1831), 179–80.

60 53 *PR* 276. The figure of 240,000 was apparently based on an average sale of 20,000 copies of each of twelve sermons. Three years later, C claimed sales of 150,000! 65 *PR* 124. The merit of the sermons, without regard to their special messages, is affirmed by their translation into French and Italian.

61 A later edition of the *Emigrant's Guide* contained "a list of articles of dress and of sea-stores necessary to the emigrant." 70 *PR* 446, 541. The letters from America, which had been published earlier in 1829 by Benjamin Smith, were reviewed in *WR* xv (July 1831), 138.

62 *Advice*, para. 119.

63 C had originally intended to sell the volume, a book of 668 pages, at 10s., but at the last minute (possibly because of his experience with a large-page edition of Protestant *"Reformation"*, which sold slowly) decided to offer it at half that figure. 70 *PR* 543.

64 The *Rural Rides* discussed in the text is the book as C published it in 1830, and the page citations in the notes that follow refer to the Penguin edition (1967) of that book. The original *Rural Rides* consisted of C's journeys on horseback during the harvest and postharvest seasons of four years (1822, 1823, 1825, and 1826), limited to the country he knew so well in the south of England, except for one excursion into Gloucestershire, Herefordshire, and Worcestershire. (The title of the first edition referred to rides in the counties of "Essex, Suffolk, Norfolk and Hertfordshire," but they were not included in the text.) After C's death, expanded editions were published which included accounts of other journeys that had appeared in the *PR* from 1821 to 1834 in which the travel was chiefly along main roads and by post chaise, often in unfamiliar country of northern England, Scotland, Ireland, and Wales – much of it nonrural. The later material was not much more than a well-written travelogue, lacking the charm of the earlier accounts, being less well provided with personal anecdotes and amusing rural encounters.

65 *Advice*, para. 75.

66 *Rural Rides*, pp. 410, 174, 207, 258–9.

67 *Rural Rides*, pp. 114–15, 137, 293, 295, 385, 453.

68 Matthew Arnold, "Future of Liberalism," *English Literature and Irish Politics*, ed. R. H. Soper (Ann Arbor 1973), p. 136. Arnold thought C "clear-headed, but rough, impatient" (p. 168).

69 *Rural Rides*, pp. 179, 181, 187; 52 *PR* 399, 462; 71 *PR* 426. C also criticized the methodist clergy for living well out of the pennies squeezed from the poor. 53 *PR* 532–9; 71 *PR* 197.

70 *Rural Rides*, p. 478. However, in large towns shopkeepers were necessary for the distribution of commodities. 69 *PR* 668.

71 46 *PR* 330; 57 *PR* 368–73; 66 *PR* 390, 473. See also *Rural Rides*, pp. 109, 225, 344, where C speaks of the "self-styled Christian, who acts the part of Jew or Quaker."

72 48 *PR* 193.

73 16 *PR* 209; 40 *PR* 1119. See also 42 *PR* 739: "Israelitish Christians"; 64 *PR* 2–3: "You money-jobbers and usurers . . . who are Jews in soul though Christians by profession"; and 84 *PR* 66: "Jews, either in religion or character, or both."

74 46 *PR* 486; 55 *PR* 80.

75 57 *PR* 132.

76 *Rural Rides*, pp. 384, 388.

77 12 *PR* 267.

78 11 *PR* 431. The unitarians, according to C, were a peculiar sect of Jews. 63 *PR* 261. He decided that he must not scold them any more when he learned that they were tolerant and friendly. 69 *PR* 104.

79 *Good Friday*, p. 21. C believed that "amongst the blasphemous rites of their synagogues" the Jews crucified Jesus in effigy twice a year. *Manchester Lectures*, p. 174. See also 66 *PR* 41; 75 *PR* 217.

C had been greatly offended by a Jewish farmer of tolls who called him an "atheist." 48 *PR* 213. C praised the czar for banishing the Jews, and thought the same should be done in England. 65 *PR* 20–4. He commended the king of Prussia for his regulations governing Jews living in Posen. 81 *PR* 145. Perhaps the picture is balanced, to some degree, by C's statement "I declare . . . that I know nothing that I would not be: Hanoverian, Jew, any thing but a Whig." 63 *PR* 661–2. After C's breakdown in 1833 he became increasingly antisemitic. 82 *PR* 479.

80 39 *PR* 188–90. C relied on "chemical processes performed by a gentleman, upon whom I can safely rely" showing that potatoes contain only "one-tenth part of nutritious matter." 67 *PR* 62. See also 29 *PR* 166. But according to Spencer Walpole (*History of England* ii:266), potatoes required half the acreage of wheat to supply the same food value.

81 "In this period bread was undoubtedly the staple of life for the 80 or 90 per cent of the population that made up the working classes." J. Burnett in Barker, McKenzie, and Yudlin, *Our Changing Fare* (London 1966), p. 70, quoted in E. J. Hobsbawm and George Rudé, *Captain Swing* (Penguin ed. 1973), p. 8n.

82 *Poor Man's Friend*, para. 59. 46 *PR* 518: The potato was a "soul-degrading root." See also Woodward, *Age of Reform*, p. 315n.

83 39 *PR* 190–1. See also 71 *PR* 406; 78 *PR* 72.

R. N. Salaman says of C: "to him should be given the credit of being the only public man of his time to proclaim openly the danger society incurred by forcing its members to adopt a standard of living based on the potato. Equally to his credit was it, that in bread and beer he saw the labourer's chief weapon of defense." *The History and Social Influence of the Potato* (Cambridge 1949), p. 524.

84 *Rural Rides*, p. 191. When C visited northern England for the first time in 1832, he thought he had discovered the "true ground of all the errors of the Scotch *feelosofers* with regard to population . . . and poor laws": the far fewer parish churches in the north. Durham and Dorset were about the same size, but Dorset had more than three times as many churches. 78 *PR* 80.

85 34 *PR* 1045–6; 42 *PR* 615; 46 *PR* 65; 49 *PR* 337, 400; 50 *PR* 798; 51 *PR* 129; 52 *PR* 131, 336; 61 *PR* 202; 69 *PR* 349; 72 *PR* 71; *Protestant "Reformation"*, para. 452. 52 *PR* 131: "I am about to prove, from the internal evidence, that one of the first two returns *must be a lie*." Mitchell and Deane (*Statistics*, p. 2) state that the first two returns may have omitted "a significant proportion of the population," but the probable error was not great enough to have affected the argument. C was plainly wrong. The principal basis for his position was the large capacity of the churches:

He pointed out that the estimate of population made by George Chalmers at the time of King John would have meant only twelve ablebodied men to each parish church. 59 *PR* 557.

86 *Rural Rides*, pp. 161, 349. 46 *PR* 66: "You found the boroughmongers greatly puzzled to account for the *increase of the paupers*; and you invented for their use this increase in population."

Britain's increase in population was urged by *The Times* as proof of her increased ability to carry on an extensive war. 61 *PR* 200–4.

87 64 *PR* 328.

88 *Rural Rides*, pp. 49–50, 161, 349. See also 39 *PR* 436–93. The government pension granted to Malthus added to C's suspicions. 72 *PR* 720.

89 52 *PR* 641–69. The "wen" was principally, but not always, used with reference to London. See 40 *PR* 1608, referring to Chatham and Portsmouth, where there had been a great swelling of population during the wars. Liverpool was "a sort of bastard wen." 59 *PR* 88.

90 45 *PR* 481. C claimed that government policy caused London living costs to be lower than those in the country. 47 *PR* 94.

91 39 *PR* 341, 435–96.

92 58 *PR* 183–6 and 66 *PR* 617–18 describe how Malthus's views stimulated C's Protestant "*Reformation*". At a later point, C stated that the book was intended "as a blow at the church-parsons." 70 *PR* 954.

The circumstances relating to the issue of the *Poor Man's Friend* are outlined in ch. 22, n. 28.

C thought that William Godwin had adequately answered Malthus, presumably in his essay *Of Population . . . in Answer to Mr. Malthus . . .* (London 1820). 72 *PR* 70, 720.

93 *Legacy to Labourers*, p. 140. The first edition shows the date as 1834, but it was not published until the following year. See also 59 *PR* 306–7, 394; 71 *PR* 47, 285.

94 *Protestant "Reformation"*, paras. 37, 192. A second volume listing the clerical establishments confiscated (the work of the Rev. Jeremiah O'Callaghan) was published in 1827. 82 *PR* 779.

95 65 *PR* 109. The regular two-volume edition offered at 8s. was supplemented by a large edition in two royal octavo volumes at £1 11s. 6d., later reduced to 10s., "making to myself the solemn promise never to publish a dear book again." 70 *PR* 541.

96 65 *PR* 108; 66 *PR* 408; 61 *PR* 262; Edward Smith, *Cobbett* II:243n.

97 Letter to the Rev. A. A. Isaacs, Jan. 4, 1885 in *The Works of John Ruskin*, ed. E. T. Cook and Alexander Wedderburn (London 1909) XXXVII:507. In an earlier letter (p. 503), Ruskin called C's history "the only true one ever written as far as it reaches."

98 Coupland, *Wilberforce*, p. 366.

99 54 *PR* 772: "It is by repetition of deeply interesting facts that an impression is made upon the people."

100 64 *PR* 134; 70 *PR* 71. C claimed that he was read by the resident ambassadors of foreign states, who sent the *PR* regularly home to their courts. 65 *PR* 359.

101 Henry Lytton Bulwer, *Historical Characters* (London 1868) II:178.

102 66 *PR* 403, 406. C claimed that "my book," i.e. *Year's Residence*, which described his method of turnip culture and was priced at 5s., "is the cheapest that ever was sold in England." 62 *PR* 293.

A catalogue of trees costing "six pence perhaps" was sold for twopence. 64 *PR* 565.

C's *Two-Penny Trash* was sold at a price "hardly paying for the paper and print," and at a price for "a very large lot" which C thought caused a loss. 71 *PR* 58, 158.

103 65 *PR* 116; 71 *PR* 166.

104 In addition to the ventures mentioned in the text, C became financially involved in (1) *The Statesman,* a London evening paper to which he contributed articles in 1822–3, some of which C reprinted in a volume entitled *Collective Commentaries* (1823); (2) the *Norfolk Yeoman's Gazette,* which was discontinued after publishing thirteen issues in 1823; (3) the sale of American books: 55 *PR* 610; 61 *PR* 227; (4) the sale of imported timber, beginning in 1827: 62 *PR* 564; (5) the publication of a number of books written by others, including those written by his sons (listed in the Epilogue) and the following: *American Slave Trade* by Jesse Torrey with preface by C (1822), *Elements of Roman History* and *An Abridged History of the Emperors* by J. H. Sievrac, translated into English by C and his sons (1828–9), *Usury* by the Rev. Jeremiah O'Callaghan (1828), and *A Compendium of the Law of Nations* by G. F. von Martens, translated into English by C (4th ed., 1829).

105 Letter to Dean, Jan. 12, 1827 (Cornell). Two years later he wrote: "If you commit burglary or larceny, or high-way robbery, you must send me six pounds; or, rather, I will call for it in about 3 hours time." Letter to [Dean], Sept. 15, 1829 (Nebraska).

106 In 1829 C was indebted to Sir Thomas Beevor for £6,000, of which half seems to have been borrowed at some earlier date. Faithfull MSS., no. 4 (Nuffield). Despite the slack interest displayed in his corn in 1828, in the following year C planted thirty acres in this crop. 67 *PR* 474.

107 July 12, 1832 (Nuffield). In 1830 the half-year rent of Barn Elm farm was overdue two months. John to Ellen, May 25, 1830 (Nuffield).

108 45 *PR* 396. See also 55 *PR* 514; 57 *PR* 393; 73 *PR* 763; *Manchester Lectures,* p. viii.

109 15 *PR* 901.

110 C had one more major indignity to undergo: his trial for libel in 1831. After his acquittal in that case, he detailed his persecutions and all the claims he had on his country which would have justified a more generous stance toward him. 73 *PR* 302–5, 761.

111 *Courier,* June 15, 1818; 34 *PR* 307.

112 44 *PR* 411, 595.

113 53 *PR* 565.

114 43 *PR* 496.

115 47 *PR* 757.

116 59 *PR* 265: "I have been . . . almost completely, in effect, out-lawed." See also 60 *PR* 664.

At a meeting of the Devon Pitt Club in 1824, the Rev. William Radford spoke of "such scoundrels as Carlile, Hone, and Cobbett – wretches who have nothing to lose but every thing to gain." 50 *PR* 165.

"No man, it was thought, with any pretensions to be a gentleman could undertake such a part as that of 'travelling reformist' or 'itinerant apostle'." William Law Mathieson, *England in Transition 1789–1832: A Study in Movements* (London 1920), 138.

117 This represents C's view. He presumably was not aware of the contemptuous reference to his *Year's Residence* and, to a lesser degree, to his *Sermons* and *Cottage Economy* in *Blackwood's* XIV (Sept. 1823), 319–26.

The notice of *Corn* in the *Westminster Review* came in 1829, after C had become firmly convinced of the prejudice against him. *WR* XI (July 1829), 54.

118 A good example is Sir James Graham's pamphlet *Corn and Currency,* discussed at 59 *PR* 641f. J. T. Ward, *Sir James Graham* (London 1967), p. 69. See also 65 *PR* 630, 826; 66 *PR* 24; 67 *PR* 327, 584, 611; 68 *PR* 307, 487, 594, 648; 70 *PR* 951; 75 *PR* 457, 620, 735. Apparently C prosecuted the *Morning Herald* sometime prior to 1825 for "purloining his words," but nothing is known about the outcome of the suit. 55 *PR* 797.

Although C was always quick to spot and proclaim plagiarism (even when it did not exist), an example of a borrowing not so identified by him is revealed in a letter of J. S. Mill in which he states that "some of the leading political economists," particularly his father, had been convinced by John Black of the *Morning Chronicle* that the poor laws should be extended to Ireland. Hugh S. R. Elliot (ed.), *The Letters of John Stuart Mill* (London 1910) II:14. C had urged this position on Black before it was taken up by him or by others. See 51 *PR* 160, heralding the conversion of the *Morning Chronicle;* 75 *PR* 282, announcing conversion of the *Quarterly Review.* Daniel O'Connell admitted that C had convinced him of the advisability of applying the poor laws to Ireland. 51 *PR* 405.

As for himself, C claimed that he never borrowed without giving credit. 39 *PR* 296.

119 "Hundreds, and I might say thousands, of men have observed to me either by letter or by word of mouth, on the studiousness with which the whole body of the 'Collective' avoid, not only in *naming,* but even *alluding to me,* even at the moment, when they are almost literally reading passages from the Register." 65 *PR* 500.

The contemporary prejudice against journalists is referred to in W. Thomas, *Philosophic Radicals,* p. 308; that against the "travelling reformist" in Mathieson, *England in Transition,* p. 138.

120 "A Political Repertory," *Political Letters and Pamphlets,* Apr. 1, 1831, p. 3.

121 Smart, *Economic Annals* II:92n.

122 73 *PR* 157. William Lovett wrote many years later: "How few of the politicians of the present day are able to estimate how much of their own views and opinions they owe to Mr. Cobbett's long teaching of the multitude, and how many of the reforms . . . are justly to be attributed to the public opinion he helped to create." *Life,* p. 45.

123 *Advice,* para. 215. C freely admitted that resentment or revenge was a motive for various of his acts: "The resentment of men of talent has been provided as a corrective of haughtiness, ignorance and insolence." 70 *PR* 22. See also 75 *PR* 323: "I have never lost sight of those injuries, nor of the authors of them."

124 In 1832 C wrote: "it has never been out of my mind for any one twenty-four hours together, from the time that the horrid sentence was passed to the present hour." 76 *PR* 723–4. C's eldest daughter asserted, long after C's death: "he never shook the impression off, as he might, and as I think he ought to have done." Anne, pp. 22–3.

125 66 *PR* 664; *Corn,* paras. 185–95; 76 *PR* 719; 77 *PR* 134. After the 1832 petition was turned down, C appealed to his friends and the public to reimburse him, which they did to the extent of £285. 77 *PR* 654; 82 *PR* 19.

126 *Corn,* para. 198; 66 *PR* 669.

127 Often he combined the two: "What a deal have I done in my life-time to produce real and solid good to my country! And how different has been the tendency of my pursuits to . . . the pursuits of the noisy, canting, jawing, popularity-hunting, newspaper-puffing fellow, Brougham." 78 *PR* 394.

128 46 *PR* 676.

129 *Corn,* paras. 5, 9, 33, 170.

130 49 *PR* 243; 64 *PR* 403. At a later point, C declared: "I overrate my capacity: the wish travels faster than the hands and legs." 68 *PR* 279.

131 62 *PR* 144; 59 *PR* 168; 71 *PR* 165. On another occasion, however, C said: "self-praise is no commendation; and . . . no man has the right to occupy the time of others by dilating on his own deeds." 58 *PR* 743.

132 41 *PR* 97; 44 *PR* 202. It was characteristic of C to reply to a lavish public address with something like: "I will not pretend to believe that I am altogether unworthy of the character you have given me." 85 *PR* 776.

133 C claims of superiority extended to Peel: 38 *PR* 429; Eldon: 53 *PR* 416; Huskis-

son: 55 *PR* 46; the bishop of Winchester: 52 *PR* 771; James Scarlett: 39 *PR* 975, 49 *PR* 193; Thomas Coke: 46 *PR* 278; Francis Horner and Henry Brougham: 43 *PR* 152; Burdett: 40 *PR* 634; and "the ministers and parliament all put together": 42 *PR* 136; 59 *PR* 274; 66 *PR* 398; 70 *PR* 68.

134 44 *PR* 195, 202, 206–7. Gordon, *Economic Doctrine*, p. 2: "Canning's often lengthy speeches were almost invariably bereft of analytical content with respect to economic processes."

135 32 *PR* 970; 42 *PR* 165, 331; 43 *PR* 465. Cf. 74 *PR* 399 and *Manchester Lectures*, p. 16: "I never have wished to possess any public power of any sort, except that of being in parliament."

136 56 *PR* 585. In a mock scene involving Peel and George IV, C predicted that the king "must have me yet" as a minister or "you have seen only the beginning of the mischief." 62 *PR* 242. See also 64 *PR* 202.

137 64 *PR* 772, 817. C repeatedly referred to his offer to serve in the government. 65 *PR* 43, 49–54, 196; 66 *PR* 464; 67 *PR* 98, 642–3, 692–5, 706–7; 68 *PR* 13, 291–2, 417–19, 590; 69 *PR* 219, 312, 324, 333, 450; 70 *PR* 1, 744, 747–8.
    Yet in 1831 C wrote: "while all these monstrous efforts have been making to *keep me down*, I have never had the smallest desire in the world to be raised up." 72 *PR* 386.

138 66 *PR* 388. See also 24 *PR* 225. C took the position that abuse never hurt the party attacked, but injured the abusing party. 18 *PR* 418; 36 *PR* 323.

139 43 *PR* 466. In 1802, when C was of the opinion that the aristocracy was above shady politics, he had praised Castlereagh's appointment to the cabinet. 2 *PR* 26. Thereafter, C regularly abused Castlereagh during his lifetime and continued the abuse after his death. 52 *PR* 397. An account of Castlereagh's suicide was reprinted to commemorate his cruelty to a reformer imprisoned for distributing pamphlets and attending a reform meeting. 59 *PR* 675.

140 62 *PR* 131, 134. See also C's comments on the deaths of Ricardo: 47 *PR* 747; Lord Liverpool: 61 *PR* 518; Canning: 63 *PR* 385, 438. In his remarks on Samuel Whitbread, C declared: "If indeed, it be of poor persons, or, of those who come to death in consequence of their offences against power, the press seems to be at full liberty to deal with them at their pleasure; while . . . the rich, or powerful, seem to find in the grave a complete shield from every thing but the praise of partial friends and hireling scribes." 28 *PR* 79–80.

141 *Cottage Economy*, para. 76.

142 Windham: 13 *PR* 686; also 13 *PR* 194. Cochrane: 30 *PR* 692; 31 *PR* 226. Folkestone: 38 *PR* 131; 40 *PR* 556, 926; 42 *PR* 221; 43 *PR* 159. O'Connell: 55 *PR* 226–34, 294, 389–91. Burdett: 53 *PR* 23. Peel: 52 *PR* 654; also 44 *PR* 199. Canning: 44 *PR* 97. Wellington: 66 *PR* 242, 302. George III: 52 *PR* 719.

143 C joined the *Courier, Post, Times,* and *New Times* (all of which he ordinarily loathed) in attacking Joseph Hume (whose work C usually praised) for Hume's alleged use of his position as commissioner of a Greek loan to promote his private interests. 60 *PR* 291, 363, 385, 449, 581. After pointing out his previous good relations with Hume, C added: "I had to write against him or lose my own character with my readers." 60 *PR* 608. C also condemned members of Earl Radnor's family (who had supported C's candidacy at Preston in 1826) for preferring an antireform candidate at Salisbury in 1831 over a reform candidate who disliked C. 72 *PR* 538–56, 707–8.

144 JPC, pp. 12, 20. "Cd. make himself most agreeable, or most disagreeable, accordg. to company" (p. 20).

145 Cf. *Advice*, para. 5: "it will not be pretended that there is another man in the kingdom who has so many cordial friends."

146 65 *PR* 499. See also 66 *PR* 14.

147 65 *PR* 115.

148 We do not have C's letter to Douce, but only a copy of Douce's reply [1825?] (Bodleian).
149 65 *PR* 54.
150 65 *PR* 500.

22. The agitator

Motto: 54 *PR* 501.

1 There were only two years (1827 and 1833) in the period 1821–34 in which C did not write of his travelling.
2 The *Norfolk Yeoman's Gazette,* a weekly periodical, published thirteen issues between February 8 and May 3, 1823, when it was discontinued. 45 *PR* 92, 163, 446, 502, 548; Pearl, *Cobbett,* p. 129.
3 49 *PR* 58, 497, 562.
4 57 *PR* 1, 387, 468, 471.
5 57 *PR* 9, 101, 151, 244, 307, 374.
6 57 *PR* 481; 58 *PR* 49, 116, 438.
7 58 *PR* 172–4. The Earl of Fingall (d. 1826) was the hereditary head of catholic nobility in Ireland.
8 59 *PR* 490. The amount raised before the election fell short of expenditures by £142, which became the subject of a postelection appeal. 59 *PR* 496; 60 *PR* 379. In 1830 C was sued by one Hoffman, Preston shoemaker, for services allegedly rendered during the 1826 election.
9 58 *PR* 372. C claimed that in 1823 Burdett had offered £500 towards C's election and in 1826 an unstated amount, but never contributed anything. 63 *PR* 725–34; 67 *PR* 799–800; 69 *PR* 476; 78 *PR* 326.
10 Before settling on Preston, a number of other constituencies were considered. C denied that he was considering Newark, and spoke of rumors of his intention to "stand for a place more conveniently situated in point of locality." 58 *PR* 238–9. He apparently had in mind either Westminster or Middlesex, which were "degraded by [their] four humbugging mummies," but finally decided on Preston in May 1826. 59 *PR* 86–7; letter to Palmer, May·6, 1826 (Nuffield).
11 All adult male inhabitants of Preston who had resided there six months were entitled to vote. William Dobson, *History of the Parliamentary Representation of Preston . . .* (Preston 1856), pp. 27–8.
12 Dobson, pp. 48–50, 75.
13 John to William junior, May 15, 1825 [1826] (Nuffield).
14 58 *PR* 577–81, from the *Morning Herald* of June 1, 1826; 59 *PR* 88–90.
15 58 *PR* 664, 676. The earlier speeches of C are given at 58 *PR* 465, 537, 555.
16 C claimed the canvass on his behalf continued for twenty-five days, involving "forty of us, or thereabouts." 59 *PR* 492.
17 58 *PR* 706, 709, 724.
18 58 *PR* 757, 782–3; 59 *PR* 5, 94. Dobson, p. 50: The "manufacturers . . . as a rule took care that the votes of their workpeople were exercised on the same side as their own."
19 The system of voting by tallies had developed during the period of the whig–tory coalition. Dobson, p. 58. C had agreed to it when it was understood that the oath of supremacy would not be put. 58 *PR* 714.
20 Seven separate protests were filed. 58 *PR* 714, 717, 719, 720, 721, 774, 777.
21 58 *PR* 722–3.
22 59 *PR* 94. At this point C used his efforts in an attempt to defeat Barrie, the tory candidate, because of his insistence that the catholics take the oath of supremacy. 59 *PR* 7, 9.

23 59 *PR* 5.

24 59 *PR* 44–8. C computed "his own voters" by (1) counting his plumpers at two votes each (they had used only one) and adding this figure to (2) the full number of split votes he had received, yielding a total of 1,446. If the "own voters" of all four candidates are similarly computed, the aggregate comes to 8,315, of which C's 1,446 is only 17 percent, obviously not the largest number of "own voters" of the four.

25 58 *PR* 804.

26 59 *PR* 94.

27 Dobson, *Preston*, p. 56. C claimed that he had caused his opponents to spend £30,000, which, if correct, would have been nearly three times the amount spent in 1820. 59 *PR* 492.

28 In his final speech at Preston C promised that an account of the election would be printed and delivered free to "each house" there. This turned out to be a publication called *Cobbett's Poor Man's Friend,* of which four numbers were issued at monthly intervals between August and November 1826; 3,350 copies of each were sent to working-class families in Preston. While the first number dealt with the Preston election, the next three related to the rights of the poor to the necessities of life. 59 *PR* 240, 373, 437, 757; 60 *PR* 54, 181, 380. A fifth and unrelated number was issued in October 1827, in which C reported that Stanley had been given a place in the government, requiring that he be reelected; C offered himself as a candidate in opposition to Stanley. 64 *PR* 193. No election was held, presumably because the place taken by Stanley (undersecretaryship of the colonies) had been created after 1705 and hence was exempt from the usual rule.

The *Poor Man's Friend* was published as a little book. At first all five numbers were included. 65 *PR* 124; 66 *PR* 405. In 1830, in the midst of an uprising against oppressive administration of the poor laws, a new edition was issued limited to the three middle numbers dealing with the rights of the poor.

29 59 *PR* 101–11; 60 *PR* 577, 686, 709; 61 *PR* 449.

30 In May 1826, the year before Liverpool's stroke, C observed that while Bathurst was speaking in the House of Lords, Liverpool was repeating, loud enough for C to hear him, "the closing nine or ten words of every sentence uttered by Lord Bathurst." 62 *PR* 390.

31 Richard L. Shiel, *Sketches of the Irish Bar* (2 vols. in 1, Chicago 1882) 1:35n, 78–82, 87, 91, 94; 11:291n, 292n.

Harriet Martineau, despite her sympathy with the catholic cause, claimed that O'Connell was constitutionally untruthful: "devoid of all compunction and all shame in regard to the random character of his representations." *Thirty Years' Peace* 1:389. Similar charges were made by others against C, but it is believed that he suffered from a milder disregard of fact than that described by Miss Martineau. C was addicted to hyperbole. His misstatements were often errors of carelessness and impetuosity; to give the mildest examples: his misquotation of poetry, or his casual use of differing numbers when describing the same situation where one can see no conceivable advantage arising from one figure rather than the other. But C had no compunction about lying when he thought it appropriate. He openly, unashamedly, and voluntarily admitted that he had lied in order to induce the whig administration to "soften them in their severe measures" toward the hungry farm laborers guilty of violent acts. *A Full and Accurate Report of the Trial of William Cobbett, Esq. (before Lord Tenterden and a Special Jury) on Thursday, July 7, 1831 . . .* (5th ed., London 1832), p. 28 (hereafter cited as *Trial of 1831*).

32 At one point C said that hearing J. P. Curran describe the wrongs of the Irish around 1812 first made him take a deep interest in their cause. 52 *PR* 392. Yet C's interest went back to 1804 at least. See, for example, 4 *PR* 255–6, 848, 949. It is not clear when C's association with O'Connell began. In 1821 C had reprinted one

597

of O'Connell's articles condemning the persecutors of Queen Caroline and declaring that Irish relief depended on parliamentary reform. 38 *PR* 193.

33 The disqualification was caused by the statutory requirement of the oath of supremacy or a declaration against transubstantiation as a condition precedent to the exercise of certain rights or the taking of office. 54 *PR* 170.

34 11 *PR* 353, 993.

35 Examples of C's comments: protestant hierarchy: 61 *PR* 656-7; 66 *PR* 810-15; 68 *PR* 260. Protestant church: 51 *PR* 681; 52 *PR* 23; 54 *PR* 463; 67 *PR* 592; 71 *PR* 242; 72 *PR* 708. There were 1,289 protestant clerical appointments in Ireland, of which 531 were nonresidents. 50 *PR* 518; 54 *PR* 774. Tithes: 61 *PR* 656-7; 62 *PR* 87-8; 66 *PR* 815. Poor laws: 51 *PR* 153; 66 *PR* 585; 68 *PR* 260; 73 *PR* 461. Malthus claimed that the excess population in England was due to the poor laws. C contended that Ireland, with no poor laws, had had a greater increase in population. 51 *PR* 15.

36 48 *PR* 747.

37 "It is the whole state of Ireland; it is the system of government in Ireland, that . . . ought to be changed." 11 *PR* 586. See also 12 *PR* 358; 16 *PR* 875-6; 23 *PR* 724; 29 *PR* 70.

38 61 *PR* 650. C tellingly cited the success of the Irish in New York: "This shows what the Irish *really are*; and it points out what they want at home: namely, good food and raiment in exchange for their labour and the use of their talents." 38 *PR* 688.

39 Shiel, *Irish Bar* 1:381.

40 Norman Gash, *Mr. Secretary Peel: The Life of Sir Robert Peel to 1830* (London 1961), pp. 386-8, 393; 53 *PR* 387-8.

41 55 *PR* 399.

42 51 *PR* 406; 52 *PR* 581.

43 53 *PR* 454, 479. Sydney Smith had said: "the measure never will be effected but by fear." Quoted in Martineau, *Thirty Years' Peace* 1:383.

44 53 *PR* 645. The bill is given in full at 54 *PR* 169-83.

45 53 *PR* 681. The bill providing for the wings was introduced by Spring-Rice on behalf of large protestant landowners in Ireland. 54 *PR* 27.

46 53 *PR* 691; 55 *PR* 399. The figure is that used by C. According to a statement by H. Grattan in the House of Commons in 1829, the total Irish electorate was 230,000, of whom 78,000 were 40-shilling freeholders. Hansard, 2nd ser. xx:1351 (Mar. 19).

In 1803 C had favored a parliamentary allowance to Irish catholic priests, but thought that it might then have been too late. 4 *PR* 949.

47 55 *PR* 399, 406, 415; 56 *PR* 73.

48 55 *PR* 214-19, 293-300, 385-443, 784; 59 *PR* 287; 66 *PR* 86.

49 Bric's comments at Cork are interspersed in C's play *Big O and Sir Glory*. 55 *PR* 773, 777-81, 792, 794.

50 55 *PR* 321, 439.

51 55 *PR* 769f; 34 *PR* 739; 56 *PR* 65.

52 56 *PR* 71; 55 *PR* 800. For the derivation of "Anna Brodie" see Appendix 1.

53 Shiel, *Irish Bar* II:292.

54 68 *PR* 71.

55 Gash, *Peel*, pp. 395-6.

56 56 *PR* 85.

57 65 *PR* 673, 705, 727.

58 66 *PR* 28, 47, 58, 97, 274; Shiel II:265-314. Parliament did not adjourn until July 28, 1828.

59 Quoted by Gash, p. 522. The following two sentences in the text are from the same source (pp. 535, 538), as is much of the balance of the paragraph.

60 67 *PR* 204. On December 11, 1828 the duke had written a cautiously worded letter

to Dr. Curtis, catholic primate of Ireland, in which he said that he was "anxious to witness the settlement" of the issue, saw no prospect of it, but did not despair of arriving at a satisfactory remedy. 67 *PR* 199. The king's speech, coming less than two months later, led C to conclude that the change had been produced by O'Connell's causing or threatening to cause a run on the Bank of Ireland. 67 *PR* 206, 247–50, 299, 302; 68 *PR* 92.

61 Martineau, *Thirty Years' Peace* 1:503.

62 In July 1830 six other Irish catholics were sworn in as king's counsel. 70 *PR* 112.

63 58 *PR* 36–8. See also 11 *PR* 995. In 1804 C rejected a manuscript for insertion in the *PR*, saying: "I will never circulate abuse of the Roman Catholics, and much less expressions of hatred or contempt of their religion." 6 *PR* 736. In 1831 C enjoyed watching stonemasons remove from the Monument the inscription charging the catholics with responsibility for the London fire of 1666. 74 *PR* 683.

64 67 *PR* 355. Because of the disenfranchisement and the oppressive regulations against the Jesuits, C "should have been disposed to vote against" the bill. 69 *PR* 407.

65 The Irish Poor Relief Act of 1838 did little to relieve the distress, since it was limited to the sick, aged, and young.

66 67 *PR* 682. C later declared that while his book "broke down the prejudices of the people," the emancipation was due to O'Connell's "personal exertions and personal influence." 84 *PR* 409.

67 The reactionaries Lord Winchelsea and the Marquis of Blandford were so upset by catholic emancipation that they threatened to vote for reform. 67 *PR* 358, 741. In moving to abolish rotten boroughs, Blandford stressed the need for protecting "the interests of the protestant community against the influx and increase of the Roman Catholic party," who might "buy up the rotten boroughs in such numbers as to imperil the Protestant Constitution." J. R. M. Butler (*The Passing of the Great Reform Bill* (London 1914), p. 57) erroneously ascribes this view to C!

68 67 *PR* 353.

69 70 *PR* 25. C exploded when Peel, in one of those hypocritical statements traditional among statesmen, declared "that we are too near to the advantages which we have derived from the mild and beneficent reign of his Majesty to be able fully to appreciate them." *Two-Penny Trash* 1:71.

70 Quoted by Mathieson, *England in Transition*, p. 264.

71 L. C. A. Knowles, *The Industrial and Commercial Revolutions in Great Britain during the Nineteenth Century* (London 1966 repr.), p. 119; Mitchell and Deane, *Statistics*, p. 282 (figures for "computed or declared values"); L. P. Adams, *Agricultural Depression and Farm Relief in England 1813–1852* (London 1965), p. 113. See C. R. Fay, *Great Britain from Adam Smith to the Present Day* . . . (2nd ed., London 1929), p. 349: The weavers and knitters were "in continuous distress for about 40 years" (1805–45).

   The debate as to whether the *average* standard of living among the laboring classes rose or fell during the first third or first half of the nineteenth century has provided an interesting exercise for statisticians. See Taylor (ed.), *Standard of Living*. It seems reasonably clear that it fell for a large enough segment of the population to make the period one of unusual distress. For example, the pay for handloom weaving at Todmorden, Lancs., was 8s. per piece in 1814, and from 1829 to 1833 averaged about 1s. 3d. 79 *PR* 678. See also 79 *PR* 723–6; 80 *PR* 9–21, 77–91, 300–11.

72 74 *PR* 798.

73 C believed that the disturbance began in July when local workmen in the Isle of Thanet in Kent drove away several score of Irishmen who had agreed to work at half price; that the "same principle which pointed out the necessity of driving out the Irish invaders pointed out the necessity of putting down the thrashing

machines." 75 *PR* 785–6; 81 *PR* 71. Hobsbawm and Rudé (*Captain Swing*, p. 61) cast doubt on the general importance of the Irish competition.

C claimed that the riots, particularly those in Sussex, were due to "the hatred in which the people held the hired overseers" employed under the poor law amendments introduced by Sturges Bourne. 85 *PR* 72. See ch. 23, n. 15.

74 The first use of the phrase "Captain Swing," or the name "Swing," apparently occurred in September 1830 when farmers in Kent began to receive letters so signed threatening to destroy their threshing machines. Threshing by hand was the standard winter employment, lasting from November through January at least. Hence, the introduction of the threshing machine created serious unemployment at the hardest time of the year. Hobsbawm and Rudé, pp. 51, 173.

The flail of the period consisted of a staff six feet long to which was attached a "swingel (as our people call it) about two feet long, and about as big around as a smallish man's wrist." *Corn*, para. 136. At a later point C stated that "swing" in some counties and "swingel" in others was the name of that part of the flail which the thrasher brings in contact with the straws. 78 *PR* 5; 81 *PR* 72.

The swing movement was virtually nonexistent in the northern counties, where wages were higher and the laborers commonly lived with the farmer. 78 *PR* 5, 404, 457–9. Hobsbawm and Rudé, App. I.

75 70 *PR* 660; 71 *PR* 279.
76 70 *PR* 844–5. Grey's cabinet included several former followers of Canning and Huskisson and one high tory, the Duke of Richmond.
77 67 *PR* 643.
78 69 *PR* 242.
79 70 *PR* 868, 898. C's first references to the new wave of fires appear at 70 *PR* 524, 590, although he referred to sporadic incidents in Suffolk and Sussex as early as 1822. 42 *PR* 186; 68 *PR* 498, 515.

Hobsbawm and Rudé, p. 61: "in the last ten days of November [1830] virtually all of Southern England seemed in flames."

80 See 70 *PR* 739, 874, 914, 974, 1081.
81 71 *PR* 2, 149, 199, 280; 73 *PR* 243, 427, 770; Hobsbawm and Rudé, App. II.
82 70 *PR* 769, 850. See also Hobsbawm and Rudé, pp. 201–2.
83 70 *PR* 723, 973; 71 *PR* 472.
84 70 *PR* 1099; 71 *PR* 39–41. See also 71 *PR* 378.
85 71 *PR* 6–9. The *Times* article appeared on December 24, 1830. In a follow-up story on January 1, 1831, *The Times* printed a report from a Brighton paper in which a correspondent claimed that C's "agent" had applied for and been refused the room at the George inn. C's "agent" appears to have been the Battle tailor James Gutsell, who shortly became C's secretary. Letter to Gutsell, July 2, 1831 (Cornell).
86 71 *PR* 81–4. The second *Times* article appeared on January 3, 1831. The spelling of the confession as given in that article is somewhat more irregular than that in the text. A third confession appeared in *The Times* of January 7, 1831, in which Goodman referred to several other unnamed instigators who had approached him. 71 *PR* 476.
87 Blandford: 71 *PR* 298, 358, 471. Benett: 71 *PR* 402.
88 70 *PR* 937–8.
89 The trial, originally set for May 11–13, was rescheduled at the request of the prosecution.

The special jury procedure called for a panel of forty-eight, from which each party could strike twelve names. A thorough canvass was made of the panel on C's behalf to determine which names to strike. Faithfull MSS., no. 9 (Nuffield).
90 C had long been an admirer of Tenterden's mildness and impartiality. 40 *PR* 688; 67 *PR* 462.
91 *Trial of 1831*, pp. 3, 24. C was particularly annoyed by the writ's description of him

as "William Cobbett, late of the parish of St. Dunstan in the west . . . labourer." Ibid. pp. 2–3, 7. See 74 *PR* 791; 75 *PR* 291, 727; 86 *PR* 470.

92 73 *PR* 131–2. C had retained the barrister Charles Phillips, but apparently used him only for pretrial advice. Letter from Faithfull, Apr. 18, 1831, Faithfull MSS., no. 9 (Nuffield).

93 *Trial of 1831*, p. 46. The *Star* had a daily circulation of only 150 copies. Aspinall, *Politics and the Press*, p. 331.

94 Melbourne, Palmerston, and Goderich were Canningite tories who had accepted positions in Grey's cabinet.

95 *Trial of 1831*, pp. 9–12.

96 Ibid. pp. 21, 33. C also claimed that Goodman had been "hurried out of the country," and produced a letter from him on board the transport ship at Portsmouth, addressed to his brother-in-law, the orthography of which (according to C) made it manifest that the pretended confessions were fabrications, and in which Goodman attributed his fate to his own bad conduct, saying nothing about C or his "lactures." Ibid. pp. 22–3.

97 Ibid. pp. 24–9, 33; *Times*, July 8, 1831.

98 *Trial of 1831*, pp. 33–4. While C was gratified by Radnor's appearance and made his gratitude known, there may have been more of a story than appears on the surface. When Radnor (Lord Folkestone) became a peer on the death of his father in 1828, he had the right to return two members for the rotten borough of Downton and to nominate one of the two for Salisbury. It was widely believed that Radnor would name C to one of the Downton seats, and apparently he had some desire to do so, but was talked out of it in 1830 by Creevey, Brougham, and perhaps some other whigs. Although C had never been promised a seat, he unquestionably was disappointed that he had not been named, and Radnor was possibly shamefaced about the affair, which had come out in the open during the election of 1831 for Salisbury, only two months before C's trial for libel. See 65 *PR* 269; 72 *PR* 547, 706; Huch, *Lord Radnor*, pp. 111–14. The latter states (p. 111) that in 1828 C "expressed his desire to have his noble friend send him to Parliament." This is a conclusion of Professor Huch, apparently based on an article by C in which he coyly stated that he had no expectation that he would be appointed, and that if appointed he would be torn between a desire not to tarnish his own fame and the greater anxiety of so acting "as not to cause disappointment, and to excite regret in the mind of his Lordship." 65 *PR* 269.

99 "The Whigs . . . were always more malignant than those whom they call the Tories. During the debates on Six Acts, Brougham, Baring, Scarlett, Calcraft, Tierney, Sir Bobby, Hobhouse, the Russells; in short the whole of them . . . voted against the Six Acts; but, they never opened their lips to speak of any of us, who were the persons to be crushed by those Acts . . . without speaking of us as wretches for whom the Six Acts were much too good!" 63 *PR* 542.

100 *Trial of 1831*, p. 32.

101 73 *PR* 132; *Trial of 1831*, p. 45. *The Times* of July 9, 1831 reported that "two of the jury were determined one way, and it was evident they would not yield." An article in the *Morning Chronicle* reported Denman as claiming that the "Government was defeated . . . owing to the perseverance of one jury-man." 76 *PR* 501.

102 *Greville Memoirs* II:161.

103 73 *PR* 257. Apart from the inscription, the portrait seems to be the same as that which C had offered at a pound a copy to "about forty friends" the year before. It was, C stated, "as perfect a likeness as an able painter can make it." Printed letter dated "Kensington, August 7th, 1830" (Yale; Cornell).

23. The Reform Act

Motto: 67 *PR* 826.

1 Austin Mitchell, *The Whigs in Opposition* (Oxford 1967), p. 241. In 1827 Brougham stated that the whigs were not "as a body" pledged to reform; that "we . . . have been . . . long divided among ourselves on that question," a statement confirmed by Lord John Russell. 62 *PR* 417–19.

2 E. P. Thompson, *English Working Class*, p. 740. T. J. Wooler, editor of the *Black Dwarf*, appears to have allied himself with Burdett after Cartwright's death. 62 *PR* 535.

3 Bentham's "Plan of Parliamentary Reform," made public in 1817, supported annual parliaments, the secret ballot, and universal suffrage (including women). The *Westminster Review* was more conservative. C nursed a grievance against Bentham ("quaint old coxcomb"), who, when arguing for universal suffrage, suggested that the people would prefer "Cartwright, of the Cartwrights of Northamptonshire" or "Brougham of Brougham" to "Cobbett with the Spa-Fields orator at his heels." Bentham, *Works* III:469, 471; 34 *PR* 360; 64 [63] *PR* 617. Conversely, Halévy suggested that Bentham's antipathy to C was due to C's refusal to publish Bentham's "Catechism of Parliamentary Reform" in 1810. Halévy, *History* II:258. But Bentham had better grounds for being annoyed at C, who had publicly proclaimed that Bentham had stolen his ideas from him and that Bentham's conversion to reform was due to Pitt's rejection of his "Panopticon." C also denounced the £23,000 that parliament voted to Bentham for his efforts on his prison project. *Year's Residence,* para. 405; 70 *PR* 147; 74 *PR* 14–15.

   In 1831 Bentham cautioned the whigs against prosecuting C for libel "lest by such a proceeding the administration would be lowered in the estimation of the people," adding that "As to Cobbett, a more odious compound of selfishness, malignity, insincerity, and mendacity, never presented itself to my memory or my imagination." Bentham, *Works* XI:68.

4 Francis Place was the motivating force behind the move to adopt contraception as a means of population control. In addition to his own book, *Illustrations and Proofs* (1822), with its vague reference to the subject, he was responsible for three anonymous (and more explicit) handbills; he probably induced James Mill to write on the subject for the *Black Dwarf;* and he stimulated Carlile to write the highly controversial article "What Is Love?" (republished as *Every Woman's Book*), which Place's editor thought violated "the canons of good taste." 58 *PR* 137–8; Norman E. Himes (ed.), *Illustrations and Proofs of the Principle of Population by Francis Place* (London 1930), pp. 44–6; *Republican* XI (May 6, 1826), 545–69. C believed that these articles were responsible for the demise of the *Black Dwarf* and the *Republican.* 64 *PR* 329, 332, 338. I have been unable to identify the "Instructive Treatise" which C claimed had been written by Place. 75 *PR* 791–4.

   In 1831 C wrote a short three-act "play" entitled *Surplus Population* in which Place ("Peter Thimble"), "the ugliest devil I ever saw," is lampooned for his Malthusian beliefs, his arrogance in calling himself "esquire," and his sycophantic adherence to Burdett. Burdett ("Sir Gripe Grindum") is ridiculed for his lechery, insincerity, and stinginess. 72 *PR* 493; *Two-Penny Trash* I:265.

   In 1835 C republished the play under the expanded name *Surplus Population and the Poor-Law Bill.* It was acted in the neighborhood of Normandy farm on March 27, 1835, and C said it was to be taken on a tour of villages of Hampshire, Sussex, and Kent. A performance at Tonbridge, Kent to be attended by C was vetoed by local authorities. 88 *PR* 92, 593. C promised to write another play called *Bastards in High Life.*

5 In 1807, responding to a proposal for "temperate reformation," C remarked: "I

am afraid, that the qualification *temperate* means *slow,* and so very slow as for no one to be able to perceive it in any way." 11 *PR* 1114.

6 John Ward, speaking in the House of Commons in 1817, stated that radical reformers included "not only those that are for annual parliaments and universal suffrage, but all that class that desire to alter the constitution upon some grand sweeping plan," while by moderate reformers he meant "those that would be content with partial alterations applicable to what they deem particular grievances." Hansard, 1st ser. xxxvi:761 (May 20, 1817). The secret ballot became a major radical reform issue sometime after 1817.

7 Hatred of the whigs and *The Times* was common among radical reformers. As to whigs see, for example, Asa Briggs, "The Background of the Parliamentary Reform Movement in Three English Cities," *Cambridge Historical Journal* x (1952), 299.

8 "For my own part, I prefer the word *radical* reform. The word radical has been interpreted to mean, amongst other horrid things, sedition and rebellion. But what does it mean? It means something belonging or appertaining to the root; and if we have an evil to remove, is it not necessary to go to the root of it?" 42 *PR* 530. See also 58 *PR* 540. In 1835, after his breakdown (ch. 24), he wrote: "Though I hate the name, I am what you call a Radical." 86 *PR* 4.

9 38 *PR* 168–70, 173; 40 *PR* 1543; 41 *PR* 82; 71 *PR* 627.

10 "Women are excluded because husbands are answerable in law for their wives, as to their civil damages, and because the very nature of the sex makes the exercise of this right incompatible with the harmony and happiness of society." 74 *PR* 328–9.

11 41 *PR* 555, 631.

12 Except to the extent that this may have resulted from a reduction in the national debt or the abolition of tithes, which C viewed as exceptional types of property.

13 11 *PR* 1115. A list of twenty-six abuses appears at 70 *PR* 751.

14 C estimated that a third of all those held in English prisons consisted of those "having killed or attempted to kill hares, pheasants or partridges." 48 *PR* 487.

15 69 *PR* 302. Amendments to the poor laws in 1819 by a bill sponsored by William Sturges Bourne (1) established a new supervisory body, the "select vestry" appointed by the ratepayers, whose vote was proportionate to the amount of property each held, and (2) allowed them to employ professional assistant overseers in place of the neighbors who formerly supervised the administration of the payments. The ancient right of the mistreated poor to appeal to the magistrates was eliminated. These changes and the harsh methods employed by the new assistant overseers "altered the whole state of rural society in England," creating a "rooted hatred between rich and poor; a thing that never was heard of before in England." 72 *PR* 612. C claimed that the 1830 riots in the south of England "were caused principally by the hired overseers." 85 *PR* 72.

16 62 *PR* 419. Russell also voted against Hume's motion to repeal one of the Six Acts. 62 *PR* 643–5; 65 *PR* 148. C made a great deal of Russell's insignificant size. 58 *PR* 542.

17 In April 1821 Lambton had moved for a committee to consider the state of representation, which lost by a vote of 55 to 43 while Lambton and Hobhouse were out "taking refreshment." 39 *PR* 22. Lambton was one of the draftsmen of the Reform Bill introduced in March 1831. But in 1827 he too had supported Canning, and later in the year accepted a peerage from the tory Goderich. See W. Thomas, *Philosophic Radicals,* pp. 342–3.

18 Hawes, *Brougham,* p. 95; 32 *PR* 242; 86 *PR* 337. See also Hawes, p. 68.

19 C noted Brougham's talents (38 *PR* 334; 44 *PR* 759; 46 *PR* 235), but always thought Brougham too glib and long-winded (41 *PR* 423; 43 *PR* 177; 63 *PR* 47, 114; 65 *PR* 324). In one passage he described Brougham as speaking in "a sort of

half hickuping voice, with the mouth three parts open and eyes like the picture of a saint that I have seen holding his hands up towards the crucifix." 61 *PR* 223.

20 61 *PR* 29. In 1834 C made several vague references, almost certainly directed at Brougham, to "laudanum and brandy, with a due spice of natural insanity." 85 *PR* 65, 199; 86 *PR* 355, 604. "Brougham was obviously not quite sane." Hawes, p. 271. C declared of Brougham: "He is the weasel, he is the nightmare, he is the deadly malady of the Ministry." 86 *PR* 334. See also 86 *PR* 537.

21 30 *PR* 687. In the instance, C was referring to a "fixed principle" regarding reform, but the remark was equally applicable to other subjects.

22 Grey: 40 *PR* 1542; 41 *PR* 81; 70 *PR* 940; 71 *PR* 664; 72 *PR* 63, 334; 75 *PR* 386; 77 *PR* 360; 78 *PR* 22. Cf. 85 *PR* 644–63, a bitter attack on Grey ("dismissing you forever") after C's breakdown in 1834.
Holland: 42 *PR* 115; 57 *PR* 305; 67 *PR* 217; 70 *PR* 940; 81 *PR* 654.
King: 44 *PR* 544, 761; 45 *PR* 388; 79 *PR* 586.
Folkestone: 41 *PR* 391; 67 *PR* 117–18; 69 *PR* 407–8; 86 *PR* 333. C became quite cross with Folkestone (Lord Radnor) for his support of the poor law amendments in 1834, but never lost his admiration for him. See e.g. 86 *PR* 157, 204, 215.
C was also an admirer of Romilly (11 *PR* 591; 15 *PR* 420; 18 *PR* 882; 19 *PR* 781) and of D. W. Harvey (80 *PR* 341; 84 *PR* 413).

23 Praise: 45 *PR* 508; 53 *PR* 23; 54 *PR* 803; 58 *PR* 43; 62 *PR* 438; 73 *PR* 484–5; 83 *PR* 210. Dispraise: 42 *PR* 441; 60 *PR* 523, 586; 68 *PR* 180; 70 *PR* 150; 86 *PR* 641.
C was highly critical, also, of Hume's involvement, along with that of Burdett, Hobhouse, Bowring, and Ellice, in the Greek loan scandal. 60 *PR* 291, 363, 385, 449, 581.

24 62 *PR* 420–1. Burdett accompanied his support of Canning with the declaration that "I do not abandon or sacrifice one iota of my principles as a friend of parliamentary reform."
One of C's recurring themes was that Canning's public "popularity" was a falsity created by Canning's manipulation of the press. 62 *PR* 72–5; 66 *PR* 301.

25 W. Thomas, *Philosophic Radicals*, pp. 72–84.

26 70 *PR* 955. It was a misdemeanor to steal a dead human body but a felony punishable by death to steal the dead body of a pig. 75 *PR* 257. In 1832 another act was passed (the Anatomy Act) allowing the dissection of paupers' bodies with the requirement of consent of the pauper's relatives.

27 See, for example, 38 *PR* 709.

28 62 *PR* 423–3.

29 57 *PR* 402; H. Hunt, *Memoirs* III:21. After suggesting that the domestic servants at the Cobbett home were not accommodating and were often changed, Hunt added: "Mrs. Cobbett, was what was called amongst the gossips, very *unfortunate* in getting maid servants." See Anne to James, May 30, 1822 (Nuffield).
The exchanges between C and Hunt reported in *The Times* for September 4, 1822 include a five-stanza poem by C entitled "To 'Saint Henry of Ilchester'," which began:

> Munchausen long has borne the prize
> From all the Quacking 'Squires
> But what are all his heaps of lies
> To thine, thou prince of liars.

30 57 *PR* 518–35. Hunt had heckled C at the Lincoln's Inn Fields meeting of February 8, 1826. 57 *PR* 399, 402, 403–6, 421–3. In 1827 C took the initiative in renewing relations with Hunt. 62 *PR* 431.

31 62 *PR* 518, 532, 535. A somewhat different version was provided by Hobhouse: C "was like a madman the latter part of the evening. He drank several glasses of wine during his first speech against Burdett, and subsequently he gesticulated

furiously, and shook his fist at us, called us bad names, and swore tremendously. There were not more than thirty of Cobbett's friends in the room, but they were posted judiciously, and our stewards had taken no pains to provide against what occurred . . . I had a note from Burdett advising silence as to the proceedings at the dinner, and saying that he did not think it a defeat." Broughton, *Recollections* III:196–7.

32 C reprinted an extended account of the meeting, not at all complimentary to himself, which had appeared in the *Morning Chronicle*. 62 *PR* 537–64.

33 Hunt had been an unsuccessful candidate for Preston in the general elections of 1820 and 1830. In the by-election of 1830, in which only one seat was at issue, there were no split votes.

34 44 *PR* 762.

35 65 *PR* 549; 70 *PR* 546. See also 67 *PR* 545; 70 *PR* 271.

36 For the history of this war and those engaged in it see Hollis, *The Pauper Press* and Wiener, *The War of the Unstamped*. C sympathized with those prosecuted for violations of the Stamp Act, and was critical of the whigs for prosecuting them, but the repeal of the act was not high on the list of his priorities. 77 *PR* 51, 476.

37 Another disciple was Thomas Wakley (founder of the *Lancet* in 1823 and a famous medical reformer until his death in 1862), who developed a lifelong interest in political reform under C's influence. From January 1831 to June 1832 Wakley published a Sunday stamped newspaper, the *Ballot*, which took on many of C's causes. See, for example, 72 *PR* 410, 633; 73 *PR* 320. C had earlier supported Wakley's medical reform activities, and continued to applaud Wakley's conduct. 67 *PR* 178; 70 *PR* 349, 382, 445; 76 *PR* 619, 823.

38 Under one of the Six Acts (60 Geo. III c. 9), adopted for the express purpose of restraining papers "tending to excite Hatred and Contempt of the Government," a tax of fourpence a copy was imposed on all periodicals that appeared more frequently than every twenty-six days, that sold for less than sixpence, and that contained "any Public News, Intelligence or Occurrences, or any Remarks or Observations thereon, or upon any matter in Church or State." A newspaper so taxed could be sent through the mails without added charge.

39 Algernon Bourke (ed.), *Correspondence of Mr Joseph Jekyll with His Sister-in-Law Lady Gertrude Sloane Stanley* (London 1894), p. 261. ". . . the advice coming from him [Cobbett] in 1830 to reform Parliament did more to prevent conflagration in this country than all the 'repressive measures' that ever were passed." George Macaulay Trevelyan, *Lord Grey of the Reform Bill* (London 1920), p. 217.

40 *Political Letters and Pamphlets*, published irregularly, but mostly at intervals of from five to nine days, continued from October 9, 1830 to May 14, 1831, for a total of thirty-four issues. On the last date Carpenter was found guilty of violating the stamp tax law and fined £120. He refused, or was unable, to pay, and was imprisoned from May to December 1831. Thereafter, he edited a number of reform publications, mostly stamped, including the evening newspaper *True Sun*, a supporter of C. Carpenter followed C in endorsing the Reform Bill.

    Penny Papers for the People was published from October 1, 1830 to July 2, 1831. This was succeeded by Hetherington's *Poor Man's Guardian*, published from 1831 to 1835. Hetherington was imprisoned from September 1831 to March 1832 and from December 1832 to June 1833 and several times thereafter. He followed Hunt in opposing the Reform Bill.

41 *Poor Man's Guardian*, no. 82 (Oct. 29, 1832). See also no. 188 (Jan. 10, 1835). Hetherington seconded the motion thanking C at the end of his lectures on the French revolution of 1830, which were taken down in shorthand by Carpenter. *French Lectures* XI:13.

42 Wiener, *The War of the Unstamped*, pp. xvii, 181n.

43 68 *PR* 33–43, wherein is set forth the joint statement of C and Hunt dated July 4, 1829.

44 68 *PR* 321, 332–3. C resigned from the association soon after the meeting of September 7, 1829 because Daniel French (see ch. 24) had been allowed to make a statement in favor of republicanism. 68 *PR* 348–50, 380–2.

The association seems to have died a natural death at the time Hunt was elected a member of parliament for Preston. Its last meeting appears to have been on December 13, 1830.

The *Westminster Review,* in its issue of January 1830, called the association one for "the defence of property" and commended the conception of the middle classes joining "their influence to the cause of the starving poor." However, the article condemned, without naming him, some of C's views, such as renouncing the national debt, and his abuse of ministers in office. "Set up a sound and honest radicalism, against an unsound and dishonest one," it advised. *WR* XII:230, 232.

45 "I really have great respect for your knowledge and talents," wrote C in 1821 (39 *PR* 290), but C lost his respect in 1830, when Attwood seemed to have allied himself with Burdett. See n. 51 below.

46 The report of the January 1830 meeting of the B.P.U. is set forth at 69 *PR* 175–91, with the renunciation of republicanism at pp. 187–8.

47 69 *PR* 173. For background to this uniting of classes at Birmingham see Briggs, "Background of Parliamentary Reform," pp. 293–302. C did not believe that the B.P.U. could be an effective instrument, because it proposed to limit itself to peaceable means: "If indeed the object were to effect it [reform] by *physical force,* combinations might succeed, but this object is most emphatically disavowed by the parties." 69 *PR* 272–3.

48 Some of the towns are listed on p. 7 of the supplement to "A Political Compendium," one of Carpenter's *Political Letters and Pamphlets.*

49 See Hollis, *The Pauper Press,* pp. 309, 311, 315; Lovett, *Life,* p. 55. According to Place, the N.P.U. made a determined effort to exclude those who were "constant attendants at the Rotunda." Wallas, *Francis Place,* pp. 283–4. Yet both Carpenter and Cleave were on the council of the N.P.U. Hollis, p. 309. On at least three occasions in 1832 C spoke to meetings of the N.U.W.C. 76 *PR* 546, 604.

50 There were twenty-six resolutions, but the final one related only to the formality of obtaining signatures to the petition being submitted to parliament. The economic background to the resolutions is discussed in Asa Briggs, "Thomas Attwood and the Economic Background of the Birmingham Political Union," *Cambridge Historical Journal* IX (1948), 190ff.

51 Since 1819, and possibly earlier, C and Thomas Attwood (and his brother, Matthias Attwood, member of parliament) had agreed on the cause of distress, but had amicably disagreed on the remedy. See 35 *PR* 196, 201; 39 *PR* 291, 352; 40 *PR* 1113–14; 44 *PR* 554, 732; 46 *PR* 279; 65 *PR* 807; 67 *PR* 630; 68 *PR* 782.

C argued for a deflated currency with an "equitable adjustment" in the nominal value of fixed obligations, including the national debt. Attwood argued for an inflated currency to effectively reduce the real value of such obligations. Both points of view were expressed in the B.P.U. resolutions. There was a wider difference, though, than appears on the surface. To C, the change in currency was a means of attaining parliamentary reform, as was shown in ch. 20. To Attwood, reform was a means of attaining a change in the currency. Briggs, "Thomas Attwood," pp. 191, 210.

C was disgusted when Attwood invited Burdett to Birmingham in 1830, declaring that he was a shoyhoy himself. 70 *PR* 87, 187. For a time, C became highly critical of Attwood, calling him, in 1832, a "bare-faced, notorious money changer." But by 1833 Attwood had regained C's respect. 77 *PR* 140; 81 *PR* 649, 778. As a result of the disappointing performance of the whigs after passage of the Reform Bill, Attwood and C worked to remove them from power. 86 *PR* 605–11.

52 A petition to parliament from the residents of Derby adopted at about the same time as the Birmingham resolutions combined economic issues with a demand for parliamentary reform. 67 *PR* 721–4.

53 Briggs, "Thomas Attwood," p. 211.

54 69 *PR* 174; Briggs, "Thomas Attwood," pp. 210–11.

55 68 *PR* 460, 636, 660, 661.

56 68 *PR* 661. C found special delight in repeating the extravagant statements of others (as well as those of his own), as, for example, Brougham's declaration that the London newspapers were the "best possible public instructor" (59 *PR* 305; 65 *PR* 9) and Sir James Graham's assertion – "by mistake, I suppose," C interposed – that the House of Commons was "the noblest assembly of freemen in the world" (*French Lectures* II:10).

57 68 *PR* 665, 719, 783–93. C later claimed that the hecklers were hired by Hunt. 72 *PR* 604.

58 68 *PR* 801; 69 *PR* 11, 33, 97, 148, 161, 220. C wanted to speak in Birmingham but could not get consent to the use of a hall. 68 *PR* 810. 70 *PR* 526: "I went in person into three-quarters of the counties of England, and delivered lectures, urging the people to demand a reform of the parliament."

59 69 *PR* 104, 224. The factory was presumably that of John Fielden, a humane employer, though C referred to it as that of "Messrs Fielding."

60 69 *PR* 33, 50, 97, 385, 417, 481, 513, 545, 634, 662. He had hoped to speak in Cambridge, but was denied the right to do so by the vice-chancellor of the university. His talk at nearby St. Ives in Huntingdonshire on March 29, 1830 was the one attended by Richard Monckton Milnes and other Cambridge men, referred to in ch. 20, n. 64.

61 69 *PR* 494.

62 70 *PR* 222. Since 1821 C had been predicting that there would be another French revolution and that eventually France would become a republic. 38 *PR* 798, 804–7.

The 1830 election and the impact of the French revolution of that year are described in Brock, *Great Reform Act*, pp. 86–118. The results of the election, although favorable to the reform cause, are confusing, because in most cases neither the candidates nor the electors had any well-defined idea of what was meant by "reform." This lack of definition caused Grey to overestimate the support he would have for the bill. Brock, pp. 152–5.

63 Letter to Mellersh, Aug. 7, 1830 (Yale).

64 69 *PR* 271, 449, 477, 618; 70 *PR* 85, 249. The money that had been subscribed was returned "except in a few cases, where they would not have it, these cases not amounting, altogether, to a hundred pounds." 82 *PR* 13. It is not known how much had been raised, so it is possible that the gesture was an easy one.

65 70 *PR* 186, 249, 320, 505, 625.

66 C's letter to Lafayette introducing Beevor and James was dated August 17, 1830. He followed this up with another letter dated September 9, 1830 for the purpose of introducing, through his son James, "three gentlemen from the town of Nottingham, who are the bearers of an address to the brave Parisians from that fine and public-spirited English Town, and also the bearers of a subscription of 5,000 fr. for the relief of the gallant wounded and the widows and orphans of the slain" (Cornell).

67 70 *PR* 185, 227; *Times*, Aug. 18, 1830; Broughton, *Recollections* IV:46.

68 70 *PR* 318–19, 341.

69 *Times*, Aug. 31, 1830.

70 The high-minded J. S. Mill wrote to his father: "I think that I have myself been of

some use in putting them on their guard against Sir Thomas Beevor and Cobbett, against Bowring and people of that kind." Francis E. Mineka (ed.), *The Earlier Letters of John Stuart Mill 1812–1848* (Toronto and London 1963), p. 66.

71 "The Town Book of Lewes 1702–1837," ed. Verena Smith, *Sussex Record Society,* LXIX (1972–3), 267–8.

72 Butler, *Great Reform Bill,* p. 85.

73 70 *PR* 285.

74 There had been some relief for the poor through elimination of the salt tax in 1825, the repeal of the tax on leather and beer in 1830 and on candles in 1831, and the reduction by half of the tax on soap in 1833. The taxation of sugar, coffee, tea, and malt continued.

75 *French Lectures* v:5.

76 C told his French lectures audience that he believed the duke would bring forth a reform measure. *French Lectures* III:1, 3; IV:9; V:11; VI:12; VIII:16; IX:13; X:15.

77 Brock, *Great Reform Act,* pp. 102, 108, 112–14.

78 The Rotunda lectures were: Oct. 25, Hunt; Oct. 27, C; Nov. 1, Hunt; Nov. 2, Carlile; Nov. 3, C; Nov. 4, Gale Jones; Nov. 6, C; Nov. 8, Hunt; Nov. 9, Carlile; Nov. 10, C; Nov. 11, Gale Jones; Nov. 12, the Rev. Robert Taylor; Nov. 15, Hunt. Advertisements in *Political Letters and Pamphlets;* 70 *PR* 609.

No talks appear to have been made by either C or Hunt for at least thirty days after November 15, although Carlile and Taylor (called the "Devil's Chaplain" by Hunt) did continue speaking.

79 Broughton, *Recollections* IV:57, 59, 73.

80 *Correspondence of Earl Grey and William IV* 1:App. A, p. 461, quoted in Asa Briggs, *The Age of Improvement 1783–1867* (London 1962), p. 240.

The story of the passage of the Reform Act of 1832 is described in detail in Butler, *Great Reform Bill* and Brock, *Great Reform Act,* from whom I have borrowed freely.

81 Wholly disenfranchised: fifty-nine boroughs with 2 seats and one (Higham Ferrers) with 1. Partly disenfranchised: one borough with 4 seats (Weymouth) to lose 2 seats; forty-seven boroughs with 2 seats to lose 1. Total: 168 seats.

Redistribution: 54 seats to counties, 1 to Isle of Wight, 43 to towns, 8 to Scotland and Ireland. Total: 106 seats (House of Commons to be reduced by 62 seats).

82 Existing electors who did not meet the new requirements would nevertheless retain their right to vote.

83 *Greville Memoirs* II:144.

84 74 *PR* 161. If the twenty-one bishops had voted the other way, the bill would have been approved by a majority of one: 178 to 179.

85 74 *PR* 179–81, 362–76, 486–501.

86 74 *PR* 481. C claimed that the London papers refused to report the fires, and they are not mentioned in Hobsbawm and Rudé, *Captain Swing.* According to C, the 1831 fires were due to "the lowering of wages." 75 *PR* 788; 86 *PR* 400.

Some fires in 1832 were reported by C at 76 *PR* 304.

In 1833 incendiarism again broke out in Scotland and in at least ten English counties. 82 *PR* 353, 372, 426, 468, 498, 524, 670.

Early in 1834 fires were reported in Suffolk, Hampshire, Durham, and Wiltshire. C claimed (without apparent justification) that they were more extensive than those in 1830. 83 *PR* 259, 333; 84 *PR* 299; 85 *PR* 357, 452. Fires appeared again at the end of 1834. 86 *PR* 456, 461, 670.

87 Hansard, 3rd ser. VIII:589–646 (Oct. 12, 1831).

88 The bishops' action precipitated a host of proposals for ecclesiastical reforms. A new *Church Reformers' Magazine* was started in February 1832 by one of C's associates, the chancery barrister William Eagle. 75 *PR* 223, 473. On C's tour of the

midlands in 1832 he arranged for booksellers to vend the magazine. Letter to John, Feb. 4, 1832 (Nuffield).

89 The *Morning Chronicle* stated flatly that "the resignation of the Ministers would have been the signal for revolution throughout the country." 74 *PR* 209.

90 The vote was 324 to 162. C thought the bill preferable to the previous one. 74 *PR* 746.

91 76 *PR* 81.

92 76 *PR* 132. Grey's statement continued with the remark that "the decision on those points would depend on the House, and not on him."

93 76 *PR* 452. Printed letter of C dated April 14, 1832 (in my possession). C mentions action taken at Glasgow, Leeds, Newcastle, Morpeth, Dudley, and, belatedly, Birmingham, but does not indicate whether these were the only petitions. 76 *PR* 455.

94 76 *PR* 391. After quoting the last sentence of the passage, M. D. George says: "Le Marchant records more soberly that on the 9th and 10th of May 'people talked very openly of civil war and even a change of dynasty'." *English Political Caricature*, p. 253.

95 76 *PR* 392–3, 399, 401, 403. C confidently asserted: "this did stop the Duke." 76 *PR* 460. See also 76 *PR* 463, 464, 486, 493.

96 76 *PR* 387, 400. The name of Wellington Street in Edinburgh was changed to Earl Grey Street, while several more public houses (and one brewery) struck "Wellington" out of their names. 76 *PR* 551.

97 76 *PR* 579. The vote was 106 to 22 (including no bishops).

98 Wholly disenfranchised: fifty-five boroughs with 2 seats and one with 1. Partly disenfranchised: one borough with 4 seats to lose 2 seats; thirty boroughs with 2 seats to lose 1. Total: 143 seats.

Redistribution: 64 seats to counties, 1 to Isle of Wight, 65 to boroughs, 13 to Scotland and Ireland. Total: 143.

99 In the counties the vote was also given to £10 copyholders, £10 leaseholders for a term originally created of not less than sixty years, £50 leaseholders for a term originally created of not less than twenty years, and occupiers of any lands and tenements liable to a clear yearly rental of £50.

In the boroughs, resident electors as the law stood prior to the act were allowed to continue to vote during their lives, despite the new higher qualifications, and the vote was granted to the occupiers of houses worth £20 per year.

100 Russell forecast a total of a million voters in the United Kingdom. The pre-1832 total has been estimated at 366,000 to 435,000 for England and Wales, and from about 420,000 to about 488,000 for the United Kingdom. The 1833 figures of 635,000 for England and Wales and 800,000 for the United Kingdom seem fairly generally accepted.

C thought that the £10 householder qualification would "give the working people some share in choosing of members of parliament" for the larger towns, although recognizing that they would be effectively excluded in counties and in small towns. 74 *PR* 322–3. He far overestimated the number of working men who would be qualified under the £10 householder rule, believing that they might elect as many as fifty to a hundred members of parliament. 74 *PR* 341, 359.

101 71 *PR* 627. C's original article, dated two days after the bill was introduced on March 1, 1830, hailed it as a personal triumph. 71 *PR* 624. The radical *Manchester Advertiser* gave C full credit for the bill. 72 *PR* 785.

102 See 72 *PR* 179–88, 220–2, 277–8, 460–4; 74 *PR* 417. Hunt attended a meeting in March 1833 at Lambeth where he spoke against the Irish Coercion Bill. 79 *PR* 688.

103 Shortly after Hunt made his first appearance in the Commons as a member for Preston he "disclaimed all connection with Messrs Carlile, Taylor, Jones, and

Cobbett, at the Rotunda meetings." 71 *PR* 433. C's heated reply (71 *PR* 682; *Two-Penny Trash* 1:215) led to a petition to the House of Commons which Hunt concocted, charging C with providing disgusting food to his employees at Barn Elm farm. 72 *PR* 19; *Two-Penny Trash* 1:236. Hunt also derided C's claims for his corn, earning from C the name "The Liar." 72 *PR* 435, 460, 634; 73 *PR* 223, 489, 589; 74 *PR* 377, 589; 75 *PR* 637; 76 *PR* 85. C dragged out some of Hunt's history (76 *PR* 105) and claimed that Hunt had sold himself to the tories. 76 *PR* 648.

104 John Plamenatz, *The English Utilitarians* (rev. ed., Oxford 1958), p. 98. That parliament responded to pressure is everywhere admitted. Butler, *Great Reform Bill*, p. 424. The more usual view is that it was the middle class "whose agitation forced it through." Dickinson, *Development of Parliament*, p. 38.

105 Both C and Hunt had been agitating in the countryside during the rural uprisings of 1830. See ch. 22.

106 72 *PR* 745; *Morning Chronicle*, June 20, 1830.

107 "The New Order of Things." Praed was a confirmed tory violently opposed to reform.

108 "Mr. Hunt was not a man of much mind." James Grant, *Recollections of the House of Commons from the Year 1830 to the Close of 1835* . . . (2nd ed., London 1836), p. 168.

109 The tories in the Commons made much of the fact that after the Lords had vetoed the bill in October 1831, Russell and Althorp had written to Attwood thanking him for his support. Hansard, 3rd ser. VIII:596–620 (Oct. 12, 1831). Wellington claimed that there was collusion relating to the creation of the Birmingham "army." Butler, *Great Reform Bill*, p. 316. Croker claimed that the conduct of the whigs toward the political unions was not free "from the marks of duplicity." 76 *PR* 594. C believed that the B.P.U. was "acting under the influence of the Ministers," presumably because the B.P.U. was one of the last to object to Grey's speech of April 1832 in which he suggested that he was willing to compromise: "there stood the Birmingham Union, gaping like a clown at a puppet-show, while all the rest of the nation from Glasgow to London, was sending up addresses, petitions and remonstrances." 76 *PR* 452–8, 530. See also 77 *PR* 13, 162. Attwood's own statement that "the road to power and honour and unhallowed glory was open to him" in October 1831 and May 1832 but that he had resisted the temptation was taken by C to mean that Attwood had been offered a place in the government and rejected it. 77 *PR* 623–9. Yet the statement might be interpreted as meaning that he had refused to exercise his power over the mob to incite rebellion. In 1833 C alleged that "office-franks" were given to Joseph Parkes of Birmingham (Brougham's associate in the Society for the Diffusion of Useful Knowledge) "to rouse the political unions in favour of Lord Grey and the whigs." As reward, Parkes was appointed secretary to the corporation commissioners. 81 *PR* 650–1.

110 In March 1832 Attwood told Althorp that "he was in a great fright at the state of his town." Broughton, *Recollections* IV:191.

111 Broughton IV:164. Before the House of Lords voted the bill down, it had received a petition from the B.P.U. urging passage of the bill adopted at a meeting of 150,000 persons at which one of the speakers argued that the Lords dared not refuse it, for in such case the people would not pay the taxes needed to support the army, and even if they did, the troops would take sides with the people rather than with the aristocracy. 74 *PR* 94. Refusal to pay taxes had been frequently put forward earlier. 74 *PR* 19, 161.

112 Brock, *Great Reform Act*, p. 254.

113 See Butler, *Great Reform Bill*, pp. 281, 295, 315–16, 384, 400; Brock, pp. 247, 254–5, 306, 307. The king by proclamation dated November 21, 1831 declared illegal all associations "under the denomination of Political Unions, to be com-

posed of separate bodies, with various divisions and sub-divisions, under leaders with a gradation of ranks . . . and distinguished by certain badges." 74 *PR* 526. C promptly declared that "men have as clear a right to form these associations as associations for circulating the bible." 74 *PR* 527.

114 Brock, p. 306.

115 Wallas, *Francis Place*, p. 309. The month before the crisis of May 1831 C had written of the disastrous impact of a run on the Bank for gold. 76 *PR* 12.

JPC, p. 84: "The Placard, 'Stop the Duke: Go for Gold', originated with Mr. John Fielden, who suggested it to Thos Attwood & others, who at first hesitated, but who had it printed. [This I am told by Mr. Jas. Whittle, who had it from Mr. F himself at the time.] – See Register, vol. 76, pp. 392, 400. (Mr. Josh. Parkes one of those present)."

116 Place's letter to Hobhouse of November 8, 1830 declares Attwood "the most influential man in England." Wallas, p. 251. See also statement of Lord Durham and others quoted by Briggs, "Thomas Attwood," p. 190.

117 Butler, *Great Reform Bill*, p. 424. Even before the Reform Bill had been finally adopted, C contemptuously suggested that the city-jobbers would vote freedom of the city to the Birmingham Council. 76 *PR* 456.

118 71 *PR* 667. See also 74 *PR* 230–1; 76 *PR* 525, 605, 652; 81 *PR* 70; *Manchester Lectures*, p. 59. Distress in trade and agriculture was also cited by C as the force behind middle-class support of reform. 74 *PR* 206–7, 231–5. The cholera epidemic of 1831–2 added to the general atmosphere of fear. Martineau, *Thirty Years' Peace* II:73.

119 76 *PR* 652, 754. See also 76 *PR* 488–9. There was nothing derisive in the word "chopstick." C proudly asserted: "I belong to the order of the chopsticks." 74 *PR* 342.

120 "It was the hypocrisy of frightened lawyers which was to turn the familiar procedure of collecting money from the upper ranks, which was widely adopted in 1830, into the crime of 'robbery' or 'extortion' for which, unlike the breaking of threshing machines, the death penalty could be given." Hobsbawm and Rudé, *Captain Swing*, p. 45.

121 Letter to Nancy, July 8, 1932 (Nuffield).

122 76 *PR* 755, 791; 77 *PR* 65; letter to Nancy, July 8, 1832 (loc. cit.).

123 76 *PR* 531.

124 Letters to Mellersh, June 4 and 11, Aug. 20, Sept. 15, 22, 25, and 27, 1832 (Yale); William junior to Akerman, Sept. 25, 1832 (Fitzwilliam); letter to Akerman, Oct. 5, 1832 (Sotheby sale in London, June 18, 1979).

Late in 1831 C had begun advertising for a farm within about forty miles of Bolt Court. 74 *PR* 504. Normandy farm, of 160 acres, in the parish of Ash, was rented at £1 an acre. 83 *PR* 149.

125 *Manchester Lectures*, p. [v]. The possibility that C might be returned for Manchester had been used as an argument by those opposing the reform legislation. 74 *PR* 397.

126 *Manchester Lectures*, p. 8; 75 *PR* 10. The lectures were not currently recorded, but their substance was written out by C from his notes. The first five were printed in the *PR* (75 *PR* 3, 65, 129, 350, 414); all six appeared in a separate volume entitled *Cobbett's Manchester Lectures, in Support of His Fourteen Reform Propositions* (1832).

127 He would end pensions and sinecures, except those for merit, and reduce government salaries; discharge the standing army; require the counties to maintain militia; abolish tithes; sell church property (except churches, churchyards, and parsonages) and crown property and apply the proceeds to the reduction of the national debt; reduce the interest on the debt by one-quarter each six months, none payable after two years; give the fundholders the proceeds of church and crown lands, but nothing more; make an equitable adjustment of private mone-

tary contracts to reflect changes in the value of money; abolish all internal taxes except those on land; impose customs duties only to the extent conducive to the navigation, commerce, and manufactures of the kingdom; provide for a powerful navy; make a fixed allowance for the king; abolish the protestant hierarchy in Ireland; hold parliament and king's court once every three years in Dublin, York, and Salisbury. *Manchester Lectures*, pp. 2–4.

128 75 *PR* 344, 407.

129 77 *PR* 129–31. There had been some move in Glasgow to name C as a candidate there, and C suggested that he might be elected at Preston and Dudley as well as at Manchester. 76 *PR* 680; 77 *PR* 129, 140, 143.

130 77 *PR* 131–2, 143–4.

131 The debate took place on August 28 and 29, 1832. Attwood and his colleague Charles Jones favored inflating the currency by issuing more paper money, while C favored a hard currency with "equitable adjustment" of existing obligations. Attwood talked for four hours and a half, followed the next day by Jones for an hour, C for two hours, and Attwood in reply for two hours. The weary crowd, probably understanding little of what was involved in either proposition, declared the home team victors. Naturally, this did not convince C. See 77 *PR* 449–52, 577–637; Pearl, *Cobbett*, pp. 180–2.

132 78 *PR* 352. Details of the tour from beginning to end appear at 77 *PR* 456, 577, 705, 769; 78 *PR* 1, 65, 129, 193, 257, 321, 385, 423, 449. In January 1833 C published a separate volume describing the trip, consisting mainly of articles from the *PR* (plus five additional pages on the Highlands), entitled *Cobbett's Tour in Scotland: And in the Four Northern Counties of England: In the Autumn of the Year 1832*, dedicated to the people of Oldham.

On visiting Robert Owen's New Lanark, C commented that the society Owen had fashioned there "is a melancholy thing to behold; that it is the reverse of domestic life; that it reverses the order of nature; that it makes minds a fiction; and, which is amongst the greatest of its evils, it fashions the rising generation to habits of implicit submission, which is only another term for civil and political slavery." 78 *PR* 391.

133 78 *PR* 469.

134 George Gilfillan, *A Second Gallery of Literary Portraits* (Edinburgh 1850), p. 298.

135 78 *PR* 715–16. C's popularity in Manchester may have been affected by the attacks made on him by Hunt, a favorite of the Manchester working class since Peterloo. Briggs, "Background of Parliamentary Reform," p. 308n.

136 Crown Street, formerly between Downing Street and King Charles Street, has disappeared and is now occupied by government offices.

A lease with a seven-year term commencing December 25, 1832 was signed in February 1832. It provided for payment of £30 and annual rent of £100. Faithfull MSS., no. 14 (Nuffield).

137 Letter to Swain, Jan. 24, 1833 (Cornell). Swain's shop was at 93 Fleet Street, a few steps from Bolt Court. Swain's advertisements in the *PR* (one of the few appearing in the paper) headed "Cheap Clothing!!" offered "for cash only" a suit of superfine clothes at £4 14s. 6d. with an added charge of 5s. 6d. if made in black or blue. 79 *PR* 64.

138 79 *PR* 267.

139 Thomas Raikes, *A Portion of the Journal Kept by Thomas Raikes, Esq. from 1831 to 1847* (2nd ed., London 1856) 1:144. Greville (*Memoirs* 11:361) reported on February 10 that Peel had been pushed from his usual seat by C. "Cobbett placed himself on the Treasury bench, next to Sir James Graham; a few days afterwards he took his seat . . . next to Sir Robert Peel." Denis Le Marchant, *Memoir of John Charles Viscount Althorp Third Earl Spencer* (London 1876), p. 451. This does not seem to have been a spur-of-the-moment decision. A month before, C had writ-

ten: "These servants of the King, being members of the House, have not the slightest claim to any particular seat or perch." 78 *PR* 772.

24. The end

Motto: *Works* 1:151.
1   77 *PR* 259. Earlier C had hoped for fifty to one hundred such members.
2   80 *PR* 148.
3   C had two close associates: John Fielden and George Faithfull, member for Brighton, brother of C's solicitor. Others who often voted with C included Daniel O'Connell and some of his following, Joseph Hume, D. W. Harvey, and Thomas Attwood.

    In December 1834 C told his Oldham constituents that he and Fielden had "hardly more power in the House than as if they had been two little robins, or a couple of sparrows." 86 *PR* 691.
4   Dickinson, *Development of Parliament*, p. 40. See also E. P. Thompson, *English Working Class*, pp. 899–900.
5   Woodward, *Age of Reform*, p. 87.
6   77 *PR* 275. See also 76 *PR* 539; 79 *PR* 587; 85 *PR* 148.
7   Not only were the reformers unable to effect any reductions in expenditure, but they found annual costs substantially increased when the Grey ministry decided to pay £20 million to the owners of the West Indies plantations as compensation for the slaves who were freed by an act adopted in August 1833. C opposed the payment, since it would increase annual taxes by £800,000.
8   Hume claimed that £39 to £40 million in tax was raised from the industrious classes, who paid as much as 50 percent on their incomes, while £10 million was paid by the higher classes, to whom taxes amounted to 15 or 20 percent of their incomes. 81 *PR* 9.
9   79 *PR* 809–10.
10   80 *PR* 324.
11   87 *PR* 763; 81 *PR* 6.
12   80 *PR* 343–4. As a concession, the ministry agreed to drop the tax on receipts for amounts under £5. 80 *PR* 322, 334.
13   83 *PR* 705–36. See also 86 *PR* 727; 87 *PR* 705. In April 1833 the malt tax had been cut by half on a Friday night and restored on the following Tuesday. 80 *PR* 263, 270–2. C repeated again and again the statement made in 1821 by John Ellman, Sussex farmer, that forty-five years before, every man in his parish brewed his own beer, and that not one man in the parish did so now. *Rural Rides*, p. 68; 44 *PR* 602. The malt tax, and its method of collection, made it difficult for the poor man to brew his own beer; hence, he was forced to purchase the far more expensive product sold at the public house or go without.
14   In April 1833, when Sadler's bill was deferred for "further inquiry" by a vote of 74 to 73, C pointed out that what was being inflicted on the children was "really very little short of murder by inches." 80 *PR* 21–2.
15   81 *PR* 181–2. See also 81 *PR* 216.
16   Hansard, 3rd ser. XIX:913 (July 19, 1833); 81 *PR* 180. The nine-hour limit was to operate in three stages: after six months it would apply to children under twelve and by thirty months to those under fourteen.
17   J. F. Bright, *A History of England . . . Period III . . . 1689–1837* (8th ed., London 1900), p. 1438. The act was passed for the period of one year. When it came up for renewal, it became a subject of disagreement within Grey's ministry which led to the fall of his government in July 1834. 85 *PR* 135.
18   The recommendations of the poor law commissioners are given at 83 *PR* 581–5; the bill, at 84 *PR* 616, 675, 736.

19 See 79 *PR* 723-6 and 80 *PR* 9-21 for a detailed survey of the wages of hand weavers in Lancashire and Yorkshire in 1833. According to John Fielden, hand weavers outnumbered weavers employed in mills by three to one in 1833. 80 *PR* 15.

20 During the discussions on the bill, C asked Althorp whether the lawyers who drew the legislation were not instructed that "one thing desired to be accomplished, was, to bring the people of England to live upon a coarser diet?" 85 *PR* 80-1. Althorp evaded the question. In 1843 a copy of the instructions was discovered and produced in the House which demonstrated that C's suspicions had been correct. Hansard, 3rd ser. LXVI:223, 1161 (Feb. 7 and 23, 1843).

21 84 *PR* 263, 616, 660, 705, 724; 85 *PR* 67, 215, 308, 321, 385, 415, 449, 470, 696, 710; 86 *PR* 55, 134, 202, 335; 87 *PR* 569; 88 *PR* 282, 489, 641, 662, 681-95.

    C pointed out the inconsistency between the principle of the poor law, which required the laboring man to save enough out of his pitifully small wage to support himself in his old age, and the regular practice of parliament to vote huge pensions for government officials who were highly paid for their services. 88 *PR* 459. The speaker of the Commons who received £6,000 a year during sixteen years of service was granted a pension of £4,000 a year for life.

22 An account of the harsh workings of the 1834 act is given in a preface written by John Cobbett to the 1872 edition of *Legacy to Labourers*.

23 *Legacy to Labourers* contains an ironic dedication to Peel which ends with the language quoted in the text. In the first month of publication 8,000 copies of *Legacy to Labourers* were sold. 87 *PR* 527.

24 Grant, *Recollections of the House of Commons*, p. 191. "Cobbett's speech in opposition was an utter failure. It did not obtain a single cheer." Le Marchant, *Memoir of Althorp*, p. 450.

    Brougham, speaking of C's career in the Commons, wrote: "He certainly did not fail, and would have had a very considerable success had he entered it at an earlier age." *Speeches of Henry, Lord Brougham* (Edinburgh 1838) 1:6.

25 Grant, pp. 338, 364, 369-70. C mentions that in parliament laughter was the "usual sequel of any statement of the grievances of the poorer classes," and refers to the "ya, ya, ya, ya, ya" that greeted him during his attack on Peel. 80 *PR* 227, 465; 88 *PR* 681. The heckling met and overcome by Hunt is described in Lovett, *Life*, p. 45n.

26 80 *PR* 141. See also 86 *PR* 694. Greville mentions as radicals "Roebuck, Faithfull, Buckingham, Major Beauclerk &c (most of whom have totally failed in point of speaking)." *Greville Memoirs* II:369.

27 Grant, p. 187.

28 This is particularly true of C's early speeches in 1833 before he was overtaken by illness. Carlile, who was at odds with C most of the time, reported C's first two speeches at length. *Gauntlet*, Feb. 17 and 24, 1833. Most of the adverse comment on C, however, refers to his total parliamentary career, including the periods of his serious illness.

    The *Annual Register* for 1835 (App., p. 226) made what appears to be an objective appraisal, saying: "In the House of Commons he was neither brilliant nor obtrusive, but was occasionally heard with indulgence and attention." The *Morning Chronicle* declared that C had "made one or two good speeches, but he repeated himself, and always made the same speech." 88 *PR* 791. Sir Henry Lytton Bulwer, who served in the Commons with C from 1833 to 1835, stated that C "wanted some physical qualifications ... necessary to the orator which he might as a younger man have naturally possessed or easily acquired," and that C "became rather a favourite with an audience which is only unforgiving when bored." Bulwer, *Historical Characters* II:174-5.

29 84 *PR* 325 for Althorp reference.

30 80 *PR* 385–421, 449–79, esp. 466. C's attempt to reply to Peel was prevented by heckling. See 80 *PR* 465. Contemporaries almost uniformly condemned C's effort and applauded that of Peel, although at this distance it seems that Peel might have been better advised to treat C's attack as a joke. As it was, he attacked C personally and claimed that C was trying to intimidate him. Somerville (*The Whistler at the Plough*, p. 258) contended that the whigs were injured in the eyes of the people "out of doors" for joining the tories in chastising C.

    The reason C gave for selecting Peel as his target was that it was the way to find out whether there was any defense to the deflationary policy embodied in the 1819 act, and selecting "the strongest man amongst all the blunderers" was the way to excite the greatest degree of interest in the subject. 80 *PR* 386.

31 84 *PR* 72, 74.

32 They include C's views on such diverse subjects as pensions and sinecures, universal suffrage, the ballot, the Septennial Act, military flogging, the sinking fund, civil servants in parliament, the game laws, equitable taxation, tithes, clerical nonresidence, multiple livings, the corn laws, the poor laws, factory laws, labor unions, laws relating to the press.

33 Letter to Sapsford, May 11, 1834 (Nuffield). Earlier C had complained of puffed ankles. Letter to John, Jan. 3, 1832 (Nuffield). C was "one of the stoutest men in the House." Grant, *Recollections of the House of Commons*, p. 191.

34 The 1833 session sat twice the number of days (142) and three times the number of hours (1,270) of former sessions. 81 *PR* 534.

    The strain of an active parliamentary life is suggested by Pitt's death when he was in his forties; the deaths of Castlereagh, Fox, and Canning when they were in their fifties; and the death of Romilly when he was in his early sixties.

35 80 *PR* 258. Except on bills of unusual importance, C and others of the reformers left around midnight, knowing they would be outvoted.

36 80 *PR* 137, 139, 154, 500. 74 *PR* 477.

37 A petition submitted by C on behalf of members of the National Political Union had disclosed Popay's activities among groups of working men. The select committee found Popay's conduct "highly reprehensible," and he was discharged. C filed a separate report critical of Popay's superiors. 80 *PR* 820; 81 *PR* 12, 105, 129, 198, 257, 321, 385.

38 Postscript to letter to Beevor, Sept. 22, 1833 (Cornell). The body of the letter is missing, and the Cornell document appears to be a copy; the original has not been found.

39 William junior seems to have been in France from 1830 to 1832 after some unexplained embarrassment. John to William, Nov. 8, 1830 (Nuffield); letter to John, Jan. 3, 1832 (loc. cit.). Our knowledge of James's falling out with his father is limited to what appeared in an obscure publication, the *Political Penny Magazine*, no. 9 (Oct. 29, 1836), of which there is only one known copy (Columbia University). The anonymous author of the article, probably Benjamin Tilly, provides the full text of a letter from twenty-eight-year-old James to his father, dated July 16, 1831, in which James claimed that he had been ridiculed by a *PR* article of that date stating that during the preparation for the 1831 libel trial James had been "engaged in the day-time with his master in town." 73 *PR* 140. The original letter has disappeared. On the face of it, James was unduly sensitive, but there may be more to the story. At some point James seems to have charged his father with adultery, which C refused to take seriously. Letter to Sapsford, Jan. 9, 1834 (Nuffield).

40 Letter to Beevor, Sept. 22, 1833 (Cornell). Later C charged Miss Blundell with embezzlement, but apparently nothing came of the charge. Letter to Sapsford, Feb. 5, 1834 (Nuffield).

41 82 *PR* 295, stating that he had slept out of the wen but five nights since parliament

was prorogued. See also 82 *PR* 375, 427, 784. C had previously announced that he would visit Oldham early in November 1833. 81 *PR* 597.

42   82 *PR* 1, 7–8. The reference to "bad book-making" probably referred to *A Geographical Dictionary of England and Wales* (1832) and *A New French and English Dictionary* (1833).

43   82 *PR* 1–37.

44   82 *PR* 769, 771, 783–6.

45   Anne, p. 19 (Nuffield).

46   At 88 *PR* 518 C says: "I had battles enough to carry on to prevent both sons and daughters being sent to school."

47   Broughton, *Recollections* III:197.

48   Defendants' brief in French case, pp. 9, 10, 15–16. Faithfull MSS., no. 20 (Nuffield).

There had been signs of disagreements of growing seriousness between C and Nancy since 1818, when Nancy went back to England leaving C on Long Island. See ch. 18, nn. 100–1. Soon after C's return to England he wrote Nancy: "fortitude is required . . . do not stay moping in the house." Jan. 4, 1820 (Nuffield). She was greatly relieved when he made arrangements to declare himself bankrupt. Anne to James, Apr. 20, 1820 (Nuffield). The month before her suicide attempt, C wrote: "cease to worry yourself about my affairs . . . it does seem monstrous to distrust my judgment; but the truth is, that the presumptuous talk about my 'crotchets' has become so habitual, that it seems to be almost impossible to eradicate the idea, or to prevent it from breaking forth into sarcastic criticism." Apr. 16, 1827 (Nuffield). In 1827 Nancy may have been concerned about C's handling of the Boxall estate, in which he was then deeply involved. See letters to Dean, Jan. 3 and 12, 1827 (Cornell) with gloss by Tilly: "something was the matter between Mr. C and his family"; to Akerman, Aug. 27, 1827 (Yale); to Nancy, Sept. 7, 1827 (Nuffield). C unabashedly records that on the day of the 1831 trial Nancy cried when he "rather hastily" criticized her for buying stockings that were too short for him. 73 *PR* 139.

49   Within the family it was believed that C left home because of beatings he received from his father. JPC Memoir, p. 47. But there is nothing to suggest this in C's public references to his father. His parents, grandparents, brothers, wife, and children were all idealized. Even after the breach in July 1833 C tried to keep the myth alive. Two months after that event he publicly proclaimed: "I should have been but a middling sort of fellow if I had not been married" (81 *PR* 721) at the same time as he was privately asserting that "the tongue" had "for more than 20 years been my great curse."

A less believable version of the suicide attempt than that given in the text was the claim by Daniel French, one of C's half-demented acquaintances, that Nancy believed that her husband had engaged in "unnatural propensities" with Riley, C's secretary, a story which French's active mind seems to have created out of the fact that C had locked himself away from the rest of the family and allowed only Riley to visit him. French's claim led to a physical assault on him by three of the Cobbett sons and an action by French against them in which he "declared in the most solemn manner his disbelief in the imputations made against Mr. Cobbett and Mr. Riley." Nancy denied that she had ever made the statement attributed to her by French. The jury found the Cobbett sons guilty of the assault, but "under strong provocation." They were fined a total of £24. *Times*, Sept. 25, 1829. See 68 *PR* 245, 415, 440; *The Singular and Unprecedented Trial of William, John, and Richard Cobbett for a Violent Assault on Daniel French, Esq.* . . . (London 1829); *French versus Cobbett. Cobbett on the Gridiron!! (Grilled to a Cinder!) Being an Answer to Cobbett's Register of October 3, 1829*, by Daniel French (London [1829]).

50   William junior to Akerman, Sept. 25, 1832 (Fitzwilliam).

51 In January 1834 C began to advertise the availability of the Crown Street house for rental. 83 *PR* 1.

52 There were, however, a few quite good things. He wrote a splendid piece on the 1833 prorogation ceremony in the House of Lords, ending with the remark: "Let republicans laugh as long as they will, at what they call 'nonsensical show'; it has a great deal more sense in it than they are aware of." 81 *PR* 543. He continued to use, as he had so often in the past, amusing analogies derived from the field and farm. 83 *PR* 134, 199, 294. Two months before he died, he wrote an article on Peel, far better than any speech he made in parliament, castigating him for speaking so well and thinking so little. 88 *PR* 129.

53 C became so intrigued by the American president that he wrote and published in 1834 *The Life of Andrew Jackson,* mainly an abridgement of a biography written by Jackson's friend and secretary of war, John Henry Eaton, to which C added an account of Jackson's fight against the Bank of the United States. 84 *PR* 2, 43, 503–4. C claimed that 10,000 copies of his life of Jackson priced at six cents a copy were sold in New York on one day. 86 *PR* 385. Some of the articles on paper money in America: 82 *PR* 257; 83 *PR* 65, 737, 783, 803, 805; 84 *PR* 1, 349, 403, 413, 489, 548, 611, 778; 85 *PR* 352, 388, 628; 86 *PR* 132, 405, 556, 680, 717, 745, 809; 87 *PR* 149, 363, 385.

54 There seem to be no reliable figures for the circulation of the *PR*. Based on the number of newspaper stamps purchased, average weekly circulation appears to have fallen from about 3,400 in the calendar year 1829 to about 1,600 in the eighteen months ended June 30, 1833. However, as the amended return for the latter period suggests, the stamp tax figures were a notoriously inaccurate source for determining circulation. *House of Commons Accounts and Papers* xxv (1830); xxxii (1833). C had earlier pointed out that the *PR* and others bought stamped paper from stationers rather than direct from the stamp office. 42 *PR* 443.

In 1828 C had an inventory of 29,000 copies of the eight titles he then had in print. Letter to John, Sept. 4, 1828 (Nuffield). Between 1828 and 1832 he published fourteen other titles, but no records have been found giving the inventory at a later date.

In 1833 C cut the price of *Two-Penny Trash* (a bound volume of almost 600 pages) from 5s. to 3s. and sent 35,000 of the separate numbers to Oldham for sale. 82 *PR* 428.

55 85 *PR* 613.

56 Faithfull MSS., no. 4 (Nuffield).

57 Faithfull MSS., no. 13 (Nuffield); John and James to Sapsford, Dec. 23, 1833. The relationship between C and Miss Boxall is not known. C had a godfather named Boxall. *Works* IV:114.

58 Letter to John, Jan. 3, 1832 (Nuffield); 78 *PR* 208.

59 77 *PR* 654; 82 *PR* 19. At the time C made his public appeal in the *PR* he also sent out "about a hundred" letters to acquaintances calling their attention to his public appeal. Letters to Akerman, Sept. 13, 1832 (Fitzwilliam); to Tubb, Sept. 15 (Bodleian); to Moore, Sept. 15 (Illinois).

60 In September 1833 C discharged Miss Blundell, as already noted; he turned over the children's books to them; and he transferred the lease of Bolt Court to John Dean, presumably to protect himself against some expected legal attack.

John had written one book: *Letters from France* (1825), and James had written three: *A Ride of Eight Hundred Miles in France* (1824), *Journal of a Tour in Italy* (1830), and *A Grammar of the Italian Language* (1830).

In 1828 C had executed a deed assigning eight books of his own authorship to members of his family, one to each of his seven children and one to Nancy. Letter to John, Sept. 4, 1828 (Nuffield).

61 Copy of C's MS. entitled "Proposals" in the handwriting of Benjamin Tilly, with his notation: "Dated abt 18 Feb. 1834" (Cornell).

62 John and James to Sapsford, Dec. 23, 1833 (Nuffield).

63 John to Gutsell, Mar. 14, 1834 (Yale); letter to Faithfull, Mar. 21, 1834 (Yale); letter from John and James, Mar. 22, 1834 (Yale). The debt to Beevor was discharged on March 22, 1834. Faithfull MSS., no. 4 (Nuffield).

64 83 *PR* 580. In April 1834, the name was changed to the *Shilling Magazine*. Pearl, *Cobbett,* pp. 185–6.

65 On several occasions C asserted that Normandy farm would become self-supporting at successively postponed future dates.

66 C refused to attend a meeting at which admission was to be charged. 81 *PR* 482. See Grant, *Recollections of the House of Commons,* p. 188.

67 84 *PR* 80, 130, 166, 193, 257, 338, 411. See also letters to Gutsell, April 13, 14, 17, 18, 22, and 24, May 16, 18, and 19 (Cornell); to Fielden, April 24 and 30, May 2 and 16, 1834 (Rutgers); to Croft, May 6, 1834 (Fordham); to Sapsford, May 11, 1834 (Nuffield).

68 84 *PR* 193; Tilly's gloss on letter to Gutsell, Apr. 18, 1834 (Cornell).

69 Macaulay's Journal, Jan. 15, 1855. I am indebted to Dr. R. Robson, Trinity College, Cambridge, for the opportunity of examining his typescript of the journal.

70 See Anthony Storr, *Human Aggression* (Penguin ed., 1976).

71 74 *PR* 400; 81 *PR* 719.

72 Letter to Gutsell, Apr. 24, 1834 (Cornell); to Oldfield, Apr. 25, 1834 (Cornell).
    The row between C and William junior had apparently started when C ordered his son's "wife" to leave Normandy farmhouse. It turned out (or so C thought) that they had not been married; William junior left shortly after she did. Letters to Gutsell, Apr. 14 and 24, 1834 (Cornell).
    In 1828 (during the great Cobbett–O'Connell feud of 1825–8) O'Connell had referred to C as a "monster, whose very home-inmates groan under the most afflicting domestic tyranny." 66 *PR* 789.

73 Hansard, 3rd ser. xxv:192, 496, 1215 (July 18 and 25, Aug. 11, 1834).

74 Letters to Gutsell, Aug. 9 and 17, 1834 (Cornell).

75 Letter to Dean, Sept. 12, 1834 (Illinois).

76 Letter to Oldfield, Aug. 29, 1834 (Illinois); to Dean, Sept. 14, 1834 (Illinois).

77 85 *PR* 213; 86 *PR* 232, 234, 237, 269.

78 The first of the ten letters to Marshall appears at 85 *PR* 769; the last, at 86 *PR* 513.

79 Letter to Gutsell [Oct. 28, 1834] (Cornell).

80 87 *PR* 65.

81 Hansard, 3rd ser. xxvi:780 (May 10, 1835); 87 *PR* 644.

82 88 *PR* 1.

83 The first edition of 5,000 copies was sold in nine days, and a second printing of 10,000 copies was ordered. At least six editions were published in 1835. 88 *PR* 455; Pearl, *Cobbett,* p. 195.

84 *Legacy to Parsons,* pp. 112, 114 (letter IV).

85 Letters to Oldfield, Mar. 18 (Illinois) and 26 (Cornell), Apr. 10, 1835 (Illinois); Agreement of May 18, 1835 between C and Oldfield (Yale); Add. MSS. 31125, fols. 158–73.
    The three new publications were *Cobbett's Legacy to Labourers* (1835); *Cobbett's Legacy to Parsons* (1835); and *Surplus Population: And Poor-Law Bill* (1835), a revision of the play originally published in 1831. According to William junior, 45,000 of these three publications had been sold by Dec. 1, 1835.

86 At the time of the transaction C owed Oldfield approximately £2,000. The £1,000 for the copyrights plus another £200 for seeds etc. sold to Oldfield was credited against the debt, so that at the time of C's death he owed Oldfield £800. William Cobbett, Jr., *Renewal of Cobbett's Register: Address and History of Normandy Farm* (Lon-

don 1836), p. 22. In February 1834 C had written that "it will be very well" if he died worth £2. 83 *PR* 295.

87 Hansard, 3rd ser. XXVIII:101, 106, 109 (May 25, 1835).
88 88 *PR* 641, 651.
89 The material from this point to the end of the chapter is derived from issue no. 9 (Oct. 26, 1836) of the *Political Penny Magazine*, letter to the editor dated Oct. 23, 1836 and signed "Philo-Cobbett" (presumably Benjamin Tilly, who was with C at Normandy farm and an eyewitness of the events described). The only known copy of this issue of the magazine is in the Columbia University library in New York. Tantalizingly, it states that C's "affairs of 1833 and 1834" would be made known in "a future number." No later numbers of this rare magazine have been found.

Epilogue

1 *Standard*, June 19, 1835; *Morning Post*, June 19, 1835; *Times*, June 20, 1835; *Tait's Edinburgh Magazine*, n.s. II (Aug. and Sept. 1835), 491–506, 583–97; *Fraser's Magazine* XII (Aug. 1835), 207–22; *Morning Chronicle*, June 19, 1835; *WR* XXIII (Oct. 1935), 451–71.

2 Pearl, *Cobbett*, p. 205. Papers relating to the Cobbett Monument Committee are held by Nuffield. Faithfull MSS. XXI:12.

3 Karl Marx wrote in 1853: "William Cobbett was the most able representative, or, rather, the creator of old English Radicalism . . . thus . . . an anticipated modern Chartist." Karl Marx and Frederick Engels, *Collected Works* XII (London 1979), 188–9.

4 Pencarrow MSS., Jan. 22, 1840, quoted by W. Thomas, *Philosophic Radicals*, p. 427. See also p. 306, which speaks of a movement of newspapers away from whiggism and radicalism: "By May 1836 a Tory writer could claim that 'the balance of newspaper power is incontestably in favour of the Conservative party'."

5 C's will, signed December 14, 1833 in the presence of Gutsell, Swain, and Tilly, declared that "if I were to die without having a will my property should be squandered amidst strife and litigation."

6 *Times*, Jan. 26, 1836; Conway, *Life of Thomas Paine*, p. 327; *Notes and Queries*, 10th ser. XII (1909), 197–8. The Letters to the Editor columns of *The Observer* for Feb. 7, 14, and 21, 1937 contain some interesting suggestions about the bones. A commonly held belief among the descendants of C (*c.* 1980) is that the bones were discreetly buried, sometime past, by one of their ancestors at an unknown location on property then owned by a member of the family.

7 Letter to William junior, Apr. 15, 1826 (Nuffield); John to William junior, Nov. 8, 1830 (Nuffield); *Cobbett* v. *Warner*, 2 L.R. 108 (1866).

8 *Times*, Jan. 14, 1878.

9 Coventry election: 80 *PR* 66, 118, 130, 135. John had tried and lost at Chichester in 1835 and 1837. He was defeated at Oldham in 1865 and 1868. William junior proposed to run for Oldham in 1852, but apparently changed his mind. William junior to Messrs. Leach and Taylor, Aug. 9, 1852 (Illinois).

10 James was an unsuccessful candidate at Bury in the 1837 election.

11 JPC. The reminiscences of Anne and Susan are in the Nuffield library.

12 JPC Memoir.

13 Richard to "my dear girls," Mar. 3, 1840 (Lathbury estate).

14 These were: Sir William Cobbett (1846–1926), Sir Walter Cobbett (1871–1955), and General Sir Gerald Lathbury (1906–78).

15 *English Grammar* letter XXIII; *Advice*, para. 355.

Sources

Manuscripts

The vast bulk of Cobbett letters and other manuscripts in the British Isles is held by the British Library and Nuffield College. Most of the material in the British Library relates to the period 1799–1811, with a considerably smaller (but nonetheless important) amount of material relating to 1819 and subsequent years. The Nuffield College correspondence extends from 1794 to 1835, with relatively little for the years 1833–5.

Original Cobbett materials, mostly letters, are also held by the Bodleian Library, the Fitzwilliam Museum, and the Public Record Office. Others with small holdings are the East Sussex Record Office, Kirklees Metropolitan Council Library, Motherwell Public Library, Lancashire Record Office, Liverpool City Library, John Rylands University Library of Manchester, the University of London, the National Library of Scotland, and the National Library of Ireland.

The two largest collections of Cobbett letters in the United States are those held by Cornell University – nearly a hundred pieces written mostly between 1830 and 1835; and by the University of Illinois – about the same number of pieces covering the period 1800–35. The University of Illinois archive includes the former collection of Arnold Muirhead. See M. L. Pearl, *William Cobbett: A Bibliographical Account of His Life and Times* (London 1953), p. 2.

Further important holdings are in the following institutions:

Adelphi University – about forty letters to Henry Hunt, 1808–29

Columbia University – the only known copy of the *Political Penny Magazine*, no. 9, of Oct. 29, 1836, containing an important article on Cobbett and his family relations 1831–5; and miscellaneous letters

Haverford College – about ten letters to Joseph Nancrede, 1818–19

Huntington Library, San Marino, Calif. – twenty-four letters to J. Mathieu, 1793–4, and several others

Rutgers University – miscellaneous Cobbett letters, and the papers of C. Rexford Davis, Cobbett scholar

Yale University – miscellaneous Cobbett letters, mostly 1833–5 but several written on his first visit to America, and two manuscripts of Cobbett's written while in the army in New Brunswick

Other American institutions holding original Cobbett materials are: American Antiquarian Society, American Philosophical Society, Boston Public Library, University of California at Los Angeles, Connecticut State Library, University of Connecticut (papers of Pierce Gaines, Cobbett bibliographer), Duke University, Fordham University, Harvard University, University of Iowa, University of Kansas, Library of Congress, Massachusetts Historical Society, University of Michigan, Pierpont Morgan Library, University of Nebraska–Lincoln, New York Historical Society, New York Public Library, New York State Library, State University of New York at Buffalo, Northwestern University, University of Notre Dame, Historical Society of Pennsylvania, Pennsylvania State University, University of Pennsylvania, Princeton University, University of Rochester, Stanford University, Swarthmore College, University of Texas, and Trinity College (Hartford).

Prints and drawings

The British Museum collection of political and personal satires includes 152 pictures from the period 1802–32 in which Cobbett appears as a principal character or is otherwise commented on. A number of these have been used as illustrations. They are nearly all critical of Cobbett's conduct, having been, in the main, instigated by the government or someone friendly to the government. Hence they reflect Cobbett's nuisance value more than his public following. Yet the varying volume of these graphic attacks provides an interesting index of the ups and downs in Cobbett's career:

Period	No. of prints	Events
1801–5	4	–
1806–10	34	Duke of York, Newgate
1811–15	7	–
1816–20	57	Spa Fields, America, Paine, Queen Caroline
1821–5	8	–
1826–30	28	Swing, grill, reform
1831–2	14	Reform

Principal published writings of Cobbett

The pamphlets Cobbett wrote in America between 1794 and 1800 were nearly all reprinted (sometimes with considerable modification) in *Porcupine's Works*, consisting of twelve volumes published in 1801. Many of Cobbett's later books and pamphlets first appeared in his weekly *Political Register*. In the following list of Cobbett's writings, those reprinted in *Porcupine's Works* are marked with an asterisk (*), and those that first appeared in the *Political Register* are marked with a dagger (†). The compilation is arranged alphabetically by the short titles that are used in the text and notes.

A Little Plain English: *A Little Plain English, Addressed to the People of the United States . . .* By Peter Porcupine. Philadelphia 1795.
Advice: Advice to Young Men and (Incidentally) to Young Women in the Middle and Higher Ranks of Life . . . London 1830. First issued in 14 monthly parts. June 1829–Sept. 1830.
American Gardener: The American Gardener; or, A Treatise on the Situation, Soil, Fencing and Laying-Out of Gardens . . . London 1821.
American PR (American Political Register): Cobbett's American Political Register. Jan.–June 1816; May 1817–Jan. 1818. New York. Published by Henry Cobbett, Cobbett's nephew.
Big O and Sir Glory: †*Big O and Sir Glory: or, "Leisure to Laugh." A Comedy. In Three Acts.* London 1825.
Bloody Buoy: *The Bloody Buoy, Thrown Out as a Warning to the Political Pilots of America; or A Faithful Relation of a Multitude of Acts of Horrid Barbarity* . . . By Peter Porcupine. Philadelphia 1796.
Bone to Gnaw: *A Bone to Gnaw, for the Democrats* . . . By Peter Porcupine. Philadelphia 1795.
Cannibals' Progress: *The Cannibals' Progress; or The Dreadful Horrors of French Invasion*

... Translated from the German by Anthony Aufrer ... republished at Philadelphia by William Cobbett. [1798.]

Collective Commentaries: Cobbett's Collective Commentaries ... London 1822. Mostly articles Cobbett published in the *Statesman* during 1822.

Corn: A Treatise on Cobbett's Corn ... London 1828.

Cottage Economy: Cottage Economy: Containing Information Relating to the Brewing of Beer, Making of Bread, Keeping of Cows, Pigs, Bees, Ewes, Goats, Poultry and Rabbits, and Relative to Other Matters Deemed Useful in the Conducting of the Affairs of a Labourer's Family. London 1822. First issued in 7 monthly parts. 1821–2.

Country Porcupine: Country Porcupine. Triweekly newspaper, March 5, 1798–Aug. 26, 1799. Philadelphia.

*Democratic Judge: *The Democratic Judge: or The Equal Liberty of the Press, as Exhibited, Explained and Exposed, in the Prosecution of William Cobbett, for a Pretended Libel against the King of Spain and His Ambassador, before Thomas M'Kean, Chief Justice of the State of Pennsylvania.* Philadelphia 1798.

*Detection of Conspiracy: *Detection of a Conspiracy, Formed by the United Irishmen, with the Evident Intention of Aiding the Tyrants of France in Subverting the Government of the United States of America.* By Peter Porcupine. Philadelphia 1798.

Emigrant's Guide: The Emigrant's Guide; In Ten Letters, Addressed to the Taxpayers of England; Containing Information of Every Kind, Necessary to Persons Who Are About to Emigrate ... London 1829.

English Gardener: The English Gardener; or, A Treatise on the Situation, Soil, Enclosing and Laying-Out, of Kitchen Gardens ... London 1828.

English Grammar: A Grammar of the English Language, in a Series of Letters. Intended for the Use of Schools and of Young Persons in General; but, More Especially for the Use of Soldiers, Sailors, Apprentices, and Plough-Boys. New York 1818.

Evening Post: Cobbett's Evening Post. Daily newspaper, Jan. 29–Apr. 1, 1820. London.

French Arrogance: French Arrogance; or, "The Cat Let Out of the Bag"; A Poetical Dialogue between the Envoys of America and X.Y.Z. and the Lady. By Peter Porcupine. Philadelphia 1798.

French Dictionary: A New French and English Dictionary. In Two Parts ... London 1833.

French Grammar: A French Grammar, or, Plain Instructions for the Learning of French. In a Series of Letters. London 1824.

French Lectures: Eleven Lectures on the French and Belgian Revolutions, and English Boroughmongering: Delivered in the Theatre of the Rotunda, Blackfriars Bridge. London 1830. First issued in 11 parts, Sept.–Oct. 1830.

Geographical Dictionary: A Geographical Dictionary of England and Wales ... London 1832.

George IV: History of the Regency and Reign of King George the Fourth. 2 vols. London 1830–4. First issued in parts, 1830–4.

Good Friday: Good Friday; or, The Murder of Jesus Christ by the Jews. London 1830.

*Gros Mousqueton: *The Gros Mousqueton Diplomatique; or Diplomatic Blunderbuss, Containing, Citizen Adet's Notes to the Secretary of State* ... By Peter Porcupine. Philadelphia 1796.

Impeachment: Impeachment of Mr. Lafayette ... Translated from the French by William Cobbett. Philadelphia 1793.

Important Considerations: Important Considerations for the People of This Kingdom. Anonymous. London 1803.

*Kick for a Bite: *A Kick for a Bite; or, Review upon Review; With a Critical Essay, on the Works of Mrs S. Rowson* ... By Peter Porcupine. Philadelphia 1795.

Legacy to Labourers: Cobbett's Legacy to Labourers; or, What Is the Right Which Lords, Baronets, and Squires Have to the Lands of England? ... London 1834 [1835].

Legacy to Parsons: Cobbett's Legacy to Parsons; or, Have the Clergy of the Established Church an Equitable Right to the Tithes, or to Any Other Thing Called Church Property, Greater Than the Dissenters Have to the Same? ... London 1835.

SOURCES

Letters to Hawkesbury: Letters to the Right Honourable Lord Hawkesbury, and to the Right Honourable Henry Addington, on the Peace with Buonaparte . . . London 1802.

Letters to Thornton: Letters from William Cobbett to Edward Thornton Written in the Years 1797 to 1800, ed. G. D. H. Cole. London 1937.

Life and Adventures: *The Life and Adventures of Peter Porcupine, with a Full and Fair Account of All His Authoring Transactions; Being a Sure and Infallible Guide for All Enterprising Young Men Who Wish to Make a Fortune by Writing Pamphlets. By Peter Porcupine Himself. Philadelphia 1796.

Life of Jackson: Life of Andrew Jackson, President of the United States of America. Abridged and compiled by William Cobbett, M.P. for Oldham . . . London 1834.

Manchester Lectures: Cobbett's Manchester Lectures, in Support of His Fourteen Reform Propositions; Which Lectures Were Delivered in the Minor Theatre in That Town, on the Last Six Days of the Year 1831 . . . London 1832.

Martens's *Law of Nations: Summary of Law of Nations* . . . by Mr Martens . . . Translated from the French by William Cobbett. Philadelphia 1795.

Mercure Anglois: Le Mercure Anglois. Feb.–Apr. 1803. London. A French version of parts of the *Political Register.*

New-Year's Gift: *A New-Year's Gift to the Democrats; or, Observations on a Pamphlet Entitled 'A Vindication of Mr. Randolph's Resignation.' By Peter Porcupine. Philadelphia 1796.

Observations on Priestley: *Observations on the Emigration of Dr. Joseph Priestley, and on the Several Addresses Delivered to Him on His Arrival at New York. Anonymous. Philadelphia [1794].

Paper against Gold: †Paper against Gold and Glory against Prosperity. Or, An Account of the Rise, Progress, Extent and Present State of the Funds, and of the Paper-Money of Great Britain . . . *Brought Down to the End of the Year 1814.* London 1815.

Parliamentary Debates: Cobbett's Parliamentary Debates. Published by Cobbett 1804–12; thereafter by T. C. Hansard, from whom it took the name "Hansard."

Parliamentary History: Cobbett's Parliamentary History of England . . . Published by Cobbett 1804–12; thereafter by T. C. Hansard.

Political Censor: *The Political Censor, or Monthly Review of the Most Interesting Political Occurrences, Relative to the United States of America. By Peter Porcupine. Nine issues, Mar. 1796–Mar. 1797. Philadelphia.

Poor Man's Friend: Cobbett's Poor Man's Friend: or, Useful Information and Advice for the Working Classes; in a Series of Letters, Addressed to the Working Classes of Preston. London. First published in parts 1826–7; shortened and revised edition 1833.

Porcupine: The Porcupine. Daily paper, Oct. 30, 1800–Oct. 12, 1801. London. Continued as *The Porcupine, and Antigallican Monitor* Oct. 13–Dec. 31, 1801.

Porcupine's Gazette: Porcupine's Gazette. Daily, Mar. 4, 1797–Aug. 28, 1799. Philadelphia. Six weekly numbers, Sept. 6–Oct. 11, 1799 and two further pamphlet issues, Oct. 19 and 26, 1799. Bustleton. Final number, Jan. 1800. New York. Selections were reprinted in *Works.*

PR (Political Register): Cobbett's Weekly Political Register, Jan. 1802–June 1835, in 88 vols., with various name changes. Vol. 89, July–Sept. 1835, published by William Cobbett junior.

Prospect from the Congress-Gallery: *A Prospect from the Congress-Gallery, during the Session, Begun December 7, 1795 . . . By Peter Porcupine. Philadelphia 1796.

Protestant "Reformation": A History of the Protestant "Reformation," in England and Ireland; Showing How That Event Has Impoverished and Degraded the Main Body of the People in Those Countries . . . First published in parts, London 1824–6. A second part, listing abbeys etc. confiscated, published 1827.

Republican Judge: *The Republican Judge: or The American Liberty of the Press . . . By Peter Porcupine. London 1798. Revision of *Democratic Judge* for English consumption.

Roman History: Elements of the Roman History, in English and French, from the Foundation of Rome to the Battle of Actium . . . The English by William Cobbett; the French by J. H.

SOURCES

Sievrac. London 1828. *An Abridged History of the Emperors, in French and English*. By the same. London 1829.

Rural Rides: †*Rural Rides in the Counties of Surrey, Kent, Sussex, Hampshire, Wiltshire, Gloucestershire, Herefordshire, Worcestershire, Somersetshire, Oxfordshire, Berkshire, Essex, Suffolk, Norfolk, and Hertfordshire: With Economical and Political Observations Relating to Matters Applicable to, and Illustrated by the State of Those Counties Respectively.* London 1830. Quotations are from the Penguin edition of 1967.

Rush-Light: *The Rush-Light. Five numbers published in New York in 1800; a sixth, after Cobbett's return to London.

Scare-Crow: *The Scare-Crow; Being an Infamous Letter, Sent to Mr. John Oldden, Threatening Destruction to His House, and Violence to the Person of His Tenant, William Cobbett, with Remarks on the same by Peter Porcupine. Philadelphia 1796.

Selections: Selections from Cobbett's Political Works: Being a Complete Abridgment of the 100 Volumes Which Comprise the Writings of "Porcupine" and the "Weekly Political Register." With Notes, Historical and Explanatory. By John M. Cobbett and James P. Cobbett. 6 vols. London: Anne Cobbett [1835–7].

Sermons: Cobbett's Sermons . . . First issued in 12 monthly parts. London 1821–2.

Soldier's Friend: The Soldier's Friend: or, Considerations on the Late Pretended Augmentation of the Subsistence of the Private Soldiers. Anonymous. London 1792.

Spelling Book: A Spelling Book, with Appropriate Lessons in Reading, and with a Stepping-Stone to English Grammar. London 1831.

Spirit of Public Journals: Cobbett's Spirit of the Public Journals. Vol. 1 for 1804. London. Not continued.

State Trials: Cobbett's Complete Collection of State Trials . . . Published by Cobbett 1809–12; thereafter by T. B. Howell, from whom it derived the name *Howell's State Trials.*

Surplus Population: †*Surplus Population: And Poor-Law Bill. A Comedy, in Three Acts.* London [1835].

Tour in Scotland: †*Cobbett's Tour in Scotland: And in the Four Northern Counties of England: In the Autumn of the Year 1832.* London 1833.

Two-Penny Trash: Cobbett's Two-Penny Trash; or, Politics for the Poor. 2 vols. London 1831–2. First appeared in monthly parts July 1830–July 1832.

Woodlands: The Woodlands: or, A Treatise on the Preparation of the Ground for Planting; on the Planting; on the Cultivating; on the Pruning; on the Cutting Down of Forest Trees and Underwoods . . . London. First published in 7 numbers Dec. 1825–Mar. 1828.

Works: Porcupine's Works; Containing Various Writings and Selections, Exhibiting a Faithful Picture of the United States of America . . . from the End of the War, in 1793, to the Election of the President, in March 1801. 12 vols. London 1801.

Year's Residence: A Year's Residence in the United States of America. Treating of the Face of the Country, the Climate, the Soil . . . In three parts. New York 1818–19.

Cobbett biographies and bibliographies

In 1835, the year of Cobbett's death, three anonymous biographies were published which are chiefly of historical interest: *The Life of William Cobbett, Esq. Late M.P. for Oldham* published by John Duncombe, London, and, with a revised title page, by William Willis, Manchester; *The Life of William Cobbett, Dedicated to His Sons* published by F. J. Mason, London; and *Memoirs of Wm. Cobbett Esq., M.P. for Oldham, and the Celebrated Author of the Political Register* published by Alice Mann, Leeds.

Huish, Robert, *Memoirs of the Late William Cobbett, Esqr. M.P. for Oldham from Private and Confidential Sources*, 2 vols., London 1836.

Watson, John S., *Biographies of John Wilkes and William Cobbett*, Edinburgh 1870.

Smith, Edward, *William Cobbett: A Biography*, 2 vols., London 1878.

Carlyle, E. I., *William Cobbett: A Study of His Life as Shown in His Writings*, London 1904.

Melville, Lewis, *The Life and Letters of William Cobbett in England & America Based upon Hitherto Unpublished Family Papers*, 2 vols., London 1913.

Cole, G. D. H., *The Life of William Cobbett with a Chapter on "Rural Rides" by the Late F. E. Green*, London 1924.

Chesterton, G. K., *William Cobbett*, London [1926].

Reitzel, William (ed.), *The Autobiography of William Cobbett: The Progress of a Plough-Boy to a Seat in Parliament*, London 1933.

Bowen, Marjorie, *Peter Porcupine: A Study of William Cobbett, 1762–1835*, London 1935.

Clark, Mary E., *Peter Porcupine in America: The Career of William Cobbett, 1792–1800*, Philadelphia 1939.

Pemberton, W. Baring, *William Cobbett*, Penguin ed., 1949.

Osborne, John W., *William Cobbett: His Thought and His Times*. New Brunswick 1966.

Briggs, Asa, *William Cobbett*, London 1967.

Sambrook, James, *William Cobbett*, London and Boston 1973.

Pearl, M. L., *William Cobbett: A Bibliographical Account of His Life and Times*, London 1953.

Gaines, Pierce W., *William Cobbett and the United States 1792–1835: A Bibliography with Notes and Extracts*, Worcester, Mass. 1971.

Other secondary sources

Adams, Charles Francis (ed.), *Letters of John Adams Addressed to His Wife*, 2 vols., Boston 1841.

(ed.), *The Works of John Adams*, 10 vols., Boston 1850–6.

Adams, Henry, *History of the United States of America*, 9 vols., New York 1889–91.

The Formative Years, condensed and ed. Herbert Agar, 2 vols., London 1948.

Adams, L. P., *Agricultural Depression and Farm Relief in England 1813–1852*, new ed., London 1965.

Aldcroft, Derek H. and Peter Fearon, *British Economic Fluctuations 1790–1939*, London 1972.

Aldred, Guy A., *Richard Carlile, Agitator: His Life and Times*, London 1923.

Arnold, Matthew, "Future of Liberalism," *English Literature and Irish Politics*, ed. R. H. Soper, Ann Arbor, Mich. 1973.

Aspinall, Arthur, *Lord Brougham and the Whig Party*, Manchester 1927.

Politics and the Press c. 1780–1850, London 1949.

(ed.), *Mrs Jordan and Her Family*, London 1951.

(ed.), *The Correspondence of George, Prince of Wales 1770–1812*, 8 vols., London 1963–71.

Bamford, Samuel, *Passages in the Life of a Radical*, ed. Henry Dunckley, 2 vols., London 1893.

Barton, John, *An Inquiry into the Causes of the Progressive Depreciation of Agricultural Labour*, London 1820.

Bathurst papers: *Report on the Manuscripts of Earl Bathurst Preserved at Cirencester Park*, London 1923.

Baugh, Albert C., *A History of the English Language*, New York 1935.

Bentham, Jeremy, *The Works of Jeremy Bentham*, published under the superintendence of his executor, John Bowring, 11 vols., Edinburgh and London 1843.

Beveridge, Albert J., *The Life of John Marshall*, 4 vols., Boston and New York 1916.

Binger, Carl, *Revolutionary Doctor: Benjamin Rush, 1746–1813*, New York 1966.

Book of Wonders, The: Part the Second, London 1821.

Boswell's Life of Johnson, ed. A. Birrell, 6 vols., London 1903.

Bourke, Algernon (ed.), *Correspondence of Mr Joseph Jekyll with His Sister-in-Law Lady Gertrude Sloane Stanley*, London 1894.

Bourne, H. R. Fox, *English Newspapers: Chapters of the History of Journalism*, 2 vols., London 1887.

Boyce, George, James Curran and Pauline Wingate (eds.), *Newspaper History from the Seventeenth Century to the Present Day*, London 1958.

Briggs, Asa, "Thomas Attwood and the Economic Background of the Birmingham Political Union," *Cambridge Historical Journal* IX (1948), 190.

"The Background of the Parliamentary Reform Movement in Three English Cities," *Cambridge Historical Journal* X (1952), 293.

The Age of Improvement 1783–1867, 3rd imp., London 1962.

Bright, J. F., *A History of England . . . Period III . . . 1689–1837*, 8th ed., London 1900.

Brock, Michael, *The Great Reform Act*, London 1973.

Brooks, Van Wyck, *The World of Washington Irving*, New York 1944.

Brougham, Henry, *Historical Sketches of Statesmen Who Flourished in the Time of George III*, 3 vols., London and Glasgow n.d.

Speeches of Henry, Lord Brougham, 4 vols., Edinburgh 1838.

The Life and Times of Henry Lord Brougham Written by Himself, 2nd ed., 3 vols., London 1871.

Broughton, Lord, *Recollections of a Long Life . . .* ed. his daughter, Lady Dorchester, 4 vols., London 1910 repr.

Brown, Esther, *The French Revolution and the American Man of Letters*, New York 1951.

Brown, Ford K., *Fathers of the Victorians*, Cambridge 1961.

Brown, Ralph Adams, *The Presidency of John Adams*, Lawrence, Kans. 1975.

Bryant, Arthur, *Years of Victory 1802–1812*, London 1944.

The Age of Elegance 1812–1822, London 1950.

Buchanan, Roberdeau, *The Life of the Hon. Thomas McKean, LL.D.*, Lancaster, Pa. 1890.

Buckle, Henry Thomas, *History of Civilization in England*, new ed., 3 vols., Toronto 1878.

Bulwer, Henry Lytton, *Historical Characters*, 2 vols., London 1868.

Burke, Edmund, *Reflections on the Revolution in France . . .* London 1795.

Butler, J. R. M., *The Passing of the Great Reform Bill*, London 1914.

Butterfield, Lyman H. (ed.), *The Letters of Benjamin Rush*, 2 vols., Princeton, N.J. 1951.

Carroll, John A. and Mary W. Ashworth, *George Washington*, New York 1957.

Cartwright, F. D. (ed.), *The Life and Correspondence of Major Cartwright*, 2 vols., London 1826.

Clapham, John H., *An Economic History of Modern Britain*, vol. 1: *The Early Railway Age 1820—1850*, Cambridge 1926.

Clive, John, *Scottish Reviewers: The "Edinburgh Review" 1802—1815*, London 1957.

Cochrane, Thomas, *The Autobiography of a Seaman by Thomas, Tenth Earl of Dundonald*, 2 vols., London 1860.

Colchester, Lord (ed.), *The Diary and Correspondence of Charles Abbot, Lord Colchester*, 3 vols., London 1861.

Coleridge, Samuel Taylor, *The Collected Works of Samuel Taylor Coleridge*, general ed. Kathleen Coburn, London and Princeton, N.J. 1969–

Commager, H. S., *The Empire of Reason*, New York 1977.

Condé, Alexander de, *The Quasi-War: The Politics and Diplomacy of the Undeclared War with France 1797—1801*, New York 1966.

Conway, Moncure D., *The Life of Thomas Paine . . .* ed. Hypatia Bradlaugh Bonner, London 1909.

Cookson, J. E., *Lord Liverpool's Administration: The Crucial Years 1815—1822*, Edinburgh 1958.

Cooper, Duff, *Talleyrand*, London 1952 repr.

Corner, George W. (ed.), *The Autobiography of Benjamin Rush . . .* Princeton, N.J. 1948.

Coupland, R., *Wilberforce: A Narrative*, Oxford 1923.

Creevey Papers . . . , The, ed. Sir Herbert Maxwell, London 1923.

Croker Papers, The: The Correspondence and Diaries of the Late Honourable John Wilson Croker, LL.D., F.R.S. . . . ed. Louis J. Jennings, 2nd ed. rev., 3 vols., London 1885.

Crosby, Travis L., *English Farmers and the Politics of Protection 1815–1892*, Hassocks 1977.

Darvall, Frank O., *Popular Disturbances and Public Order in Regency England* . . . London 1934.

Davis, H. W. C., *The Age of Grey and Peel*, Oxford 1967 repr.

Defoe, Daniel, *A Tour through the Whole Island of Great Britain*, 2 vols., Everyman ed.

Derry, Warren, *Dr Parr: A Portrait of the Whig Dr Johnson*, Oxford 1966.

Dickinson, G. Lowes, *The Development of Parliament during the Nineteenth Century*, London 1895.

Dobson, William, *History of the Parliamentary Representation of Preston* . . . Preston 1856.

Dowell, Stephen, *A History of Taxation and Taxes in England from the Earliest Times to the Present Day*, 3rd ed., 4 vols., London 1965.

Dropmore papers: *Report on the Manuscripts of J. B. Fortescue, Esq. Preserved at Dropmore*, 10 vols., London 1892–1927.

Elliot, Hugh S. R. (ed.), *The Letters of John Stuart Mill*, 2 vols., London 1910.

Elwes, H. J. and Henry A. Elwes, *Trees of Great Britain and Ireland*, Edinburgh 1912.

Fay, C. R., *Great Britain from Adam Smith to the Present Day* . . . 2nd ed., London 1929.

Huskisson and His Age, London 1951.

Fearon, Henry B., *Sketches of America* . . . 2nd ed., London 1818.

Feiling, Keith, *Sketches in Nineteenth Century Biography*, London 1930.

Fetter, Frank Whitson, *Development of British Monetary Orthodoxy*, Cambridge, Mass. 1965.

Fischer, David H., *The Revolution of American Conservatism*, New York 1962.

Fitzpatrick, John C. (ed.), *The Writings of George Washington from the Original Manuscript Sources 1745–1799*, 39 vols., Washington 1931–44.

Flexner, James Thomas, *Doctors on Horseback*, New York 1937.

States Dyckman: American Loyalist, Boston 1980.

Ford, W. C. (ed.), *Writings of John Quincy Adams*, 7 vols., New York 1913–17.

(ed.), *Statesman and Friend: Correspondence of John Adams and Benjamin Waterhouse, 1784–1822*, Boston 1927.

Freneau, Philip, "The Royal Cockneys in America," *The Poems of Philip Freneau*, ed. F. L. Pattee (3 vols., New York 1963) III: 185.

Furber, Holden, *Henry Dundas First Viscount Melville 1742–1811* . . . London 1931.

Furneaux, Robin, *William Wilberforce*, London 1974.

Gash, Norman, *Mr. Secretary Peel: The Life of Sir Robert Peel to 1830*, London 1961.

Aristocracy and People: Britain 1815–1865, London 1979.

Gayer, Arthur D., W. W. Rostow and A. J. Schwartz, *The Growth and Fluctuation of the British Economy*, 2 vols., Oxford 1953.

George, M. Dorothy, *English Political Caricature 1793–1832: A Study of Opinion and Propaganda*, Oxford 1959.

Gilfillan, George, *A Second Gallery of Literary Portraits*, Edinburgh 1850.

Gillen, Mollie, *Assassination of the Prime Minister: The Shocking Death of Spencer Perceval*, London 1972.

Glover, Richard, *Britain at Bay: Defence against Bonaparte 1803–14*, London 1973.

Gordon, Barry, *Political Economy in Parliament 1819–1823*, London 1976.

Economic Doctrine and Tory Liberalism 1824–1830, London 1979.

Grant, James, *Recollections of the House of Commons from the Year 1830 to the Close of 1835* . . . 2nd ed., London 1836.

Granville Leveson-Gower, Lord (1st Earl Granville), *Private Correspondence 1781 to 1821*, ed. Countess Granville, 2 vols., London 1916.

Gray, Denis, *Spencer Perceval: The Evangelical Prime Minister 1762–1812*, Manchester 1963.

Greville, Charles C. F., *The Greville Memoirs: A Journal of the Reigns of King George IV* . . . ed. Henry Reeve, new ed., 8 vols., London 1888.
Grey, Lord, *The Correspondence of the Late Earl Grey with H.M. King William IV*, ed. Henry, Earl Grey, 1867.
Griffin, P. C., *A Catalogue of the Washington Collection in the Boston Atheneum*, Boston 1897.
Griggs, Earl Leslie (ed.), *Collected Letters of Samuel Taylor Coleridge*, 6 vols., Oxford 1956–71.
Gronow, R. H., *Recollections and Anecdotes: Being a Second Series of Reminiscences* . . . London 1863.
Halévy, Elie, *A History of the English People in the Nineteenth Century*, 6 vols., London 1924–47.
Hammond, J. L. and B. Hammond, *The Village Labourer*, new ed., London 1920.
Hardcastle, Mrs. (ed.), *Life of John, Lord Campbell, Lord High Chancellor of Great Britain*, 2 vols., London 1881.
Hawes, Frances, *Henry Brougham*, New York n.d.
Hawke, David F., *Benjamin Rush: Revolutionary Gadfly*, Indianapolis and New York 1973.
Hazen, Charles Downer, *Contemporary American Opinion of the French Revolution*, Baltimore, Md. 1897.
Hazlitt, William, *The Spirit of the Age: or Contemporary Portraits*, 2nd ed., London 1835.
Himes, Norman E. (ed.), *Illustrations and Proofs of the Principle of Population* by Francis Place, London 1930.
Hobsbawm, Eric J., *Labouring Men: Studies in the History of Labour*, 6th imp., London 1969.
Hobsbawm, Eric J. and George Rudé, *Captain Swing*, Penguin ed., 1973.
Hobson, Bulmer (ed.), *The Letters of Wolfe Tone* (1821), Dublin 1920.
Holland, Lord, *Memoirs of the Whig Party during My Time* by Henry Richard Lord Holland, ed. his son Henry Edward Lord Holland, 2 vols., London 1852–4.
Further Memoirs of the Whig Party, 1807–1821 . . . ed. Lord Stavordale, London 1905.
Holland House Diaries 1831–1840, The, ed. A. D. Kriegel, London 1977.
Hollis, Patricia, *The Pauper Press: A Study in Working-Class Radicalism in the 1830s*, London 1970.
Holmes, Richard, *Shelley: The Pursuit*, New York 1975.
Hoskins, W. G., *The Age of Plunder: King Henry's England 1500–1547*, London 1976.
Huch, Ronald K., *The Radical Lord Radnor: The Public Life of Viscount Folkestone, Third Earl of Radnor*, Minneapolis, Minn. 1977.
Hunt, Henry, *Memoirs of Henry Hunt Esq. Written by Himself in His Majesty's Jail at Ilchester*, 3 vols., London 1820.
Hunt, Leigh, *The Autobiography of Leigh Hunt*, ed. J. E. Morpurgo, London 1959.
Huntia: A Yearbook of Botanical and Horticultural Bibliography, vol. II, Pittsburgh, Pa. 1965.
Inaugural Addresses of the Presidents of the United States, House Doc. 540, 82nd Congress, Second Session.
Jephson, Henry, *The Platform: Its Rise and Progress*, 2 vols., London 1892.
Johnson, David, *Regency Revolution: The Case of Arthur Thistlewood*, Salisbury 1974.
Jones, Howard Mumford, *America and French Culture 1750–1848*, Chapel Hill, N.C. 1927.
Kent, C. B. Roylance, *The English Radicals: An Historical Sketch*, London 1899.
Keynes, John Maynard, *A Tract on Monetary Reform*, London 1923.
Knowles, L. C. A., *The Industrial and Commercial Revolutions in Great Britain during the Nineteenth Century*, London 1966 repr.
Koch, Adrienne, *Adams and Jefferson: "Posterity Must Judge"*, Chicago 1963.
Konkle, Burton Alva, *Joseph Hopkinson 1770–1842*, Philadelphia 1931.
Le Marchant, Denis, *Memoir of John Charles Viscount Althorp Third Earl Spencer*, London 1876.

Lean, E. Tangye, *The Napoleonists*, London 1970.

Lloyd, Christopher, *Lord Cochrane* . . . London 1947.

Loudon, J. C., *Arboretum et Fructicetum Britannicum*, 8 vols., London 1830.

Lovett, William, *The Life and Struggles of William Lovett* . . . with a preface by R. H. Tawney, London 1967.

McRee, Griffith J., *Life and Correspondence of James Iredell* . . . 2 vols. in 1, New York 1949.

Marlow, Joyce, *The Peterloo Massacre*, London 1969.

Marshall, John, *The Life of George Washington*, 5 vols., Fredericksburg, Va. 1926.

Martin, J. A., *Martin's Bench and Bar of Philadelphia*, Philadelphia 1883.

Martineau, Harriet, *The History of England during the Thirty Years' Peace 1816–1846*, 3 vols., London 1849.

Marx, Karl and Frederick Engels, *Selected Works*, 3 vols., Moscow 1969.

Mathieson, William Law, *England in Transition 1789–1832: A Study in Movements*, London 1920.

Miller, John C., *Crisis in Freedom*, Boston 1951.

Alexander Hamilton: Portrait in Paradox, New York 1959.

The Federalist Era 1789–1801, New York 1960.

Mineka, Francis E. (ed.), *The Earlier Letters of John Stuart Mill 1812–1848*, Toronto and London 1963.

Mingay, G. E., *Enclosure and the Small Farmer in the Age of the Industrial Revolution*, London 1976 repr.

Mitchell, Austin, *The Whigs in Opposition*, Oxford 1967.

Mitchell, B. R. and Phyllis Deane, *Abstract of British Historical Statistics*, Cambridge 1971.

Mitchell, Stewart (ed.), *New Letters of Abigail Adams*, Boston 1947.

Mitford, Mary Russell, *Recollections of a Literary Life*, London 1859.

Moore, Thomas, *Memoirs of the Life of the Rt. Hon. Richard Brinsley Sheridan*, 4th ed., 2 vols., London 1826.

Memoirs, Journals and Correspondence of Thomas Moore, ed. Lord John Russell, 8 vols., London 1856.

The Life, Letters and Journals of Lord Byron, London 1860.

Morison, Samuel Eliot, *The Oxford History of the American People*, 2 vols., New York 1972.

Morley, Edith J. (ed.), *Henry Crabb Robinson on Books and Their Writers*, 3 vols., London 1938.

Morris, Richard B., *Encyclopedia of American History*, New York 1953.

Namier, Lewis, *The Structure of Politics at the Accession of George III*, 2nd ed., London 1961.

Nevins, Allan and Frank Weitenkampf, *A Century of Political Cartoons: Caricature in the United States from 1800 to 1900*, New York 1944.

New, Chester, *The Life of Henry Brougham to 1830*, Oxford 1961.

O'Connell, John, *Recollections and Experiences during a Parliamentary Career from 1833 to 1848*, 2 vols., London 1849.

O'Connell, Maurice R. (ed.), *The Correspondence of Daniel O'Connell*, Dublin.

Oldfield, Thomas, *An Entire and Complete History, Political and Personal, of the Boroughs of Great Britain*, 3 vols., London 1792.

Paine, Thomas, *The Political Works of Thomas Paine Complete in One Volume* . . . London [1844].

Rights of Man, Penguin ed., 1976.

Pares, Richard, *King George III and the Politicians*, Oxford 1953.

The Historian's Business and Other Essays, Oxford 1961.

Patterson, M. W., *Sir Francis Burdett and His Times (1770–1844)*, 2 vols., London 1931.

Peacock, Thomas Love, *Thomas Love Peacock Letters to Edward Hookham and Percy B. Shelley* . . . ed. Richard Garrett, Boston 1910.

Perkins, Bradford, *The First Rapprochement: England and the United States 1795–1805*, Philadelphia 1955.

Peterson, Svend, *A Statistical History of American Presidential Elections*, New York 1963.

Pickering, Octavius and C. W. Upham, *Life of Timothy Pickering*, 4 vols., Boston 1867–73.

Pitkin, Timothy, *A Political and Civil History of the United States of America* . . . 2 vols., New Haven, Conn. 1828.

Plamenatz, John, *The English Utilitarians*, rev. ed., Oxford 1958.

Plummer, Charles (ed.), *The Governance of England* . . . by Sir John Fortescue . . . Oxford 1926.

Plunket, David, *The Life, Letters, and Speeches of Lord Plunket*, 2 vols., London 1867.

Poetry of the Anti-Jacobin . . . with explanatory notes by Charles Edmonds, 2nd ed., London 1854.

Political Letters and Pamphlets Published for the Avowed Purpose of Trying with the Government the Question of Law . . . by William Carpenter, London 1830–1.

Porritt, Edward, *The Unreformed House of Commons: Parliamentary Representation before 1832*, 2 vols., New York 1903; repr. 1963.

Post, John D., *The Last Great Subsistence Crisis in the Western World*, Baltimore and London 1977.

Quennell, Peter (ed.), *The Private Letters of Princess Lieven to Prince Metternich 1820–1826*, London n.d.

Raikes, Thomas, *A Portion of the Journal Kept by Thomas Raikes, Esq. from 1831 to 1847*, 2nd ed., 4 vols., London 1856.

Reid, T. Wemyss (ed.), *The Life, Letters and Friendships of Richard Monckton Milnes, First Lord Houghton*, 2 vols., New York 1891.

Rhodes, R. Compton, *Harlequin Sheridan: The Man and the Legend*, Oxford 1933.

Ricardo, David, *Letters of David Ricardo to Thomas Robert Malthus 1810–1823*, ed. James Bonar, Oxford 1887.

Letters of David Ricardo to Hutches Trower and Others, 1811–1823, ed. James Bonar and J. H. Hollander, Oxford 1899.

The Works and Correspondence of David Ricardo, ed. Piero Straffa, 11 vols., Cambridge 1951–73.

Roberts, Michael, *The Whig Party 1807–1812*, 2nd ed., London 1865.

Robertson, Charles Grant, *England under the Hanoverians*, London 1953 repr.

Robinson, Henry Crabb, *Diary, Reminiscences, and Correspondence of Henry Crabb Robinson*, ed. Thomas Sadler, 2 vols., London 1872.

Rogers, Samuel, *Recollections of the Table-Talk of Samuel Rogers* . . . ed. Morchard Bishop, London 1952.

Romilly, Samuel, *Memoirs of the Life of Sir Samuel Romilly*, ed. his sons, 3rd ed., 3 vols., London 1840.

Rose, George, *The Diaries and Correspondence of the Right Hon. George Rose*, ed. L. V. Harcourt, 2 vols., London 1860.

Rosebery, Lord, *Pitt*, London 1902 repr.

Rowe, G. S., *Thomas McKean: The Shaping of an American Republicanism*, Boulder, Colo. 1978.

Rudé, George (ed.), *The Eighteenth Century*, London 1965.

Ruskin, John, *The Works of John Ruskin*, ed. E. T. Cook and Alexander Wedderburn, vol. xxxvii, London 1909.

Rutt, J. T., *Life and Correspondence of Joseph Priestley*, 2 vols., London 1831–2.

Salaman, R. N., *The History and Social Influence of the Potato*, Cambridge 1949.

Salvemini, Gaetano, *The French Revolution 1788–1792*, London 1954.

Scott, James Brown (ed.), *The Controversy over Neutral Rights between the United States and France 1797–1800*, New York 1917.

Sheridan, Richard Brinsley, *The Letters*, ed. Cecil Price, 3 vols., Oxford 1960.

Shiel, Richard L., *Sketches of the Irish Bar,* 2 vols. in 1, Chicago 1882.

Simond, Louis, *An American in Regency England* . . . ed. Christopher Hibbert, London 1968.

Smart, William, *Economic Annals of the Nineteenth Century,* 2 vols. New York 1964 repr.

Smith, David B. (ed.), *Letters of Admiral of the Fleet the Earl of St. Vincent,* 2 vols., London 1927.

Smith, E. P., *Whig Principles and Party Politics: Earl Fitzwilliam and the Whig Party,* Manchester 1975.

Smith, George Gregory, *The Dramatic Works of the Right Honourable Richard Brinsley Sheridan with a Memoir of His Life* by G.G.S., London 1872.

Smith, Henry Stooks, *The Parliaments of England from 1715 to 1847,* ed. F. W. S. Craig, 2nd ed., Chichester 1973.

Smith, Sydney, *The Letters of Peter Plymley* . . . by Sydney Smith with an introduction by G. C. Heseltine, London 1929.

Somerville, Alexander, *The Whistler at the Plough,* London 1852.

Southey, Robert, *Letters from England,* ed. Jack Simmons, London 1951.

Stephen Leslie, *Swift,* London 1903 repr.

Stevenson, John, *Popular Disturbances in England 1700–1870,* London 1979.

Swinnerton, Frank, *A Galaxy of Fathers,* London 1966.

Taylor, Arthur J. (ed.), *The Standard of Living in Britain in the Industrial Revolution,* London 1975.

Thomas, Malcolm I. and Peter Holt, *Threats of Revolution in Britain 1789–1848,* London 1977.

Thomas, William, *The Philosophic Radicals: Nine Studies in Theory and Practice 1817–1821,* Oxford 1979.

Thompson, E. P., *The Making of the English Working Class,* Penguin ed., 1975.

Thompson, F. M. L., *English Landed Society in the Nineteenth Century,* London, 1971 repr.

Thorburn, Grant, *Forty Years' Residence in America,* London 1834.

Times, The, The History of "The Times": "The Thunderer" in the Making 1785–1841, London 1935.

Tinkcom, Harry M., *The Republicans and Federalists in Pennsylvania 1790–1801,* Harrisburg, Pa. 1950.

Toynbee, Arnold, *The Industrial Revolution of the Eighteenth Century in England,* new ed., London 1908.

Trevelyan, George Macaulay, *Lord Grey of the Reform Bill,* London 1920.

History of England, London 1926.

Trevelyan, George Otto, *The Life and Letters of Lord Macaulay,* London, ed. 1959.

Trial of 1831: A Full and Accurate Report of the Trial of William Cobbett, Esq. (before Lord Tenterden and a Special Jury) on Thursday, July 7, 1831 . . . 5th ed., London 1832.

Twiss, Horace, *The Public and Private Life of Lord Chancellor Eldon,* 3 vols., London 1844.

Veitch, G. S., *The Genesis of Parliamentary Reform,* London 1965 repr.

Wadsworth, A. P., *Newspaper Circulations, 1800–1954, Trans. Manchester Statistical Society,* 1955.

Wallas, Graham, *The Life of Francis Place,* rev. ed., London 1918.

Walmsley, Robert, *Peterloo: The Case Reopened,* Manchester 1969.

Walpole, Spencer, *A History of England from the Conclusion of the Great War in 1815,* 6 vols., London 1890.

Ward, J. T., *Sir James Graham,* London 1967.

Warfel, Harry R., *Noah Webster: Schoolmaster to America,* New York 1936.

(ed.), *Letters of Noah Webster,* New York 1953.

Warren, Charles, *Jacobin and Junto* . . . Cambridge 1931.

Watson, Steven J., *The Reign of George III 1760–1815,* Oxford 1960.

Welch, Richard E., Jr., *Theodore Sedgwick, Federalist: A Political Portrait,* Middletown, Conn. 1965.

Wharton, Francis (ed.), *State Trials of the United States during the Administrations of Washington and Adams*, Philadelphia 1849.

Wickwar, William H., *The Struggle for the Freedom of the Press 1819–1832*, London 1928.

Wiener, Joel H., *The War of the Unstamped*, Ithaca, N.Y. and London 1969.

Wilberforce, R. I. and Samuel Wilberforce, *The Life of William Wilberforce*, 5 vols., London 1838.

Williams, Orlo, *Life and Letters of John Rickman*, London 1911.

Winch, Donald (ed.), James Mill, *Selected Economic Writings*, Edinburgh 1966.

Windham, William, *The Diary of the Right Hon. William Windham 1784 to 1810*, ed. Mrs. Henry Baring, London 1866.

Windham Papers, The: Life and Correspondence of the Right Honourable William Windham 1750–1810, ed. Archibald Primrose, 2 vols., London 1913.

Woodward, E. L., *The Age of Reform 1815–1870*, Oxford 1939 repr.

Yonge, C. D., *Life and Administration of Robert Banks Jenkinson, 2d Earl of Liverpool*, 3 vols., London 1868.

Ziegler, Philip, *A Life of Henry Addington, First Viscount Sidmouth*, London 1965.

Index

Volume 1 includes pp. i–xvii and 1–310; volume 2, pp. 311–633. *ER =Edinburgh Review;* HC = House of Commons; M.P. = Member of Parliament; *PR =Cobbett's Weekly Political Register.*

Abbot, Charles (later 1st Baron Colchester), 134, 224, 226–7, 229, 237, 301n8
Abbott, Charles (later Lord Tenterden), 428, 477–81
Abercrombie, James, 67, 264n75
Adam, William, 130, 218, 220, 221, 296n62, 297n70
Adams, Abigail, 79, 82, 85, 91
Adams, Charles, 246
Adams, Henry Brooks, 105, 320
Adams, John: on U.S. government, 39; on terrorism of 1793, 46; presidential candidate, 73–4, 88, 267n64; character, 77; as president, 77–81, 87–9, 266n54; C's views, 87–9, 106, 266–7nn62, 64 & 65, 272n19; mentioned, 100, 268n38
Adams, John Quincy, 74, 85, 92, 349, 567n152
Adams, Samuel, 44
Addington, Henry (later Lord Sidmouth): as prime minister, 118–19, 126, 128, 131, 132, 137–42, 274n8, 275n20; stand against Melville, 134, 145; harsh home secretary, 342, 353, 380, 391, 565n130, 567nn148 & 149, 572n68; retires, 463; appearance, 141; mentioned, 133, 155, 174, 208, 223, 348, 351, 368, 369–70
Addison, Joseph, 18, 72, 249
Adet, Pierre-Auguste, 73–5, 94
Akerman, John Y., 589n37
Alexander the Great, 333
Alien and Sedition Acts of 1798 (U.S.), 84, 102, 266n34, 373
Aliva, René, 589n40
All the Talents, ministry of, 135, 137, 138, 145, 155, 182, 194, 465, 558n48
Althorp, Lord, 425, 506, 508, 513, 514, 539, 610nn109–10
Ambigu, L', 125, 274n2

American Monthly Review, 57
American Slave Trade by Jesse Torrey, 592–3n104
Ames, Fisher, 64
Amiens, peace of, 119–21, 123–6, 137, 142, 227
Amity and Commerce, French–American treaty of, 43, 73, 80, 95
André, Major John, 577n27
Anti-Gallican Monitor, 298n25
Anti-Jacobin; or, Weekly Examiner, 113, 235, 264 motto
Anti-Jacobin Review and Magazine, 113, 124
"Anti-Scoundrel," 230–1
Appeal to the Public and a Farewell Address to the Army, An, by Brevet Major Hogan, 215–16, 296n49
Arbuthnot, John, 56
Archambault, Monsieur, 355
Arden, Lord, 208, 210, 221
Argus, 147
aristocracy, *see* monarchy and aristocracy
army, standing, 345, 411, 419, 571n45
Arnold, Matthew, 441, 446, 590n68
Ashley, Lord (later Lord Shaftesbury), 511
Ashley, John, 107, 270n81
Association of Friends of Radical Reform, 489–90
Astor, John Jacob, 355
Attwood, Mathias, 562n68, 606n51
Attwood, Thomas, 490–1, 501–2, 504, 606n51, 610nn109–13, 611n116, 613n3
Auckland, Lord, 41, 147, 279n66
Aurora: defends violence of French revolution, 58; attacks C, 70, 95, 268n15; publishes Adet, 73; on Washington, 77; publishes Paine, 78; on Adams, 79; mentioned, 72, 91, 267n1, 268n15, 269n46
Austen, Jane, 12

Carlyle, Thomas, 446

Caroline of Brunswick (later Queen Caroline): "delicate investigation" (1806), 399; in Europe (1814–20), 399–400; charged with adultery, 402; charges dropped, 406, but innocence not established, 580n79; excluded from coronation, 407, 581n106; dies, 407, 581n107; character, 399, 579–80nn72 & 81. C offered release from prison for silence, 557n31; induces publication of "The Book" (1813), 399; advises her (1820), 402–7; writes her letter to king, 403–4; rededicates *English Grammar*, 582n113; attends her court, 408, 480, 582n114; later says vindictive feeling played part in conduct, 580n86. Mentioned, 580n87, 581nn97, 101–3 & 110, 582n112

Carpenter, William, 450, 488–90, 531, 605nn40 & 41, 606n49

Cartwright, John: keeps reform cause alive (1797–1806), 192–3; condemns Perceval, 294n1; founds Hampden clubs, 344; favors universal suffrage, 345, 563n91; approves of C's flight to America, 357; contests Westminster seat (1818), 364; breaks with Burdett, 366, 572n59; urges C to return to England, 370; cut by C, 388; fined over protest against Peterloo massacre, 380; dies, ending *Black Dwarf*, 483; mentioned, 209, 326, 566n140, 571n40

Cashman, John, 566n136

Castle, John, 367, 369–70, 566nn131 & 132

Castlereagh, Lord: arranges sale of parliamentary seats, 223–5; fights duel with Canning, 236; deserts catholic emancipation and leads ministerial party in HC, 332; makes secret alliance with Austria and France, 560n32; condemned by Shelley over Peterloo, 381; leads attacks on Queen Caroline in HC, 402; says C aspires to high office, 452; takes own life, 463–4; C's views, 332, 369–70, 452, 595n139, 615n34; mentioned, 241, 360, 368, 372, 391, 567n145, 584n27

Catholic Association, 449, 466–7

catholic emancipation: opposition of George III, 138, 211, 465; issue at Preston election (1820), 461; history of legislation, 464–72; C's views, 465–72; catholic disqualifications at issue, 465; allowance to catholic priests, 467, 598n46; C's defense of catholics, 211, 471–2, 599n63

"catholic rent," 466, 469

Cato Street conspiracy, 393, 578n57

Cervantes Saavedra, Miguel de, 18, 249

Chadwick, Edwin, 512

Chalmers, George, 591n85

Champion and Weekly Herald, 534

Charles X, 473

Charlotte, Queen, 114

Charlotte, Princess, 343, 399, 580n81

chartists, 531, 619n3

Chatham, Lord (1708–1778), 573n73

Chatham, Lord (1756–1835), 236, 300n62

Chesapeake (U.S. frigate), 319

cholera epidemic, 611n118

Chopstick Festival, 503

Christie, Gabriel, 64

Churchill, Charles, 18

church of England: Queen Caroline's name excluded from liturgy, 401; C urges reform, 524–5, but resolves to stick with church, 544–9, objecting only to its temporalities, 204–5, 548; advocates sale of church property, 419, 586n69; *see also* clergy

church of Ireland: C proposes to remove tithes, 524

Church Reformers' Magazine, 608n88

Cintra convention, 212–15, 299n32, 358

civil list, 150

Clancarty, Lord, 223–4

Chanricarde, Lord, 174

Clarence, Duke of, *see* William IV

Clarke, Mary Anne, 217–20, 296nn55–60, 555n3

Clarke, Samuel, 415

classical languages, 538–9

Claude Lorrain, 343

Clavering, General, 296n57

Cleary, Thomas, 363, 364–6, 427–8, 572n54

Cleave, John, 488–90, 531, 606n49

Clement, William, 569n27, 587n5

clergy: sale of church livings, 143, 223; worldly conduct, 204, 446, 548; catholic emancipation, 206; nonresidency, 208, 548; wickedness, 294n90; mentioned, 202, 553

Clifford, Henry, 236, 272n28, 275n19, 301n7

Clifton, Lord, 417

Cloncurry, Lord, 458

Cobb, Nathan, 376

Cobbett, Anne (1795–1877; C's eldest child): returns to England (1800), 108; acts as C's amanuensis, 159, 403; attends school, 280–1n7; accompanies C on leaving Newgate, 328–9; during Coventry election, 393–7; during bankruptcy proceedings, 398; viewing queen's arrival in London (1820), 401; thinks C should be queen's prime minister, 408; is ill

Grey, Lord Charles (*cont.*)
  doubts nation's ability to repay debt,
  583–4n23; becomes prime minister
  (1831), 464, 473, 495; promises reform and to put down disorders with
  severity, 473–4; C calls as witness in
  1831 trial, 478; puts reform through
  parliament, 495–501; C's views, 486,
  604n22; mentioned, 210, 241, 450,
  498
gridiron: C offers to be roasted if financial
  system does not break down, 365;
  adds to masthead of *PR*, 413, 424;
  denies condition fulfilled, 421, 424,
  586nn72 & 85
  Feast of the Gridiron, 413, 423–5,
  587n88
Grinnell, Captain, 37
Grimshaw, Nicholas, 462
Grote, George, 502–3
Gutsell, James, 523, 524, 589n37, 600n85

habeas corpus suspended in England, 84,
  113, 353, 357, 369, 370, 402; in Ire-
  land, 128, 511
Hall, Charles, 202, 552
Hall, Lieutenant John, 30
Hallett, William, 298n26, 563n87
Hamilton, Alexander, 39–41, 65, 83, 87,
  88, 107
Hamilton, Lord Archibald, 224
Hamlin, Philip, 223–4, 233, 236
Hammond, George, 114, 271n6, 326
Hampden clubs, 344, 351, 363, 563n86
Hannibal, 333
Hansard, *see* Cobbett, William: published
  writings: *Parliamentary Debates*
Hansard, T. C., 171, 235, 244, 253–4,
  304nn65 & 67
Harding, Edward, 272n16, 283n85
Hardwicke, Earl, 128–30
Hardy, Thomas, 252
Hare, James, 119, 141
Harper, Robert G., 104–6, 269nn57 & 64
harvests: *1794*, 53; *1793–1800*, 112; *1804*,
  194; *1809–12*, 561n46; *1813–15*, 342,
  410; *1816*, 346, 582n9; *1829–30*, 473;
  conflicting reports, 562n64; *see also*
  little ice age
Harvey, D. W., 529, 604n22, 613n3
Haswell, Anthony, 262n21
Hawkesbury, Lord, *see* Liverpool, Lord
Hay and Turner, 398
Hayes [or Heyes], John, 576n11
Hazlitt, William, 2, 298n24, 311, 446, 553,
  585n64
Heathcote, Sir Gilbert, 560n32
Heine, Heinrich, 446
Henry, Patrick, 268n38
Heriot, John, 118

Hetherington, Henry, 488, 531, 605nn40
  & 41
Hewlings, Mr., 182
Hill, Rowland, 256n18
Hinxman, John, 575n104
Hippisley, Sir John, 339, 561n39
"History of the Last Hundred Days of
  English Freedom, A," 361
Hobhouse, John Cam (later Lord
  Broughton): contests Westminster
  (1819), 366; addresses meeting on
  Peterloo and is sent to Newgate, 380; a
  sham reformer, 486; threatens C at
  Crown and Anchor dinner (1827),
  486–7; involved in Greek loan scan-
  dal, 604n23; mentioned, 458, 495,
  601n99, 603n17
Hogan, Brevet Major, 215–16
Holbach, Baron d', see *Ecce Homo*
Holland, Lady, 191
Holland, Lord, 2, 301n1, 486, 579n68,
  604n22
Holland, Mr., 14–15, 66
Hone, William, 367, 381–4, 483, 567n150,
  572n63, 581n98, 593n116
Honeywood, W. P., 417
Hood, Sir Samuel, 179, 181–2
Hopkinson, Joseph, 103
Horace, 18
Horace in London by James and Horace
  Smith, 447
Horner, Francis, 227, 314, 594–5n133
Horse-Hoeing Husbandry by Jethro Tull,
  438
Horsley, Bishop, 176, 225
Houston, George, 547–8
Howe, Lord, 68
Howell, Thomas Bayly, 170, 254, 300n80,
  304n66
Howell's State Trials, see Cobbett, William:
  published writings: *State Trials*
Hughan, Thomas, 171, 283n83
Hulme, Thomas, 371, 569n27
Hume, David, 200, 291n57
Hume, Joseph, 422–3, 486, 498, 595n143,
  604n23, 613n3
Hunt, Henry: meets C, 288n11; occupies
  obscure role until 1816, 192–3, 344;
  views on Cobbetts, 162–3, 281n35;
  visits C in Newgate, 326; attends Spa
  Fields meetings, 349–50; supports C
  on flight to America, 357; violent
  style, 361, 570n33; appeals for funds
  to defend participants in Pentrich
  rising, 363; contests Westminster
  (1818) and is confronted with C's
  letter, 364–6, 571–2nn51–4; urges C
  to return to England, 370; principal
  speaker at Peterloo, is arrested, returns to London as hero, 379–81, 483;
  chairs dinner for C (1819), 386–7;

C's old letter about Hunt, 365; heals breach with Burdett, 483, 572n55; condemns Wilberforce, 573n78; blames Queen Caroline for decline of royalty in public esteem, 581n103; allies himself with Bentham and philosophical radicals, 483; plays behind-the-scenes part in passage of Reform Bill, 502; promotes contraception, 552, 602n4; views of C, 366, 557–8n47; mentioned, 192, 286n28, 301nn7–8, 364–5, 468, 490, 565n126, 572n60

Plamenatz, John, 500

Plumb Pudding for the Humane, Valiant, Chaste, Enlightened Peter Porcupine, A, by Mathew Carey, 267n14

Plumer, William, 62

Plunket, William, 128

Pole, Charles, 132

Political House That Jack Built by William Hone, 381–4

Political Letters and Pamphlets edited by William Carpenter, 450, 489, 605n40

political parties, C's views, 156, 175, 177, 280n100, 284 motto, 297n14; *see also* tories; whigs

Political Penny Magazine, 615n139, 619n89

Political Progress of Britain by James Callender, 55

Political Proteus: A View of the Public Character and Conduct of R. B. Sheridan, Esq., 286n48

political unions: formed (1829–31), 490; outlawed (1831), 610n113

Ponsonby, George, 225

Ponsonby, J. W., 495

poor, the: definition, 293n73; deteriorating conditions, 201, 292n72; discrimination, 486, 494, 525, 540, 595n140, 614nn20 & 21; C assumes patronage, 194–206, 426; *see also* taxation

poor laws, 443, 474, 485, 494, 512, 525, 552–3, 599–600n73, 603n15, 614n22; for Ireland, 552, 593–4n118, 598n35

Poor Man's Guardian, 605n40

Popay, William, 515, 615n37

Pope, Alexander, 18, 56, 72, 184, 249

popular disturbances
U.S., 46; *see also* Whiskey Rebellion
Birmingham (1791), 49–50
Nore and Spithead (1797), 112
Luddites and food riots (1811–16), 313, 341–2, 349, 561nn46 & 50
"bread or blood" (1816), 346
Spa Fields (1816), 349–50, 353, 565n130, 566nn131–2, 578n57
Pentrich rising (1817), 362–3
Peterloo (1819), 379–84

Reform Bill (1831), 495–7, 499, 609n94
Captain Swing and other rural (1830–4), 473–5, 496, 503, 600n74, 608n86

population, 412, 442, 552–3, 591–2nn84–6

Porcupine, and Antigallican Monitor, 273n41

Porcupiniad by Mathew Carey, 267n14

Portland, Duke of, 176, 207, 208, 236

Portugal, 211, 235

post office, *see* newspapers: post office control

potatoes, 441–2, 537, 549, 591nn80–3

Powell, Richard, 30–1, 35

Praed, W. M., 501

Preston elections, 458–63, 488, 500

Prevost, Sir George, 337

prices, 112, 194, 342, 343, 346, 409–11, 418, 421, 473–4, 582n1, 583n15, 586n71

Priestley, Joseph, 1, 49–51, 53, 86, 94, 112, 124, 270n71

privy council, 112, 494

"puff-out," *see under* banks and banking

quakers, 199, 291n52, 441, 591n71

Quarterly Review, 298n25, 348, 358, 392, 565n126, 567nn148 & 150, 593–4n118

Radford, the Rev. William, 593n116

Radical Reform Association *or* Society, *see* Association of Friends of Radical Reform

Radnor, Earl, *see* Folkestone, Lord

Raleigh, Sir Walter, 249

Randolph, Edmund, 60–2

Reading Mercury, 587n88

Redesdale, Lord, 128–30, 131, 246, 275n20, 302n18, 578n38

Reeves, John, 116, 129, 235, 243, 271n5, 272n20, 283n83, 302n18, 579n68

Reformists' Register, 360

reform legislation, *see* parliamentary reform

regency, 317–18

Reid, Eleanor (Mrs. James Warner), 569n19

Reid, Frederick, 393

Rejected Addresses by James and Horace Smith, 446

Rejected Articles by P. G. Patmore, 447

Republican, 483
venge, 369, 557–8n47, 573n74, 580n86, 594n123
:ynolds, Sir Joshua, 100

Ricardo, David: praises C's letter to Luddites, 565n123; astonished by C's success at Norfolk county meeting (1823), 420; supports return to gold standard, 584n39; proposes paying